DEMOCRACY IN THE OLD SOUTH

Fletcher Melvin Green in his study at home in Chapel Hill, North Carolina.

Photograph by Wallace Patterson.

DEMOCRACY IN THE OLD SOUTH *and Other Essays*

by Fletcher Melvin Green

Edited by J. ISAAC COPELAND

VANDERBILT UNIVERSITY PRESS · 1969

"Gold Mining: A Forgotten Industry of Antebellum North Carolina,"
"Listen to the Eagle Scream: One Hundred Years of the Fourth of July in North Carolina, 1776–1876," and "Resurgent Southern Sectionalism, 1933–1955" Copyright 1937, 1954, and 1956 by the *North Carolina Historical Review*
"Duff Green: Industrial Promoter" and "Democracy in the Old South" Copyright 1936 and 1946 by the *Journal of Southern History*, Southern Historical Association
"Cycles of American Democracy" Copyright 1961 by the *Mississippi Valley Historical Review* (now the *Journal of American History*)
"On Tour with President Andrew Jackson" Copyright 1963 by the *New England Quarterly*
"Thomas Prentice Kettell: Economist, Editor, and Historian," from *Southern Wealth and Northern Profits* by Thomas Prentice Kettell Copyright 1965 by the University of Alabama Press
"William Watson Davis," from *The Civil War and Reconstruction in Florida* by William Watson Davis Copyright 1964 by the University of Florida Press
"Some Aspects of the Convict Lease System in the Southern States," from *Essays in Southern History* edited by Fletcher Melvin Green Copyright 1949 by the University of North Carolina Press

Material reprinted by permission of the copyright holders

Printed in the United States of America
by Kingsport Press, Inc., Kingsport, Tennessee

Standard Book Number 8265-1128-7

Library of Congress Catalogue Card Number 68-9268

For

MARY FRANCES GREEN

Devoted wife, gracious hostess,
and,
to a host of former graduate students,
a faithful friend

Hers in full measure are those charms
associated with the Old South

Foreword

T H E choice of essays to be included in this volume
was my own and the editing has consisted princi-
pally of bringing the footnotes into a consistent form; the reader
must remember that these essays were written over a period of
three decades and published in various places. When the collection was first assembled, minor inconsistencies in style were
evident throughout, the natural consequence of such a varied
publishing history. Stylistic changes—in capitalization, in punc-
tuation, in paragraphing—were made for the sake of uniformity by the editorial staff of Vanderbilt University Press, who
also made minor, clarifying changes in the wording of one or two
essays. This was done with the approval of the author; in no case
has a change involved emphasis or meaning.

To bring uniformity to the footnotes has required time and a
certain amount of care, but it was not difficult; in fact, it was a
pleasant undertaking, since it afforded me an insight into Green
the scholar such as I would never have gained otherwise. But the
essay on Green was not easy to write. How does one write about
his mentor, a person for whom he has great respect and affection?
After many rewritings, the essay must stand as written; it is my
own, it was written honestly, and I accept responsibility for it.

My debts are many. Most of all, I am indebted to Professor and
Mrs. Green for their cooperation and especially to Professor
Green for making available the two previously unpublished essays. Dewey W. Grantham, Jr., of Vanderbilt University, offered
encouragement from the beginning, and his support of my efforts
never diminished. Mrs. Pattie McIntyre and Mrs. Phyllis An-
drews, of the University of North Carolina Library staff, were of

invaluable help with the footnotes; William S. Powell, Lawrence F. London, Miss Anna Brooke Allan, Mrs. Carolyn Wallace, and Clyde N. Wilson, Jr.—all of the library staff and the latter three from my department—offered valuable suggestions on more than one occasion. Edwin A. Miles, of the University of Houston; Hugh F. Rankin, of Tulane University; Clifton L. Hall, of the University of Tennessee; and Ernest W. Hooper, of Middle Tennessee State University, have, with patience and interest, talked with and listened to me as we discussed ideas and polished phrases for inclusion in the essay on Green. Finally, I want to thank Miss Martha I. Strayhorn, Assistant Editor of Vanderbilt University Press, and to say that it was a joy to work with her.

Chapel Hill, North Carolina   J. Isaac Copeland
September 1968

SPECIAL ACKNOWLEDGMENT is made to the following, who have granted permission for the reprinting of copyrighted material from the periodicals and books that are listed below:

"Gold Mining: A Forgotten Industry of Antebellum North Carolina," "Listen to the Eagle Scream: One Hundred Years of the Fourth of July in North Carolina, 1776–1876," and "Resurgent Southern Sectionalism, 1933–1955" appeared in the *North Carolina Historical Review* (January and April 1937, July and October 1954, and April 1956). Reprinted by permission of the *North Carolina Historical Review*, State of North Carolina, Department of Archives and History.

"Duff Green: Industrial Promoter" and "Democracy in the Old South" appeared in the *Journal of Southern History* (February 1936 and February 1946). Reprinted by permission of the *Journal of Southern History* and the Southern Historical Association.

"Cycles of American Democracy" appeared in the June 1961 issue of the *Mississippi Valley Historical Review*, now the *Journal of American History*. Reprinted by permission of the *Journal of American History* and the Organization of American Historians.

"On Tour with President Andrew Jackson" appeared in the *New England Quarterly* (June 1963). Reprinted by permission of the *New England Quarterly*.

"Thomas Prentice Kettell: Economist, Editor, and Historian" is the introduction to *Southern Wealth and Northern Profits* by Thomas Prentice Kettell. Copyright 1965 by the University of Alabama Press. Reprinted by permission of the University of Alabama Press.

"William Watson Davis" is the introduction to the 1964 facsimile edition of *The Civil War and Reconstruction in Florida* by William Watson Davis (New York: Columbia University Press, 1913). Copyright 1964 by the University of Florida Press. Reprinted by permission of the University of Florida Press.

"Some Aspects of the Convict Lease System in the Southern States" appeared in *Essays in Southern History Presented to Joseph Grégoire de Roulhac Hamilton . . .* edited by Fletcher Melvin Green. Copyright 1949 by the University of North Carolina Press. Reprinted by permission of the University of North Carolina Press.

Contents

Introduction: Fletcher Melvin Green

F LETCHER Melvin Green's official retirement from
the University of North Carolina in June 1966
brought to a close one phase of a long and distinguished career.
During this period, he had exerted a deep influence upon the
teaching of American history and upon southern history in particular. Fortunately for the scholarly world, his retirement has not
led to inactivity because, since 1966, he has been busily engaged
in completing research and writing projects that were begun
earlier. In the fall semesters of 1966 and 1967, he taught classes on
the Chapel Hill campus; in the spring semester of 1967, he was a
research fellow at the Henry E. Huntington Library in San Ma-
rino, California; and in April 1968, he delivered the Eugenia
Dorothy Blount Lamar Lectures at Mercer University. For the
academic year 1968/69, he will be in England as Harmsworth
Professor of American History at Oxford University. In view of
this record of activity and the fact that he has a host of former
students teaching in colleges and universities throughout the nation, it is evident that Green will continue to exert considerable
influence upon the historical profession for years to come.

It is difficult to characterize Green. He is a scholar, a teacher,
and a warm and loyal friend, but there are qualities of strength
and character in him that these words fail to convey. Whenever a
group of his former students are together for any length of time,
the conversation is likely to turn to the secret of "Uncle Fletcher's" skill with students—his ability to inspire them and to win
their loyalty. No one is ever satisfied with the discussion, but
reference is almost always made to his genuine interest in what
each student is doing and to his uncanny sensitivity to what each

student needs at a given point in his work. This latter gift has produced a remarkable store of reminiscences that range from praise when a student was discouraged, to the comment, "This is not up to your standard, nor is it up to mine," when a student has done less than his best.

After graduating from Emory University and teaching in a preparatory school for one year, Green enrolled as a graduate student at the University of North Carolina in the fall of 1921. Here, he came under the influence of Joseph Grégoire de Roulhac Hamilton, one of the ablest of William A. Dunning's students, and it was Hamilton who trained him and who watched his progress with almost paternal pride. Green's journeys away from Chapel Hill brought him into contact with two other distinguished historians of the South—William E. Dodd, under whom he studied briefly at the University of Chicago, and Walter Lynwood Fleming, with whom he taught for a year at Vanderbilt University. The year 1923/24 was spent teaching in a junior college and was followed by the year at Vanderbilt. He returned to the University of North Carolina in 1925, received his Ph.D. in 1927, and remained as a member of the Department of History. From this date, his career at Carolina was interrupted only by the acceptance in 1933 of a professorship at Emory, but he returned in 1936 to Chapel Hill, where he continued as a member of the faculty until his retirement to emeritus status thirty years later. In 1946, he was appointed Kenan Professor of History; and from 1953 to 1960, he served as department chairman.

During his career at Carolina, Green was a Visiting Professor at Harvard in 1944/45 and taught in the summers at the College of William and Mary, the University of Tennessee, Duke, the University of Missouri, Stanford, Columbia, and Northwestern. In 1949, he delivered the Walter Lynwood Fleming Lectures at Louisiana State University; in 1962, he was one of the lecturers for the Institute of Southern Culture at Longwood College; and in 1964, he gave the J. P. Young Lectures at Memphis State University. He has also lectured at the U. S. Military Academy, Connecticut College, Agnes Scott College, the University of Houston, and a number of other institutions.

Historical societies and boards have honored Green with various offices. He was for many years a member of the executive board of the North Carolina Department of Archives and History; secretary-treasurer, member of the executive council, and, in 1945, president of the Southern Historical Association; president of both the Historical Society of North Carolina and the North Carolina Literary and Historical Association; and member of the executive council and president, in 1961, of the Mississippi Valley Historical Association—now the Organization of American Historians. Also, he has served on three different occasions as a member of the board of editors of the *Journal of Southern History* and for one term on the board of editors of the *Mississippi Valley Historical Review.*

In any assessment of Green, the most impressive quality is the man's absolute integrity. In his career as a teacher, Green has never tolerated work representing less than a student's best, nor does he allow himself any compromise in his own work; the lecture to a class, the grading of a set of quiz papers, the reading of a student's manuscript—all receive infinite care, with never a thought that one of these duties might be treated in a casual or routine fashion.

But insistence upon superior performance is only one aspect of Green's honesty. In a day when professors are busily engaged in research and rarely available to their students, Green remains unique; his students and his teaching always come first. At the University of North Carolina, his best-known courses were "The Old South" and "The South Since Reconstruction." These were repeated many times, yet never did they become routine. On more than one occasion, students must have experienced the feeling that, in the hour preceding his lecture, Green had communed with the spirit of Andrew Jackson, talked with a plantation owner or a slave trader, or discussed life in the 1840s with a free Negro or a slave. This feeling came not from any dramatic presentation, but because Green displayed complete familiarity with his topic; furthermore, his lecture had been carefully prepared, and it was delivered in clear, effective English, with seldom a repetitious phrase and never a pause for the next word. Green's lectures were so meaty, in fact, as to provoke one innocent coed to ask, "What do you expect us to do with all this stuff?" It should be noted also that he has never used a "joke" as a filler or as a distraction, though his asides after a point has been made are a delight.

Green has always endeavored to revise his courses to take note of the latest historiographical developments. His lectures are apt to include some new fact gleaned from a book just published or from the most recent issue of a scholarly journal. When he taught the course dealing with the "New South," he often referred in his lectures to pertinent articles or editorials that had appeared in the morning newspaper.

Green's talent in the classroom appeals to undergraduates and graduates alike, but his reputation rests largely upon his work with graduate students. This reputation began with his return from Emory and continued to grow until his retirement. For three decades, graduate students flocked to his classes, and his majors left to establish themselves, not only at leading institutions in the South, but at ranking institutions across the nation—from Princeton, Virginia, and Johns Hopkins, on the East Coast, to the Claremont Graduate School and the University of California at Berkeley, on the West. In all, the number of his doctoral graduates totals almost one hundred, and his masters number more than one hundred and fifty.

When Green is asked if he can account for his phenomenal success as a director of graduate studies, he always answers "No." It is true that finding an answer is not simple; but any number of his former students can testify that it was Green who imbued them with a desire to search for the facts, taught them the importance of an open mind, and schooled them in the ways of accuracy. In his *Southern History in the Making,* Wendell H. Stephenson calls the reader's attention to the amount of research and scholarly writing done by Green's students. A number of their books and articles have won prizes, and, in all, the group has published 100 books and 225 articles; in addition, thirty former students have received Guggenheim, Ford, Rosenwald, Social Science Research Council, Fulbright, and Institute for Advanced Study fellowships. Taking the group as a whole, they have taught in half the states and in England, Germany, Japan, and India. Stephenson closes the passage by saying that the record of the group equals, if it does not surpass, that attained by students at Johns Hopkins directed by Herbert Baxter Adams. This was written in 1964, and, in the years since, there have been additions to the list. In the Stephenson Papers in the Manuscripts Department of the Duke University Library are several letters giving different versions of a story that places Green at the Gates of the Kingdom of Heaven, greeting each of his former students with the question, "And what research have you been doing lately?"

One of Green's rare qualities has been his ability to guide students into research areas of their own interest. The result is that among them there is no concentration in one field or one period; and in the large group of doctors and masters majoring with him, there developed no school of interpretation or theory of history. By example, he had taught them to search for the facts and to interpret the facts as they saw them. In his association with students, perhaps one of the finest tributes to Green is the fact that, with all the research they have done, neither they nor their research have ever been used by him for his writings or to promote something in which he is interested.

Few teachers have better understood the mood of their students. Green has known when and how far to push, and he has possessed the ability to draw from a student his best performance and even to prod him into a performance better than he thought himself capable of. In his dealings with everyone, but particularly with students, Green has always been perceptive; he has seen the good points and the weaknesses, and he has been charitable, but few have ever deceived him.

In the years immediately following the Second World War, the students majoring with Green forged a remarkable circle of friendship among themselves and with him. Though these men and women have now long been out of graduate school, the friendship has continued, and it includes both those who completed their work in earlier years and those who did so later. When these people gather at professional meetings, it is interesting to note their good-humored teasing of one another and of Green, their interest in each other's research, and the absence of rivalries and jealousies. Fletcher Green did much to create this atmosphere.

The affection and respect that Green's students have for him is, in part, shown by the *Festschrift, Writing Southern History,* published by the Louisiana State University Press and presented to Green in the fall of 1965. It was prepared as a labor of love; all of the ex-students were consulted in choosing the committee to supervise the operation, very few declined when asked to prepare an essay, and none approached the task in a perfunctory manner. The truth is that some felt the result would have been better if the essays could have had the advantage of Green's critical suggestions.

The picture of Fletcher Green used as a frontispiece in this volume has some sentimental value—at least for his students, many of whom have copies of it. The photograph was taken in his study at home, and the desk is a handsome Williamsburg reproduction that was given to him by his former students in 1961, at the time of his presidency of the Mississippi Valley Historical Association. On the upper right corner of the desk, not shown in the picture here, is an engraved silver plate denoting the gift.

Green has devoted untold hours to his graduate students, some part of which might have been spent on his own research and writing. But in spite of this, his bibliography as published in *Writing Southern History* has 225 entries, and its most notable feature is the range of topics presented. Green has articles that treat the American Revolution, the antebellum South, the Civil War, the post-Civil War South, general American history, social and cultural history, and business history. Some of his best contributions have been in the form of editorial work, beginning with Henry Kyd Douglas's *I Rode With Stonewall* and extending through the more recently published *Memorials of a Southern Planter* by Susan Dabney Smedes. He obviously enjoys this work, because he does it with care and thoroughness. In both the works that he has edited and in his articles, Green has been attracted to neglected people and topics—those who were important in their day, yet slipped from the pages of history. His editing of Thomas Prentice Kettell's *Southern Wealth and Northern Profits* and his three articles on gold mining in the Old South are excellent examples.

In addition to the completely serious writing, there are some lighter pieces, such as "Listen to the Eagle Scream," "On Tour with President Andrew Jackson," and "Johnny Reb Could Read," that show Green's appreciation of humor and his ability to write. His greatest talents, however, lie in research and his use of the spoken word in the classroom.

The world of sports and the great outdoors afford Green much pleasure. As a young man, he played baseball; and as a young teacher, he coached football and basketball and once won a district championship with a girls' basketball team. This interest in sports has continued, for he is today an ardent fan of the University's athletic teams. Fishing has at times been a favorite recreation, but golf has come more and more to assume first place. From the late 1940s on, golfing with his sons, with his graduate students, or with faculty friends has been the favorite pastime. But to be out of doors is sometimes sufficient. Green knows his plant, animal, and bird life, and it is a source of pleasure to him merely to walk and observe the beauty of nature and the changing seasons. On a cold, snowy day when younger members of the faculty may find themselves unable to reach the campus, no one is surprised to see Green calmly walking along the snow-covered street on the way to his office.

Green's graduate students have afforded him much satisfaction, but his greatest pleasure has come from his family. Mrs. Green has made their home a place for gracious living, and the two sons and two daughters share the fine qualities of their mother and father. And there are the grandchildren. To see Green with his granddaughter, a charming young miss "of almost six summers," is to realize his warmth and humanness. Also, the children of faculty members and of graduate students have always found him to be a friend. Some members of the history department remember an occasion when Green, playing amateur herpetologist, caught a small green snake which he placed in a bottle and brought to a young faculty son. For several days thereafter, the lad referred to his prize as the "Doctor Green Snake." Fletcher

Green, distinguished historian that he is, has never been too busy to take an interest in others, especially young children.

Constitutional Development in the South Atlantic States, 1776–1860, written by Fletcher Green and published by the University of North Carolina Press in 1930, was dedicated to Dr. Hamilton with the simple words, "Director, Teacher, and Friend." As Green has always felt toward Hamilton, so now his students feel toward him. Perhaps Charles Sellers, Jr., of the University of California at Berkeley, spoke for each of them when he wrote in the preface to the first volume of his *James K. Polk,* "Finally I am deeply grateful to Professor Fletcher M. Green of the University of North Carolina who guided the early evolution of this project as a doctoral dissertation, and, by precept, example, and friendship, continues to make historical scholarship exciting for his many present and former students."

J.I.C.

DEMOCRACY IN THE OLD SOUTH

1

Gold Mining: A Forgotten Industry of Antebellum North Carolina

As a young historian only a few years removed from graduate school, Green published three articles on gold mining in the Old South. He referred to the industry as a forgotten one; and he is correct, because few twentieth-century Americans—or southerners, for that matter—realize that North Carolina, Georgia, and Virginia were early centers of the nation's gold mining. This essay was published in the *North Carolina Historical Review*, XIV (January and April, 1937), 1–19, 135–155.

T HE YEARS OF THE GREAT DEPRESSION have led the people of the South, North Carolina in particular, to renew their efforts to wrest from the earth its store of precious metal. Numerous news items of recent date testify to this awakened interest. One news story in a daily paper says:

Mecklenburg County seems well along toward having a full-fledged gold rush. Since the American Smelting and Refining Company became interested in the renewal of gold mining activities in the vicinity of Hopewell Church, calls and letters have been pouring in at the Charlotte chamber of commerce from prospectors and others interested in the location of some of the old abandoned mines of the county and sections considered likely for attempts at gold digging.[1]

In some cases, at least, the miners have been successful, for they discovered at the Nugget Gold Mine in Mecklenburg County a nugget weighing about twelve pounds,[2] while the Hedrich Mining

1. Charlotte *Observer*, 15 August 1931.
2. Greensboro *Daily News*, 15 August 1932.

3

Company of Montgomery County produced twenty pounds of gold in its first week of operation in 1932.[3] The latter company opened a fifty-five-foot shaft at the Black Ankle Mine, and the engineer estimated that the ore developed had a gross value of $900,000. The Overton Mine, operated by the Randolph Mining Company, has been worked on shifts twenty-four hours per day and, with a thirty-stamp mill running, has proven quite successful.[4] Around many of the mines in Randolph, Montgomery, and Mecklenburg counties are to be found miners and prospectors from other states, drawn by the news of new gold strikes as well as the tradition of the richness of the mines when worked in earlier years.

Many large companies have been interested in the reopening of the old mines of western North Carolina. One paper announced that "Big Companies have engineers in the field looking into Gold and Copper Prospects."[5] Among such companies in 1930 were the Anaconda Copper, American Smelting and Refining, Tennessee Copper, United States Smelting, Mining and Refining, Ducktown Chemical and Iron, Jackson Mining Company, and the Condor Consolidated Mines, Ltd., of Toronto.[6] The Asheville *Citizen* announced that a "New York company would spend $2,500,000 on development of mines, erection of concentration plant and smelter in the Swain County area."[7]

So much interest has been aroused in the southern gold fields that the Civil Works Administration granted Georgia $9,000 with which to make a gold survey of the state;[8] and the director of re-employment in North Carolina was urged to apply to the federal government for a grant from the Public Works fund with

---

3. *Ibid.,* 6 March 1932.

4. *Loc. cit.*

5. Charlotte *Observer,* 23 February 1930.

6. *Ibid.*

7. For other news stories of mining activities, see the Charlotte *Observer,* 8 April 1929, and Greensboro *Daily News,* 13 June, 6 December, and 16 December 1931, and 14 February 1932.

8. For gold mining in antebellum Georgia, see Fletcher M. Green, "Georgia's Forgotten Industry: Gold Mining," *Georgia Historical Quarterly,* XIX (June and September 1935), 93–111, 210–228 (hereafter, "Georgia's Forgotten Industry").

which to open a mammoth ore-reducing plant somewhere in the gold region of either Georgia or North Carolina.[9]

There had been little or no gold mining in North Carolina since 1907 until this new interest was aroused in 1929,[10] but these facts serve to recall the days of a real gold rush in the South which took place about one hundred years ago. An eyewitness wrote, at the time of the California rush:

In 1830 nearly as great excitement prevailed in relation to them [the mines of the southern states], as does now in reference to California. Persons from all quarters crowded into these regions, and the product was then estimated at $5,000,000 per annum.[11]

The excitement spread throughout the entire Southeast, and prospectors were found in every southern state. A group of scientific miners and engineers toured the region in 1831 and found Georgia and North Carolina the richest fields. Their report concluded, "After all, North Carolina is the place for Mining;—it is the real Potosi of North America."[12]

As a consequence of the discoveries and such publicity, the Tarheel state came to be known as the "golden state, from the great lumps of precious metal found there"[13]—and, indeed, the title "golden state" was not so absurd as one might think. Prior to 1829, all the gold mined in the United States and coined at the Philadelphia Mint was taken from North Carolina mines. The industry developed in the 1830s to such a degree that it ranked second to agriculture,[14] and it continued to be of considerable importance down to the Civil War. The total production from 1799 to 1860 was estimated at above $60,000,000.

9. Raleigh *News and Observer*, 10 November 1933.

10. Charlotte *Observer*, 8 April 1929.

11. "Commercial and Financial Review," *Hunt's Merchants' Magazine*, XX (January 1849) , 79.

12. Salisbury *Western Carolinian*, 29 August 1831.

13. Tarborough *Free Press*, 17 October 1828. [In this essay, the older spelling of the North Carolina cities "Tarborough" and "Hillsborough" is kept intact, since that spelling is used in the newspapers of that day which are cited here. Other essays in this volume reflect the changes which later took place, and use the revised spellings, "Tarboro" and "Hillsboro." Still later, in 1965, with state and federal approval, the latter returned to the earlier spelling of its name.—J.I.C.]

14. Salisbury *Western Carolinian*, 29 August 1831.

The gold mining industry of North Carolina is now little more than a memory, for while contemporary newspapers, journals, and other avenues of public expression teemed with news of the activities, little effort has been made to collect and preserve the records. Most of the mining companies kept records of their mines, but few of these have been preserved; at least, few have been located. Several newspapers were established in the mining region and one of them was definitely a miners' journal—yet, there is no complete file of it available. Again, the branch mint at Charlotte kept records; but—other than the formal annual reports to the director of the mint—none of these are known to be extant. The student of the mining industry in North Carolina is forced, therefore, to rely upon fugitive material, incomplete newspaper files, contemporary descriptive articles, and the prospectus which almost every company published.

The story of gold mining in North Carolina prior to 1860 logically divides itself into five major sections: an account of the early interest in an attempt to locate the supposedly rich mines; the first modern discovery in 1799 and the gradual spread of the interest in the state down to the middle 1820s; the period of the great rush and the development and stabilization of the industry down to 1837; the establishment of the branch mint at Charlotte and the exploitation of the mines down to their desertion for the California fields in 1849; and a revival of interest just prior to the Civil War.

The discovery of rich gold and silver mines in her South American colonies made Spain, for the time being, the most powerful and influential of the European colonial powers. This led explorers and missionaries to visit Florida and other parts of North America, "impelled by the desire to acquire gold while saving souls."[15] As early as 1513, Ponce de Leon reported that a cacique in Florida had an abundance of gold.[16] Mirvelo in 1518, Narváez

15. Fletcher M. Green, "Georgia's Forgotten Industry," p. 95.

16. G. F. Becker, *Gold Fields of the Southern Appalachians*, U.S. Congress, House of Representatives, 54th Cong., 1st sess., 1895, House Document No. 5, p. 253 (hereafter, *Gold Fields*) ; Joseph Seawell Jones, *Memorials of North Carolina* (n.p.: [Printed by Scatcherd & Adams], 1838) , pp. 82–83 (hereafter, *Memorials*) .

in 1528, De Soto in 1540, and Laudonnière in 1564 all heard reports of gold in the Southern Appalachian regions.[17] This evidence led James Mooney to conclude that

Long before the end of the sixteenth century . . . the existence of mines of gold and other metals in the Cherokee country was a matter of common knowledge among the Spaniards at St. Augustine and Santa Elena, and more than one expedition had been fitted out to explore the interior. Numerous traces of ancient mining operations with remains of old shafts and fortifications, evidently of European origin, show that these discoveries were followed up, although the policy of Spain concealed the fact from the outside world.[18]

If the Spaniards attempted to conceal the fact, mining operations in the 1830s disclosed their efforts. An English diplomatic agent wrote of North Carolina mines that there was

indubitable evidence that these mines were known and *worked* by the aboriginal inhabitants, or some other people, at a remote period. Many pieces of machinery which were used for this purpose have been found. Among them are several *crucibles* of earthenware, and far better than these now in use.[19]

In fact, the news of Spanish discoveries found its way to the English colonists. William Byrd wrote that

The Spaniards had lately discovered Rich Mines in their Part of the West Indies, which made their Maritime neighbours eager to do so too.

17. W. S. Yeates, S. W. McCallie, and Francis P. King, *A Preliminary Report on a Part of the Gold Deposits of Georgia*, Bulletin No. 4-A, Geological Survey of Georgia (Atlanta: George W. Harrison, 1896), p. 26; "The Narrative of Alvar Nuñez Cabeça de Vaca," edited by Frederick W. Hodge, in *Spanish Explorers in the Southern United States, 1528–1543* (New York: C. Scribner's Sons, 1907), p. 21; "The Narrative of the Expedition of Hernando de Soto. By the Gentleman of Elvas," edited by Theodore H. Lewis, in *Spanish Explorers in the Southern United States, 1528–1543*, p. 154; Frederick Moore, "Gold in North Carolina," *Scientific American Supplement*, LIII (22 March 1902), 21918; Becker, *Gold Fields*, p. 253.

18. James Mooney, *Myths of the Cherokee* (Washington: Government Printing Office, 1902), p. 25.

19. Sir William Gore Ouseley, *Remarks on the Statistics and Political Institutions of the United States* (Philadelphia: Carey & Lea, 1832), p. 174 (hereafter, *Statistics*). See also J. S. Jones, *Memorials*, p. 85; James S. Buckingham, *The Slave States of America*, 2 vols. (London: Fisher, Son & Co. [1842]), 1, 42; Charles Lanman, *Letters from the Alleghany Mountains* (New York: Geo. P. Putnam, 1849), p. 189; "Gold Mines," *American Almanac* (1832), p. 228; and Hillsborough *Recorder*, 24 June 1829.

This Modish Frenzy being still more Inflam'd by the Charming Account given of Virginia, by the first Adventurers, made many fond of removeing to such a Paradise.

Happy was he, and still happier She, that cou'd get themselves transported, fondly expecting their Coarsest Utensils, in that happy place, would be of Massy Silver.[20]

The Raleigh colonists heard of the existence of gold in the very region where it was later discovered; and Sir Walter Raleigh, in assigning territorial rights, reserved to himself one-fifth of the gold and silver that might be discovered. Sir Ralph Lane is reported to have

made a voyage in small boats in 1586 up the Albermarle Sound, and penetrated four days' journey up the Roanoke (Moratock) river in quest of information as to a country called *Chaunis Temoatan, where,* from the accounts of the Indians, there was an abundance of the precious metals.[21]

The Indians gave a fairly accurate description of mining operations which they said were carried on twenty days' journey from the coast. Sir Francis Drake captured two Spaniards, Nicholas Burgoignon and Pedro Morales, who reported that they had seen quantities of gold in the mountains of North Carolina.[22] And the Indians related to the English settlers in North Carolina that a company of Spaniards from Florida had mined gold very successfully in that region for two or three summers. The Indians, fearing that the whites would drive them from their lands if this became generally known, put the entire party of Spanish miners to death. Senator Thomas L. Clingman did not believe this tradition entitled to credit,[23] but it does accord with Indian practices.

So firmly did the English expect to find gold that Charles II specified "all veins, mines . . . of gold, silver, gems, precious

20. William Byrd, *William Byrd's Histories of the Dividing Line betwixt Virginia and North Carolina,* edited by William K. Boyd (Raleigh: The North Carolina Historical Commission, 1929), p. 2.

21. J. S. Jones, *Memorials,* p. 82.

22. *Ibid.,* p. 83.

23. Thomas L. Clingman, to the Asheville *Highland Messenger.* The letter is reprinted in Lanman, *Letters,* p. 189.

stones"[24] in his grant of Carolina to the Lords Proprietors in 1663: and he reserved for himself "the fourth part of all gold or silver ore, which, within the limits, shall from time to time happen to be found."[25] The charter of 1665 required of the Proprietors "the fourth part of gold and silver ore . . . over and besides the fourth part of the gold and silver ore"[26] reserved in the Letters Patent of 1663. And the Lords Proprietors, in the Fundamental Constitutions of 1669, reserved to themselves all the "mines, minerals, quarries of gems, and precious stones."[27]

The early English settlers made many efforts to locate the mines which the Spaniards and Indians were thought to have operated, but all failed until the beginning of the nineteenth century. Sir William Berkeley, governor of Virginia, sent out an expedition in 1669, expecting to find silver mines in North Carolina, "for certain it is that the Spaniard in the same degree of latitude has found many."[28] James Moore, secretary of the colony of South Carolina, made an expedition from Charlestown in 1690 and, led by Indian guides, reached the mountains where he found evidence of Spanish mines, but failed to discover gold.[29] Governor Josiah Martin secured native gold from Guilford County in 1774.[30] Mines had been worked in Chesterfield County, South Carolina, and in Gaston, Cherokee, and Mecklenburg counties, North Carolina, before the Revolution.[31] And

as early as the Revolutionary War, perhaps before that period, shafts had been sunk on Fisher Hill (about six miles south of Greensboro)

24. Francis N. Thorpe, *The Federal and State Constitutions, Colonial Charters, and Other Organic Laws of the States, Territories, and Colonies now or heretofore forming the United States of America,* 7 vols. (Washington: Government Printing Office, 1909), V, 2744.

25. *Ibid.,* 2745.

26. *Ibid.,* 2763.

27. *Ibid.,* 2785.

28. Foster A. Sondley, *Asheville and Buncombe County* (Asheville, N.C.: Asheville Citizen, 1922), p. 29.

29. *Ibid.*

30. J. S. Jones, *Memorials,* p. 84.

31. Henry B. C. Nitze and H. A. J. Wilkins, *Gold Mining in North Carolina and Adjacent South Appalachian Regions,* North Carolina Geological Survey, Bulletin No. 10 (Raleigh: G. V. Barnes, public printer, 1897), p. 26 (hereafter, *Gold Mining in North Carolina*).

which show a good degree of skill and experience in mining matters.
. . . These shafts have long been known as the "Revolutionary Diggings."[32]

One old German miner was frightened away from these mines by
Lord Cornwallis's troops in 1780. Thomas Jefferson reports in his
Notes on Virginia (1782) the finding of a seventeen-pennyweight
nugget near the Rappahannock River. So sure were some of the
inhabitants of North Carolina that there was gold on their lands
that they reserved the gold mines to their heirs by their wills.[33]
But these sporadic efforts availed nothing, and St. Jean de
Crèvecoeur predicted in 1793 that it would

require the industry of subsequent ages, the energy of future generations, ere mankind here will have leisure and abilities to penetrate
deep, and in the bowels of this continent, search for the subterranean
riches it no doubt contains.[34]

De Crèvecoeur's prophecy was wide of the mark, however, for
in six years from the time he wrote, gold had been discovered in
North Carolina; and within ten years, great interest had been
aroused in developing the industry. The first discovery was made
in 1799 in Meadow Creek on the farm of John Reed,[35] a Hessian
soldier who had settled in Cabarrus County at the close of the
Revolution. There are several different accounts of this first discovery. According to one, two miners, on their way north from the
South American mines, stopped overnight with Reed. They no-
ticed in the clay, used to chink the space between the logs of the

32. James T. Foster, *A Brief Sketch of the Early Discoveries of Gold Mines and
Mining in North Carolina, down to the Present Period* (Greensboro, N.C.: [n.p.],
1883), p. 3 (hereafter, *Early Discoveries*). See also Thomas G. Clemson, "Gold and
the Gold Region," in the *Orion* (April 1844), IV, 62–63; J. D. Whitney, *The
Metallic Wealth of the United States, Described and Compared with that of other
countries* (Philadelphia: Lippincott, Grambo & Co., 1854), p. 115 (hereafter,
Metallic Wealth).

33. J. S. Jones, *Memorials*, p. 84.

34. Michel Guillaume St. Jean de Crèvecoeur, *Letters from an American Farmer,
Describing Certain Provincial Situations, Manners, and Customs, and Covering some
Idea of the State of the People of North America* (Philadelphia: From the press of
Matthew Carey, 1793), p. 15.

35. "John Reed," *Dictionary of American Biography*, 20 vols. (New York: Charles
Scribner's Sons, 1928–1936), XV, 450.

cabin, shining particles which they believed to be gold. They inquired of Reed where he had obtained the dirt; he pointed to Meadow Creek, a small stream flowing into Rocky River, and the miners began to pan the sand and soon discovered a large nugget.[36]

The more authentic account, however, says that Conrad Reed, twelve-year-old son of John, accompanied by a younger brother and sister, was shooting fish with bow and arrow one Sunday while their parents were at church. Conrad saw a shining piece of metal in the water, recovered it and took it home. The lump of metal, about the size of a small smoothing iron, was carried by John Reed to William Atkinson, a silversmith of Concord, who was unable to identify it. Reed took the nugget home and used it for three years as a doorstop. In 1802, he carried it to a jeweler in Fayetteville, who fluxed the gold and ran it into a bar about six inches long. Reed, not knowing the value of the metal, asked and received from the jeweler what he thought was a big price, namely $3.50.[37] The real value of the nugget, which weighed about seventeen pounds after three years of wear, was about $8,000, and one account says that Reed later sued the jeweler and recovered $1,000.[38]

Reed now began to search for gold and, in 1803 and 1804, several nuggets were found, weighing from one to twenty-eight pounds.[39] The largest of these pieces was found by a Negro boy.

36. Don Maquire, "The Discovery of Placer Gold in North Carolina," in the *Salt Lake Mining Review,* 30 August 1924.

37. The earliest recorded story of the discovery is found in "Native Gold Discovered in North Carolina," in *Medical Repository* (November-January 1803–1804), 2d series, I, 307. George Barnhardt, a miner of Cabarrus County, well-acquainted with the Reeds, made a sworn statement in 1848, which is generally in accord with the first account. See John Hill Wheeler, *Historical Sketches of North Carolina from 1584 to 1851* (New York: F. H. Hitchcock, 1925), II, 63–64. For a modified version, see the Raleigh *Star and North Carolina Gazette,* 16 January 1824. The *Star* says the Reed children were shooting fish at night and that the light of their torches reflected on the gold and caused it to be discovered.

38. J. F. Shinn, "Discovery of Gold in North Carolina," *Trinity Archive,* VI (May 1893), 335–337.

39. Dr. Stephen Ayers, "Description of the Region in North Carolina where Gold has been Found," *Medical Repository,* 2d series, IV (August-October 1806), 149–150. The Reed mine was said in 1900 to "hold the world's record for the

Naturally, the excitement spread, and people began to search madly for the precious metal. The large, loose nuggets were soon picked up, and the workers began to wash and pan the sand for smaller particles. Reed formed a company with Frederic Kisor, James Love, and Martin Pfifer and worked his mine for some years. In 1831, a vein mine was opened, and Reed leased it for one-fourth the gold found. In 1835, he brought suit for alleged fraudulent returns, and the mine was temporarily closed. The yield of the Reed mine from 1799 to 1848 was reported to have been in excess of $10,000,000.[40] Other companies were formed and mining took on some of the characteristics of an organized business. People from other states, Maryland and Massachusetts in particular, became interested in investing in the Cabarrus County gold lands as early as 1807.[41]

The early mining operations were almost entirely lacking in system, skill, and scientific method. Placer mines only were worked, and pick, shovel, and pan were about the only tools used. Later, crude wooden boxes, washers, and rockers were used. Still later, a Baltimore miner made a machine in which quicksilver was mixed with the sand, and the loose particles of the dust were thus saved. Mercury was used as early as 1809 and, in 1829,

---

greatest production of gold nuggets, both as to size, value, and quantity." Thomas Jefferson Hurley, *Famous Gold Nuggets of the World* ([New York?]: n.p., 1900) , pp. 16–18. From this mine came nuggets weighing 28, 17, 16, 13, 10, 9, 8, 7, 5, 4, 3, 2, and 1 pounds. These were, of course, small ones compared with the 161-pound California nugget and the 184-pound Australian one. See "Australian Monster Nugget" and "Australia Nugget," *Hunt's Merchants' Magazine*, XXXVIII (June 1858) , 771, and XLI (December 1859) , 756.

40. "Gold and Silver Produced by the Mines of America from 1492 to 1848," Art. 4, No. 2, *Mining Magazine*, I (October 1853) , 371–373. On the Reed mine, see also Denison Olmsted, *Report on the Geology of North-Carolina, Conducted under the Direction of the Board of Agriculture* ([Raleigh?]: n.p., 1824) , Part I, pp. 34–35; "Geology and Mineralogy of North-Carolina," *The Southern Review*, I (February 1828) , 251–252; North Carolina, Geological Survey, 1852–1863, *Geological Report of the Midland Counties of North Carolina*, [prepared] by Ebenezer Emmons (New York: G. P. Putnam & Co., 1856) , pp. 166–167 (hereafter, Emmons, *Geological Report*) .

41. John Steele, *The Papers of John Steele*, edited by H. M. Wagstaff (Raleigh: Edwards & Broughton Printing Co., 1924) , II, 505, 506, 876–879. See also Archibald Debow Murphey, *The Papers of Archibald D. Murphey*, edited by William H. Hoyt (Raleigh: Uzzle & Co., 1914) , I, 154–155 (hereafter, *Murphey Papers*) .

sufficient quantities were found in Burke County to supply the demand.[42] A contemporary description of the mining operations reads as follows:

The common mode of working is . . . first, to pick out all the visible grains they can find, and throw by the remaining mass into a heap, and afterwards, at some convenient time, to separate the minuter particles thoroughly by means of mercury. The amalgam so obtained is then put into a proper vessel, and exposed to the action of fire; by which the quicksilver is distilled off in vapour, while the gold remains behind.[43]

The work was carried on largely "whenever the corn is hoed, the cotton weeded, and agricultural business which engages them will permit."[44] In fact, it was said, as late as 1823, that not a single "person of science is engaged in the business."[45] Under such conditions, bare wages were about all the laborer could expect unless he were the lucky finder of large nuggets. But "were the business conducted with proper skill, it might prove a source of wealth to its proprietors, and be of great advantage to the state, in adding to its metallic medium."[46] In spite of the inefficient methods and lack of system, gold was discovered in Cabarrus, Anson, Mecklenburg, Montgomery, and several other counties of western North Carolina by 1820.

In the 1820s, newspapers of the state made reference to almost daily discoveries of gold. These notices were copied by the papers of Washington, New York, and Boston, and in little county and frontier weeklies, and even in European papers. A North Carolina editor wrote:

The account we gave of the mine in Anson County, N.C., seems to excite much interest throughout the country, and some of the New York

42. Hillsborough *Recorder,* 20 May 1829; "Miscellaneous," *American Farmer,* XI (5 June 1829) , 95.

43. Ayers, "Description of the Region in North Carolina where Gold has been Found," *Medical Repository,* 2d series, IV (August-October 1806) , 150.

44. *Ibid.,* VI, 193.

45. Columbia *Missouri Intelligencer,* 29 January 1824, quoting the Raleigh *Register.*

46. *Ibid.*

editors appear rather incredulous on the subject. We have taken some pains to obtain further information. . . .[47]

Another paper reported that

It having been doubted by many that gold has been found in this state . . . Benjamin G. Baker, a merchant of New York . . . procured in Cabarrus County a piece weighing nearly 400 pennyweight . . . [which he] intends to take with him to New York, that the incredulous in that city may have occular [sic] proof that the precious metal is actually found, in large masses, in North Carolina.[48]

The discoveries of gold were so numerous, and the publicity given them so widespread, that "in 1825 the North Carolina gold fever began to rage," and a real rush to the fields began. William G. Graham, on a tour of the state in 1829, wrote Judge Thomas Ruffin as follows:

I have heard scarce anything since my arrival, except gold. Nothing before has ever so completely engrossed the attention of all classes of the community in this section, since my earliest recollection. . . . Those who have been esteemed prudent and cautious, embark in speculation with the greatest enthusiasm—bankrupts have been restored to affluence, and paupers turned nabobs.[49]

47. Hillsborough *Recorder*, 23 July 1823.

48. Raleigh *Star and North Carolina Gazette*, 16 January 1824. For accounts of widespread discoveries, see the following: for 1826, Tarborough *Free Press*, 12 September, 24 October; for 1827, *ibid.*, 21 April, 12 May, 1 September, 22 September; for 1828, *ibid.*, 18 January, 1 February, 9 May, 4 July; for 1829, Salisbury *Yadkin and Catawba Journal*, 3 February, 12 May, 14 July, 8 September; for 1830, Tarborough *Free Press*, 19 February, 30 April, 21 May, 16 July, 21 September, 12 October, 23 November, 7 December; for 1831, *ibid.*, 11 January, 22 February, 19 April, 3 May, 10 May, 7 June, 19 July, 23 August, and 15 November. Distant papers which copied or carried notices were the Cheraw, S.C., *Intelligencer;* Columbia *Missouri Intelligencer;* Charleston, S.C., *Gazette;* New York *Daily Advertiser;* New York *Journal of Commerce;* Fredericksburg, Va., *Political Arena;* Greenville, S.C., *Mountaineer;* New York *Observer;* Macon, Ga., *Telegraph;* Washington *National Intelligencer;* and Washington *United States Telegraph.*

49. Thomas Ruffin, *The Papers of Thomas Ruffin*, edited by J. G. deR. Hamilton (Raleigh: Edwards & Broughton Printing Co., 1918), I, 509–510 (hereafter, *Ruffin Papers*). See also the Rutherfordton *North Carolina Spectator and Western Advertiser*, 10 September 1830, which speaks of the great "height . . . of the gold fever." This paper also quotes the Fredericksburg, Va., *Political Arena* and the Richmond, Va., *Compiler* on the spread of the North Carolina "gold fever."

During the earlier period, mining had been carried on chiefly in and along the streams. The second period was to be characterized by ridge and vein mining, though of course the placers were still worked. Charles E. Rothe, an experienced mining engineer from Saxony who made a mineralogical survey of the state in 1826, foreshadowed this change when he reported that "several different formations" had been discovered "which are of greater extent than the thin alluvial layers of mud which have been hitherto worked."[50] The formations were "gold in veins of iron ore," "gold in veins of quartz," and a "variety of different ores containing gold in a state of mechanical mixture."[51] Rothe concluded his report by saying that a systematic search for and a scientific development of the veins were necessary for success. The first gold mines "in regular, well-defined veins" were discovered by accident in Montgomery County, when miners, following a placer, discovered the vein in the bank where the placer ended. In the vein was found a "nest of pure virgin gold"[52] weighing 15,000 pennyweight. The product of this vein

was so great as to excite general notice; and stimulated the land-owners in that section to search for these hidden treasures. The mines now began to attract the attention of the public; and several persons of enterprise, and some of capital, repaired to the spot. Some of them made investments, began to erect machinery, and worked the veins with system and regularity.[53]

Systematic search for the mines was then begun. Miners of many nationalities and of all degrees of skill, from the trained and experienced mining engineer to the unskilled laborer, flocked to the region. The prospector, or " 'Gold Hunter,' one of an order of people that begin already to be accounted a distinct race,"[54] was a familiar figure in the entire western half of the state. And "the population of the country for nearly 100 miles square" was

50. Charlotte *Catawba Journal*, 7 March 1826. Rothe's report is dated Salisbury, 15 February 1826.

51. *Ibid.*

52. Godfrey T. Vigne, *Six Months in America* (London: Whittaker, Treacher, & Co., 1832) , I, 223.

53. *Ibid.*, p. 225.

54. Olmsted, *Geology of North Carolina*, Part I, p. 84.

"agonized under the increased and increasing fever for gold."[55] New gold mines were

discovered almost every week; and in fact, well nigh every day. . . . These discoveries . . . produced considerable spirit and animation among our citizens. They have called many lazy, lounging fellows, who once hung as a heavy weight upon society, into active and manly exertion.[56]

Gold finding became the all-absorbing topic of the day; capitalists invested in mines, and the gold region expanded daily. A mining engineer from England estimated that 100,000 laborers might be profitably employed in the industry.[57] The *American Farmer* began to fear that the new impulse given to mining, the ingenious methods of extracting gold, and the large number of laborers employed in the industry, would prove injurious to the great agricultural interests of the South.[58]

The discovery, near Charlotte in 1831, of a nest or bed of gold containing pieces weighing five, seven, and eight pounds, the entire find weighing one hundred and twenty pounds and valued at $20,000, produced a frenzy of excitement.[59] Many of the mines were worked on an extensive scale, some employing more than 1,000 laborers; and there were more than 30,000 men engaged in the industry. Mills for grinding the ore were erected, water and steam power were utilized, and a vast amount of capital was invested.[60] So extensive was the industry that a Congressional committee which investigated the mines in 1831 reported to Congress

55. Tarborough *Free Press*, 19 June 1829. This item appeared also in the St. Louis, Mo., *Beacon* of 4 July 1829, copied from the Richmond, Va., *Enquirer*.

56. Hillsborough *Recorder*, 10 June 1829. See also Salisbury *Yadkin and Catawba Journal*, 16 June 1829; Tarborough *Free Press*, 3 April 1829; Greensboro *Patriot*, 10 June 1829.

57. Hillsborough *Recorder*, 8 July 1829. See also *ibid.*, 20 May, 24 June, 2 September 1829; and *Ruffin Papers*, I, 503.

58. "The Precious Metal," *American Farmer*, XI (25 September 1829) , 222–223.

59. Charlotte *Journal*, 14 April 1831; Macon, Ga., *Advertiser*, 29 April 1831; Tarborough *Free Press*, 3 May 1831; Washington *United States Telegraph*, 5 April 1831. The latter paper gives the value at $200,000.

60. Ouseley, *Statistics*, pp. 172–174; Buckingham, *The Slave States*, II, 221–222.

that the high expectation that has been formed of the extent and richness of these mines (North Carolina and Georgia) is confirmed by daily experience and more accurate examination; so that it is evident that the product must become more and more abundant, and cannot but have a material influence upon the wealth, arts, commerce, and currency of the whole Union.[61]

So long as the mines worked were placers, and pick, shovel, and pan the only tools used, miners worked individually or in small groups. Little science, skill, or capital was necessary, and the individual miner was often more successful than the organized group. There were more than 1,000 such miners in Burke County alone.[62] But before very long, individual laborers were unable to make good wages. Colonel James Grant wrote Judge Thomas Ruffin in 1830 that, of the 2,800 laborers in Burke and Montgomery counties, only about one-fourth were making wages.[63] The ridge mines necessitated tools for digging the gravel and wagons for transporting it to water for washing. Long toms, arastras, and other tools for separating the gold from gravel were expensive, and the individual miners largely gave way to groups.[64] Farmers worked their mines in off seasons between harvesting and planting and between the "laying-by" season and harvesting. Some planters transferred their slaves from the plantation to the mine, which they worked on shares.[65] Some owners dug their gravel and

61. U.S., Congress, House of Representatives, *Assay Offices, Gold Districts [of] North Carolina and Georgia*, 21st Cong., 2d sess., 1831, House Report No. 82, p. 1.

62. "Intelligence and Miscellanies," *American Journal of Science*, XVI (July 1829), 361–362; "Miscellaneous," *American Farmer*, XI (5 June and 25 September 1829), 95, 223.

63. *Ruffin Papers*, II, 10–11.

64. Rutherfordton *North Carolina Spectator and Western Advertiser*, 26 March 1830; *Act of Incorporation of the Mecklenburg Gold Mining Company in the State of North-Carolina; and Report of the Secretary of the Company on the State of its Concern; with Accompanying Documents* (New York: W. Solefree, 1833), p. 9 (hereafter, *Incorporation, Mecklenburg Co.*).

65. Mooney, *Myths of the Cherokee*, p. 220; "Intelligence and Miscellanies," *American Journal of Science*, XVI (July 1829), 363; Charlotte, N.C., Mining Board, *Statistics of Mines and Minerals in North Carolina, Collected by the Mining Board of Charlotte* (Charlotte, N.C.: Observer Printing House, 1878), p. 4 (hereafter, *N.C. Statistics of Mines and Minerals*).

had it washed on shares by owners of machinery.[66] On the other hand, some of the

more intelligent, wealthy, and enterprising citizens of the State, after personal examination, are withdrawing their slaves entirely from the cultivation of cotton and tobacco, and removing them to the deposit mines of this [Burke] county.[67]

But because planters preferred to invest in land and Negro slaves, their mining operations were carried on with small capital and in a desultory, careless, extravagant, and unskillful manner.[68]

When the vein and quartz mines were opened and machinery, steam engines, and capital became necessary, local labor was replaced by foreign labor. Local workmen were declared incompetent to run the machinery and the papers carried advertisements for skilled laborers and mechanics.[69] Such machines as John Woody's "Gold Cradle" and Lewis Eisenmenger's "Gold Machine" were sold to the miners.[70] Shafts were sunk from 100 to 150 feet to get at the veins, and lateral passages extended "great distances" on every side. The passages were roofed with boards and supported by heavy timbers. The ore was drawn from the shafts in buckets by mules or steam engines. It was then pounded by stamps and the gold separated by quicksilver. To operate such a mine successfully required from 25 to 150 hands.[71]

The expensive character of vein and underground mining led to the organization of chartered mining companies and the importation of foreign capital. The Cabarrus Gold Mining Company, chartered in 1832 with a capitalization of $200,000,[72] was a

66. *Ruffin Papers*, II, 12.

67. Isaac T. Avery to Hon. S. P. Carson, in *Assay Offices, Gold Districts, North Carolina, Georgia, Etc., to Accompany Bill H.R. 84*, U.S., Congress, House of Representatives, 22d Cong., 1st sess., 1831, *House Report No. 39*, p. 23.

68. "The Mining Interest at the South," *Russell's Magazine*, III (August 1858), 442.

69. *Ruffin Papers*, II, 11; Salisbury *Western Carolinian*, 1 August 1831; "The Mining Interest at the South," *Russell's Magazine*, III (August 1858), 443.

70. Rutherfordton *North Carolina Spectator and Western Advertiser*, 10 September, 24 September 1830; *Murphey Papers*, I, 354–355.

71. Macon, Ga., *Advertiser*, 24 August 1831; Ouseley, *Statistics*, pp. 170–172; Tarborough *Free Press*, 11 January 1831; Vigne, *Six Months in America*, I, 232–234.

72. Charlotte *Miners' and Farmers' Journal*, 28 March 1832.

typical one, although several companies were capitalized as high as $1,500,000. Nine companies were chartered by the legislature of 1834 for the county of Mecklenburg alone.[73] Speculation in mining stock was general, and newspapers and journals were filled with advertisements of mines for sale, lease, or exchange, and of those who wanted to buy.[74]

Speculation was not always honest, for owners and agents early learned to lead the prospective purchaser to the place where the richest ore was being worked, and some were not averse to "salting" their mines. One agent so deceived an investigator from New York that, upon his return to that city, he began to buy stock in the mine which jumped from $100 par to $1,000. It was later learned that the agent owned shares in the mine and made a profit of $150,000 on his stock.[75] Charles Fisher, a member of Congress from North Carolina, was engaged in mining, and his correspondence discloses that people from Charleston, Baltimore, and New York consulted him on investments. Fisher proposed to buy rather than lease the mines and also to purchase Negro slaves with which to work them. He desired that his plans be kept from the newspapers so as to avoid competition, and also to prevent the owners from raising their prices.[76] The New York *Observer* sent a correspondent to the gold fields, who kept the readers of that paper informed of the development of the mines.[77]

One of the most distinctive features of the gold region was the development of a number of boom towns, where thousands of laborers were assembled and a rough, crude society was established. When a rich strike became known, miners flocked to the

73. D. A. Tompkins, *History of Mecklenburg County and the City of Charlotte* (Charlotte, N.C.: Observer Printing House, 1903), I, 131.

74. For typical advertisements, see Charlotte *Catawba Journal,* 9 September 1828; Charlotte *Miners' and Farmers' Journal,* 28 March 1832; Rutherfordton *North Carolina Spectator,* 18 June 1831.

75. Tarborough *Free Press,* 23 July 1830; 20 November 1832; "The Gold of California and its Effects on Prices," *Hunt's Merchants' Magazine,* XXXIV (May 1856), 536–540.

76. Charles Fisher to Henry W. Connor, 14 January 1828; Andrew Kerr to Fisher, 23 September 1828. From the Fisher Family Papers, in the Southern Historical Collection at the University of North Carolina Library, Chapel Hill, N.C.

77. "Gold Mines," *American Almanac* (1832), p. 226.

region; almost overnight, a town would spring up, only to be deserted as soon as its more accessible mines were exhausted or the news of a new and richer strike reached the camp. Among the most important of these mines and towns were Brindletown, Bissell, Capps, Jamestown, Washington, Morganton, Gold Hill, and Charlotte. The last was not only in the center of the gold region but was also the seat of the branch mint. It and Morganton are the only towns which retain any importance at the present time. The miners in these towns ranged from 600 to 5,000.

Charlotte, Brindletown, Washington, and Gold Hill each employed from 3,000 to 5,000 laborers.[78] These laborers were not, of course, all engaged at one mine but were distributed in several mines. Many of the laborers were local people, both men and women. The women were said to "develop great acumen in selecting the best gold-bearing lands and became very expert in panning it."[79] One "young lady," working at Dismuke's mine in Anson County, found a thirteen-pound, seven-ounce nugget, and by the terms of the contract received one-half of the find.[80] There were also hundreds of Negro slaves employed in the mines. They seem to have worked side by side with the white men and women, though at a lower wage scale, without any race difficulties.[81] There were employed in the Lincoln County mines alone more than 5,000 slaves in 1833.[82] Negroes were often used to cut timber, build fences and dams, and cultivate the food crops for the miners. The superintendent of the Mecklenburg Mining Company

78. Nitze and Wilkins, *Gold Mining in North Carolina*, p. 29; U.S., Congress, Senate, *Use of Senate Stationery in Promoting Gold Hill Consolidated Company*, 63d Cong., 2d sess., 1914, Senate Report No. 688, p. 9.

79. Moore, "Gold in North Carolina," *Scientific American Supplement*, LIII (22 March 1902) , p. 21918.

80. Tarborough *Free Press*, 5 September 1828.

81. "Report Made by the Honorable G. C. Vernplanck of the Select Committee for the Purpose of Inquiring into the Expediency of Establishing Assay Offices in the Gold Districts of North and South Carolina and Georgia," in *American Quarterly Review*, XI (March 1832) , 89 (hereafter, Verplanck, *Report*) ; Bannister, Cowan & Co., *The Resources of North Carolina* (Wilmington, N.C.: privately printed, 1869) , pp. 47–51.

82. Henry Barnard, "The South Atlantic States in 1833, as seen by a New Englander," edited by B. C. Steiner, in *Maryland Historical Magazine*, XIII (1918) , 347 (hereafter, "South Atlantic States") .

used six slaves who raised "hay, corn and oats, . . . much more than we can use; besides the advantage of placing us beyond the combination of the country people, which is sometimes a great evil."[83] Slaves were permitted to search for gold on Sundays and holidays on shares, and many secured enough money in this way to buy freedom for themselves and families.[84]

But by far the larger part of the laborers in the mines, at least from 1830 to 1845, were foreigners. Many of them were poor, ignorant, and morally degenerate. They included Jew and Gentile, Latin and Nordic. In the mining towns were found Negroes, Americans, English, Welsh, Scotch, Cornish, Irish, Spaniards, Swedes, Germans, Swiss, Poles, Austrians, Brazilians, Turks, Mexicans, Hungarians, Italians, and Portuguese; and in one mine, some thirteen different languages were spoken.[85] Some of the mine owners, however, preferred to employ "diggers of the country," for the mine would not then be

liable to be stopped by a turn-out of the English miners for higher wages, as they will at time do, now by their being *seduced* away by other companies: besides in case of necessity, negroes could be employed.[86]

Many of the mining towns sprang up on the frontier of the southern states, where a few log huts, surrounded by a few acres of corn and other foodstuffs, marked the only improvement made by man. The horde of miners with their machinery and the bustle of industry soon changed the face of the earth. Jamestown had been a straggling place in a small valley but was "turned topsy-turvey by the gold diggers, who had utterly ruined the beautiful valley for agricultural purposes."[87] Roads in the mining region were

83. *Mecklenburg Gold Mining Company,* pp. 17–18.

84. Washington *United States Telegraph,* 11 November 1826.

85. Tarborough *Free Press,* 7 June 1832; "Gold Mines," *American Almanac* (1832), p. 227; Buckingham, *Slave States,* II, 222; Clarence Griffin, *The Bechtlers and Bechtler Coinage and Gold Mining in North Carolina* (Forest City, N.C.: Forest City *Courier,* 1929), pp. 10–11 (hereafter, *The Bechtlers*).

86. *Mecklenburg Gold Mining Company,* pp. 22–23.

87. G. W. Featherstonhaugh, *A Canoe Voyage up the Minnay-Sotor, with an Account of the Lead and Copper Mines of Wisconsin, of the Gold Region in the Cherokee Country and Sketches of Popular Manners* (London: R. Bentley, 1847), II, 231.

intolerable, and travel was almost impossible. Henry Barnard found the going very difficult, even with "easy riding horses and a double chair."[88] The stage from Lincolnton to Morganton was "drawn by a mule and a little pony . . . a queer looking outfit," but the ill-matched team was preferable to the one which replaced it, for the latter "gave out in about two miles, and we were obliged to wait two hours before we could get the old mule again."[89]

Charlotte, the center of the gold region and the resort of many foreigners, was a "beautiful village." Some of the mining companies had built "substantial and comfortable dwelling houses" for the "white persons and officers" besides "excellent houses for the black hands." Stables, store houses, carpenter shops, a smelting and assay house, a saw and grist mill were also found at the St. Catherine mine.[90]

The mine, however, was not "worked in a very scientific manner." It had been opened to a depth of 100 feet and had tunnels radiating in every direction for several hundred yards. The tunnels were lighted only with candles and were so low that the miners had to creep on hands and knees. One hundred men were working in the mine and the ore was raised by horsepower. Blast mining filled the tunnels with smoke and the sound almost deafened the miners.[91]

This mine had once belonged to "James Capps, who was a poor drunken devil, and after the discovery of the gold, he lived so fast and drank so much whiskey that he died in a year. His wife is a poor beast and his children not much better."[92]

---

88. Barnard, "South Atlantic States," pp. 338, 344.

89. *Ibid.;* John Taylor, *Some Account of the Discovery of Gold in the United States* ([n.p.: n.p., 1831?]) , p. 2 (hereafter, *Gold in the U.S.*) .

90. Barnard, "South Atlantic States," p. 342; *Mecklenburg Gold Mining Company,* pp. 28–29. [The Barnard account uses the words "St. Catherine mills." Green has changed this to "St. Catherine mine," and with apparent correctness, because this particular mine, near Charlotte, was one of North Carolina's best known and most productive mines.—J.I.C.]

91. Barnard, "South Atlantic States," p. 341.

92. *Ibid.,* p. 340.

At another mine, the people were "a set of cut throats and savages, with some exceptions."[93] The worthless fellows gathered around the mine and worked enough to buy bread and whiskey and spent the remainder of their time in gambling and fighting. One poor fellow who had committed murder was so troubled by his act that he could not bear to be alone. Whiskey carts and hucksters' wagons loaded with whiskey and provisions were always to be seen near such mines.[94] But all the men at the mines were not such a tough and crude lot. Henry Barnard met at one mine "Mr. Hall, a pedagogue," and "Doctor Baskerville, a very good-looking man," as well as twenty other "young men engaged in the mining business . . . and a fine set they were, too. In the course of the evening champagne and Madeira were brought in and a right merry time we had of it."[95] Barnard also found "pretty young ladies" and "very beautiful women" who played the piano and sang sweetly even though they lived in "log houses, one story having two rooms."[96] He found the accommodations at McIntyre's Tavern in Morganton "miserable" and those at Tate's so bad that he became "mad as a hornet"; but at Mitchell's, he had a "fine toddy" and a dinner with which he could find no fault: it consisted of "cold bacon, fried bacon, cold beef and fowl . . . egg and corn bread."[97]

At the larger mines and towns, "the state of morals" was "deplorably bad." This was attributed to

the absence of any general organization as yet for the police and regulation of the mines, combined with the usual effects of gold upon the uneducated and needy classes of men . . . who generally seek employment in the gold district.[98]

93. Charles E. Rothe, "Remarks on the Gold Mines of North Carolina," *American Journal of Science*, XIII (January 1828), 201–217 (hereafter, Rothe, "Remarks"). This article was written by Charles E. Rothe, a German metallurgist and mining engineer, for and at the request of the people of Germany.

94. *Ibid.*

95. Barnard, "South Atlantic States," p. 346.

96. *Ibid.*

97. *Ibid.*, 347.

98. "North Carolina Gold Mines," *Hunt's Merchants' Magazine*, XXXI (October 1854), 517; Ouseley, *Statistics*, p. 173.

Gold Hill, a company with a million-dollar capitalization, was opened in 1842. A town meeting was held to select a name for the post office, and Colonel George Barnhardt suggested the name of the company. In 1848, there were employed in the fifteen or more mines 1,000 laborers. The town at that time contained five stores, one tavern, four doctors, besides mechanics, blacksmiths, carriage makers, boot, shoe, saddle, and harness makers, and brick- and stonemasons. It was the best market for produce in all western and middle North Carolina. The houses of the Gold Hill Company were valued at $50,000. The industry continued to develop and, in 1856, there were 3,000 laborers employed. Shafts were sunk 700 and 800 feet deep. The value of the mine at one time was estimated at $6,000,000, although it had already produced some $5,000,000 in gold. At the height of its production, it ran night and day and utilized steam hammers, Chilean and Drag mills, Burke rockers, and Tyrolese bowls, all driven by seven steam engines.[99]

The owners of the Washington mine attempted a model establishment. A small hill, with a gentle slope in every direction, was selected for the town. This was enclosed by a board fence seven or eight feet high. Within the enclosure,

the various working establishments, the mine, smelting and roasting furnaces, mechanics' shops, coal houses, crushing, baking and washing houses, shaft houses, offices, laboratory, officers' dwellings, and other essential buildings[100]

were erected. The miners' houses, store, schoolhouse, stables, etc., to the number of sixty, were arranged externally around the mine.[101] In spite of such precaution, lack of organization and

99. Wheeler, *Historical Sketches,* II, 395–397; Charles Upham Shepard, *Description of Gold and Copper Mines at Gold Hill, Rowan Co., North Carolina* (n.p.: n.p., [1853]) , pp. 1–2; T. J. Cram, *Report Upon the Mine and Mills of the North Carolina Gold Amalgamating Company* (Philadelphia: Collins, 1874) , pp. 8–9; U.S., Congress, Senate, *Use of Senate Stationery in Promoting Gold Hill Consolidated Company,* 63d Cong., 2d sess., 1914, Senate Report No. 688, pp. 8–9; Emmons, *Geological Report,* pp. 160–162.

100. Richard Cowling Taylor, *Reports on the Washington Silver Mine in Davidson County, North Carolina* (Philadelphia: E. G. Dorsey, printer, 1845) , pp. 10–11.

101. *Ibid.*

order and decorum led to disturbances, and the owners demanded reform and improvement on the part of the superintendents, James Bell and George Greenfield. One year later, they reported as follows:

We have used every means in our power to improve the condition of your establishment by improvement in different ways. We have built several excellent and convenient houses; we have expelled several dissipated and unruly characters from our neighborhood; we have encouraged industry and sobriety; and are most happy to say that the present condition of the place is better than we could reasonably expect. The establishment of a store has answered a good purpose; it has given great satisfaction to your workmen and the country around us.[102]

The mining towns "afforded a valuable market to the producers of corn, pork, etc. in the parts adjacent"[103] to the gold region. Traders as far away as Connecticut drove their wagons in caravans, "loaded with all kinds of tin ware, dry goods, cutlery, and various wares and merchandise"[104] to the gold fields of North Carolina.

While the life of the miner was rough and crude, there were certain compensations other than the hope of gain and the excitement of a rich find. Social and political gatherings furnished an avenue or outlet for pent-up emotions. The motif of such gatherings, as well as the patriotic celebration of the Fourth of July, centered around gold and the mining industry.[105] Several newspapers in the region were concerned chiefly with the mining interest and one, the *Miners' and Farmers' Journal,* was established as the organ of those interests. The paper was begun in 1831 and catered to the interests of the miners. Thomas J. Hatton, the editor, said "the *Journal* having been established for the disseminating correct information on that subject, we shall insert such articles as shall be interesting."[106] This paper, as well as others in the gold region, was filled with notices of new discoveries, leading articles

---

102. *Ibid.,* p. 36.

103. *Niles' Weekly Register,* XLVIII (16 May 1835) , 188.

104. Washington *United States Telegraph,* 11 November 1826.

105. Rutherfordton *North Carolina Spectator and Western Advertiser,* 9 July 1830.

106. Charlotte *Miners' and Farmers' Journal,* 28 March 1832.

on mines and mining, advertisements of mines for lease or sale, and of miners' tools, machinery, and supplies.

Foreign influences played a major role in developing the North Carolina gold mines, although "enterprising strangers" were not always trusted, nor did they always receive a warm welcome.[107] As already noted, many foreign laborers worked in the mines; many mines were owned by foreigners; native owners often employed foreign engineers and mineralogists as superintendents; some owners went to Germany to study foreign mining methods; and many of the new machines were of foreign make. Humphrey Bissell, a leading miner, studied at Frieburg and Swansea and brought back a German engineer for his mine. Gugnot, a Frenchman, introduced the first stamp mill in the state. Douvergene, another Frenchman, was employed by the North Carolina Company as a consultant chemist. Godfrey T. Vigne made use of the services of "Mr. Damm, a Swedish gentleman." The English Gold Mining Company employed Vincent Rivifinoli, an Italian experienced in South American mines, as superintendent, but he proved unsuccessful in managing southern whites and Negroes and was "forcibly dispossessed" of his job.[108] John H. Wheeler, superintendent of the Charlotte mint, reported in 1840 that

many of the mines, in their most productive state, belonged to foreigners or were leased by them; the agents or managers were also foreigners; and the capital, also, was from abroad. The agents, then, often made prompt returns, by remitting the bullion direct to Europe. This was the case with Chevalier Rivifinoli.[109]

The dislike of foreigners and the export of gold led to efforts to exclude foreigners from the mines. Higher taxes on foreign investments were levied, and the native laborers refused to work for

107. Tompkins, *Mecklenburg County*, II, 120; Rothe, "Remarks," *American Journal of Science*, XIII (January 1828), p. 210.

108. Tompkins, *Mecklenburg County*, II, 120–123; *Murphey Papers*, I, 382–383; Vigne, *Six Months in America*, I, 221; Franklin L. Smith, "Notice of Some Facts Connected with the Gold of a Portion of North Carolina," *American Journal of Science*, XXXII (July 1837), 132; *Mecklenburg Gold Mining Company*, pp. 3, 7; "The Gold Mines of North Carolina," *Hunt's Merchants' Magazine*, XI (July 1844), 65.

109. *Hazard's United States Commercial and Statistical Register*, III (July 1840), 2.

foreign owners and superintendents. Riots and pitched battles sometimes took place between native and foreign laborers and complicated the problem of order.[110] To escape such disturbances, and with the hope of larger profits in the Cherokee country in Georgia, some of the North Carolina miners sent a petition to President Jackson asking permission to work the Georgia mines. The President replied that Georgia had sovereign power within the state and also possessed the "domain in fee." Since the mines and minerals belonged to the state, not the federal government, the President refused to intervene in favor of the North Carolinians.[111]

The fact that Georgia claimed and exercised control over the mines in that state suggested the same practice to North Carolinians. Some proposed the formation of a "North Carolina Gold Company" to buy and work the mines as a state enterprise, but with private subscription to the stock.[112] Others proposed that foreign investors be kept from the state. That this might be more efficiently accomplished, they suggested that the mines and water courses be seized under the right of eminent domain. Colonel Joseph Graham added to this proposition the idea of a state mining engineer and a director of mines, and also proposed that the government provide instruction in mining engineering and mineralogy, so that it would have skilled native miners.[113] The legislature appointed a committee to investigate and report how North Carolina might best combine "private and public interest" in the mines, and whether the state should lend its aid to corporate associations engaged in mining. The committee reported that private individuals could not develop the mines because of the expense of mills, machinery, houses for workmen, and salaries for skilled engineers and mechanics, and because of the hazardous character of mining operations. It recommended, therefore, the

110. *Ruffin Papers*, II, 12–13; Verplanck, *Report*, p. 90; Rutherfordton *North Carolina Spectator and Western Advertiser*, 21 May 1830.

111. Andrew Jackson, *Correspondence of Andrew Jackson*, edited by John Spencer Bassett (Washington, D.C.: Carnegie Institution of Washington, 1926–1935), IV, 376, 377, 382.

112. Charlotte *Catawba Journal*, 13 September 1825.

113. *Ruffin Papers*, II, 13.

incorporated companies.[114] The director of the United States Mint further recommended that North Carolina encourage the mining industry by granting special privileges to banks which bought and assayed the gold.[115] But beyond the incorporation of mining companies, the state did not go.

Either the encouragement given by their government or the richness of the placer mines caused the industrious North Carolinians and others to develop the mines, greatly to the financial and economic advantage of the citizens and the state. A legislative committee reported that while the mining business was in its infancy, the people were indebted to it for

the restoration of the greatly depreciated currency of the country to a sound and safe circulating medium. The bills of the Bank of North Carolina, at a discount, but three years since of more than eight percent, are now at par.[116]

A report to Congress stated that a great change was

perceptibly taking place in the monied concerns of the people. The upper part of North Carolina has very severely felt the pressure so generally complained of throughout the South. These difficulties are rapidly disappearing from the gold districts. The gold that is found and put into circulation, and the sums that are expended in making experiments, erecting machinery, procuring labor and provisions, are producing important changes, and greatly improving the condition of the country.[117]

The gold mined in the state was used extensively in local trade.

The dust became a considerable medium of circulation, and miners were accustomed to carry about with them quills filled with gold, and a pair of small hand scales on which they weighed out gold at regular rates; for instance, three and one-half grains of gold was the customary equivalent of a pint of whiskey.[118]

114. *Incorporation, Mecklenburg Co.*, pp. 3–4.

115. U.S., Congress, House of Representatives, *Assay Offices, Gold Districts [of] North Carolina and Georgia*, 21st Cong., 2d sess., 1831, House Report No. 82, p. 3.

116. John Taylor, *Gold in the U.S.*, p. 6.

117. U.S., Congress, House of Representatives, *Assay Offices, Gold Districts, North Carolina, Georgia, Etc., to Accompany Bill H.R. No. 84*, 22d Cong., 1st sess., 1831, House Report No. 39, p. 15.

118. Mooney, *Myths of the Cherokee*, p. 221.

Local merchants exchanged merchandise, miners' tools, and supplies for the gold; farmers sold meat, corn, and foodstuffs to the
miners and took gold dust and nuggets in exchange; drovers from
Tennessee and Kentucky received pay for their livestock in gold
which they carried with them into those states;[119] and the goods
which local merchants bought on the eastern markets were often
paid for in gold.[120] Many of the banks sent agents into the region
to purchase gold. Colonel J. T. Avery, agent of the Bank of the
State located at Morganton, bought much of the gold mined in
Burke and Rutherford counties prior to 1832, which he estimated
to be worth $6,000,000. The miners, however, said it was nearer
$12,000,000. The price paid by the banks was 90 to 97 cents per
pennyweight.[121]

Large quantities of the gold were used by jewelers and artisans.
A Macon, Georgia, jeweler purchased his gold from North Carolina rather than from Georgia, in order to obtain a finer color and
grade. The amount of gold used in the arts of 1832 was estimated
at $600,000; and the director of the mint said in 1833 that fully
one-fifth of the gold produced in North Carolina was diverted to
the arts.[122] Again, much of the gold was exported as bullion direct
to the European countries, chiefly to London and Paris. Some
journals estimated that one-half of the gold produced in 1832 was
so exported.[123]

119. Foster, *Early Discoveries,* p. 3.

120. "Bills of exchange drawn on the house of James Hamilton & Son, by the
Gold Mining Company of Burke . . . payable at the Chemical Bank at New York,
have been put in circulation in the western part of the State and . . . are answering
a great public convenience." Tarborough *Free Press,* 15 November 1833. The
Washington *United States Telegraph,* 16 May 1829, says that merchants from
Fayetteville, Cheraw, and Charleston brought gold and carried it north in quantities
of from ten to forty pounds each year.

121. "North Carolina: Gold Mines of North Carolina," *American Almanac*
(1841), p. 216; Tarborough *Free Press,* 19 February 1830.

122. Athens, Ga., *Southern Banner,* 8 February 1834; Vigne, *Six Months in
America,* I, 231; Macon, Ga., *Advertiser,* 17 June 1831; *Niles' Weekly Register,* XLIV
(10 August 1833), 392; U.S., Congress, House of Representatives, *Assay Offices, Gold
Districts [of] North Carolina and Georgia,* 21st Cong., 2d sess., 1831, House Report
No. 82, p. 1.

123. "North Carolina: Gold Mines," *American Almanac* (1832), p. 227; "North
Carolina: Gold Mines of North Carolina," *American Almanac* (1841), p. 214;
Athens, Ga., *Southern Banner,* 8 February 1834.

One would naturally suppose that most of the gold would have gone to the mint at Philadelphia for coinage, but the above facts show that such was not the case. Yet, the total amount of North Carolina gold coined at the Philadelphia mint from 1799 to 1860 was $9,100,591.37. The highest amount deposited in any one year was $475,000 in 1833.[124]

But a large part of the North Carolina gold was stamped and coined by private assayers and minters, some of whom were counterfeiters, while others were honest if illegal. A Congressional committee reported that a "considerable amount of gold, in bullion or under private stamps, [was] circulating as a sort of imperfect currency."[125] Henry Barnard reported a set of counterfeiters in Burke County in 1833, one of whom was apprehended after several years of illegal coinage.[126] Several skillful assayers established themselves in the gold region and stamped their pieces "five dollars" so accurately that there was no penalty attached thereto, as there was to counterfeiting the United States coinage.[127]

Most important of all the private mints was that of the Bechtlers in Rutherford County. Christopher Bechtler, born in 1782 in Pfortzheim, Grand Duchy of Baden, came to the United States in 1829 and settled in Rutherford County, North Carolina.[128] Bechtler opened his mint at Rutherfordton in 1831, at the urgent request of several miners, after Congress had rejected their petition for a branch of the United States Mint. The petition to Congress complained of the risk and expense of transporting gold to the Philadelphia mint and decried the fact that much of the gold was being exported to Europe, and hence lost to American coinage.[129] Bechtler was an accomplished and honest goldsmith and his mint immediately won favor. He carried on business until

124. "Statistics of Coinage," *Hunt's Merchants' Magazine,* VII (July 1842), 90; "Coinage of the United States," *Hunt's Merchants' Magazine,* XLIV (March 1861), 338; "Comparative Purity of Gold from Modern Mints," *Hunt's Merchants' Magazine,* XLIV (March 1861), 340–341.

125. U.S., Congress, House of Representatives, *Assay Offices, Gold Districts [of] North Carolina and Georgia,* 21st Cong., 2d sess., 1831, House Report No. 82, p. 1.

126. Barnard, "South Atlantic States," p. 345.

127. Tarborough *Free Press,* 10 October 1834.

128. *The Numismatist,* XXV (August 1912), 261.

129. Rutherfordton *North Carolina Spectator and Western Advertiser,* 2 July 1831.

1843, when his sons, Charles and Augustus, and a nephew, Christopher, Jr., succeeded him. The mint continued operation until 1857.[130] The Bechtlers also made collar buttons, cuff links, necklaces, rings, brooches, and watch chains of the native gold.[131]

Bechtler advertised his work in the papers and called upon the miners in North Carolina, South Carolina, and Georgia to bring their gold to him for assaying and coinage. He coined $1.00, $2.50, and $5.00 pieces, charging 2½ percent for seigniorage; he fluxed gold at the rate of $1.00 per 1,000 pennyweight.[132] The Bechtler coins constituted a chief part of the circulating medium of the gold region. Much of it was also carried by traders, travelers, and emigrants into the West and North and even abroad, for its intrinsic value was slightly above its nominal value. Foreign miners took their gold to Bechtler and had him flux and run it into bars of $500, $1,000, and $2,000 value, so that it could be more easily exported.[133] Some of the Bechtler coins found their way to the mint and were recoined, but the superintendent of the branch at Charlotte reported very little at that place. Bechtler had several competitors in his work, chief of whom was Templeton Reid of Georgia.[134]

The Bechtler coins carried not only their value, but also his name and the name of the state from whence the gold was taken. They were still in circulation in 1860, and one occasionally turns up even today. Just how much gold passed through the mint it is impossible to say. Bechtler reported in 1840 that he had coined $2,241,840.50 and fluxed an additional 1,729,988 pennyweights.[135]

130. Nitze and Wilkins, *Gold Mining in North Carolina,* pp. 41–42.

131. Griffin, *The Bechtlers,* pp. 1, 9.

132. Rutherfordton *North Carolina Spectator and Western Advertiser,* 27 August 1831. See also Thomas Featherstonhaugh, "A Private Mint in North Carolina," reprinted from Southern History Association, *Publications,* X (March 1906), 67–77; G. W. Featherstonhaugh, *A Canoe Voyage,* II, 327–330.

133. James Graham, *Speech on the Proposition to Abolish the Branch Mints* (Washington: Gales and Seaton, 1842), pp. 4–5; "The Gold Mines of North Carolina," *Hunt's Merchants' Magazine,* XI (July 1844), 64.

134. Fletcher M. Green, "Georgia's Forgotten Industry," p. 220; Alexander E. Outerbridge, Jr., "Curiosities of American Coinage," *Popular Science Monthly,* LIII (September 1898), pp. 599–600.

135. "Coinage of the United States," *Hunt's Merchants' Magazine,* III (July 1840), 87. See also Raleigh *Sentinel,* 13 September 1836.

How much he had prepared for export he did not say. From 1840 on, the Bechtler coinage declined because of the establishment of the branch mint at Charlotte, but the fact that the Bechtlers continued operations until 1857 indicates that they did a profitable business.

The discovery of the southern gold and the export of much of it to Europe led to congressional action. The press of North Carolina in 1829 urged a change in the ratio of gold and silver so that the former might be kept in circulation at home. The state papers quoted the Washington and Philadelphia papers to the same effect.[136] This view fitted in with Thomas Hart Benton's idea of hard money and his opposition to bank paper, and he introduced a bill in the United States Senate to establish the ratio of 16 to 1. Campbell Patrick White led the fight in the House of Representatives, although he had formerly favored 15.625 to 1.[137] This shift was the direct result of the discovery of southern gold. The argument that prosperity would be restored by retaining the gold in circulation was effective, and the bill passed. And, according to Senator Hill, the increase of 6 percent in the value of gold stimulated its production.[138]

In 1830, the inhabitants of the southern gold fields began to urge the establishment of a branch mint in the region. They maintained that adulteration and counterfeiting had become so general that people feared to accept the bullion; ingots could not be estimated, so that accounts had to run at interest until remittances to and returns from Philadelphia could be had; the distance to Philadelphia necessitated a delay of from four to six months and the consequent loss of interest for that period. Letters were written to members of Congress and memorials and petitions were

136. Tarborough *Free Press*, 17 July, 14 August 1829; Salisbury *Western Carolinian*, 28 July 1829.

137. Thomas Hart Benton, *Thirty Years' View: or A History of the Working of the American Government for Thirty Years, from 1820 to 1850* (New York: D. Appleton and Co., 1854) , I, 436–439; Alonzo Barton Hepburn, *A History of the Currency and the Perennial Contest for Sound Money in the United States* (New York: Macmillan Co., 1903) , pp. 58–59.

138. U.S., Congress, *Register of Debates in Congress* . . . , 23d Cong., 2d sess., 1835 (Washington: Gales and Seaton, 1835) , XI, pt. 1, 597.

submitted to Congress urging that at least an assay office be established. The concerted action led Samuel Price Carson to call for a committee of investigation. Carson argued that the miners suffered much loss from robbers in transporting gold to Philadelphia. The committee was appointed and circulated a questionnaire among the miners soliciting information.[139] Upon the information obtained, the committee recommended the establishment of one or more assay offices so as to "stimulate the enterprise and industry of all employed in the business and to increase its value to them and the country."[140] The assay offices would not only prove advantageous to the industry, but would also "give steadier supplies and greater regularity to the operations of the mint."[141]

The matter dragged along until December 1833, when all the papers were submitted to a select committee. This committee reported a bill for four assay offices, one each in Virginia, North Carolina, South Carolina, and Georgia. The director of the mint opposed the establishment of assay offices, for fear the gold would be diverted to the arts and recommended, instead, the establishment of branch mints. His recommendation was accepted, and a bill to that effect passed the House by a vote of 115 to 60.[142] Considerable opposition developed in the Senate, where the bill was attacked as a sectional measure. Some senators opposed the bill because most of the Georgia gold region was in the Cherokee country, and others argued that the mints were not needed.[143]

The debate on the bill was largely sectional, with the South and West supporting and the North and East opposing its passage.

---

139. Foster, *Early Discoveries*, p. 7; *American Farmer*, XI (12 February 1830), 383–384; Rutherfordton *North Carolina Spectator and Western Advertiser*, 26 March 1830; Tarborough *Free Press*, 19 February 1830.

140. Verplanck, *Report*, p. 5.

141. *Ibid.*

142. U.S., Congress, House of Representatives, *Assay Offices, Gold Region, South, to Accompany Bill H.R. No. 407*, 23rd Cong., 1st sess., 1834, House Report No. 391, pp. 1–2; U.S., Congress, *Register of Debates in Congress . . .* , 23rd Cong., 2d sess., 1835 (Washington: Gales and Seaton, 1835), XI, pt. 2, 1655–1656, and Appendix, p. 159; U.S., Congress, House of Representatives, 23rd Cong., 1st sess., 1834, House Report No. 391, p. 13.

143. U.S., Congress, *Register of Debates in Congress . . .* , 23rd Cong., 2d sess., 1835 (Washington: Gales and Seaton, 1835), XI, pt. 1, p. 604.

Willie P. Mangum, Bedford Brown, Thomas Hart Benton, G. A. Waggaman, and John C. Calhoun were pitted against Henry Clay and Theodore Frelinghuysen. Brown argued for hard money and urged the mints as a balance for northern protective tariff. Waggaman centered his argument around the expense, loss, and difficulty of transporting the gold to Philadelphia. Calhoun decried the sectional opposition and supported the bill as an act of justice to the South, and as one which would extend equal benefits to the entire country. But Benton was the warmest advocate of the bill. He stressed the constitutional right of the people of Georgia and North Carolina to the mint. He pointed out that there were six hundred machines (the banks) printing paper money and only one coining hard money. He believed the question vital to the well-being of the South and West. Gold coin would circulate throughout the country and drive out the bank paper if only the mints were established. Stock drivers of Ohio, Tennessee, and Kentucky would carry the gold back with them, and it would become the circulating medium of the Mississippi Valley.

Benton reiterated that this was a question of currency; of hard money against paper; of gold against United States Bank notes. It was a struggle with the paper system. He said the gold bill was one step; the branching of the mint would be the second step; the suppression of all notes under twenty dollars would be the third step towards getting a gold and silver coinage.[144]

The bill passed the Senate, 24 to 19, and became a law on March 3, 1835. It provided for three branch mints, one each at New Orleans, Charlotte, and Dahlonega. The one at New Orleans was to coin both gold and silver, while the other two were restricted to gold coinage. Congress appropriated $56,000 for building and equipping the mint at Charlotte. The contract was let by competitive bidding, and Reuben Perry and Thomas P. Ligon of Charlotte secured the contract at $29,700.[145] The cornerstone was

144. Benton, *Thirty Years' View*, I, 550–553; U.S., Congress, *Register of Debates in Congress* . . . , 23d Cong., 2d sess., 1835 (Washington: Gales and Seaton, 1835) , XI, pt. 1, 551–552, 580.

145. U.S., Congress, House of Representatives, *Mint of the United States and Branches*, 25th Cong., 2d sess., 1838, Document No. 273; Raleigh *Register,* 27 October 1835.

laid January 8, 1836, and the mint opened for business December 4, 1837.[146] In addition to the main building, there were rooms for the superintendent, a kitchen, smokehouse, laundry, stables, carriage house, woodhouse, summer house, and—most remarkable of all—a bathhouse. The latter was eight feet square, with one door and window, transom lights, and fixtures for a shower bath.[147] Some of the items of equipment were as follows: ink-stands, $13.75; office chair, $34.00; sofa, $81.50; three lamps, $15.00; fine carpet and rugs, $150.49; a clock, $65.00; and fences and shrubbery, nearly $500.00. Such extravagance during the hard times of the panic of 1837 led to bitter criticism in Congress. A committee of investigation reported that it saw no connection between such buildings and equipment and the coining of gold.[148] The original building was burned in July 1844, and D. M. Barringer was given a contract for rebuilding it at $25,000. Another fire in February 1845 gave H. C. Owen a contract for repairs at $20,000.[149]

The mint was opened with appropriate ceremonies. Crowds of excited and enthusiastic miners and citizens shouted their approval. Colonel John H. Wheeler, whom the *Western Carolinian* described as "the gentleman who knocked Mr. Hutchinson's nose out of joint, and kicked over Dr. Fox's pail of milk,"[150] was the first superintendent. He was expected to *"wheel* out the *yellow boys,* not slowly," but as fast as the *"Great Benton* himself could wish."[151] Associated with Wheeler were John H. Gibbon, assayer; John R. Bolton, coiner; and William F. Strange, chief clerk. In addition, there were several unskilled laborers. The

146. U.S., Congress, House of Representatives, *Mint of the United States and Branches,* 25th Cong., 2d sess., 1838, Document No. 273; Tompkins, *Mecklenburg County,* I, 132.

147. U.S., Congress, House of Representatives, *Expenditures—Branch Mint at Charlotte, N.C.,* 26th Cong., 2d sess., House Report No. 18, pp. 4–6.

148. *Ibid.,* pp. 7–8.

149. Tompkins, *Mecklenburg County,* I, 132.

150. Salisbury *Western Carolinian,* 13 May 1837. Other superintendents were Colonel Burgess S. Gaither in 1841; Greene W. Caldwell in 1844 and again in 1853; William J. Alexander in 1846; and James W. Osborne in 1849. Wheeler, *Historical Sketches,* II, 268.

151. *Ibid.*

annual expenditure of the mint was about $11,000 and the total expenditure prior to 1850 was $143,963.15.[152]

The opening of the mint stimulated, temporarily, the mining and coining of gold. It also greatly benefited farming, encouraged the sciences, led to the improvement of roads, and generally imparted a spirit of successful enterprise to the country.[153] But in a short time the amount of gold offered for coinage declined. R. M. Patterson, director of the mint at Philadelphia, said the decline was due to the exhaustion of the placer mines and lack of machinery, capital, and skill with which to develop the vein and underground mines; to the high price of cotton, which drew farmers from mines; to the coinage of private mints like that of Bechtler; and to over-valuation of foreign gold by the Act of 1834. He recommended the repeal of the latter and the coinage of small change by the mints.[154] The North Carolina legislature instructed the state's delegation to introduce and support such a bill, for, according to the instructions, the scarcity of such coin was injurious to all the great productive branches of trade and industry.[155] Nothing, however, came of these efforts.

The expense of the mint, together with the decline of its coinage, led to an effort to discontinue it. Willis Green, a Whig Representative from Kentucky, moved for its discontinuance in 1841. He attacked the "branch mints as useless establishments, cumbering the machinery of Government, wasting the money of the people, and increasing the fearful power and patronage of the Executive."[156] Jesse A. Bynum and James Graham of North Caro-

152. U.S., Congress, House of Representatives, *Branch Mint—Charlotte, N.C.,* 25th Cong., 3d sess., 1839, House Document No. 189, p. 3; "Expenses of the United States Mint and Branches," *Hunt's Merchants' Magazine,* XXIV (January 1851), 100.

153. Asheboro, N.C., *Southern Citizen,* 29 November 1839; *Hazard's United States Commercial and Statistical Register,* II (July 1840), 2; Clemson, "Gold and the Gold Region," *Orion* (April 1844), IV, 57–66; Lanman, *Letters,* pp. 190–192.

154. U.S., Congress, House of Representatives, *Annual Report of the Director of the Mint,* 24th Cong., 2d sess., 1837, Executive Doc. No. 96, p. 2; "Statistics of Coinage," *Hunt's Merchants' Magazine,* IV (April 1841), 382–383.

155. U.S., Congress, House of Representatives, *Resolution of the Legislature of North Carolina for a Law Directing the Coinage of Small Change at the Mint at Charlotte,* 25th Cong., 3d sess., 1839, House Document No. 142, p. 1.

156. Willis Green, *Remarks on the General Appropriations Bill,* delivered in the House of Representatives, 18 February 1841, pp. 1, 2, 4.

lina replied to Green and defended the mint. Bynum claimed that
the movement was a Whig effort to overthrow hard money and
re-establish the United States Bank. To effect this, the "mint must
first be destroyed, and all idea of a solid, permanent currency,
founded on a *specie basis,* discountenanced and discouraged
amongst the *laboring, mechanical, planting* and *producing classes*
of this country."[157]

James Graham denounced the motion as anti-southern. He said
the mint, like the army, navy, and post office, was a service
institution and not expected to pay its cost. The United States
should encourage the miners so that they would not be subject to
the "merchants, banks, and speculators."[158] The press of North
Carolina was aroused and ardently defended the mint. One editor
said that "to do away with the branch mints would deprive the
South—especially the gold region of North Carolina and Georgia
—of all the advantages and facilities which they afford."[159] The
director of the mint came to the defense of the branches. He
reported that, while the mines were not worked as extensively as
formerly, they were very rich and had deposited more than
$2,000,000 of gold for coinage in the two years just preceding.[160]
The southern Whigs, while attacking the extravagance of the
branch mints, refused to support Green's resolution, and it failed
to pass.[161]

In 1847, Robert J. Walker, Secretary of the Treasury, ordered
that all United States funds then in deposit banks be transferred
to the nearest branch mint. Thomas Corwin, his Whig successor,
recommended in 1851 that, since the coinage of the branch mints
had declined without any decrease in expenditure, they should be

157. Jesse A. Bynum, *Speech in the Committee of the Whole on a Motion to
Strike out the Appropriation to Continue the Branch Mint in North Carolina,*
delivered in the House of Representatives, 17 February 1841, pp. 1, 2, 9.

158. Graham, *Speech on the Proposition to Abolish the Branch Mints,* pp. 3, 6, 7.

159. Salisbury *Western Carolinian,* 6 May 1842.

160. U.S., Congress, House of Representatives, *Report of the Operations of the
Mint and Branch Mints,* 28th Cong., 2d sess., 1845, Executive *Document No. 99,* pp.
1–6.

161. Edward Stanly, *Sketch of the Remarks of Mr. Stanly on the Branch Mint of
North Carolina* (Washington: Gales and Seaton, 1840) , p. [3] and *passim.*

reduced to assay offices only.[162] This was not done, however, and the Charlotte mint continued in operation until its seizure in 1861 by the Confederate forces.

It is possible to ascertain approximately the amount of gold which North Carolina offered for coinage. The director's report for 1860 shows that there had been sent to the Philadelphia mint from North Carolina a total of $9,100,591.37. The Charlotte branch mint coined a total of $4,663,273.35. And add to this the Bechtler coinage prior to 1840 of $3,746,930.06, and we get a grand total of $17,510,794.78.

The establishment of the mint at Charlotte in 1837 gave nation-wide publicity and importance to the North Carolina mines, and speculation in mining stock became rife in the 1840s. Some capitalists sought honest investments and made considerable fortunes. On the other hand, many invested for the mere sake of speculation. Stocks were quoted regularly on the New York exchange where the speculation ran into the "double game as played by the Bulls and Bears." More than $40,000,000 was invested in North Carolina mining stock.[163] During the 1840s, the capital came largely from the North, whereas in the early period it had come chiefly from abroad. New York and Boston capitalists became largely interested in 1846. Commodore R. F. Stockton was a leading investor. He bought the famous Gold Hill, the Rudisill, and the Huey mines in North Carolina and the Dorn and Brewer mines in South Carolina.

Speculation was not always profitable to the speculators and often brought ruin to the industry.

Led on by bankrupt merchants, broken-down lawyers, quack doctors, clergymen whose political fanaticism had robbed them of their churches—in short, officered by men who had failed in every pursuit they had undertaken—how could it be otherwise than that the operations conducted by them in this new field of enterprise should have

162. "United States Treasury Circular," *Hunt's Merchants' Magazine*, XVI (March 1847), 308; "United States Mint," *Hunt's Merchants' Magazine*, XXVI (February 1852), 236.

163. Emmons, *Geological Report*, p. 163; Friedrich A. Genth, *The Mineral Resources of North Carolina* (Philadelphia: [n.p.], 1871), p. 1; *Niles' Weekly Register*, XLVI (10 May 1834), 172; Foster, *Early Discoveries*, pp. 4, 7, 9.

been attended with the same failures which had marked all their former doings?[164]

But the leaders generally escaped, and innocent shareholders were the chief losers. "Indeed it was the very wildest gambling, compared with which a stake on the faro table almost appears a safe investment."[165] The general effect on the southern mines was bad, as absentee ownership has so often been.

The evil effects of speculation, together with the discovery of gold in California, led to a noticeable decline of mining operations in North Carolina. One stream in McDowell County which had 3,000 miners at work in 1848 was practically deserted in 1850. The miners left individually and in groups for California. Many carried their slaves with them to the new fields. Their experience in the southern mines gave them an advantage over inexperienced miners. They were not only more adept at locating likely placers, but they were also more skillful in working them. Many southern miners made valuable contributions to the development of western mining and reaped rich harvests for themselves. Others failed in the new fields and gradually trooped back to their old diggings with others of the "Busted by Gosh" group.[166]

In an effort to revive the industry, the legislature, in 1852, passed an act to "encourage the investment of capital for mining and manufacturing purposes."[167] Under this act, a group of not less than five persons might be incorporated, provided the shares were not less than $1.00 par and provided such stock was advertised in the state papers.[168] Geologists and mining engineers published reports which proclaimed anew the valuable mineral resources of the state.[169] Gradually, the industry was renewed: old

164. "The Mining Interest at the South," *Russell's Magazine*, III (August 1858), 443–445.

165. *Ibid.*

166. *The Gold Fields of North Carolina*, p. 16; Tompkins, *Mecklenburg County*, I, 130; George D. Hubbard, *Gold and Silver Mining as a Geographic Factor in the Development of the United States* ([Oberlin?]: n.p., 1912), p. 105; Whitney, *Metallic Wealth*, p. 115; Nitze and Wilkins, *Gold Mining in North Carolina*, p. 27.

167. *Prospectus of the Ward Gold Mining Company* (1854), pp. 1, 9.

168. *Ibid.*

169. Shepard, *Gold and Copper Mines*, p. 8; Emmons, *Geological Report*, p. 176.

mines, ruined by wildcat speculation of the 1840s, were re-opened and, under more scientific management, yielded a profit; and new companies were organized. Typical of such undertakings was the Ward Gold Mining Company, with a capital stock of $1,500,000. The more reputable investors expanded their holdings and applied the new scientific methods which had been developed in California. Commodore Stockton, for instance, purchased several new mines, including the Howie and Lawson mines in Union County.[170]

One writer advised the southern people that, while forming Southern Rights Associations and withdrawing students and trade from northern schools and markets, they should not forget their mining interests. He urged that southern schools teach mining engineering so that the southern mine owners might "not be dependent upon foreigners as they now are to manage their mines."[171] People turned their attention from politics to mining after the election of 1856, and considerable excitement developed, which continued down to the Civil War. In fact, "the five years preceding the war witnessed a revival of mining industry and real progress was made toward a mastery of the methods of sulfurets in an economical and thorough manner."[172] One newspaper editor said that "the mining interest of this region of country has assumed an importance which it has never enjoyed before."[173]

One of the chief factors in this revival of mining in the 1850s was the discovery and development of silver and copper mines. Both silver and copper had been found in small quantities in several of the mines in earlier years, but had been neglected

170. Henry Martyn Chance, *The Auriferous Gravels of North Carolina* ([n.p.]: [n.p.], 1881), p. 478. Paper read before the American Philosophical Society, 15 July 1881.

171. J. Bridge, *The Practical Miner's Own Book and Guide, with Additions by Job Atkins* (Richmond, Va.: J. W. Randolph, 1860), pp. 6–7.

172. *N.C. Statistics of Mines and Minerals*, p. 4. See also Raleigh *Register*, 1 September 1858; Salisbury *Carolina Watchman*, 31 August 1858; Montroville W. Dickeson, *Report of the Geological Survey and Condition of the Twin Mine in the County of Guilford, North Carolina* (Philadelphia: J. B. Chandler, 1860), p. 1, and *passim*.

173. Raleigh *North Carolina Star*, 12 April 1854.

because of the greater importance of gold.[174] In 1838, copper was found at the Deep River Gold Mine in Guilford County, and 100 tons of the ore were shipped to Liverpool; and the superintendent of the Charlotte mint made requisition for a silver assayer in 1839.[175] The Washington Silver Mining Company, located ten miles from Lexington, mined ore which, over a twenty-seven-month period, averaged $100 per ton; and, in 1841, six furnaces were in full operation at the mine.[176] That same year, domestic silver was for the first time deposited at the Philadelphia mint.

The discovery of copper at Ducktown, in East Tennessee, in 1850, aroused the wildest excitement in that state. Captain Harris, an English engineer in charge of the Ducktown mine, shipped from that mine 14,291 tons of ore for which the company received more than $1,000,000. The Hiwassee Company was organized and purchased 600 acres of mineral lands, for which it paid $680,000.[177] The "copper fever" spread "extensively throughout the gold mining region" of North Carolina and a "species of contagious insanity broke out: the monomaniacal feature of which was now copper, as it had on former occasions been gold."[178]

Mines were opened in Guilford County which were said to have produced $1,000,000 the first year of operation. Newspapers began to proclaim the new riches, and copper was pronounced more valuable than all the gold, silver, iron, and coal deposits combined.[179] One writer in *Hunt's Merchants' Magazine* com-

174. *Ibid.*, 1 June, 3 August 1853.

175. Raleigh *Register*, 7 May 1853; U.S., Congress, House of Representatives, *Branch Mint—Charlotte, N.C.*, 25th Cong., 3d sess., 1839, House Document No. 189, p. 2.

176. R. C. Taylor, *Washington Silver Mine*, p. 30; "Statistics of Coinage," *Hunt's Merchants' Magazine*, VI (April 1842) , 375–376.

177. Nantahala and Tuckasege Land and Mineral Company, *Second Preliminary Report of the Nantahala and Tuckasege Land and Mining Company* (Cincinnati: Wrightson & Co., 1858) , pp. 17–18 (hereafter, *Nantahala and Tuckasege Report*) .

178. Raleigh *North Carolina Star*, 4 May 1853; Washington *National Intelligencer*, 19 July 1854; "The Mining Interest at the South," *Russell's Magazine*, III (August 1858) , 445–446.

179. Charles T. Jackson, *Report on the Copper Mine of the North Carolina Company in Guilford County, North Carolina* (New York: Nesbitt, 1853) , pp. 6, 7.

pared the North Carolina copper region with the Lake Superior belt and, while he found the latter the richer, he said the North Carolina region was the more valuable because of the food supply, timber, climate, and conditions of the soil and ore.[180] The North Carolina Copper Company was organized under Charles T. Jackson, famous for his geological reports on Maine, New Hampshire, and Rhode Island. The Nantahala and Tuckasege companies were chartered in 1857, and the Nantahala was organized in Cincinnati with a capital stock of $2,000,000. The company purchased 100,000 acres of land and employed F. F. Orom of Cornwall, England, experienced in the Ducktown mines, as superintendent.[181]

Throughout the earlier period, lack of science, skill, and system had characterized mining in North Carolina. Present and immediate gains had been sought, rather than permanent and continued operations. The 1850s saw more permanent works constructed and more scientific methods, greater skill, more system, and better machinery applied to the industry. As early as 1843, miners on the Catawba River developed a crude method of mine dredging.[182] Stamp mills were introduced in 1836, and the roasting process was developed in 1847.[183] In 1854, Chilean mills and engines were introduced at the Russell and Lupton mines, at an expense of $85,000; but lack of a skilled manager brought failure.[184] At other mines, however, machinery under the new conditions proved successful. At the Gardner mine, vertical shafts, five in number, were sunk 258 feet, and lateral passages followed the veins more than 5,000 feet.[185] An observer at the Gold Hill Mine reported that shafts were from 425 to 800 feet deep. They were

180. "The Mineral Resources of the United States," *Hunt's Merchants' Magazine,* XXXI (December 1854) , 764.

181. *Nantahala and Tuckasege Report,* pp. 3–7, 15.

182. Tompkins, *Mecklenburg County,* II, 120; "Miscellanies: Gold of North Carolina," *American Journal of Science,* XLVIII (April 1845) , 398.

183. Nitze and Wilkins, *Gold Mining in North Carolina,* pp. 32, 35, 36.

184. Philip L. Lyons to Charles Fisher, 4 July 1854, from the Fisher Family Papers in the Southern Historical Collection at the University of North Carolina Library, Chapel Hill, N.C.; Raleigh *North Carolina Star,* 11 May 1853.

185. Greensboro *Daily News,* 6 December 1931.

braced with heavy timbers and had ledges or platforms every twenty feet. Ladders twenty inches wide enabled the miners to ascend or descend. A steam pump was used to keep the shaft clear of water. At the 270-foot level, Negro laborers were observed boring in the rock with sledge and drill. At the 330-foot level, twenty white miners were found standing on one narrow ledge and twenty Negroes on another, awaiting the explosion of a number of blasts in the main tunnel. The ore was drawn from the depths, in buckets made of whiskey barrels, by a double-action windlass. While a full bucket came up, an empty one went down. The motive power for the windlass was a blind horse, but steam power was used elsewhere in the mine. Among the three hundred laborers in the pit were women, white and black, barefooted boys and girls from twelve to fifteen years of age, and white and Negro men. A Cornish foreman directed the work. The mining costume

consisted of a coat with short sleeves and tail, and overalls of white duck. A round-topped, wide-brimmed hat of indurated felt protected the head like a helmet. In lieu of crest or plume each wore a lighted candle in front, stuck upon the hat with a wad of clay.[186]

The writer has had access to the manuscript records of one mine, the High Shoal Gold Mining Company, covering the period from 1848 to 1859. From these records, one can reconstruct the economic life of the mine and miners. They show that the company ran a commissary and bought produce with which to feed its hands. Corn, bacon, flour, tallow, potatoes, beef, and meal were purchased and furnished to the miners. Shoes, tobacco, sugar, and tea were also supplied. Corn sold at 40 to 53 cents per bushel, and bacon at 8 cents, beef at 3 cents, and flour at 2 cents per pound. Powder for blasting was bought at $3.34 per keg. Male laborers were paid from $8 to $35 per month. No distinction was drawn between white and black labor, so far as wages were concerned. White and black women received half pay. Boys and girls, some twelve years of age, were paid $6 per month. Many slaves were employed. In 1850, eleven masters hired 123 slaves to the mine.

186. David H. Strother, "North Carolina Illustrated," in *Harper's Magazine*, XV (August 1857), 292–294, 296–298.

The smallest number hired by any master was 9 and the highest 15. At least one free Negro was employed, a girl, at twenty-five cents per day. If laborers lost time, their wages were cut accordingly. Teamsters were hired by the day at $2.50 or at $1.25 per load of ore hauled. Five cents per bushel was the charge for hauling sand. During the ten-year period, at least five blind horses and three blind mules were purchased, at prices ranging from $15 to $38. These animals were used at the High Shoal mine, as was the case at mines generally, to draw the ore from the mine. Eleven men were shareholders in the business. On April 4, 1850, they divided $9,966.85 as dividends; and one of them drew $428 on July 1, 1850, and an additional $2,750 on July 25, 1851.[187]

The most significant of the new methods of the period of revival was hydraulic mining. This method was tried in North Carolina in the 1840s, but failed. Miners who returned from California were able, however, to apply it successfully in the 1850s. The man to whom most of the credit was due was Dr. M. H. VanDyke, a practical and expert mining engineer, who was much interested in developing the mineral resources of the South. The mines in Burke and McDowell counties were worked extensively by this method during the closing years of the decade. William P. Blake[188] found at the Burke County mines

an aqueduct for supplying water to the placers, which for extent and execution compares favorably with those in the Gold Region in California. The water is carried for miles around the summit of the hills, and across a valley half a mile wide, in a flume supported by trestle work a hundred feet high.[189]

187. "Record Book of the High Shoal Gold Mining Company, 1848–1859." Bound ledger, 81 pages. From the William Alexander Hoke Papers in the Southern Historical Collection at the University of North Carolina Library, Chapel Hill, N.C.

188. Blake, a noted geologist, mineralogist, and mining engineer, was connected with the United States Pacific Railway Survey and later with the War Department in Washington. During the 1850s, he made mineralogical surveys for several mining companies in Georgia and North Carolina.

189. Chestatee Hydraulic Company, *Prospectus of the Chestatee Hydraulic Company* (New York: John F. Trow, printer, 1858), pp. 3–5, 15, 23; Nitze and Wilkins, *Gold Mining in North Carolina*, p. 31; William P. Blake and Charles T. Jackson, *The Gold Placers of the Vicinity of Dahlonega, Georgia* (Boston: [n.p.], 1859), p. 19.

At the Jamestown mine, Captain Stokes used a pipe to shoot water into the mine pits, and the suction not only carried out the water but the gravel and sand as well. Many of the placers, which had already been worked by the old method, were now re-worked once or even twice with the hydraulic method and yielded from 6,000 to 50,000 pennyweights per acre. While the application of hydraulic mining was still in its infancy, Blake reported that

districts previously unavailable for want of water are, by this new method, made to yield rich returns. One effect of this method is to change the uncertain, lottery-like character of mining, to the conditions of a regular business, yielding its assured and certain average of monthly or quarterly returns.[190]

Whether or not Blake's view was correct was not to be learned, for, before the new science, skill, machinery, and methods could be proven, the Civil War put an end to all mining in the South. Hermann Credner, an expert mining engineer who made a survey of the North Carolina gold region in 1866, gave an interesting explanation for the failure of the North Carolina mines in the antebellum period. He said:

The advantages offered by these mining fields are too evident not to have been appreciated a long time ago; but the indifference of the Southern people to this branch of industry, and the impossibility of carrying on, successfully, under the institution of Slavery, operations requiring intelligent & skillful labor, were hindrances not easy to overcome.[191]

The gold-mining industry of antebellum North Carolina had a marked influence upon the life of the people and the development of the state. For some fifty years, it had engaged the attention of the people generally, and for more than half that period, it had been of prime importance. For several years, upwards of 30,000 people were engaged in the industry, and many others were indi-

---

190. Blake and Jackson, *Gold Placers,* p. 19.

191. [Hermann Credner], "Report on Certain Mineral Lands in Cabarrus and Mecklenburg Counties, North Carolina (1866)," translated from the German by Adelberg and Raymond, p. 1. Unpublished manuscript in the North Carolina Collection of the University of North Carolina Library, Chapel Hill, N.C. Both the German and English texts are given.

rectly connected with it. Something like $100,000,000 had been invested, and upwards of $50,000,000 of gold had been produced. Such an industry could not but have affected the life of a rural, thinly populated, and relatively backward state, such as North Carolina then was. Contemporary accounts pay glowing tribute to the good influences of the mining industry. Naturally, newspapers, observers, and travelers tended to exaggerate its importance, but such tributes do indicate an influence upon the people.

Writing in 1829, the editor of the Tarborough *Free Press* said that the mining industry

infuses life and activity into all branches of business. The heavy pressure which is bowing down the necks of the people of this state bears but lightly on our brethren in Mecklenburg; and will soon, according to the present course of things, scarcely be felt by them. We are told that every branch of industry seems to be revived there; mechanics, merchants, and farmers, begin to wear countenances as pleasing as they did in better times.[192]

The Hillsborough *Recorder* and the *Western Carolinian* both copied this editorial with approving comments. One of Judge Ruffin's correspondents wrote that "invaluable benefits" had come to the state as a result of the investment of capital in the mines. He thought "the Western part of the State particularly" had been "greatly benefited by the great and increasing demands for their supplies produced, and great amount of money left among them by Capitalists, and Travellers."[193]

Some of the newspapers and "some persons of intelligence, but most at a distance," expressed a fear that mining would "retard the prosperity and advancement of the country in the arts, public improvements, and the moral happiness of the people."[194] Their fears led them to hold up the picture of conditions in Spain, Mexico, and South America as an example of what gold mining did for a people and a state. These ill-boding prophets claimed that the search for the precious metals debased the mind and

192. Tarborough *Free Press*, 10 April 1829.
193. Colonel Joseph Grant to Judge Thomas Ruffin in *Ruffin Papers*, II, 12.
194. Rutherfordton *North Carolina Spectator and Western Advertiser*, 11 June 1830.

destroyed the principles of patriotism and liberty.[195] But Roswell Elmer, Jr., editor of the *North Carolina Spectator and Western Advertiser,* in replying to the critics, said that it did not

matter much what occupation is followed so long as it is productive of wealth and tending to add to the resources of the nation—keeping all classes employed and consequently benefitting all. The effect produced on this section of the state has been favorable to the interest of the farmers as well as those engaged in mining, in the ready sale of their produce at higher prices than they would have formerly obtained, and that too in "shining dust." Many whose affairs a year since were in a state of embarrassment have collected the "hidden treasures" from their own soil, and made themselves independent and happy. And many enterprising adventurers who have engaged in it, have been rewarded with a plentiful golden harvest.[196]

All industrial pursuits seem to have been stimulated: iron mining was encouraged, mechanics found employment, trade was increased, and vacant buildings were occupied and new ones constructed.

There was a close relationship between mining and agriculture. As before noted, the one was a sort of handmaiden to the other. In 1828, when the price of cotton was low, many laborers went into the gold mines. This, in turn, stimulated the production of corn, the small grains, and other food crops to supply the miners who were able to pay high cash prices. Likewise, it tended to check the overproduction of cotton and bring up the price of that staple.[197] Godfrey T. Vigne, touring the gold region, noted that among the advantages that followed the development of the mines was the encouragement given to agriculture "in the withdrawal of some of its surplus labor, and giving it new employment."[198] This created "home markets for the surplus products of the farmer" and encouraged him to "improve his farm, and increase the produc-

195. Vigne, *Six Months in America,* I, 236; Tompkins, *Mecklenburg County,* I, 130.

196. Rutherfordton *North Carolina Spectator and Western Advertiser,* 11 June 1830.

197. Tarborough *Free Press,* 18 January 1828; "Miscellanies: Projected Branch Mint of North Carolina," *American Journal of Science,* XX (July 1831), 401; *Niles' Weekly Register,* XLII (30 June 1832), 325.

198. *Six Months in America,* I, 238–239.

tiveness of his land."[199] Important changes also took place "in the staples of the gold country; cotton will be less and less cultivated in the mining districts, while the foodstuffs, farinaceous, succulent vegetables—and the starch will claim the chief attention."[200]

On the other hand, when cotton prices advanced, the farmers left the mines for the fields, and there came a decline in the gold produced. But while native labor deserted the mines, foreign laborers came in and kept them going.[201]

Hezekiah Niles estimated that the foreign capital invested in southern mines yielded about 10 percent. Even so, Niles was glad to see the *foreign* investments, for

Every dollars worth of gold collected in North Carolina or Georgia, etc., represents at least 75 dollars worth of *American* corn, beef, pork, etc., consumed by the various laborers employed, and 10 or perhaps 15% more, goes into the general stock of *American* wealth, produced by *other* labor.[202]

Charles Fisher, a miner and one-time member of Congress from North Carolina, summed up the benefits of mining in the following manner. Agriculture was benefited by the withdrawal of surplus labor which found profitable employment elsewhere. "Home markets" were created for the surplus agricultural products, and thus better agricultural methods were encouraged. The farmers turned from cotton and other staples to grains, vegetables, and live stock. Emigration, which had "been carrying off so many of our most enterprising and useful citizens," was checked, and many foreigners of wealth, intelligence, and business habits were drawn to the state. Mechanical arts were improved and an enterprising spirit was developed.[203] Another North Carolinian said that the state could not profitably grow the staple crops—cotton, sugar, rice, and tobacco—with slave labor and that free labor was

199. *Ibid.*

200. *Ibid.*

201. "Gold Mines of North Carolina," *Hunt's Merchants' Magazine,* XI (July 1844), 65; "Commercial Chronicle and Review," *Hunt's Merchants' Magazine,* XX (January 1849), 79; Raleigh *Sentinel,* 16 February 1836.

202. *Niles' Weekly Register,* XLII (7 April 1832), 91. [Italics mine.—F.M.G.]

203. U.S., Congress, House of Representatives, *Assay Offices, Gold Districts, North Carolina, Georgia, Etc., to Accompany Bill H.R. 84,* 22d Cong., 1st sess., 1831, House Report No. 39, pp. 17–18, quoting a letter from Charles Fisher to the Honorable S. P. Carson, chairman of the Select Committee.

not sufficiently promoted. Mining, he said, held out a "healthful occupation for every excess of free population."[204]

The state legislature also defended mining as a beneficial occupation, and a committee drew up a report recounting at length the advantages derived from the development of the gold mines. It reads, in part, as follows:

To a State without foreign commerce, for want of seaports, or a staple, without internal communications by rivers, roads or canals—without a cash home market for any article of agricultural produce—without manufacturers—in short without any object to which native industry and active enterprise could be directed, or which could offer a stimulus to exertion—the discovery and development of her gold mines are events, which, more than the lapse of inert centuries, will advance her influence, prosperity and happiness. . . . [Her] citizens were before the opening of the mines, in general involved in debt, seemingly beyond a possibility of extraction. Valuable farming possessions were sold under execution and under trust deeds for insignificant prices, it being as impracticable in many instances to procure 50 dollars as 500 dollars, especially when the Bank was pressing collections and withholding loans. The sums since extracted from the mines by the native population, and the sums since expended by the adventurers for mining purposes have materially changed the aspect of things. There are few debts; emigration has nearly or quite ceased; land has greatly risen in real, and not merely nominal value; and there is a spirit of contentedness and honest pride in the inhabitants. There is an increased attention to the domestic comforts of life, a rapid extension of education —jealousy of foreigners has given place to liberal and friendly feelings —mechanics of all descriptions receive high wages and constant employ[ment]—farmers find a ready and cash market for their produce, and there is not known to be any class of worthy persons, upon whose interest the working of the gold mines has not exerted a favorable and happy influence.

Your Committee cannot ascertain that any of the evil consequences which were predicted as the inevitable attendants upon gold mining have ensued. North Carolina has not [been] impoverished, but enriched; her citizens have not become indolent, but industrious; intercourse with strangers, if it has not improved, has not contaminated the native population; all the arts of civilized life are beginning rapidly to be appreciated, and innumerable new paths of enterprise, and avenues to fortune and fame are now opening to her youths.[205]

204. *Ibid.,* pp. 5–6.
205. *N.C. Statistics of Mines and Minerals,* pp. 6–7.

2

Duff Green: Industrial Promoter

> Duff Green is not related to the author, but Green's interest in
> him is of long standing. In the early 1930s, while on a trip
> to the mountains of North Georgia, Green had the opportunity
> of meeting the daughter of Duff Green and learned that a large
> collection of family papers was still in her possession. Through
> his efforts, these were purchased for the Southern Historical
> Collection of the University of North Carolina Library, and he
> used them to write a number of articles about Duff and his son,
> Benjamin Edwards Green. This essay was published in the
> *Journal of Southern History,* II (February, 1936), 29–42.

ALMOST FORGOTTEN TODAY, DUFF
Green was, in his own time, as well known as Francis P. Blair or Horace Greeley; and his name was for nearly half a century a household word throughout the nation.[1] A man of versatile interests, wide information, shrewd insight, and unflagging industry, he had an interesting and varied career. Born in Kentucky in 1791, Green was successively a schoolteacher; a captain in the War of 1812; an associate of René Paul in mercantile interests in the West; a government land surveyor in Missouri; a lawyer; a member of the Missouri constitutional convention of 1820, and of both houses of the state legislature; a brigadier general in the state militia; a government mail contractor; the owner

1. J. L. P. Smith to Asa Packer, 18 October 1867. This letter, other manuscripts, newspaper clippings, and pamphlets cited in this article are in the Duff Green Papers in the Southern Historical Collection of the University of North Carolina Library, Chapel Hill, North Carolina. The Papers contain several letter books, together with many loose letters to and from Green, newspaper clippings concerning Green and his activities, a large number of manuscripts varying in length from a few to more than one hundred pages, and many pamphlets.

and editor of several newspapers, including the St. Louis *Enquirer,* the Washington, D.C., *United States Telegraph,* the Washington *Examiner,* the Baltimore *Pilot,* and the New York *Republic;* the special agent of President Tyler in England, France, and Mexico; a United States consul at Galveston, Texas; the promoter, organizer, and contractor of numerous industrial enterprises; and a writer on finance and currency.[2] He died in Dalton, Georgia, in 1875.

Throughout his long and distinguished career, Green was dominated by three great passions: to make money; to secure the election of his friend, John C. Calhoun, to the Presidency; and to unify and develop the interests of the South as a section in the Union. All three of these, Green thought, might be advanced by a program of industrial development. Certainly money was to be made in coal and iron mining, in canal and railway construction, and through industrial organizations and commercial agencies. Green believed that Calhoun might further his candidacy for the Presidency by attending and taking an active part in the Chicago internal improvements convention of 1847. He wrote Calhoun that the bank and the tariff issues had passed away but that the Memphis railroad convention and President Polk's vetoes of rivers and harbors bills had given a new impulse to the question of internal improvements. Green believed that the Chicago convention, if rightly directed, would do much to control the question. He said:

There is no other mode of touching the pocket nerve so efficiently as the system of Internal Improvement and it is with you now to say what direction that quesion shall take. By going to Chicago you can do much to control it.[3]

Green feared that if the South opposed appropriations for rivers and harbors and other internal improvement projects, the West and East would carry the measures. And

In that case Abolition and improvements go together & strengthen each other. On the other hand if the South unite with the West *now*

2. "Duff Green," *Dictionary of American Biography,* 20 vols. (New York: Charles Scribner's Sons, 1928–1936) , VII, 540–541.
3. Green to Calhoun, 28 May 1847.

and by entering into this convention moderate and regulate the system, they command the West as allies and secure their aid in denouncing and suppressing abolition.[4]

In a letter to the Governor of Alabama, Green warned against the "fanaticism and ambition" of the North which would inevitably lead to an "unholy war upon the South." He said:

We must prepare for this conflict . . . How? Not by Disunion . . . for that will accelerate the crisis. Our only hope lies in this . . . that mind and money govern the world. We must educate our sons and our daughters in reference to their duty, and we must avail ourselves of all the proper means of acquiring wealth. . . . We must develop our resources and increase our wealth by stimulating the industry of our people. As one means of doing this we must make good Roads that our people may associate more with each other and increase the profits of labor by diminishing the expense of transportating its products to market. . . . Give us good Roads, and union & concert and we need fear no danger.[5]

In line with this theory, Green devoted more than thirty-five years of his life to the industrial development of the South.

First of his industrial projects was a combination of land speculation and coal mining. Acting upon the advice of his physician, Green in 1835 gave up the sedentary life of an editor and went to the Sulphur Springs of Virginia for a rest cure.[6] Riding over the mountains, he observed outcroppings of coal and purchased 60,000 acres of mineral lands in Virginia and Maryland. He secured charters from these two states for the Union and the Union Potomac companies, sold stock, and organized the companies, with the privilege of constructing canals and railroads to connect his mines with the Chesapeake and Ohio Canal.[7] The

4. Green to F. H. Elmore, 29 May 1847; Green to R. K. Cralle, 30 May 1847.

5. Duff Green, "To the Governor of Alabama." This open letter is undated, but internal evidence indicates that it was written in the 1850s and that it was addressed either to J. A. Winston or to A. B. Moore.

6. Duff Green, "To the Editor of the *Times*, St. Louis, Missouri," 1 May 1873, p. 3; Ben E. Green MS. The latter document is a review of the business relations of Ben E. and Duff Green, covering the years from about 1835 to 1875, and contains about sixty unnumbered pages.

7. *Charters of the Union Company and Union Potomac Company* (Baltimore: Printed by John Murphy, 1840) , p. 1.

panic of 1837 caused the work to be suspended, but Green later combined the two companies, secured the aid of engineers and capitalists,[8] and renewed the enterprise. A canal was constructed from the mouth of the Savage River to the Chesapeake and Ohio Canal; and the New Creek, the Potomac Mining Company, and the Cumberland Coal Mining Company successfully mined and marketed the coal.

At one time, Green and his associates controlled more than 2.5 million acres of mining lands in Maryland, Virginia, Kentucky, and Pennsylvania. The construction of canals to his mines aroused Green's interest in the possibility of that means of transportation; and during the 1840s, he became interested in various canal projects. He contracted with the Chesapeake and Ohio Canal Company for the completion of that work;[9] he was interested in and secured charters from Texas and Louisiana for canals connecting the Sabine and Rio Grande rivers, and the Sabine with the Red and Mississippi rivers;[10] he also projected a ship canal from Newark, New Jersey, to the Atlantic Ocean.[11] He secured a patent on a process for deepening the channel of streams and building embankments, and applied to both Louisiana and Virginia for charters to carry out such work on the Mississippi River and in Norfolk Harbor.[12]

Green's mining operations, while on an extensive scale, were not very profitable because of the lack of transportation facilities, and most of his canal projects never materialized. He therefore turned to railroads as a more feasible means of transportation. When the Baltimore and Ohio Railroad decided, in 1847, to extend its line west from the Cumberland, Green bid for and secured the contract for the construction of sixty miles of the road. He agreed to take bonds of the road in payment and asked also

8. Among his associates were James W. McCulloh, D. B. Douglas, Charles F. Mayer, James H. Hamilton, James Renwick, J. J. A. Ebbetts, and R. W. Latham.

9. J. M. Coale, president of the Chesapeake and Ohio, to Green, 6 January 1844; Green to Everett & Kettle, 17 March 1844.

10. Green to Thomas F. McKinney, 9 January 1846; McKinney to Green, 19 January 1846.

11. Andrew Talcott to Green, 4 May 1846.

12. Green to E. Burke, 4 September 1846; Ben E. Green MS.

for a special rate for the transportation of his coal. Failing to secure the latter, he sublet his contract to others.[13] Through his friendship with John Y. Mason, Secretary of the Navy, Green secured the contract to construct and repair vessels of the government. He obtained capital from Simon Cameron and employed A. Mehaffy to conduct the work and opened the Gosport Navy Yard.[14] Here were built, among others, the famous *Powhatan*.

Green's contract with the Baltimore and Ohio had demonstrated to him, in his own words,

that a proper development of our railways would so increase the value of our property & especially of our agricultural products as to enable us to organize a financial system competent for our protection. I saw that it was the purpose of the English party in Boston to use their influence financially & politically to give such strength to the *Northern* feeling & prejudice, as to create a controling *Northern* influence, sectional, financial & political & that with this view they were making extraordinary efforts to identify the North West with the North East.[15]

Green determined to counteract this sectional influence by bringing about a consolidation of the railroad lines in the South and began, in 1846, to interest capitalists in the idea of a great southern system of railways.[16] Backed by eastern capitalists, he began to buy up key roads in the South.[17] The purpose of this program was to give, ultimately, a main line connecting Washington and New Orleans by way of Lynchburg, the Holston Valley, and Nash-

13. Green to Moreau Delano, 24 May 1847; Green to Edward Learned, Jr., 24 May 1847; Green to J. Gonder, Jr., 24 May 1847; Green to S. R. Brooks, 24 May 1847; Green to Louis McLane, 17 June 1847; Green to R. M. McLane, 6 September 1847; Green to Charles Gould, 31 July 1847.

14. Green to Simon Cameron, 9, 10, and 26 August 1847; Green to A. Mehaffey, 2, 7, 22, 23, and 28 September 1847.

15. Green, "To the Editor of the *Times*, St. Louis, Missouri," p. 5.

16. Edward Learned, Jr., William Ward, David Henshaw, and Daniel Carmichael were all interested in purchases.

17. They were interested in the following roads: East Tennessee and Georgia; Nashville, Portsmouth, and Roanoke; Gaston and Raleigh; Wilmington and Raleigh; Virginia and Tennessee; Seaboard and Roanoke; and the Montgomery. Green to Charles L. Hinton, 9 April 1847; Green to Thomas B. Frick, 13 November 1846; William Ward to Green, 10 April 1847; Green to Ward, 22 April, 18 November, 17 December 1847, and 26 March 1848; Green to John Bell, 4 April 1848.

ville;[18] and another from Washington to Mobile by way of Richmond, Raleigh, Columbia, Augusta, Atlanta, and Montgomery.[19]

In 1848, Green revived interest in the East Tennessee and Georgia Railroad, took the contract for the construction of a part of it, and was instrumental in completing the line from Knoxville, Tennessee, to Dalton, Georgia.[20] Supplementary to this project, Green secured a charter for the Georgia Exporting Company for engaging in export trade. He attempted to secure a contract with the federal government for five vessels to carry on this trade.[21]

In the hope of obtaining a better economic alliance of the South and West, Green called a meeting, which assembled in Washington on December 3, 1851, of all those interested in the development of railroads in these sections. He formulated a program for governmental aid to railway construction based on mail contracts. The convention approved the plan and a memorial to Congress was prepared. Congress gave the project a favorable report and took the matter under advisement but never carried the plan into action.[22]

Failing to obtain the financial support he desired, Green, nevertheless, proceeded during the next ten years to secure charters and organize companies for the building of several railroads in the South and West. First, he secured charters for roads in Georgia and Alabama, and some of the roads were constructed.[23] Working on the idea of a Southern Pacific road, he entered into

18. Green to L. A. Cazenove, 19 April 1848.

19. Green to Charles T. Pollard, 3 June 1847.

20. Duff Green, *To the People of East Tennessee* (n.p., n.d.), pp. 2, 5; *Records of the Bills, Answers, and Exhibits, Duff Green vs. E. T. & Ga. R. R. Co.* (New York: [n.p.] 1856), pp. 3–10.

21. U.S., Congress, Senate, *Journal,* 31st Cong., 1st sess., 22 August 1850, p. 570; U.S., Congress, Senate, *Memorial of the Georgia Exporting Company,* 31st Cong., 1st sess., 1849–1850, Misc. Doc. No. 122.

22. Washington *Daily American Telegraph,* 12 January 1852; Washington *Southern Press,* 8 March 1852; U.S., Congress, House, "New Mexican Railway Company," 36th Cong., 1st sess., 1859–1860, Misc. Doc. No. 85; Washington *National Intelligencer,* 15 August 1857.

23. Among the roads were the Dalton and Gadsden, the Georgia and Alabama, and the Alabama and Tennessee River.

communication with President Arista of Mexico and asked for a charter for a road to connect the Rio Grande with the Pacific by way of Mexico City, with branches from that city to Vera Cruz, Acapulco, and Matamoros. Green urged Arista to send an able minister to Washington, hoping to get the support of both the Mexican and United States governments. In 1854, Mexico chartered the Rio Grande, Mexican, and Pacific Railway.[24]

To link this road with those of the Gulf Coast states, Green secured a charter from Texas for the Sabine and Rio Grande Railroad Company. This company was authorized to construct a road from near the thirty-first degree on the Sabine by way of San Antonio to the Rio Grande near the Presidio del Rio Grande. By the terms of the charter and subsequent acts, Texas granted the road 10,240 acres of land and a loan of $6,000 per mile. The road was organized with Duff Green as president, and a contract was made, in 1856, with the Lester L. Robinson Company for its construction. Robinson forfeited his contract in 1858, and Green secured the contract for his American Improvement Company. Green then made arrangements with the Rio Grande, Mexican, and Pacific Railway Company for the union of the two roads.[25] Another link in the Southern Pacific line was the New Orleans, Opelousas, and Great Western Railroad Company. This road was chartered by Louisiana and, supported by state, municipal, and private subscriptions, was well on the road to completion in 1854. It was to be joined with the Sabine and Rio Grande, giving connection from New Orleans to the Pacific.[26] Two other lines in which Green was a prime mover were the Florida Central, Atlan-

24. Green to President Arista (n.d.); Proposed Charter of the Mexican International Railroad Company (MS); *Charter of the Rio Grande, Mexican, and Pacific Railroad Company* (n.p., n.d.), pp. 10–19.

25. Duff Green (MS), "The Sabine and Rio Grande Railroad Company"; U.S., Congress, Senate, *Memorial of Duff Green, President of the Sabine and Rio Grande Railroad Company*, 36th Cong., 1st sess., 1860, Misc. Doc. No. 48, p. 1; "Journal of the Proceedings of the Sabine and Rio Grande Railroad Company," 1854, 1856, 1857 (MS).

26. Duff Green (MS), "Southern Railroads"; *Second Annual Report of the New Orleans, Opelousas, and Great Western Railroad Company* (New Orleans: [n.p.] 1854), pp. 3, 4; Green, *Memorial of the President of the Sabine and Rio Grande Railroad Company*, p. 1.

tic and Gulf Railroad, chartered in 1852; and the New Mexican Railway, chartered in 1860.[27]

This comprehensive scheme for southern railroads would have given a main line from Washington to the Pacific coast by way of Lynchburg, Knoxville, Nashville, Birmingham, Montgomery, Mobile, New Orleans, San Antonio, and Mexico City, and another from Washington to Montgomery by way of Richmond, Raleigh, Columbia, Augusta, and Atlanta. There would also have been connecting lines to Wilmington, Charleston, Savannah, and Jacksonville. To buy up the roads already built and to construct the line from New Orleans to the Pacific and other connecting lines would require enormous capital. Green set himself to the task of organizing some agency which might provide the corporate capital based on railroad stock, and manipulated by a general holding company. Neither did he ignore the idea of government aid in land grants, loans, and mail contracts.

Believing that railroad bonds might be an efficient basis of credit to secure money for developing the mineral resources and the construction of railroads, and thus aid labor and increase the wealth of the South, Green applied to the legislature of New Jersey for a charter for a "Railroad Trust Company." The bill was defeated, according to Green, "by the influence of gamblers and speculators in Wall Street."[28] He then applied to the legislature of Pennsylvania for a charter for the "Pennsylvania Fiscal Agency." While the bill passed by a nearly unanimous vote, Governor Asa Packer hesitated to approve it for fear that Green's plan for the Southern Pacific could not be carried through. The promoter then prepared *An Argument Addressed to his Excellency the Governor of Pennsylvania, in Support of the Bill to Incorporate the Pennsylvania Fiscal Agency*, which induced Packer to agree to sign the bill, provided Green could get the Mexican government to acquiesce and European bondholders to subscribe their Mexican bonds to the road through the agency.

27. Governor R. K. Call to Green, 11 February 1852; "Book of Subscription for the New Mexican Railway Company" (MS), p. 9.

28. Clipping from the Trenton, N.J., *True American* (date line torn), ? February 1856; Newark, N.J., *Daily Advertiser,* 18 February 1856; Green, *To the Editor of the Times,* p. 6.

Green prevailed on the Mexican Minister, Jose Mata, to go to Mexico and secure the consent of his government. The minister returned to Washington with Lerdo y Tejada, Minister of Finance, and the promise of Mexican support. Green then procured letters from President Buchanan and sailed from Boston, September 6, 1859. He conferred with George M. Dallas, United States minister to England, Richard Cobden, and Lord John Russell, and they obtained for him a hearing before a committee of the Mexican bondholders. Green assured the committee that he was acting with the knowledge and approval of both the Mexican and United States governments, and the Mexican creditors accepted the arrangements. Other British capitalists also agreed to subscribe for stock in the agency.[29]

Upon Green's return, in October, Governor Packer signed the bill and the agency was organized with Green as president and William Halsted treasurer.[30] Green then went to Mexico and sent David R. Porter, one of his associates, to Texas to secure certain desired changes in their charters. This was accomplished, and Green wrote his wife that it was "no small triumph to have devised the means of building the first road to the Pacific."[31] But like other best-laid plans of mice and men, Green's road program was cut short by the election of Lincoln and the secession of the southern states. In 1862, Oliver W. Barnes, David R. Porter, and others reorganized the agency, although Halsted, the treasurer, opposed reorganization on the ground that Green, as president and owner of 42,000 of the 50,000 shares of stock, could not be present.[32] But the legislature of Pennsylvania was not disposed to favor a "rebel" and passed an act reorganizing and changing the

29. Duff Green, *An Argument Addressed to His Excellency the Governor of Pennsylvania* (Philadelphia: C. Sherman & Son, 1859), p. 1 and *passim;* Green, *An Address to the People of Pennsylvania* (Philadelphia: [n.p.] 1859), p. 1 and *passim;* Green, *An Address to the People of the United States,* pp. 191–192; Green, *To the Editor of the Times,* pp. 6–7; "Bill of Particulars in the Pennsylvania Fiscal Agency Case," pp. 2–3; Green to Mrs. Lucretia M. Green, 24 and 25 August, 30 September 1859 (from London); Samuel R. Brooks to Green, 11 July 1859.

30. Green to Lucretia M. Green, 31 October, 1, 8, 9, and 12 November 1859; David R. Porter to Green, 18 November 1859; Duff Green, Reply to Interrogations in the *Credit Mobilier Case* (n.p., n.d.), p. 8.

31. Green to Lucretia M. Green, 8 November 1859.

32. William Halsted to Green, 3 April, 11 and 20 November 1865.

name of the agency to the Credit Mobilier of America. It was this reorganized company which financed the Union Pacific Railroad, and under Oakes Ames and others filched millions of dollars from the American people. After the war, Green sought to recover his rights under the original charter, but the governor of Pennsylvania removed Ben H. Brewster, the attorney general who favored Green, and forbade the suit to be brought. Green then employed counsel and brought suit against the company, which at first offered to compromise but later refused any settlement.[33] Whereupon, Green wrote B. H. Bristow, Secretary of the Treasury, and offered his interests in the company to the United States, provided the government would push the case. This was refused, and Green, without further recourse, dropped the matter.[34]

Though opposed to secession, Green threw in his lot with the Confederacy. He published a pamphlet, *Facts and Suggestions on Currency and Direct Trade,* in which he urged the South to develop manufacturing, internal improvements, and natural resources as the only hope of defeating the North. Green immediately began the manufacture of iron in the Coosa Valley, Georgia. He secured a contract with the Departments of War and Navy for the manufacture of carbines and imported skilled English laborers from New York to run the works. In 1862, he bought the Embreeville Iron Works in Washington County, Tennessee, and made a contract with Josiah Gorgas, Chief of Ordnance, to furnish one-half of the output of the iron works to the Confederate government; the remaining half he was permitted to sell in the open market.[35] At the Confederate Iron Works, Green manufactured guns, shot, shells, horseshoes, chains, nails, railroad iron, and iron for farm implements. Six new furnaces were opened at the Confederate Works and others in the Coosa Valley. Sawmills, railroads, flat and keel boats were constructed; iron and coal

33. Included among his lawyers were B. H. Brewster, Edward Learned, Jr., R. J. and J. L. Brent, and Charles O'Connor.

34. *Commonwealth of Pennsylvania* vs. *Sidney Dillon et al.* (Philadelphia: [n.p., 1868]) , pp. 1–10; Green, *Bill of Particulars,* pp. 3–7; Green, *Prospectus of the Credit Mobilier* (n.p., n.d.) , pp. 1–3; *The Credit Mobilier* vs. *Oakes Ames* (n.p., n.d.) , pp. 1–4; Green to B. H. Brewster, 17 March 1875; Philadelphia *Times,* 1 May 1877.

35. Contract of Duff Green and Josiah Gorgas, 1 April 1863; contract of Duff Green and William K. Blair, 28 October 1862, 22 May 1863.

mines and a stone quarry were opened, and a thriving settlement was developed. In addition to civilian labor, Green was furnished a detail of disabled soldiers and was permitted to conscript up to fifty-four laborers for each furnace opened. The government detailed commissioned officers to preserve order and discipline at the works. The Ordnance Department reported that the Confederate Iron Works were of immense importance to Generals Bragg and Longstreet in their East Tennessee campaigns.[36]

A competing company, the Vulcan Iron Works of Chattanooga, claimed that Secretary of State Judah P. Benjamin was one of its stockholders and used this argument to spirit laborers away from the Confederate Iron Works. Green appealed directly to President Davis, Secretary of State Benjamin, and Secretary of War James A. Seddon. Benjamin denied any interest in, or knowledge of, the Vulcan Works, and General A. E. Jackson reprimanded Captain A. L. Whitley and Colonel T. H. Logwood, who had been getting Green's laborers.[37]

The iron mines offered possibilities for further development after the war, and Green took steps in that direction. He secured a charter for the Tennessee Mining and Manufacturing Company and planned to expand the works. On the 45,000 acres, he proposed to develop iron and coal mining; to cultivate some 8,000 acres of the fertile valley land in foodstuffs; to open flax, cotton, and woolen mills; to run sawmills, gristmills, and blacksmith shops; and to lay out a model self-sufficient village to accommodate some 20,000 people engaged in the mines, farms, and factories.[38] This plan was cut short, however, by the Blair heirs, who

36. Green to Captain W. F. Stone, 29 March, 10 June, 7 and 12 August 1836; Green to Major J. M. St. John, 10 April 1863; Green to Colonel T. H. Logwood, 12 May 1863; Second Auditor's Report, 15 September 1863.

37. Green to St. John, 11 May 1863; Green to Benjamin, 11 May 1863; Benjamin to Green, 15 May 1863; General A. E. Jackson to Green, 21 May 1863; Green to President Davis, 10 November 1863, with endorsements of Jefferson Davis, Lieutenant Colonel J. M. St. John, and J. A. Seddon.

38. Green to the Planters Insurance, Trust and Loan Company, 3 June 1864; *Prospectus of the Tennessee Mining and Manufacturing Company* (Washington: Printed by Lemuel Towers, 1865), pp. 3, 5; *The East Tennessee Industrial Company*, (n.p., n.d.), pp. 1, 2, 4, 7. Many letters between Green and C. F. L. Smith, the engineer in charge of the plant, are in the Green Papers.

sued and recovered the property on the ground that the contract for the sale of the Embreeville Works had called for payment in current bank notes or Confederate treasury notes no longer legal tender.[39]

Long a student of and a prolific writer on the subject of finance and currency,[40] Green earnestly sought an answer to the question facing the devastated South: namely, where might the capital necessary for the rebuilding of the South's economic order be found? He believed that the chief source of credit was land, and he determined to organize an association to which southern landowners might subscribe up to fifty percent of the value of their lands and borrow from the association fifty percent of their subscriptions. He secured a charter for the American Industrial Agency with the Maryland branch as the clearinghouse for branch agencies in all the southern states.[41] The chief object of these agencies was "to aid the development of agriculture, mining, manufactures, and commerce in the United States, and especially of the South and Western States";[42] or, as one of the charters stated it:

for the purpose of reviving the industry and restoring the prosperity of the Southern States, by so organizing the associated credit of Southern

39. R. S. Blair vs. Duff Green, 19 May 1866; Affidavit of Thomas A. R. Nelson, 28 April 1866.

40. Among others, Green published the following: *Facts and Suggestions on the Subject of Currency and Direct Trade* (Macon: Printed for the Chamber of Commerce, 1861); *Facts and Suggestions Relative to Finance and Currency addressed to the President of the Confederate States* (Augusta: J. T. Patterson & Co., 1864); *A Memorial and a Bill Relating to Finance, National Currency, Debt, Revenue* (Memphis: Southwestern Publishing Co., 1869); *How to Pay off the National Debt, Regulate the Value of Money, and Maintain Stability in the Values of Property and Labor* (Philadelphia: Claxton, Remsen & Haffelfinger, 1872).

41. Other companies chartered were the Contractors Association, the American Improvement Company, the Planters Insurance, Trust, and Loan Company, the Central Transit Company, and the Mississippi American Industrial Agency, the last affiliated with the London Mississippi Valley Association. States granting charters to one or more of Green's agencies were Texas, Mississippi, Alabama, Georgia, Tennessee, Virginia, Maryland, and New Jersey. Branches were organized in other states and one at least in England.

42. Green, Memorial to Congress, 15 March 1866; Green to the Corporators of the American Industrial Agency, 15 February 1866.

land owners, as to put an end to the ornerous [*sic*] conditions enacted at present for advances to enable them to cultivate their lands.[43]

Newspaper comment was generally favorable to the plan. A Texas editor thought the

enterprise . . . worthy of confidence and as promising largely and safely to advance our material interests. . . . It offers to the capitalist ample security and large returns, and speedy civil recourse in realizing their money when due. It offers, on the other hand, to the land owner and laborer, money upon moderate interest, and upon time that will not jeopardise his property interest.[44]

Another editor wrote as follows: "after careful consideration of the subject, it appears to us that the plan here proposed is the best that has been suggested as a means of restoring the industrial prosperity of the South."[45] The Memphis *Avalanche* (March 23, 1869) thought the agency "the most practical scheme for the development of the interests of the Southern States." And a correspondent of Governor Packer said that he knew of "nothing at this moment more likely to save the nation from total ruin than such a support of the truth as . . . [Green] will be able to afford if . . . [he gets his] association & its organ into full operation in good time."[46]

British capitalists were interested and sent M. J. McHaffie to investigate the agency. McHaffie was reported to have "arranged to make advances on cotton shipped to Liverpool."[47] In fact, the British capitalists desired to subscribe to a majority of the stock and thus get control of the agency.[48] Southern planters were likewise anxious to subscribe their lands. One agent in Alabama sent in a subscription of $140,000 and said he was confident of raising half a million.[49] A committee of the National Labor Union investigated the agency and was so favorably impressed that J. C. C. Whaley, president of the Union, supported Green as editor of the

43. *Prospectus Maryland Industrial Agency* (n.p., n.d.) , p. 5.
44. Houston *Telegraph,* 11 January 1867.
45. Trenton, N.J., *Daily State Gazette,* 5 March 1867.
46. J. L. P. Smith to Asa Packer, 18 October 1867.
47. Houston *Journal,* 10 January 1867.
48. Green to S. R. Brooks, 9 May 1866; Green to General W. M. Lawton (London) , 2 April 1875.
49. W. H. Kimbrough to Green, 18 June, 19 July 1867.

People's Weekly, a joint Union-Agency paper.[50] Branch agencies were even organized among the freedmen, though they were primarily savings bank clubs.[51]

In spite of such favorable reception, the agencies failed. Among the factors to which Green attributed failure were the following: the uncertainty in regard to the resumption of specie payments; the refusal of Congress to provide for the early restoration of the southern states into the Union; and the hesitancy of planters and capitalists "to engage in any Southern enterprises, which might be paralyzed by hostile and destructive legislation."[52]

In his last years, Green revived his earlier scheme of a southern railway system. Not only did he attempt the union of various roads in Virginia, North Carolina, Georgia, and Alabama, but he was also instrumental in building the Dalton, Rome, and Selma, the Dalton and Southwestern, and the Dalton and Jacksonville roads, all now a part of the Southern Railroad system.[53] He also revived his old plan of a Southern Pacific railway. He and A. K. Owen organized the Great Southern Trans-Oceanic and International Air Line Railroad. They petitioned Congress and secured the promise of land-grant aid, they obtained the support of capitalists, and were ready to begin the surveys of the route when the failure of Jay Cooke and Company brought an end to their program. The route of the road would have been from Austin, Texas, to the Bay of Topolobampo in the Gulf of California.[54]

While most of Green's industrial enterprises failed of their

50. Baltimore *People's Weekly,* 11 April 1868; Washington *United States Telegraph and Weekly Visitor,* 2 November 1868; Duff Green to Ben E. Green, 11, 21, and 24 June 1868.

51. Green to Ben E. Green, 24 October 1868. Green says that Henry Braddock, a well-educated Negro preacher of Baltimore, was taking the lead in organizing the Negro agencies.

52. *Prospectus of the American Industrial Agency* (New York: John F. Trow & Co., 1866) , p. 5.

53. *Plan for a Great Trunk Railway Line* (New York: [n.p.], 1868) , pp. 6–12; Green to John Tucker, 18 December 1873; Green to Ben E. Green, 5 May 1871, 22 August 1873, 14 April 1874; R. K. Ford to Green, 18 October 1871; Certificate of Organization of the Dalton and Southwestern Railroad, 12 April 1872.

54. *The Austin-Topolobampo Railroad Route* (n.p., n.d.) , p. 1; Albert K. Owen, *The Great Southern Trans-Oceanic and International Air Line* (Philadelphia: Rowley & Chew, 1873) , pp. 3, 4; Agreement of Duff Green and Albert K. Owen, 2 August 1873; Minneapolis *Tribune,* 13 April 1884.

ultimate goal during his own lifetime, he must nevertheless be given credit for his wisdom and foresight. His mining interests, especially, were forerunners of present-day developments, and today a railroad follows almost every line in which Green was interested. His program for economic solidarity in the South bears a striking parallel to that of Count Cavour in the Italian states of the 1850s. A prophet of better things, a pioneer industrial builder, and a promoter without a superior was Duff Green. But as the Philadelphia *Times* said of him, "Like all great men he was a visionary, or, rather in advance of his times."

3

Democracy in the Old South

In his book, *Constitutional Development in the South Atlantic
States, 1776–1860* (Chapel Hill: University of North Carolina
Press, 1930), Green dealt with the gradual and continual
development of the democratic principle in the southern states.
This is a fuller treatment of the theme, its main point being
that the South, like the North, shared in the development of
political democracy in the early nineteenth century.

   In 1945, Green was president of the Southern Historical
Association, but exigencies of the Second World War brought
cancellation of the meeting. This essay had been prepared
as the presidential address. It was published in the
Journal of Southern History, XII (February 1946), 2–23.

THE AMERICAN DREAM OF DEMOCRACY
and equality, based upon the philosophy of natural
rights and popular sovereignty, found full, free, and adequate
expression in such Revolutionary documents as the Declaration of
Independence and the bills of rights of the state constitutions:
"We hold these truths to be self-evident, that all men are created
equal, that they are endowed by their Creator with certain unalienable Rights, that among these are Life, Liberty and the
pursuit of Happiness." [And from Sections 2 and 4 of the Virginia
Bill of Rights:] "All power is vested in, and consequently derived
from, the people; . . . magistrates are their trustees and servants,
and at all times amenable to them." "No man, or set of men, are
entitled to exclusive or separate emoluments or privileges from
the community but in consideration of publick services." These
and similar expressions of democratic equalitarianism were familiar to the people in all the states of the American Union.

The mere declaration of these ideals did not insure their acceptance and enforcement; a vigorous and continuous defense of liberty is essential if it is to be preserved. Thomas Jefferson, spokesman for democracy, early observed that men were by their constitutions naturally divided into two classes: those who fear and distrust the people and seek to draw all power into their own hands; and those who have confidence in the people and consider the people the safest depository of public happiness and general well-being. These two classes he called aristocrats and democrats. From the very beginning of American independence, these two groups began a contest for control of the governments. This contest between the forces of aristocracy and democracy was one of the most important issues in the political development of the American nation during the first half-century of its existence. In the northern states, it was fought between the commercial-financial aristocracy and the working men; in the southern states, between the aristocratic, slaveholding planters and the yeoman farmers.

The first state constitutions were framed in an atmosphere of equality and the recognition of human rights, without hint of race or class distinctions; but they established property and freehold qualifications for voting and officeholding, and a system of representation that gave control of the state governments to the wealthy, conservative, aristocratic classes. The power and influence of the aristocracy were further enhanced by the victory of the conservative group that established the Federal Constitution. The Jeffersonian democrats, accepting—in theory, at least—the doctrines of natural rights, popular sovereignty, government by compact and contract, and the perfectability of mankind, began a militant assault upon the strongholds of aristocracy. They demanded and obtained a bill of rights to the Federal Constitution, and an extended suffrage and a greater equality of representation in the state governments. Under their attacks, the powers of aristocracy were gradually whittled away. Finally, with the accession of Andrew Jackson to the Presidency in 1829, it seemed that democracy would certainly triumph. Most American people agreed with Alexis de Tocqueville that the democratic revolution was an irresistible one, and that to attempt to check it "would be to resist the will of God."[1]

As democratic reform moved into high gear, under Jackson, its forces were divided by the emergence of the bitter sectional controversy over slavery. The northern abolitionists saw in the institution of slavery the absolute negation of liberty and equality, and they began to weigh and to find wanting almost every feature of southern society. In particular, they condemned the southern state governments, declaring that in them political democracy was being overthrown by a slaveholding aristocracy. This change, said they, was the result not of caprice or political accident but of deliberate design on the part of the aristocracy; and it was succeeding, because *"the non-slave-holding people of the South lacked the enterprise, intelligence and daring to demand and extract their democratic rights."*[2] In other words, they held that the masses of free whites were incapable of understanding or maintaining their rights, and that the planter aristocracy was bitterly hostile to free institutions and the democratic theory of government universally.

By the time the sectional controversy reached the breaking point, the abolitionists had decided that the slaveholders had become a

DOMINANT CLASS, having positive control of the . . . political power of those States. . . . the system of slavery concentrating, as it does all political influence in a few men who are virtually absolute in their respective States.[3]

Contrasting the two sections, Richard Hildreth, the historian, declared:

The Northern States of the Union are unquestionable Democracies, and every day they are verging nearer and nearer towards the simple

1. Alexis de Tocqueville, *Democracy in America,* translated by Henry Reeve, 4th ed., 2 vols. (New York: Henry G. Langley, 1845), I, 1–2, 5.

2. Thomas S. Goodwin, *The Natural History of Secession; Or, Despotism and Democracy at Necessary, Eternal, Exterminating War* (New York: Derby & Miller, 1865), pp. 40–41.

3. Elhanon W. Reynolds, *The True Story of the Barons of the South; Or, The Rationale of the American Conflict* (Boston: Walker, Wise and Co., 1862), pp. 34–35.

idea and theoretic perfection of that form of government. The Southern States of the Union, though certain democratic principles are to be
found in their constitutions and their laws, are in no modern sense of
the word entitled to the appellation of Democracies: They are Aristocracies; and aristocracies of the sternest and most odious kind.[4]

This interpretation of southern society and government was
based upon moral hatred of Negro slavery, rather than a true
knowledge of southern state governments or a philosophical or
realistic understanding of democracy. Its appeal to the excited
and hostile North was so powerful that most people accepted it as
unquestionably accurate; and the general historians of the United
States incorporated it into their writings. For instance, James
Ford Rhodes says, in his *History of the United States from the
Compromise of 1850,* that the "slaveholders, and the members of
that society which clustered round them, took the offices. . . . The
political system of the South was an oligarchy under the republican form."[5] And Lord Acton, the British historian and publicist,
wrote that secession was an aristocratic rebellion against a democratic government.[6]

The abolitionist promoters of the theory of the aristocratic
nature of southern governments never attempted to define just
what they meant by either aristocracy or democracy. Indeed,
democracy has always been difficult of definition. It is a relative
term, and has had various meanings among different peoples and
for the same people at different stages of their political development. Here, it will be used in its general sense as a form of
government in which the sovereign power is held by the people
and exercised through a system of representation in which the
representatives are chosen by a fairly large electorate. The electorate has not been a fixed one in the United States. In the early

4. Richard Hildreth, *Despotism in America: An Inquiry into the Nature, Results,
and Legal Basis of the Slave-Holding System of the United States* (Boston: J. P.
Jewett and Co., 1854) , p. 8.

5. James Ford Rhodes, *History of the United States from the Compromise of 1850,*
7 vols. (New York: Macmillan Co., 1906–1907) , I, 345. See also Hermann E. Von
Holst, *The Constitutional and Political History of the United States,* 8 vols.
(Chicago: Callaghan and Co., 1876–1892) , I, 348–349.

6. [The sentiment is expressed in "The Civil War in America," in his *Historical
Essays & Studies* (London: Macmillan, 1907) , pp. 123–142.—J.I.C.]

days of the American republic, the suffrage was bestowed upon adult male property owners; in the second quarter of the nineteenth century, it was extended to all adult white males; during Reconstruction, the Negro was given the ballot; and, in 1920, women were permitted to vote in all elections. Recently, Georgia has given the ballot to youths eighteen years of age.[7] No one would say that the state governments were undemocratic in 1850 simply because women did not vote; but they were *more* democratic in 1920 because women did vote. The same may be said in regard to Negro suffrage. Furthermore, up to the Civil War, the emphasis on democracy was placed on *political* equality; since that time, greater emphasis has been placed on social and economic equality. Modern thought presupposes that institutions, in order to be understood, must be seen in relation to the conditions of time, place, and thought in which they appear. It is difficult to look at democracy in this way, for one is prone to judge democracy of the past by the criteria of today. Yet the degree of democracy prevailing under the constitutions and governments of the Old South must be judged by the democracy of that era, not of the present. George Sidney Camp was but speaking for his generation, when he wrote, in 1840, that democracy

is not of an agrarian character or spirit. Its immediate object is an equal division of political rights, not of property. . . . But republicanism does aim a death blow at all those laws and usages the object of which is . . . to give it a particular and exclusive direction as a means of political power.[8]

As noted above, the Revolutionary state constitutions utilized to a large degree the framework of colonial governments and constitutional practices of the colonial period which had recognized and established a governing class of the wealthy aristocracy. Only eight of the thirteen states made any change in suffrage

7. [Since this essay was first published, in 1946, the voting age has been lowered to 18 years in Kentucky, also; to 19, in Alaska; and to 20, in Hawaii.—J.I.C.]

8. George Sidney Camp, *Democracy* (New York: Harper and Brothers, 1841), p. 155. Harper and Brothers were so anxious to spread the influence of this first general analysis of the principles of democracy by a native American that they brought it out in their Family Library.

requirements, and these changes did not abolish the principle that only property holders should vote—they merely reduced the amount of property required. Property and freedhold qualifications for voting and officeholding meant that the governing class in the southern states was in large measure a planter aristocracy. The system of representation also favored the planter group of the eastern section. Though democratic in form, these constitutions were certainly not democratic in fact. They did, however, lay the basis for the expansion of popular control, the chief element in a political democracy, to the majority of the people.

Hardly had the landed aristocracy established themselves in power when demands for revision and readjustment were heard in each of the states. Among the specific reforms called for were the disestablishment of the church and the abolition of religious qualifications for officeholding; the abolition of the laws of entail and primogeniture; the broadening of the suffrage; the equalization of representation; and the reduction of property qualifications for officeholding. All looked toward the curbing of the powers of the landed aristocracy. Piecemeal amendment and revision of the constitutions partially satisfied these demands.

In South Carolina, the dissenting Presbyterians and Congregationalists, led by William Tennent, a Presbyterian minister, and Christopher Gadsden, prepared a memorial which was signed by thousands of people and presented a petition to the legislature in 1777, asking "free and equal privileges, both religious and civil" for all Protestants. Another group of reformers joined forces with the dissenters and demanded an elective upper house of the legislature, rather than the appointive council. These changes were too democratic for the conservative and aristocratic element; but when the next elections showed a majority of the people favorable to the reform, and after the popular party had blocked an appropriation bill, the conservatives yielded. Even then, Edward Rutledge and Arthur Middleton resigned the governorship, rather than approve the changes. Maryland, too, modified her constitution in favor of Quakers, Mennonites, and other minor religious groups. Jefferson, Madison, and Richard Henry Lee succeeded in securing the disestablishment of the Episcopal Church in Virginia by legislative enactment.

South Carolina amended her constitution and joined Georgia and North Carolina in prohibiting entails and primogeniture. While no change was made in the Virginia constitution, the democratic element led by Jefferson forced measures through the legislature abolishing entails in 1776 and primogeniture in 1785. Jefferson believed that this legislation formed part of a system by which "every fibre would be eradicated of ancient or future aristocracy and a foundation laid for a government truly republican."[9] The Virginia aristocracy never forgave him for this action.

The aristocracy made some slight concessions to the democrats in regard to suffrage and representation. South Carolina reduced the property requirements for voting from one hundred to fifty acres of land, and Georgia reduced it from ten pounds to the payment of all taxes levied by the state. Both states reduced considerably the property qualifications for officeholding. And the up-country counties, inhabited largely by small farmers, were given a more nearly equal share of representation in the state legislatures. All efforts at change in these particulars failed in Maryland, Virginia, and North Carolina. In spite of the concessions granted, the conservative aristocracy was still in control of all five of the original southern states at the close of the eighteenth century.

The constitutions of the two new southern states added to the Union during this period of readjustment, Kentucky and Tennessee, show some influence of the frontier ideals of democracy. Kentucky gave the suffrage in 1792 to all free adult male citizens, but limited it to free white males in 1799. Representation was apportioned to free adult male inhabitants in 1792, and to qualified electors in 1799. No property or religious qualifications for office were prescribed, and the governor, after 1799, was to be elected by popular vote rather than indirectly by an electoral

9. Jefferson, Thomas, *The Complete Jefferson,* assembled and arranged by Saul K. Padover (New York: Duell, Sloan & Pearce, 1943), p. 1150.

college, as in 1792. Tennessee showed somewhat more aristocratic leanings in her constitution of 1796. Suffrage was limited to freemen possessed of a freehold; legislators and the governor were required to possess freeholds of 200 and 500 acres of land, respectively; representation was apportioned to the counties according to taxable inhabitants; and no person who denied the existence of God was eligible for any civil office. Though somewhat more democratic than the seaboard states, Tennessee nevertheless belongs with the group of older states controlled by the landed aristocracy. It should be pointed out, however, that, in all these states, there was much cheap land to be had; hence, it was no great burden to qualify for voting in any of these states.

The political revolution of 1800 which brought Jefferson and his party to power in most of the southern states, as well as in the federal government, led to the demand that the principles of the bills of rights be translated into realistic democracy, rather than to stand as mere glittering generalities. In every state, democratic leaders condemned the discrimination made between those who had property and those who had none. They declared that, where property had representation, the people could not be free; and they were able to show that under the existing system of representation a minority of wealthy men of the east had absolute control of the state governments. They appealed to the philosophy of natural rights and demanded equality of political rights and privileges. This movement came largely from the small farmer or yeoman class concentrated in the newer counties of the up-country or the western parts of the states; hence, it took on something of the nature of an intrastate sectional fight. It naturally involved social and economic issues, as well as political rights.

The rapid settlement of the piedmont and mountain region of these states in the first quarter of the nineteenth century gave to the up-country a majority of the white population. These small farmers had somewhat different interests from the low-country planters. They desired internal improvements—roads, canals, and railroads—at state expense, in order that they might have an economic outlet for their farm produce, cattle, and domestic manufactures. A supporter of reform predicted that, if the westerners were given their way, roads and canals would be built, domestic manufactures would increase, wealth would multiply, and that the "Old Families . . . imbecile and incorrigible," would be replaced by a "happy, bold and intelligent middle class."[10] But the legislatures were controlled by the planter aristocracy of the east, who feared heavier taxation if the western farmers were given equal representation, and resisted all change.

The yeoman farmers were joined by a small class of industrial laborers of the eastern cities. These people were smarting under the provisions of the constitutions that required a freehold for voting just as the yeoman farmers were smarting under the unequal system of representation. The laborers demanded manhood suffrage. The aristocratic planters feared to grant their demands lest the laborers join the small farmers in taxing the wealth of the East.

The democratic reformers demanded conventions fresh from the people with power to rewrite completely the constitutions. But since most of the constitutions left it to the legislature or made no provision for calling a constituent assembly, and since the aristocracy, with their control over the legislatures, could prevent a call through that body, the democrats were blocked at the very threshold of reform. The aristocratic minority fought doggedly to maintain its favored position, contesting every move of the democrats, and yielding only in the face of an open revolt. In Maryland, they permitted a series of amendments between 1805 and 1810 that brought reorganization of the judicial system so as to bring justice closer to the people and make the courts more expeditious and less expensive. Property qualifications for officers were swept away; the suffrage was extended to adult white males, the written ballot was required, and the plural vote was abolished; and some minor officials were made elective. In South Carolina, representation was reapportioned in the house on the basis of white inhabitants and taxes combined. By this method, the large slaveholding districts and parishes lost some of their representatives as allotted under the earlier constitutions. Suf-

10. *Niles' Weekly Register*, XXXVII (31 October 1829), 145.

frage was extended to include all white adult males who had resided in the state two years and were possessed of a freehold of fifty acres or a town lot, or who, if possessed of neither, had lived six months in the election district. This, in reality, meant white manhood suffrage. A series of amendments in Georgia, between 1808 and 1824, made all officers from constable to governor, including judges of all the courts, elective by popular vote. These changes looked toward a greater participation in governmental affairs by the people and made the governments more responsive to the public will; but except in South Carolina, they did not appease the democratic reform spirit. The conservatives had prevented any change in North Carolina and Virginia.

Four new southern states, Louisiana, Mississippi, Alabama, and Missouri, were admitted to the Union during these years. Louisiana, admitted in 1812, fell to the control of the landed aristocracy. Only free white males were permitted to vote, and they were required to pay a state tax before qualifying. Members of the legislature and the governor were required to possess freeholds ranging in value from $500 to $5,000. Representation was apportioned according to qualified voters, or property holders. The governor and other officers were chosen by popular vote. Mississippi, too, was controlled by property holders. All officers were elected by popular vote; voting was limited to free white males who were enrolled in the militia or paid a tax; representation was based on white population; but members of the legislature and the governor were required to possess land ranging from 50 to 600 acres, or real estate ranging in value from $500 to $2,000. Alabama greatly broadened the base of political power. Suffrage was granted to all adult white male citizens; no property qualifications were required for state officials who were elected by popular vote; and representation was according to white inhabitants. Both Mississippi and Alabama declared that freemen only were possessed of equal rights. Missouri required no property qualifications for voting or officeholding, though members of the legislature must pay taxes. Only whites could vote, and representation was based on free white male inhabitants.

Thwarted by the aristocratic minority in calling legitimate

conventions, the democratic majority in the old states now threatened to take the matter in their own hands and call extra-legal conventions. Mass meetings were held in Georgia, North Carolina, Virginia, and Maryland; polls were conducted in various counties, all of which voted overwhelmingly for calling conventions; grand jury presentments called attention to the need for reform and recommended direct action if the legislatures failed to act; the voters in many counties instructed their representatives in the legislature to support a bill calling a constitutional convention; and hundreds of petitions went to the legislatures demanding relief. Typical of the sentiment for calling extra-legal conventions is the statement of a North Carolinian that if the legislature failed "to comply with the wishes of a great majority of the State," then "A convention will be assembled in the west, and the constitution amended without the concurrence of the east; and this being the act of a majority, and the legal act, will consequently be obligatory on the whole State. The constitution *will be amended.*"[11]

A statewide reform convention assembled at Milledgeville, Ga., on May 10, 1832, and issued a call for an election of delegates to a convention to meet at the capital in February 1833, to alter, revise, or amend the constitution, or write a new one. It issued an address to the people, in which it declared

that the people have an undoubted right, in their sovereign capacity, to alter or change their form of government, whenever in their opinion it becomes too obnoxious or oppressive to be borne. That crisis . . . has arrived, when the people should assert their rights, and boldly and fearlessly maintain them.[12]

The legislature now capitulated and called a convention to meet at the same time and place as that called extra-legally. Comparable action took place in Maryland in 1836, but the legislature passed a series of amendments similar to those proposed by the reform convention and forestalled extra-legal action. In like manner, the legislatures of Virginia and North Carolina capitulated to the reform party and submitted the question of a "Convention

11. Salisbury *Western Carolinian,* 17 July 1821.
12. Milledgeville, Ga., *Southern Recorder,* 31 May 1832.

or No Convention" to the voters. In both states, the call was
adopted by large majorities. Mississippi and Tennessee, too, at
the demand of the people, called conventions to revise their constitutions. This was one of the most signal victories for majority or
popular rule in American history. In these states, the people
without political voice had, by threat of appeal to numerical
majority action, forced the landed aristocracy who possessed the
legitimate and constitutional political power to submit the fundamental law to the scrutiny and revision of delegates elected from
the people for that purpose alone.

Democracy had won a victory over aristocracy. The people had
compelled the wealthy planter class in control of the legislatures
to call conventions to revise the fundamental law of the states.
Majority rule had exerted its power and justified its right. One
democratic spokesman declared that the freemen had united their
forces "to break to pieces the trammels of aristocracy, and show to
the enemies of republican equality that the sons of freemen will
still be free."[13]

John C. Calhoun, Abel P. Upshur,[14] and other aristocratic
leaders of the South openly denied the Jeffersonian ideal of equality of all men and bitterly condemned majority rule as the tyranny of King Numbers; and they had their supporters in the
North among such men as James Kent, Joseph Story, and Orestes
A. Brownson.[15] The less famous and little-known leaders of democracy just as boldly proclaimed the doctrine of political equality. The views of the former have been given much attention by
the historian; those of the latter have been generally ignored. The
significant thing about the controversy, however, is that the views
of the latter prevailed. The bills of rights remained unchanged,
and the majority forced the aristocracy to grant all white men an
equal voice in the state governments. Charles James Faulkner,

13. Salisbury *Western Carolinian*, 22 October 1822.
14. Virginia, Constitutional Convention, 1829–1830, *Proceedings and Debates of
the Convention of the Virginia State Convention of 1829-30* (Richmond: Printed by
S. Shepherd & Co. for Ritchie & Cook, 1830), pp. 68–71 and *passim*.
15. For Brownson's opposition to majority rule, see his "Democracy and Liberty,"
in *United States Magazine and Democratic Review*, XII (April 1843), 374–387, and
his "Unpopular Government," *ibid.*, XII (May 1843), 529–537.

spokesman for the Virginia democracy in 1850, said that nothing short of a radical and fundamental change in the structure of the state constitution "could satisfy the progressive aspirations of a people who felt that their energies were held in subjugation by artificial restraints inconsistent with the true principles of republican freedom and equality."[16] And, after the Virginia convention of 1850 had adjourned, he declared:

Its results was one of the proudest triumphs of popular government which the records of history can attest. A revolution as decided in its results as any of those which for the last century have deluged the monarchies of Europe with blood, passed off under the influence of the acknowledged principles of popular supremacy as quietly and tranquilly as the most ordinary county election.[17]

The reform movement begun about 1800 now bore fruit in numerous constitutional conventions,[18] and these conventions rewrote the state constitutions in line with the ideals of Jacksonian democracy. Many writers have attributed the democratic reforms of the 1830s to the influence of the western frontier. A study of the movement in the southern states gives an emphatic denial to this assumption. The people of the southern states were cognizant of what was going on in the West, but the demands for reform grew out of local conditions and would have arisen had there been no "New West" beyond the Appalachians. In fact, it would be more nearly accurate to say that many of the ideas and motives of Jacksonian democracy were southern in origin.

To what extent was aristocracy weakened and democracy strengthened by the work of the conventions of the 1830s? In the first place, property qualifications for voting were abolished in all southern states except Virginia and North Carolina, and Louisiana

16. "Hon. Charles James Faulkner, Member of Congress from Virginia," *United States Democratic Review,* XLI (March 1858) , 227.

17. *Ibid.,* 227–228.

18. Conventions were held in Virginia in 1829–1830, Mississippi in 1832, Georgia in 1833 and 1839, Tennessee in 1834, North Carolina in 1835, and an abortive or revolutionary one in Maryland in 1836. There is a close parallel in the action of the northern states. Beginning with Connecticut in 1818, Massachusetts, New York, Delaware, Vermont, and Pennsylvania all held general constitutional conventions by the end of the 1830s; and in Rhode Island, there was an unconstitutional convention in 1842 that went beyond the extra-legal action in the southern states.

still required the payment of taxes.[19] The last of the religious restrictions were also abolished. In a similar manner, property qualifications for officeholding were wiped out, except for South Carolina and Louisiana, and age and residence requirements were reduced. A large number of officers heretofore selected by the legislature or appointed by the governor were now elected by popular vote. These included civil and militia officers, justices of the peace, superior court judges, and governors in all the states except Virginia and South Carolina. Rotation in office was generally applied through short terms and restricted re-eligibility. Progress was also made in the equalization of representation. There was no uniformity in the states, however. Some used white population; some, qualified voters; some, federal population returns; and some, a combination of population and taxation. Those states that had heretofore granted special borough representation abolished it.

In still another way, these changes broadened the base of democracy. For the first time, the people had been consulted as to the revision and amendment of their constitutions. The conventions were called directly or indirectly by action of the people. The revised constitutions were, in turn, submitted back to them for ratification or rejection. In at least one state, the people twice rejected the changes and forced the desired reforms through by legislative amendments. And the new constitutions provided for future amendment and revision.

In one matter there was a definite reactionary movement. This was the issue of free-Negro suffrage. Virginia and North Carolina joined Maryland and Kentucky in taking from the free Negro the ballot he had heretofore possessed. In like manner, all new states of the period, North as well as South, denied suffrage to free Negroes. The action of the old southern states was paralleled by that of the northern states. Delaware, Connecticut, New Jersey, and Pennsylvania took the ballot from the Negro. And New York, in 1821, limited Negro suffrage by requiring that the Negro voter

19. Among northern states, New Jersey and Rhode Island retained property qualifications, and Connecticut, Massachusetts, Pennsylvania, and Ohio retained the tax-paying requirement.

possess a freehold valued at $250 over and above all indebtedness. Hence, only five of the northern states granted equal suffrage to Negroes. Whether or not Jefferson, Mason, and other Revolutionary proponents of natural rights philosophy intended to include Negroes in the statement that "all men are created equal and endowed with certain unalienable rights" is a debatable question;[20] but in actual practice, the American people had decided by their constitutional provisions that Negroes were not included in the *political people.* From the very day of the Declaration of Independence, the race problem had caused the American people to make an exception to the doctrine that "all men are created equal." But the partial exclusion of the Negro from the promises of democracy did not impair the faith of the whites in those promises.

The influence of the democratic reforms of the Jacksonian period were far-reaching. Evidence of this is to be seen in many phases of southern life—social, intellectual, economic, and political. But the people were not satisfied with their partial victory, and the signs of progress only made them more determined to complete the democratization of their state governments. Their increased political power made the task of securing additional amendments and revision of their constitutions easier than had been that of calling the conventions of the 1830s. In the first case, they had threatened extra-legal action; in the second, they simply used the powers already possessed to put through additional reforms. This time, they determined to take from the aristocratic class its last remnants of special political privileges. Important amendments in Georgia, Missouri, and North Carolina, and revision by convention in Louisiana, Kentucky, Maryland, and Virginia,[21] brought those states in line with the most democratic ones. Virginia, in 1851, was the last state to provide for popular election of the governor; and North Carolina, in 1856, abolished the

---

20. Samuel E. Morison and Henry S. Commager, *The Growth of the American Republic,* 2 vols. (New York: Oxford University Press, 1937), I, 82, state that "Jefferson did not mean to include slaves as men."

21. Louisiana in 1844 and 1852, Kentucky in 1849, and Maryland and Virginia in 1850.

fifty-acre freehold required to vote for members of the state senate. The three new states, Arkansas, Florida, and Texas, all established complete equality of the whites in political affairs, and
made all officials elective by popular vote. The *United States
Magazine and Democratic Review,* analyzing the progress of constitutional reform in the nation, declared that the constitution of
Louisiana showed "more political insight, and a more absolute
reliance upon the principle upon which popular governments are
based, then appears in the fundamental law of any other state in
the Union"; but the Missouri constitution "affords more efficient
guarantees to individual rights, and leaves fewer opportunities for
political corruption and for intercepting the fair expression of the
wishes of the people"[22] than that of any other state.

These changes left South Carolina the one remaining stronghold of the landed aristocracy in the South. While she had
granted manhood suffrage in 1810, she continued to require her
governor to possess a freehold until after the Civil War; the
governor and presidential electors were chosen by the legislature;
and representation was apportioned on a combination of white
population and taxation. But among the northern states, Massachusetts continued to apportion representation in her senate on
property until 1853; and Rhode Island continued to require voters and officeholders to possess real estate valued at $134 over and
above all incumbrances, or with a rental value of $7.00, until
1888.

The establishment of white manhood suffrage, the abolition of
property qualifications for officeholders, the elections of all officers
by popular vote, and the apportionment of representation on
population rather than wealth, with periodic reapportionment,
dealt a death blow to the political power of the landed, slaveholding aristocracy of the Old South. No longer could the members of
that class dictate to the great majority of free white men. The
aristocracy still had influence, as the wealthy merchant and indus-
trialist of the northern states had influence, and as men of property in all times and places have influence, but they did not

22. "The Progress of Constitutional Reform in the United States," *United States
Magazine and Democratic Review,* XVIII (April 1846) , 247, 253.

possess that influence because of special political privileges. Some southern planters possessed baronial wealth, but this wealth no longer gave them political control. They constituted a social, not a political, aristocracy. "Such an aristocracy, although it may confer personal independence, cannot create political authority."[23]

If the landed aristocrat wished to sit in the seat of power and administer the affairs of state, he must seek the support of the voter, his master. He must recognize every voter, however poor, as his political equal. And in the political hustings, landlord and squatter, wealthy planter and poor white, did mingle as equals.[24]

The political revolution also meant that large numbers of the small farmer and yeoman classes began to enter politics, and win seats in legislature, Congress, and the governor's office. The first governor chosen by popular vote in Virginia, in 1851, was Joseph Johnson, whose childhood had been spent in abject poverty without the opportunity for formal schooling. Despite these handicaps, he had served in the legislature and Congress, beating some of the most wealthy men of his district.[25] Indeed, six of the eight men who served Virginia as governor in the years just prior to the Civil War came from the plain people; two began life as farm hands, one as a tailor, one as a mill hand, and another as a mail contractor. Henry County, Virginia, had the second-highest percentage of large slaveholders in the state, yet only two justices of the peace, chosen between 1853 and 1858, possessed as many as ten slaves, while seven owned none, and five owned only two each.[26]

Few studies of southern leadership have been made, but prelim-

23. Frederick Grimké, *Considerations upon the Nature and Tendency of Free Institutions* (Cincinnati: H. W. Derby & Co., 1848) , pp. 311, 314; Camp, *Democracy,* pp. 220–221.

24. For descriptions of the equality of all classes at the polls, see Hamilton W. Pierson, *In the Bush; Or, Old-Time Social, Political, and Religious Life in the Southwest* (New York: D. Appleton & Co., 1881, pp. 131–146; and Henry Benjamin Whipple, *Bishop Whipple's Southern Diary, 1843–1844,* edited by Lester B. Shippee (Minneapolis: Oxford University Press, 1937) , pp. 22–23, 52.

25. "Joseph Johnson," in *Southern Historical Magazine,* I (April 1892) , 185–187.

26. Gustavus W. Dyer, *Democracy in the South Before the Civil War* (Nashville: Publishing House of the Methodist Episcopal Church, South, 1905) , pp. 80–82.

inary investigations suggest that a majority of the political leaders
of the Old South between 1830 and 1860 came from the plain
people, rather than from the large planter class. Many such men
received aid from wealthy planters to secure their education, as
did George McDuffie and Alexander H. Stephens. The literary
societies at the University of North Carolina paid all expenses of
one "penniless student" each year. Several of these students rose
to high rank in the state, one becoming a United States senator.[27]
Dozens of the men who rank at the very top in political leadership
began as poor boys, and became planters and men of wealth by
their own efforts. Let one of these men tell his own story:

> When I was a boy—a very little boy—an honest but poor man settled
> (squatted is a better word) in a country where I yet reside. . . . Day
> by day he might have been seen following his plough, while his two
> sons plied the hoe. . . . The younger [of the sons] studied law and . . .
> was drawn into politics. He was elected to the State Legislature, to
> Congress, Judge of the Circuit Court, Governor of his State, to Con-
> gress again and again, but he never forgot that he was a squatter's son.
> He stands before you today.[28]

Like Albert Gallatin Brown, many of the leaders of the Old South
grew up on the frontier, where free men could not and did not
recognize any political superior. In fact, much of the South was
only one generation removed from frontier society in 1860. Aristocracy takes more time to establish itself than one generation.

One test of the effectiveness of democracy is the exercise of the
suffrage by those qualified to vote. The southern states met this
test to about the same degree that the northern states did. There
was considerable variation from state to state in both the North
and the South, but the percentage of votes cast, according to the
voting population, in the southern states exceeded that of the
North as often, and to about the same degree, as it failed to reach
it. For instance, in the presidential election of 1828, Georgia, with
a white population of 296,806, cast 18,790 votes; and Connecticut,

27. Kemp P. Battle, *Memories of an Old-Time Tar Heel,* edited by William
James Battle (Chapel Hill: University of North Carolina Press, 1945), p. 93.

28. Albert Gallatin Brown, *Speech . . . in the House of Representatives, 14 March
1852, on the Southern Movement and Mississippi Politics* (Washington: Printed at
the Globe Office, 1852).

with a white population of 289,603, cast 18,277 votes; Alabama, however, with a white population of 190,406, cast 19,076 votes. Thus, the vote of Georgia and Connecticut was 6.3 percent of the voting people, but that of Alabama was 10.1 percent. In the same election, Massachusetts, with 603,351 free people, cast 35,855 votes; Virginia, with 694,300 whites, cast 38,853 votes; but Tennessee, with only 535,746 whites, cast 46,330 votes. The percentages of these states were 5.9, 5.5, and 8.2, respectively. In the presidential election of 1860, Georgia, with a white population of 595,088, cast 106,365 votes; Connecticut, with 406,147 white people, cast 77,146 votes; and Alabama, with 529,121 whites, cast 90,307 votes. The percentages for the three states were 18.0, 16.7, and 17.0, respectively. In this election, Massachusetts had 1,231,066 free people and cast 169,175 votes; Virginia had 1,105,453 whites and cast 167,223 votes; and Tennessee, with 834,082 whites, cast 145,333 votes. The percentages were 13.7, 15.1, and 17.4, respectively. A comparison of all the southern with all the northern states shows a white population of 7,614,018 casting 1,260,509 votes and 18,736,849 people casting 3,369,134 votes, or a percentage of 16.6 for the South and 17.9 for the North. The western states gave the North the advantage in the over-all comparison. But if one uses adult white male population, which is more accurate for voting percentages, then the South had a percentage of 69.5 and the North of 69.7.[29]

The vote of the southern states was almost equally divided between the Whig and the Democratic parties in the presidential elections from 1836 to 1852 inclusive. In the five elections, the total popular vote of the Whig candidates was 1,745,884, that of the Democratic candidates was 1,760,452, or a majority for the Democrats of only 14,568. The Whigs had a majority in three elections; but in 1836, it was only 1,862 votes, and its biggest

29. White population is used as a basis for all these calculations except that free population is used for the six states that permitted Negroes to vote. South Carolina is excluded, since the presidential electors of that state were chosen by the legislature. Population figures are taken from the United States Census reports; the votes from Thomas H. McKee, *The National Conventions and Platforms of All Political Parties, 1789–1900; Convention, Popular, and Electoral Vote*, 3d ed. (Baltimore: The Friedenwald Co., 1900).

majority was in 1840, with 52,851. The Democratic majority in 1844 was only 23,766; and in 1852, when the Whigs were weakened by the Compromise issue, it was 79,690. There was a total of twenty-seven states in the Whig column and thirty-seven in the Democratic column for the five elections; but, except for the election of 1852, there was no overwhelming majority for either party; and in 1848, the parties divided the states equally. Such an equal division of party strength prevented any one group from dominating the political situation in the South. The states were shifting back and forth between the two parties so rapidly that no one could hope to retain power long enough to consolidate party, much less planter class, control. This situation also enabled the southern states to exert popular control over the United States senators who were elected by the state legislatures. With party changes in the states, the senators were often instructed by the legislature how to vote on major issues in Congress. While the purpose of instruction was partisan, it nevertheless resulted in the senators being made responsible to the majority will as expressed in state elections, for many senators voted according to instructions, and others resigned rather than do so.

With the coming of manhood suffrage came the demand for popular education so that the voter might cast a more intelligent ballot. It was recognized that democracy and republicanism could work effectively only with an educated electorate. Since "The chief object of constitutions and laws" is "to render its citizens secure in their lives, liberty and prosperity," the importance of "a good education to each individual, to every community, and to the State, cannot be too highly valued," declared a report of the Louisiana constitutional convention of 1844.[30] Popular education, wrote James M. Garnett of Virginia,

is of most importance in all governments. But it is indispensible in ours where all political power emanates immediately from the people, who must be themselves both intelligent and virtuous, or it will rarely

30. Louisiana, Constitutional Convention, 1844–1845, *Proceedings and Debates of the Convention of Louisiana, Which Assembled at the City of New Orleans, 14 January 1844* (New Orleans: Besancon, Ferguson & Co., 1845), pp. 316–319.

happen that their public functionaries will be any better than themselves.[31]

Even the aristocratic element recognized the principle that they must now educate their masters, although many did not wish to support education by taxation. One of them declared

that in adopting universal suffrage, we took necessarily the consequences that would flow from it were any portion of the people ignorant and debased. . . . Without you enlighten the sources of political power, we shall have no government. . . . You have adopted the principle of universal suffrage, but the basis is public education.[32]

Recognizing the need, every southern state, with the exception of South Carolina, where a system of poor schools existed, provided for the establishment of a public school system of education before 1860. North Carolina led off in 1839; the question had first been submitted to popular vote and carried by a large majority. In some states—Louisiana, for instance—the constitution required the legislature to provide a state system and to support it by taxation. All the states except Virginia and South Carolina provided for a state superintendent of public instruction; in most states, the superintendent was elected by popular vote. The systems of public education in the southern states, in provisions for administration, support, and general results, compare favorably with those in the northern states in 1860.[33]

In like manner, popular control of southern state governments brought measures designed to minister to the economic wants of the people. In fact, some leaders of democratic reform boldly proclaimed that this was one of the major purposes of government.[34] Boards of public works, popularly elected, were created to supervise internal improvements and to further the economic progress of the states. They were interested also in the public

31. James M. Garnett, "Popular Education," in *Southern Literary Messenger,* VIII (February 1842), 115.

32. *Proceedings and Debates of the Convention of Louisiana* (1844), p. 909.

33. Edgar W. Knight, *The Influence of Reconstruction on Education in the South* (New York: Teachers College, Columbia University, 1913), pp. 94, 98.

34. See, for instance, "Hon. Charles J. Faulkner, Member of Congress from Virginia," in *United States Democratic Review,* XLI (March 1858), 218.

utilization of the natural resources of the states. Imprisonment for debt was prohibited; banks were brought under state control; provision was made for chartering corporations; monopolies were prohibited; and provisions were made for uniform and equal taxation of property according to value. All these measures were included in the state constitutions. The states, too, safeguarded the rights and interests of the unfortunate classes. State asylums for the insane and schools for the deaf, the dumb, and the blind were established at state expense.

The history of the southern state constitutions and governments from 1776 to 1860 reveals a progressive expansion in the application of the doctrine of political equality. By 1860, the aristocratic planter class had been shorn of its special privileges and political power. It still gave tone and color to political life, but it no longer dominated and controlled the political order. On the other hand, the great mass of the whites had been given more and more authority, and majority rule had been definitely established. The interpretation of the southern states as "political aristocracies of the sternest and most odious kind" had no basis in fact. With the exceptions already noted, the southern state governments were as democratic in 1860 as their northern sister states. They had not attained the ideal goal of absolute equality; but in spirit and administration, as well as in form, they had progressively become more and more concerned with the rights and interests of the people.

4

Cycles of American Democracy

> As in the preceding essay, Green warns us that the word
> *democracy* is a relative term and that it has had various meanings
> at different times. This paper was presented in April 1961, in
> Detroit, Michigan, as the presidential address to the Mississippi
> Valley Historical Association, now the Organization of
> American Historians. It was published in the *Mississippi Valley
> Historical Review,* XLVIII (June 1961), 3–23.

DEMOCRACY IS A TERM WITH WHICH the American people are so familiar that they rarely attempt to define it; and whenever they do so, they find the undertaking most difficult. Leading authorities in philosophy and political science are unable to agree upon its meaning.

James Bryce defined it as a "form of government in which the ruling power of a state is legally vested, not in any particular class or classes, but in the members of the community as a whole," that is, "a government in which the will of the majority of qualified citizens rules." Not so, says Walter Lippmann: "We must abandon the notion that the people govern. Instead, we must adopt the theory that, by their occasional mobilizing as a majority, the people support or oppose the individuals who actually govern." Another authority, Robert M. MacIver, says that "Democracy is not a way of governing, whether by a majority or otherwise, but primarily a way of determining who shall govern and, broadly, to what ends." And Harold J. Laski has said that "No definition of democracy can adequately comprise the vast history which the concept connotes. To some, it is a form of government, to others a way of social life."[1]

---

1. Hillman M. Bishop and Samuel Hendel, editors, *Basic Issues of American Democracy: A Book of Readings* (New York: Appleton-Century-Crofts, 1948), pp. 14–18.

We may conclude, then, that democracy has no precise meaning, that there can be no one correct definition. Democracy is a relative term, one that has various meanings among different peoples and for the same peoples at different stages of their political development. In this paper, the term will be used, as generally accepted by historians, to mean a form of government in which the ultimate sovereign power is held by the people and exercised through a system of representation in which the representatives are chosen by a large electorate and are responsible to the electors.[2]

In America, democratic government has been an evolving and expanding institution. It has grown with the country. Its origins, of course, may be traced back beyond the American Revolution to our colonial heritage; yet, the Revolution itself was a struggle for political democracy, for government by "the consent of the governed," and it is from the Revolutionary era that we can date the beginning of a series of cycles in the growth of American democracy. In the course of our history, from then until the present, four cycles are clearly discernible. The first was the era of the Revolution and of our first constitutions, when the people assumed authority to establish the governments by which they were to be governed. During the second cycle, from the close of the eighteenth century to 1860, the several states, acting as agents for the people, were responsible for democratic advance, with the federal government playing an insignificant or minor role. Since 1860, however, the situation has been reversed. When federalism gave way to nationalism in the years after the Civil War, the United States government assumed the dominant role and has held it ever since, and the states have contributed less and less to democracy's advance. During the latter third of the nineteenth century, the Congress exercised a controlling influence in shaping American democracy, and the judiciary served as a check to slow down progress. During the early years of the twentieth century, as the fourth cycle began, the Executive seemed destined to replace Congress as the leader, but since the 1930s, the judiciary has been in the ascendancy.

2. See Carl Becker, *Modern Democracy* (New Haven: Yale University Press, 1941) , pp. 4–6.

The developments of the nineteenth and twentieth centuries have been the working out of principles first enunciated as the tenets of American democracy during the Revolutionary era. Our fundamental concepts and principles, based upon the philosophy of natural rights and popular sovereignty, found full and adequate expression in such Revolutionary documents as the Virginia Bill of Rights of June 12, 1776, the Declaration of Independence of July 4, 1776, and the Massachusetts Bill of Rights of 1780.[3] In Virginia, it was declared that

All men are by nature equally free and independent, and have certain inherent rights, of which . . . they cannot by any compact deprive or divest their posterity; namely, the enjoyment of life and liberty, with the means of acquiring and possessing property, and pursuing and obtaining happiness and safety.

In the same spirit, and in that same summer of 1776, Congress proclaimed the self-evident "truths" that

all men are created equal, that they are endowed by their Creator with certain unalienable rights, that among these are life, liberty and the pursuit of happiness. That to secure these rights, governments are instituted among men, deriving their just powers from the consent of the governed.

In Massachusetts, provisions of the bill of rights were clear and detailed:

The people . . . have the sole and exclusive right of governing themselves. . . . Government is instituted for the common good, for the protection, safety, prosperity, and happiness of the people and not for the profit, honor, or private interest of any one man, family, or class of men. . . . All elections ought to be free; and all the inhabitants of this commonwealth, having such qualifications as they shall establish by their frame of government, have an equal right to elect officers, and to be elected, for public employments.

These and similar expressions of democratic equalitarianism were familiar to the American people during the last quarter of

3. The introduction here draws on the author's *Constitutional Development in the South Atlantic States, 1776–1860* (Chapel Hill: University of North Carolina Press, 1930) and "Democracy in the Old South," an essay which first appeared in the *Journal of Southern History*, XII (February 1946), 3–23, and is reprinted on pp. 65–86 of this volume.

the eighteenth century, but they were not fully incorporated into the framework of government, either state or federal. Two of the original states chose to continue under the colonial charters, and the new constitutions were far from radical experiments in democratic self-government. Only one original state constitution was submitted to the people for popular approval; the others were promulgated by the bodies that framed them. Five of the constitutions contained no provision for amendment or revision, and some had no separate bill of rights. Nor was the principle of religious freedom fully recognized. Even the Pennsylvania constitution, generally conceded to have been most democratic of all, required each member of the legislature to take an oath that he believed "in one God, the creator and governor of the universe, the rewarder of the good and the punisher of the wicked," and to acknowledge that the Old and New Testament had been "given by Divine inspiration." Suffrage was limited to free white males by property qualifications ranging from tax payments to freeholds of 100 acres or £60 in value. High property qualifications for officeholding prevailed. Members of the legislatures were required to be possessed of freeholds of 250 to 500 acres; and governors, of freeholds of 1,000 acres to property worth £5,000. Members of the legislatures and some local officials were elected by popular vote, but governors and other state officials were chosen by the legislature.

Among democratic tendencies found in the first constitutions was the conscious move toward liberalizing suffrage by shifting from the freehold to tax payments. Some forbade imprisonment for debt after the delivery of all property; some, the entailment of estates. Some provided for the separation of church and state and for state support of education. Georgia, for instance, declared that "Schools shall be erected in each county and supported at the general expense of the state." Most important of all were the "inherent rights" enumerated in the bills of rights. That of Virginia, written by George Mason, was the first adopted, and it served as a model for those that followed. The most characteristic feature of the bills of rights was their reflection of eighteenth-century natural-rights philosophy. They spoke of founding government by "compact only," of "natural and unalienable right," and of men being "by nature equally free and independent." They declared that freemen could not be deprived of liberty except by the law of the land. Trial by jury was safeguarded. When prosecuted, freemen were to be presented with an indictment, were to have the right to counsel and evidence, could not be compelled to give evidence against themselves, and could be convicted only by a jury of their peers. Excessive bail and fines, cruel and unusual punishments, bills of attainder, general warrants, and ex post facto laws were forbidden, as were perpetuities, monopolies, hereditary honors, special privileges, titles of nobility, standing armies in time of peace, and the suspension of the writ of habeas corpus. They proclaimed the right of free exercise of religion, of freemen to bear arms, and the supremacy of the civil over military power. They guaranteed freedom of elections, speech, and press; and recognized the right of people to assemble, to petition for redress of grievances, to instruct their representatives, and to participate in legislation. Taxation without consent was forbidden. They declared that the purpose of government was to promote the welfare and happiness of the people, that all political power was vested in the people, and that a majority of the people had the right to alter, change, or abolish the government when it became subversive of the purposes for which it was established.

Shadowy and indistinct as some of these concepts may be, they were the foundation stones upon which the superstructure of American democracy was to be erected. And while political leaders, North and South, were, during the 1830s and 1840s, to condemn the political axioms of the natural-rights philosophy as "glittering and sounding generalities,"[4] they were proclaimed anew in the state constitutions of that period. And the philosophical concept that all men are born equal and are possessed of

4. Rufus Choate, United States senator from Massachusetts, used this particular phrase. Samuel G. Brown, *Life of Rufus Choate,* 2d ed. (Boston: Little, Brown, and Company 1870), p. 328. See also Carl Becker, *The Declaration of Independence: A Study in the History of Political Ideas* (New York: Vintage Books, 1958), pp. 240–244. Rhode Island included a bill of rights in her first constitution in 1842; Virginia incorporated her Bill of Rights of 1776 in her revised constitution of 1850; and Minnesota included one in her constitution of 1858.

inherent and unalienable rights continues, even in 1961, to inspire and justify American democracy.

The Articles of Confederation, ratified in 1781, had little direct bearing on the establishment and development of democracy in the United States. Little more than a league of sovereign states, the Confederation had no authority to act upon the individual citizen. In the same decade, Congress, in adopting the Northwest Ordinance of 1787, set up property qualifications for voting and officeholding higher than those in most of the states. The elector was required to possess a freehold of 50 acres; members of the legislature, 200; the secretary, judges, and councillors, 500; and the governor, 1,000 acres. The Ordinance contained a few provisions similar to those in the state bills of rights and provided for the encouragement and support of education. Unlike any of the original state constitutions, the Ordinance, however, excluded slavery from the Territory.

The delegates who assembled in Philadelphia in 1787 feared the excesses of democracy they professed to see in the state constitutions. Although they failed to include a formal bill of rights, they did incorporate some of the provisions of the state bills of rights into the Constitution. It forbade Congress to suspend the writ of habeas corpus except in case of rebellion or invasion, to pass bills of attainder or ex post facto laws, or to confer titles of nobility. And it provided for jury trial, except in impeachment cases. It left the qualifications of voters for members of the House of Representatives to be determined by the individual states. Critics of the Constitution forced the adoption of ten amendments in 1791, which guaranteed freedom of speech, press, and assembly, the right of petition, and trial by jury with counsel and witnesses, and forbade excessive bail, fines, cruel and unjust punishments. The federal Constitution and government were somewhat less inclined toward democracy, equality, and individual rights than were the state governments. The first cycle in American democracy had come to an end.

To the extent that democracy depends upon constitutional guarantees of individual rights, the United States had embraced democracy. But these guarantees had not been fully implemented, and the principles and ideas associated with popular government had not gained wide acceptance. To a numerous and influential upper class, popularly called aristocrats, the word *democracy* stood for leveling tendencies, radicalism, and mobocracy. They hoped and expected that the conservative interests would overcome the democratic trends. John Adams called upon the aristocrats to "Remember, democracy never lasts long. It soon wastes, exhausts and murders itself. There never was a democracy that did not commit suicide."[5] James Fenimore Cooper maintained that equality was "no where laid down as a governing principle of the institutions of the United States, neither the word, nor any inference that can be fairly deduced from its meaning, occurring in the constitution."[6]

The democrats realized that democracy could not stand still, that a static democracy, like a static society, was a dying one, and that, to live, democracy must constantly change and grow. As one of their number expressed it, "Nothing is clearer than that genuine democracy must ever be progressive."[7] And from the beginning, American citizens, individually and in organized groups, have constantly striven to broaden the base of democracy and to attain their full liberty and equal rights and opportunities. Progress has been made, not by revolutionary action, but through the orderly processes of governmental action. The evolution of democracy in the United States has been greatly influenced by the dual system of state and federal governments and by the separation of governmental powers between the three branches—legislative, executive, and judicial. At times, the two governments and the three branches of each have worked at cross purposes; at others, they have supported each other in efforts to broaden and develop democracy.

The second cycle, from 1790 to 1860, can best be studied in the

5. Morris L. Ernst, *The Ultimate Power* (Garden City, N.Y.: Doubleday, Doran & Co., 1937), p. 70.

6. James Fenimore Cooper, *The American Democrat*, with an Introduction by H. L. Mencken (New York: A. A. Knopf, 1936), p. 42.

7. Ohio, Constitutional Convention, 1850–1851, *Report of the Debates and Proceedings of the Convention for the Revision of the Constitution of Ohio*, 2 vols. (Columbus: S. Medary, Printer to the Convention, 1851), II, 551.

state constitutions which "so reflect the changing conditions and varied interests of the United States, that a study of them affords a perfect mirror of American democracy."[8] Lord Bryce found them "a mine of instruction for the natural history of democratic communities."[9] In the period before 1860, the rights, privileges, and immunities of the citizen were much more dependent upon the political institutions of the several states than they were upon those of the federal government. In fact, during most of this period, the United States seemed to ignore the individual, left to the states nearly all the functions that affected individual rights, and in at least one case (the Dorr Rebellion in Rhode Island), failed to intervene or support the citizens in their effort to carry through a democratic reorganization of their state government. When the citizen voted for his representative in Congress, he did so under suffrage qualifications established by his state. Federal relations with the individual were generally negative, rather than positive. The First Amendment to the Constitution forbade Congress to enact a law respecting the establishment of religion but did not restrain a state from doing so. Hence, up to 1835, the North Carolina constitution forbade Catholics to hold office; and as late as 1930, those New Jersey citizens who did not profess to a belief in God were denied the right of testifying in the state courts.[10]

The major goal of the democratic reformers of the first half of the nineteenth century was political equality. This they hoped to attain by the abolition of religious and property tests for voting and officeholding, the adoption of the written ballot, the popular election of all state and local officials, and the more equitable distribution of representation. These reforms were generally opposed by the wealthy, aristocratic, conservative classes and supported by the lower classes, or plain people. Many of the leaders for reform, however, came from the upper class. Generally speak-

---

8. James Q. Dealey, *Growth of American State Constitutions from 1776 to the End of the Year 1914* (Boston: Ginn and Co., 1915), p. 117.

9. James Bryce, *The American Commonwealth*, 2d ed., 2 vols. (London: Macmillan and Co., 1891), I, 434.

10. Ernst, *The Ultimate Power*, p. 195.

ing, the Federalist and Whig parties opposed, while the Jeffersonian Republican and Jacksonian Democratic parties supported reform, although there was considerable criss-crossing of individuals within the parties. Minor parties—the workingmen's and labor groups, for instance—were supporters of the democratic revolution.

Constitutional revision designed to promote democracy was a never-ending process. The thirteen original states had grown to thirty-four by 1860, and each of them held a convention—some, two, three, or even four; several had periodic revisions by a council established for that purpose; and many of them added amendments through legislative action. In the later period, all new constitutions, as well as revisals and some amendments, were submitted to a popular referendum. In several cases, the voters, disappointed with the extent of reforms offered, rejected the revision and forced another convention. The territories forced Congress to keep step with state democracy in constitution-making. The Northwest Ordinance had established a freehold of fifty acres of land for voting, but the Mississippi Territory protested this as undemocratic, and pre-emptioners were added to the list of voters in 1807. This did not satisfy the democrats, and they demanded that all taxpayers be permitted to vote. Congress acquiesced and abandoned the freehold in 1811. All new states carved out of the public domain between 1830 and 1860, except one, called a convention and drafted a constitution without waiting for Congress to pass an enabling act.

The older states generally followed orderly and legal processes in constitutional revision, but the people were not averse to taking power into their own hands in order to secure their rights. One or two examples will suffice. In North Carolina, after the legislature had refused to call a convention, the reformers called upon the whole people to join forces and "by an unanimity and promptness of action, break to pieces the trammels of aristocracy, and show to the enemy of republican equality that the sons of freemen will still be free."[11] They declared that "a convention

11. Salisbury *Western North Carolinian,* 17 July 1821, 22 October 1822.

will be assembled . . . [and] the constitution *will be* amended."
But they did not get the convention for more than a decade. The
Georgia democrats went a step further. They issued a call for a
convention that declared, "The people have an undoubted right,
in their sovereign capacity, to alter or change the form of their
government, whenever in their opinion it becomes too obnoxious
or oppressive to be borne."[12] The people elected delegates to meet
in an extralegal constitutional convention, whereupon the legislature capitulated and called for a legal convention to assemble at
the place and time specified in the people's call. In Rhode Island,
the action resulted in the well-known Dorr Rebellion. The reformers called a people's convention, which adopted a constitution providing for white manhood suffrage to replace the freehold
requirement of the old charter-constitution. Thomas W. Dorr was
elected and inaugurated governor. Both he and the legally elected
governor, Samuel W. King, appealed to President John Tyler,
who made it clear that the federal government would intervene if
necessary to guarantee a republican form of government for the
state. Dorr's Rebellion was crushed, but a legally assembled convention extended the suffrage to adult male citizens who were
possessed of real estate worth $134 or who paid a rental of $7.00
per annum, and to native-born male citizens who paid a tax of
$1.00, or contributed $1.00 for the support of public schools.[13]

In spite of the bitter controversy over slavery and abolition
from 1830 to 1860, there was little sentiment to include the Negro
in the free suffrage group. In fact, the pendulum swung in the
other direction. Between 1790 and 1838, ten states—six slave and
four free—which had permitted limited Negro suffrage abolished
it. New York abolished Negro suffrage in 1807 but re-established
it in 1821 for those who owned a freehold worth $250 clear of
debt and on which they had paid tax. Efforts to re-establish equal
Negro suffrage were defeated in 1846 and 1860. Wisconsin rejected a Negro suffrage amendment in 1848, but the state supreme court ruled, in 1866, that the action had been ratified.
Ohio also defeated a Negro suffrage amendment, in 1851. The

12. Milledgeville, Ga., *Southern Recorder,* 31 May 1832.
13. See Arthur M. Mowry, *The Dorr War: Or, The Constitutional Struggle in
Rhode Island* (Providence, R. I.: Preston & Rounds Co., 1901).

slavery issue was used by the reformers in some of the slave states, who argued that the extension of suffrage to all white males would unite the whites in support of the institution of slavery. Slavery advocates championed the continued use of the federal ratio for apportioning representation in the legislatures, on the ground that it would strengthen the South in its defense against abolitionism.

There is little evidence that sectionalism, North or South, East or West, had any material influence on the advance of democracy. Of the original states, South Carolina, generally conceded to have been controlled by the planter aristocracy, was the first to amend her constitution to establish adult white male suffrage, whereas Rhode Island was the last to abolish the freehold requirement. North Carolina, less dominated by a planter aristocracy than any southern state, was the last state to abolish the dual suffrage requirement for the two houses of the legislature. The new western states consciously drew the more liberal suffrage qualifications from eastern states. They also followed the eastern states in setting up different requirements for voting in local and general elections. New states north of the Ohio River did not seem to move any more rapidly forward in establishing adult manhood suffrage than those south of it. Mississippi abolished property qualifications for suffrage in 1817, whereas Illinois retained a taxpaying requirement until 1837. Furthermore, the new upper western states excluded Negroes as well as Indians from the suffrage. One recent scholar has concluded that

In view of the extent to which western suffrage history was a recapitulation of the suffrage history of the eastern seaboard, it is difficult to believe that the New West was unique or that it made any new contribution to the growth of suffrage democracy.[14]

By 1860, the states had practically completed their campaign for political democracy as the term was then understood. Property qualifications for voting and officeholding had been abolished.

14. Chilton Williamson, *American Suffrage; from Property to Democracy, 1760–1860* (Princeton: Princeton University Press, 1960), pp. 221–222. For an older and conflicting view, see John D. Barnhart, *Valley of Democracy: The Frontier Versus the Plantation in the Ohio Valley, 1775–1818* (Bloomington: Indiana University Press, 1953).

Popular elections of governors, other state officials, and in many cases the judiciary, prevailed; and every state, with the exception of South Carolina, now chose presidential electors by popular vote. The written ballot had been provided in all states except Virginia and Illinois. Polling places had been brought near the voter, an improvement as important as the discontinuing of the requirement that voters be freeholders. Primogeniture and entail had been abolished, and imprisonment for debt had been drastically restricted. Church and state had been separated, and religious tests for voting and officeholding had been abolished. Representation had been more equitably reapportioned, rotten boroughs had been abolished, and the larger urban centers had been given greater representation.

Having established political democracy, the people began to use their power for their greater good. Banks and other corporations were brought under regulation; and, of far greater importance, the states began to implement the provisions in their constitutions which provided for state-supported public schools. Varying from state to state, this movement got under way, north, south, and west. Along with funds for public schools came funds for internal improvements. One North Carolina farmer expressed a general feeling when he wrote that such state support would provide

a large fund to be laid out in the improvement of roads and rivers; in the creation of schools for the education of the children . . . ; in ameliorating our penal code by the establishment of a penitentiary, and in various other ways for the state as the wisdom of the people may, from time to time prescribe and direct.[15]

Alexis de Tocqueville wrote in the first edition of his *Democracy in America* that "the gradual development of the principle of equality is a providential fact. . . . It is universal, it is durable, it constantly eludes all human interference, and all events as well as all men contribute to its progress." Fifteen years later, he con-

15. [In some instances among these essays, the time lapse between Fletcher Green's original research, the writing of the essay, and subsequent publication has resulted in the separation of notes from essays, with an occasional complete loss. This reference is the only one from a previously published work for which it has been impossible to trace the proper documentation.—J.I.C.]

cluded that his prophecy, at least for the United States, had been fulfilled. Democracy was an established and going concern.[16] The states had played the lead role in this successful enterprise, but their major task had been completed. Democracy was soon to shift its concern to minority groups—Negroes, women, and Indians— whose political rights had been largely ignored and neglected. This shift was accompanied by another, which was to place major emphasis on civil rights and economic democracy. The United States government was to lead in this new venture.

The American Civil War was fought, according to official statements of President Lincoln and the Congress, to save the Union. The Union was saved, but the war transformed it from a federal into a national government, and the victorious North determined that the new Union should use its national power not only to free itself from the sinful stain of slavery, but also to further the cause of political democracy. The states were to be shorn of much of their power and to become, as time went on, more and more the mere administrative units of national authority until, today, little is left of the federal system as established in 1789.[17] Looking at the problem from the vantage point of the present, one might make a good case for the view that the nation would have been better off if Alexander Hamilton's program for a national state had been accepted by the Constitutional Convention.

The changes wrought by the war in the nature and spirit of the Union were accompanied by another significant change—the shift in the attitude of the people toward government. A large part of the American people no longer accepted the Jeffersonian view that that government is best which governs least. They wanted more and more services from their government. Furthermore, the development of transportation and communication, the expansion of industry and commerce, and the rise of cities contributed to the growth of a large industrial labor class that looked to the

16. Alexis de Tocqueville, *Democracy in America*, edited by Phillips Bradley, 2 vols. (New York: Vintage Books, 1957), I, ix.
17. See Roy F. Nichols, "Federalism Versus Democracy," in *Federalism as a Democratic Process*, by Roscoe Pound and others (New Brunswick: Rutgers University Press, 1942), pp. 49, 74–75.

national government for economic equality as well as political democracy.

The advocates of freedom for the slave and suffrage for the Negro still looked back to the Revolutionary philosophy of natural rights and human equality. Negroes, like white men, were created equal and possessed unalienable rights to life, liberty, and the pursuit of happiness. President Lincoln had taken the first steps toward this goal during the war; but since his authority was based upon the exercise of war powers of doubtful constitutionality, control shifted to a more radical group in Congress, which determined to destroy the institution, root and branch, and to give the freedmen full citizenship rights. By special acts, Congress liberated the slaves in the District of Columbia and the territories in 1862, and required gradual emancipation of West Virginia as the price of her admission into the Union. In 1865, congressional leaders decided on the bold plan of abolishing slavery everywhere in the Union by an amendment to the United States Constitution. This "was the first example of the use of the amending process to accomplish a specific reform on a nation-wide scale,"[18] and it aroused considerable opposition, even in the northern states. Of the thirty-six states, three-fourths were necessary for ratification. Five of the states failed to ratify. The eleven former Confederate states, constituting more than one-fourth of the total number, were not yet back in the Union, but they were required to ratify the Thirteenth Amendment as a prerequisite to re-admission. Secretary of State William H. Seward included eight of them in the proclamation which declared the amendment in force. This was only the first instance of what Thomas Reed Powell has called "complete coercion" by the national government "to secure ratification . . . [of amendments] by the unreconstructed states."[19]

The slaves having been freed, Congress moved to secure suffrage for the Negro. The Reconstruction Act of 1867 required the secession states to "permit all male citizens . . . of whatever race,

18. James G. Randall, *The Civil War and Reconstruction* (Boston: D. C. Heath and Co., 1937), p. 508.

19. Thomas Reed Powell, *Vagaries and Varieties in Constitutional Interpretation* (New York: Columbia University Press, 1956), p. 215.

color, or previous condition of servitude" to vote for delegates to the conventions, which, in turn, were required to incorporate a provision into the constitution guaranteeing the "elective franchise . . . to all such persons as have qualifications herein stated for electors." Finally, the state was required to pledge that its constitution should "never be so altered as to deprive any citizen or class of citizens of the United States of the right to vote who are entitled to vote by the constitution herein ratified."

The Congress had concern for the political rights of Negroes in states other than the secession states. In 1867, it bestowed suffrage on the Negroes in the District of Columbia and the territories. Likewise, Congress required Nebraska and Colorado, whose constitutions confined voting privileges to whites, to amend their organic laws so as to permit Negro suffrage. More sweeping was the action of Congress in proposing the Fourteenth and Fifteenth Amendments. The first made of the freedmen citizens of the United States and forbade any state to make or enforce any law "which would abridge the privileges of citizens"; the second declared that "The right of citizens of the United States to vote shall not be denied or abridged by the United States or by any State on account of race, color, or previous condition of servitude." It should be remembered that only six states had permitted Negro suffrage in 1860. That Negro suffrage was advocated by the Radical Republicans for partisan purposes detracts not at all from the importance of the enfranchisement of the Negro. It still stands as one of the most significant steps in the development of political democracy in America. There may be some truth in the statement of a well-known scholar that

In the United States, suffrage came to the Negro like a bolt from the blue sky, confusing both friend and foe as to its meaning. The law did not fit the social system. It was a façade concealing a hollow interior so far as any real freedom for the Negro was concerned.[20]

There are explanations for the failure of Negro suffrage not mentioned by the author. Among them were the fact that the

20. Harold F. Gosnell, *Democracy, the Threshold of Freedom* (New York: Ronald Press Co., 1948) , p. 28.

Negro was thrown into the sea of politics before he had been taught to swim; that misguided southern whites threw stumbling blocks in the path of the unlettered, newly enfranchised voter, and illegally prevented him from exercising his rights; and that unscrupulous politicians everywhere deliberately exploited the Negro voter.

Under congressional Reconstruction, the southern states added other democratic provisions to their constitutions. Among the more important were the prohibition of imprisonment for debt, a homestead exemption from seizure and sale for debt, the guarantee of married women's property rights, the requirement that taxes should be levied for public schools open to Negroes as well as whites, albeit most of them provided for segregated schools, and the admission of Negroes to the militia. South Carolina provided for the popular election of presidential electors, and Louisiana for the first time included a separate bill of rights in her constitution. Congress also influenced some revision in states outside the South. It required all new states to establish and support public schools free from sectarian control; required Arizona to drop from her constitution a provision for the recall of judges but, like the southern states and their pledge on Negro suffrage, she later violated the pledge; and Indiana dropped the provision from her pre-Civil War constitution that forbade Negroes to settle in the state. Without pressure from Congress, other states completed the democratic reforms begun before the Civil War. Among such changes were the popular election of the judiciary; the final dropping of the Protestant religion as a requirement for holding state office, and the remnants of property requirements for office-holding. The over-all significance of congressional influence on political democracy in the last half of the nineteenth century constitutes one of the great landmarks in the history of democracy. In 1915, one constitutional historian wrote that

So powerful has been the democratic influence of Congress in reconstruction and in the formation of states out of territories, that one might almost wish that the New England and smaller middle states would attempt to secede from the Union, so that Congress might have the pleasure of reconstructing them on democratic lines.[21]

21. Dealey, *Growth of American State Constitutions*, pp. 110–111.

Congress played a role in the successful campaign for direct election of United States senators and suffrage for women similar to that it played in the abolition of slavery and the enfranchisement of the Negro, namely, by drafting and proposing constitutional amendments to be ratified by the states. The system of electing senators by state legislatures, originally provided by the United States Constitution, was subject to many criticisms, chief of which was that it violated a basic concept of American democracy—the popular election of governmental officials. Conservatives generally opposed any change, and southerners opposed popular election of senators for fear that it might interfere with white supremacy in the South. Some states began to hold preferential primaries for senators, and the movement gained favor. Finally, in 1912, Congress passed a resolution that was ratified in 1913. Other than conforming to and satisfying the demand of the democratic concept of popular elections, the change has been of little significance on American democracy.

The demand for woman suffrage had its roots deep in natural-rights philosophy. From the beginning of our nation, there had been a continuing demand for a broader suffrage. Religious, property, and race or color qualifications fell by the way, but sex, which barred a larger number than either of these, was last to fall. New Jersey had inadvertently permitted women to vote under her constitution of 1776, which gave the suffrage to "all inhabitants of full age worth fifty pounds." Few women took advantage of the opportunity, and the constitution was soon changed so as to limit suffrage to males. In 1838, Kentucky gave widows with children of school age the right to vote in all school elections, and Kansas extended this right to all women in 1861. The enfranchisement of Negroes by congressional action shortly after the Civil War gave renewed strength to the woman-suffrage movement, and in 1878, a resolution for a constitutional amendment was introduced in Congress. It gained little headway, at first. The early victories came in the states, chiefly in the West. Finally, in 1916, the two major parties endorsed woman suffrage in their platforms; and in 1918, President Woodrow Wilson gave his support to the proposed amendment as a war measure. Both houses of Congress passed a resolution in 1919 which declared that "the right of citizens to vote shall not be denied or abridged by the United States or by any State on account of sex." Ratified by the necessary states in 1920, it became the Nineteenth Amendment to the Constitution. Chief opposition came in the southern states, which were about equally divided on the issue. The southern argument against the change was that it would interfere with white-supremacy control of elections. Constitutional historians hold that woman suffrage has not greatly affected either the course of legislation or political practices. Women seem to vote in about the same proportion and for similar reasons as men.[22] Progress has been made, however, in that the number of women who go into active politics has been gradually increasing and, in recent years, they have occupied high positions in both state and national government.

Congress made vigorous efforts during the Reconstruction period to enlarge and secure equal rights of all citizens through legislation and constitutional guarantees. These efforts were closely related to the liberation and enfranchisement of the Negro and were aimed chiefly against state discrimination. Speaking for a civil rights measure, Lyman Trumbull, senator from Illinois, frankly said, "if [a man] is discriminated against under . . . state laws, because he is colored, then it becomes necessary to interfere for his protection."[23] These measures, however, were broad enough to include all people who were discriminated against, although some were specifically designed for the protection of the Negro.

A broad civil rights act of the latter class was enacted in 1866, but doubt of its constitutionality led Congress to incorporate its major provisions into Section 1 of the Fourteenth Amendment, where its protection was guaranteed to all citizens. The Amendment for the first time defined citizenship and also for the first time gave national protection to rights that might be invaded by a state. In doing so, it reversed the traditional relationship of the

22. Carl B. Swisher, *American Constitutional Development*, 2d ed. (Boston: Houghton Mifflin, 1954) , p. 702.

23. *The American Annual Cyclopaedia and Register of Important Events, 1866* (New York: D. Appleton & Co., 1870) , p. 204.

citizen to the two governments. This amendment was followed by several other civil rights acts, one of which, that of 1875, was designed to protect the Negro's social rights, or to establish his social equality, by guaranteeing his admission to hotels, theaters, restaurants, public conveyances, places of amusement, and other semi-public establishments.

This broad program of civil and social rights and equal opportunities was largely thwarted by the decisions of a conservative Supreme Court. In a series of decisions, from 1876 to the well-known Civil Rights cases of 1883, the Court found that the rights which the acts were attempting to protect were social rather than civil and that the national government had no jurisdiction over such matters.

By 1890, the southern states came to the conclusion that the national guarantees of Negro suffrage, like those of civil and social rights, might safely be ignored, and they devised constitutional provisions—educational tests, good moral character, poll tax payments, and registration procedures—which almost entirely disfranchised the Negro. They safeguarded white suffrage by various *or* clauses, including property ownership, ability to read or understand the Constitution when read, and the grandfather clauses. At first, the national courts upheld the new constitutional provisions, but in 1915, the grandfather clause was held unconstitutional. By that time, however, its benefits to whites had expired in all states except Oklahoma. The exclusions against the Negro were still enforced. By the end of the century, Congress had largely lost its enthusiasm for democratic leadership. A new cycle was ready to begin.

During the Progressive era, the states temporarily reassumed their former position as leaders in liberal democratic reforms. Various schemes were devised to regain power that had slipped into the hands of the political bosses and interests. They were more numerous and popular in the western states, where Populism had been strong. Most notable of these new devices or programs were the initiative, referendum, recall, and the direct and preferential primaries. The initiative and referendum enabled the voters to propose legislation which the interest-controlled legislatures had refused to consider, and the referendum placed laws on the ballot for approval or rejection by the voters. Oregon was the leader in this program. It might be noted that some states in the pre-Civil War period utilized this principle in constitutional revision. The direct primary, first used in Wisconsin, became widespread in state and local elections. Those in the South were restricted to white voters in the Democratic primaries. The preferential primary was used, in some states, to give the voter a chance to express his preference for senatorial candidates before they had become elective by popular vote, and his choice for the Presidency. The recall was used in various states to recall officials, both local and state, who were thought to have failed the people. During the latter part of the nineteenth and in the early twentieth century, many states adopted educational qualifications for voting. Generally, they were designed to improve popular government, but southern states used them, as they did their primaries, to restrict Negro voting. These state reforms constituted no major revolution in the American democratic system. They merely buttressed the long-accepted idea that the people had the right to govern themselves and should participate in the making of legislation and elect officials who were responsible to the people.

A new era, or cycle, in the development of American democracy, involving social, economic, political, and civil rights, got under way in the second quarter of the twentieth century. Working together as a team to effect the new measures were the states, the President, the Congress, and the Supreme Court. The efforts of the first three were somewhat sporadic, and for the first time the Supreme Court assumed the leadership in effecting democratic advances. This was the more interesting because the Court had heretofore been a conservative check on the more liberal and democratic branches of government. In the period following the Civil War, it had limited some congressional legislative action, disallowed in toto some of the more promising provisions of the civil rights acts, and had interpreted the section of the Fourteenth Amendment which prohibited a state to "deprive any person of life, liberty, or property" so as to give protection to business interests rather than human rights. The personnel of the Court changed rapidly in the New Deal period, and the Court's philosophy became much more liberal. The Court shifted from support of laissez faire in regard to freedom of contract and rights of property, began to sanction legislation designed to regulate economic life in terms of human and national interest, and to apply "due process of law" as a protection to persons rather than corporations.

State action varied from state to state and region to region. Southern public opinion had been partially awakened to the evils of a restricted electorate and to discrimination against the lower economic class, whites and Negroes. In urging the abolition of the poll tax, Chief Justice Grafton Green of the Tennessee Supreme Court said:

Universal exercise of the right of suffrage must be regarded as the ideal support of democratic institutions. . . . Elections were designed to put into effective operation the underlying principle of democracy which makes the will of an unfettered majority controlling. So it is that restraint upon plenary participation in a primary election, as well as a regular election, is destructive of the basis of either system.[24]

Unfortunately, Green's state did not heed his plea and, along with other southern states, it continued to require payments of poll taxes for voting. Influenced by the call of eighteen-year-old boys into the armed services during World War II, two southern states [Georgia and Kentucky] have given the franchise to qualified citizens eighteen years of age.

Eastern and western states have been more concerned with individual rights than political action, and many have enacted civil rights and anti-bias legislation. Some forbid "religious or racial discrimination" in the sale or rental of dwelling and apartment houses; others guarantee "full and equal service and treatment" to persons of any race or color in hotels, restaurants, barber shops, swimming pools, skating rinks, theaters, and public conveyances.[25]

Presidents Franklin D. Roosevelt, Harry S. Truman, and

24. Jennings Perry, *Democracy Begins at Home* (Philadelphia: J. B. Lippincott Co., 1944), flyleaf.
25. See New York *Times,* 18 February 1961, for recent enactments.

Dwight D. Eisenhower gave support to civil rights. Roosevelt popularized the idea of equal rights to all regardless of race or color, but his accomplishments were not notable. Truman, opposed by a hostile Congress, accomplished more than Roosevelt. He appointed a committee on civil rights that, after much study, prepared a report which revealed widespread discrimination against minority groups in all parts of the country. The committee recommended a series of measures designed to curb the evils, but Truman was unable to get any action from Congress. Eisenhower, less vocal on the issue than either Roosevelt or Truman, accomplished more in the field of civil rights than either. He abolished segregation in the armed services, in schools on army posts, and in institutions maintained by the Veterans' Administration. His administration was instrumental in breaking the color line in hotels and theaters in Washington. And he, very hesitantly, sent troops to Little Rock to preserve order in the integration of the public high schools of that city.

In 1957, Congress enacted a Civil Rights Act, the first since Reconstruction, which provided for a Bi-Partisan Commission on Civil Rights with power to investigate the denial of suffrage and equal protection of the law because of race, color, or religion. An assistant attorney general was given power to initiate suit by injunction where there was evidence of interference with voting rights. Federal judges were empowered to enjoin state officials from refusing to register qualified voters, and punish them with fine and imprisonment, if guilty, without jury trial. This measure promises to be a major victory for racial equality at the polls.

The Supreme Court decisions since 1925 have worked what might be called a democratic revolution in the United States. The Court has accepted the basic principles of the civil rights acts and the Fourteenth Amendment and translated them into reality. At last, it has given the American people the assurance that they will have their day in court. It has found that freedom of speech, press, teaching, and learning are included in the liberty which the state may not take from a citizen without due process of law. After half a century, it learned that separate accommodations for the Negro on trains, Pullman and dining cars, and other common carriers, isolating a Negro student from his fellows in a state university, and denying Negro citizens the use of parks and swimming pools owned by the public was a denial of equal protection of the law. In *Smith* v. *Allwright* (1944), it discovered that party primaries are instruments of the state, and as such are limited by constitutional provisions with respect to due process and equal protection of the laws. Finally, in 1961, it learned that the Civil Rights Act of 1871 is constitutional and valid. Most important of all, in *Brown* v. *Board of Education* (1954), it found that the decision in *Plessy* v. *Ferguson* (1896) was in error. It discovered that segregation of children in public schools solely on the basis of race, even though physical facilities and other tangible factors were equal, deprived children of the minor group of equal protection of the laws. In other words, segregation, per se, is unconstitutional. This decision heralded a new epoch in the search for equality. In short, it is a lesson in democracy directed to all United States citizens. And, as Federal Judge Irving R. Kaufman recently said, the lesson is to be learned and applied in the North as well as the South, in the East and in the West.[26]

The present cycle of democratic development, concerned chiefly with the recognition, implementation, and attainment of political and civil rights of minority groups already guaranteed by law and constitution, in which the Supreme Court has played the leading role, has not yet run its course. The courts are continuously broadening and strengthening these rights. And it is not inconceivable that it might yet reverse the decision in the civil rights cases of 1883, as it has already reversed that of *Plessy* v. *Ferguson,* so as to secure the Negro and other minority groups equal rights in hotels, theaters, and all places of amusement and entertainment.

Democracy has been tested in the United States longer than in any other country; but while the United States has gone further down the democratic road than most countries, much remains to be done before complete democracy can be achieved. For example, the poll tax in five southern states still prevents the lower

26. *Ibid.,* 25 January 1961.

economic class, both white and Negro, from voting. The urban centers are discriminated against in many states in regard to representation. And the people of the District of Columbia are denied both the suffrage and representation. These political evils are already under attack and may be eliminated in the not too distant future.[27] But other evils will appear, and it is as true today as when first expressed by Patrick Henry that "Eternal vigilance is the price of liberty." Furthermore, since democracy is progressive in nature, ever growing, ever changing, it may never be completed. Like the mirage, the goal when approached may recede into the future.

27. Since the above was written, three significant developments have taken place. First, an amendment to the United States Constitution giving suffrage to the citizens of the District of Columbia has been ratified; second, a United States District Court judge has ordered the registration officials of Macon County, Alabama, to register forthwith a group of Negro citizens and has issued an injunction prohibiting future discrimination against any prospective Negro voters; and, third, the United States Supreme Court has agreed to hear a suit from citizens of Tennessee requiring the state legislature to redistrict the state for representation.

5

Listen to the Eagle Scream:
One Hundred Years of the Fourth of July
in North Carolina, 1776-1876

In this essay, Green touches some of the lighter moments in history. Published in the *North Carolina Historical Review*, XXXI (July and October 1954), 295–320, 529–549, it is one of two that he has written that deal with the Fourth of July celebration, the other being "The Spirit of '76," which was published in the *Emory University Quarterly*, XI (June 1955), 65–82.

THE DAY AFTER THE CONTINENTAL CONgress had agreed upon a declaration of independence, John Adams, writing to his beloved Abigail, predicted that "The second day of July, 1776, will be the most memorable epocha in the history of America."[1]

I am apt to believe [said he] that it will be celebrated by succeeding generations as the great anniversary festival. It ought to be commemorated, as the day of deliverance, by solemn acts of devotion to God Almighty. It ought to be solemnized with pomp and parade, with shows, games, sports, guns, bells, bonfires, and illuminations, from one end of this continent to the other, from this time forward, forevermore.[2]

But it was to be July 4, the day Congress adopted the Declaration drafted by Thomas Jefferson—not July 2—that was to be celebrated "as the great anniversary festival." And had Adams added

1. John Adams, *The Works of John Adams, Second President of the United States; With a Life of the Author, Notes and Illustrations*, edited by Charles Francis Adams, 10 vols. (Boston: Little, Brown and Co., 1850–1856), IX, 420.
2. *Ibid.*

dinners, orations, the drinking of toasts, the reading of the Declaration, an evening ball or dance, and the shooting of firecrackers to his list of the means by which the day was to be celebrated, his prophecy would have been more nearly accurate.

Charles Warren, distinguished historian of the Supreme Court of the United States, writing in 1945, said:

> It is a singular fact that the greatest event in American history—the Declaration of Independence—has been the subject of more incorrect popular belief, more bad memory on the part of participants, and more false history than any other occurrence in our national life.[3]

Warren cleared up some of the misconceptions concerning the date of the adoption and signing of the Declaration, the ringing of the Liberty Bell, the early celebration myth, and the poor memory of John Adams, Thomas Jefferson, and other participants in that historic event.[4]

It is my purpose in this essay to discuss the celebration of Independence Day from 1776 to 1876 in North Carolina and, incidentally, in the South. Today, little attention is paid to July Fourth by the people of North Carolina; but during the first century of our national existence, it was almost universally observed. A study of the orations and toasts delivered at those celebrations will throw light on public opinion and attitudes on the major problems—state, regional, and national—of the day and help to clear up some of the "false history" referred to by Charles Warren.

The American states received official news of the Declaration of Independence from the Continental Congress in July 1776, and joyously proclaimed it to the people. Some legislatures ordered the Declaration to be printed in the state gazettes and to be proclaimed in each county by the sheriff. Others held public meetings in the capital cities, where the Declaration was read and celebrated by a dinner, a toast to each of the thirteen states,

---

3. Charles Warren, "Fourth of July Myths," *The William and Mary Quarterly: A Magazine of Early American History, Institutions and Culture,* 3d ser., II (July 1945) , 237.

4. *Ibid.,* 237–272.

illuminations, and ceremony in which an effigy of George III was either burned or buried.[5]

In Georgia, public officials, gentlemen, and the militia drank a toast "to the prosperity and perpetuity of the United Free and Independent States of America."[6] And the President of the Council pronounced a funeral oration over King George, in which he said:

For as much as George the Third, of Great Britain, hath most flagrantly violated his Coronation Oath, and trampled upon the Constitution of our Country, and the sacred rights of mankind: We, therefore, commit his political existence to the ground—corruption to corruption—tyranny to the grave—and oppression to eternal infamy; in sure and certain hope that he will never obtain a resurrection to rule again over the United States of America. But, my friends and fellow citizens, let us not be sorry, as men without hope, for tyrants that thus depart—rather let us remember that America is free and independent; and that she is, and will be, with the blessing of the Almighty, Great among the nations of the earth.[7]

The North Carolina Council of Safety received news of the Declaration on July 22, 1776, and ordered

the committees of the respective Towns and Counties in this Colony on receiving the Declaration, do cause the same to be proclaimed in the most public manner, in Order that the good people of this Colony may be fully informed thereof.[8]

On July 25, the Council adopted a resolution requiring the people to take a loyalty oath in which they were to declare that they "do absolutely believe" in independence, recognize no English authority, and promise to obey the Continental Congress.

At a meeting of the citizens of the town of Halifax on August 1, the Declaration was officially proclaimed to the state. On that day,

5. Charles D. Deshler, "How the Declaration Was Received in the Old Thirteen," *Harper's New Monthly Magazine*, LXXXV (July 1892), 165–187.

6. Charles Colcock Jones, Jr., *History of Savannah, Georgia* (Syracuse: D. Mason and Co., 1890), 234–235.

7. *Ibid.*

8. North Carolina (Colony), *The Colonial Records of North Carolina*, collected and edited by William L. Saunders, 10 vols. (Raleigh: P. M. Hale and Josephus Daniels, 1886–1890), X, 682–684.

"an immense concourse of people" and soldiers having gathered, Cornelius Harnett "read the Declaration to the mute and impassioned multitude with the solemnity of an appeal to Heaven."[9] When he had finished, "the enthusiasm of the immense crowd broke into one swell of rejoicing and prayer." The soldiers seized Harnett and "bore him on their shoulders through the streets, applauding him as their champion, and swearing allegiance to the instrument he had read."

Celebrations of the Fourth in 1777 were few in number but were widely scattered throughout the country. The day was observed by an unofficial celebration at Philadelphia, which included a dinner for members of Congress, state officials, and the officers of the army. A number of toasts were drunk to the Fourth, to liberty, and to the memory of fallen troops. Throughout the city, bells were rung; ships in the harbor fired thirteen cannon each; there was a parade, followed by fireworks. And music was furnished by a Hessian band that had been captured at Trenton.[10] A similar celebration was held in Boston.

The most elaborate celebration held anywhere in the country took place at Charleston, South Carolina. A newspaper reported it as follows:

Friday last being the first anniversary of the glorious formation of the American empire . . . the same was commemorated by every demonstration of joy. Ringing of bells ushered in the day. At sunrise, American colors were displayed from all the forts and batteries, and vessels in the harbor. The Charleston regiment of militia, commanded by the Honorable Colonel Charles Pinckney, and the Charleston artillery company, commanded by Captain Thomas Grimball, were assembled upon the parade, and reviewed by his excellency the President. . . . At one o'clock in the several forts, beginning with Fort Moultrie, on Sullivan's Island, discharged seventy-six pieces of cannon, alluding to the glorious year 1776, and the militia and artillery three general volleys. His Excellency the President then gave a most elegant enter-

9. The description of the celebration at Halifax is taken from Joseph Seawell Jones, *A Defence of the Revolutionary History of the State of North Carolina from the Aspersions of Mr. Jefferson* (Raleigh: Turner and Hughes, 1834), 268–269. Jones says he received the account of this ceremony "from a pious elderly lady, who was present on the occasion."

10. Warren, "Fourth of July Myths," p. 254.

tainment in the council chamber, at which were present all the members of the Legislature then in town, all the public officers civil and military, the clergy, and many strangers of note to the amount of more than double the number that ever observed the birthday of the present misguided and unfortunate King of Great Britain. After dinner the following toasts were drank, viz: '1. The free, and independent, and sovereign States of America. 2. The great council of America—may wisdom preside in all its deliberations. 3. General Washington. 4. The American army and navy—may they be victorious and invincible. 5. The nations in friendship or alliance with America. 6. The American ambassadors at foreign courts. 7. The Fourth of July, 1776. 8. The memory of the officers and soldiers who have bravely fallen in defense of America. 9. South Carolina. 10. May only those Americans enjoy freedom who are ready to die for its defence. 11. Liberty triumphant. 12. Confusion, shame, and disgrace to our enemies—may the foes to America (slaves to tyranny) humble and fall before her. 13. May the rising States of America reach the summit of human power and grandeur, and enjoy every blessing.' Each toast was succeeded by a salute of thirteen guns, which were fired by Captain Grimball's company from their two field-pieces, with admirable regularity. The day having been spent in festivity, and the most conspicuous harmony, the evening was concluded with illuminations, etc., far exceeding any that had ever been exhibited before.[11]

The 1777 celebrations were unofficial gatherings; but on June 24, 1778, Congress gave official recognition to the day and appointed a committee which arranged for a celebration, including a sermon. Under federal sponsorship, the celebration became firmly established by 1783. The first celebration in North Carolina under federal authorization was held at Newbern in 1778. John Adams, who observed the festivities of the day, wrote Governor Richard Caswell on July 10 describing the celebration.

On Saturday last [said he] the ever-memorable Fourth of July, the Rising United States of America entered the Third year of their Independence, in spite of numerous fleets and armies; in spite of tomahawks and scalping knife; in spite of the numerous wicked and diabolical engines of cruelty and revenge, played off against us by the magnanimous and heroic, humane and merciful George the Third, the father of his people, and his wicked and abandoned soldiery. On this day, the bright morning star of this western world arose in the east and

11. Boston *Continental Journal and Weekly Advertiser,* 31 July 1777.

warned us to emerge from the slavish tyranny and servile dependence on a venal and corrupt court, and to assume to ourselves a name among nations, a name terrible to tyrants, and wrote in indelible characters by the Almighty as a refuge from persecution. This day was observed here with every possible mark and demonstration of joy and reverence; triple salutes were fired from the batteries in town, and on board the ship Cornell, and the privateer brig Bellona, belonging to this port, the gentlemen of the town met, where many toasts suitable to the importance of the day were drunk, and the evening happily concluded.[12]

Captain R. Cogdell, also an observer, added some details in a letter which he wrote the governor. Said he:

In celebration of this day great numbers of Guns have been fired, at Stanley's wharf, and Mr. Ellis' ship three different firings from each from early in the morning midday and evening, and Liquor given to the populace. Stanley and Ellis seem to vie with each other, in a contest who should do the most honor to the day, but Mr. Ellis had the most artillery.[13]

The recognition of American independence by England in the Treaty of Paris of 1783 gave additional meaning to the Fourth of July. The action of Congress "declaring the cessation of arms as well by sea as land" reached North Carolina on April 30, 1783. "A great wave of rejoicing and gratitude thrilled through the Legislature," and on May 16, "it recommended a Statewide observance of the Fourth of July," and called upon Governor Alexander Martin to issue a proclamation to that effect.[14] Whereupon, Governor Martin, on June 18, 1783, issued a proclamation, declaring that in accordance with the legislature's resolution that he appoint "the Fourth of July next, being the anniversary of the Declaration of American Independence, as a Day of Solemn Thanksgiving to Almighty God," he strictly commanded

all Good Citizens of this State to set apart the said Day from bodily labour, and employ the same in devout and religious exercises. And I do require all Ministers of the Gospel of every Denomination to convene

12. North Carolina, *The State Records of North Carolina,* collected and edited by Walter Clark, 16 vols. (Winston and Goldsboro: M. I. & J. C. Stewart and Nash Brothers, 1895–1907) , XIII, 456.

13. *Ibid.,* XIII, 187.

14. *Ibid.,* XIX, 223, 287.

their congregations at the same time, and deliver to them Discourses suitable to the important Occasion, recommending in general the Practice of Virtue & true Religion, as the great foundation of private Blessings as well as National Happiness & prosperity.[15]

The Moravians were the only group in the state to act on the governor's proclamation. They assembled at Salem at ten o'clock on the Fourth and celebrated with wind instruments, a Te Deum, a sermon, and a prayer. At two o'clock, there was a dinner, after which songs were sung; later in the afternoon, the congregation marched in a procession; and in the evening, the houses were illuminated, and bells were rung. The Bethabara congregation "favored making it as impressive as our circumstances allow," and ordered all members do no work on the day. They assembled at ten o'clock, read the proclamation, and had prayers. The Friedland group "solemnly and happily celebrated" the day.[16] According to Adelaide L. Fries, late lamented member and former president of the Historical Society of North Carolina, this was "the first celebration of the Fourth of July by state Legislative enactment in the United States."[17] But the Moravians were the only group in the state to obey the governor's proclamation. In the same year, Boston became the first municipality to order an official celebration.[18] Boston also claimed the distinction of having the first orator of the day in 1783, but this claim was disputed by David Ramsey, South Carolina's distinguished historian of the Revolution, who said he "delivered the first oration that was spoken in the United States, to celebrate this great event" in Charleston in 1778.[19]

15. The proclamation is not found in the *State Records,* but is printed in full in Adelaide L. Fries, editor, *Records of the Moravians in North Carolina,* 7 vols. (Raleigh: Edwards and Broughton, and North Carolina Department of Archives and History, 1922–1947), IV, 1919–1920.

16. Fries, *Records of the Moravians,* IV, 1834, 1835, 1863, 1868, 1885.

17. Adelaide L. Fries, "An Early Fourth of July Celebration," *Journal of American History,* IX (September 1915), 469–474. Warren, "Fourth of July Myths," p. 258, states that the legislature of Massachusetts had requested the governor of that state "to direct that a suitable preparation be made for the celebration" of 4 July 1781.

18. Warren, "Fourth of July Myths," p. 258.

19. David Ramsey, *An Oration Delivered on the Anniversary of American Independence, July 4, 1794, in Saint Michael's Church, to the Inhabitants of Charleston, South Carolina* (London: W. Winterbotham, 1795), 1–2.

Prior to the adoption of the Constitution, the celebration of July Fourth had been nonpartisan; but, according to Charles Warren, that event transformed the day in the northern states into a political holiday, celebrated chiefly by the Federalists. The orators of the day were Federalists; Jefferson was seldom toasted, and his part in the drafting of the Declaration was minimized. Such was not the case in the South, where Federalists and Republicans jointly celebrated the day. There are few references to celebrations in North Carolina from 1785 to 1790; but after the state ratified the Constitution, the people once again began to celebrate Independence Day. The Edenton *State Gazette,* on July 2, 1790, published an ode titled "The American Union Completed," which proclaimed:

> 'Tis done. 'tis finish'd! guardian Union binds,
> In voluntary bands, a nation's minds:
>
> . . .
>
> Now the *new* world shall mighty scenes unfold
> Shall rise the imperial rival of the *old.*
>
> . . .
>
> O happy land! O ever sacred dome!
> Where PEACE and INDEPENDENCE own their home:
> COMMERCE and TILLAGE, hail the Queen of *Marts,*
> Th' Asylum of the world, the residence of ARTS.

The toast at the 1790 celebration generally emphasized the bonds of union. For instance, among the fourteen toasts drunk at New-bern was one to "the Federal Union, may it be Perpetual."[20]

Others of similar nature were "Energy to Government and a Federal Head"; and "May our Sister State, Rhode Island, be convinced of her error without the necessity of coercion." As the rivalry between Federalists and Jeffersonian Republicans became more bitter, the representatives of each used the Fourth of July celebrations as a means of publicizing their party's position. A Federalist toast to

The Hon. John Jay—may that worthy citizen in the execution of the mission committed to his charge, secure to his fellow-citizens the invaluable blessings of peace, and in every other act, excell their most sanguine expectations,

20. Edenton *State Gazette of North Carolina,* 16 July 1790.

was balanced by a Republican toast: "An honorable negociation or a decided and vigorous opposition to the measures of the British Court." The Republican toast, "The Republic of France —may her sons persevere in their glorious efforts for Liberty, until they obtain complete victory and permanent peace," was matched by a Federalist one: "The State of North Carolina—may the virtuous union of her citizens baffle the boasted SKILL of the French and their emissaries." If a Federalist, with the Whiskey Rebellion in mind, toasted "The forces of the Union! May their bayonets push home the argument when remonstrance fails," one Republican was ready with "May the spirit of wisdom dictate our laws, and impartial justice enforce them," and another with "May the snowy mantle of American Freedom, never be stained with the black corruption of monarchical sway."[21]

Both Federalists and Republicans endorsed the sentiments expressed in many toasts. They jointly drank to "The progress of useful knowledge! May the arts and sciences be cultivated with success, and their great end be directed to the improvement of social happiness." And both cheered the toast on the Revolution: "The wisdom that planned, the spirit that upheld, and the bravery that achieved the American Revolution." Both fervently hoped that American citizens "may . . . justly prize the blessing we enjoy." Both were interested in prosperity, so they drank to the various economic interests in the following: "The farmers and manufacturers of America"; "May the sails of American Commerce be filled with the winds of prosperity"; "The agricultural, manufacturing and commercial interests of the United States; may they be cherished with wisdom, . . . protected with valor, [and] support and cherish each other." Both, too, were hopeful that liberty would endure and be expanded. Hence they drank to many versions of a toast to liberty. "May the tree of Liberty never wither, but be immovable as the Appalachians"; may it "take root in the center of the earth, and its branches spread from pole

21. These toasts, with several variants, and many others, may be found in the Halifax *North Carolina Journal,* 9 July 1794 and 9 July 1798; Fayetteville *North Carolina Minerva and Advertiser,* 9 July 1796; and the Wilmington *Chronicle and North Carolina Weekly Advertiser,* 17 July 1795.

to pole"; and "may its roots be cherished in this its native land, until its branches extend themselves over the remotest corners of the earth." Both Federalists and Republicans claimed to be gentlemen, hence they were chivalrous and considerate of the ladies. They might require the ladies to leave the dinner before the men began to drink, but they invariably toasted the fair sex. Typical of their sentiments are the following: "The American *Fair!* May the perfections of their minds excell the beauties of their persons"; "May they bestow their smiles on none but the friends of their country"; and, more seriously, "May they impress on the rising generation the value of the prize their fathers fought and bled for."[22]

The victory of the Jeffersonian Democratic Republican party in the elections of 1800 changed somewhat the mood and spirit of the Fourth of July celebrations. Quite naturally, the orations, and especially the toasts, put more emphasis on Jeffersonian ideas and principles and less on Federalism. In 1799, for the first time since the 1770s, the Declaration of Independence was read in North Carolina celebrations. Gradually, the practice developed, and from 1805 until 1860, it was regularly read at all celebrations. Numerous odes were written on the Declaration and read on the Fourth. One by Alexander Lucas, editor of the Raleigh *Minerva,* written at the request of the citizens of Raleigh, was sung with much gusto. Describing the utopia which would follow the general acceptance of the principles of the Declaration, Lucas declared:

> Discord no more shall roam abroad,
> > The fire and sword no more destroy,
> But friendship smile o'er all mankind,
> > And all their sorrows end in joy.[23]

Republicans emphasized Jefferson's authorship of the Declaration. In one of the many such toasts, Joseph Gales, editor of the Raleigh *Register,* toasted Jefferson "as the sage and patriotic author of the Declaration of Independence." William Boylan, a

22. Fayetteville *North Carolina Minerva and Advertiser,* 9 July 1799.
23. The ode is printed in full in the Raleigh *Star* of 5 July 1811.

Federalist editor of the Raleigh *Minerva,* corrected Gales; he contended that John Adams and other members of the Committee that wrote the Declaration should have equal recognition with Jefferson. The controversy, complicated by rivalry over state printing, finally ended in a fight between the two editors, in which Gales was severely beaten.[24]

The orators, generally Republican, the leaders who offered the regular toasts, and most of those who gave voluntary toasts reflected Jefferson's views on party unity. Among the numerous toasts that expressed this sentiment are the following: "Union. Let the bickerings of party be heard no more. . . . We are all Americans, and belong to the great family of the Republic"; "Goodwill—may the fervor of political zeal never disturb the harmony of social intercourse"; "Parties. There is not talismanic virtue in names. Let us appreciate men for their deeds"; and "National Unanimity—may the hateful demon of discord be banished from our land and the name of American absorb all other distinctions."[25] During the Jeffersonian period, North Carolinians also toasted "Freedom of the Press" and "Trial by Jury," and emphasized Jeffersonian principles and philosophy by reading the Bill of Rights as well as the Declaration of Independence on July Fourth.[26]

As the controversy with England over neutral rights became more and more bitter, it largely absorbed the attention of the Fourth of July celebrants. A Raleigh meeting drew up a long resolution on the *Leopard* affair and transmitted it and an address to President Jefferson. One of the toasts drunk on that occasion was:

The memory of the seamen who fell a sacrifice to British outrage— May the atrocity of this act produce the adoption of such measures as shall secure us from future violence, and establish our maritime rights on a firm foundation.[27]

24. Raleigh *Register,* 16 July, 3 December, 10 December 1804.
25. *Ibid.,* 17 July 1812; Raleigh *Minerva,* 7 July 1808; Raleigh *Star,* 26 July 1810, 17 July 1812.
26. Halifax *North Carolina Journal,* 8 July 1805; Raleigh *Register,* 24 July 1812.
27. Halifax *North Carolina Journal,* 8 July 1805.

But such measures were not immediately adopted, and the next year the Raleigh citizens toasted *"Neutral Rights.* The surrender of an inch only countenances a claim for an ell; may a hair's breadth never be yielded, till the conqueror is led to make his sword the yard stick." But France, too, was violating neutral rights, so North Carolinians toasted *"The French Tiger and British Shark.* Paring to the nails of one, and a file to the teeth of the other."[28]

When war came, Wilmington citizens cheered a toast to "The 4th of July 1776. The sword of America again drawn from its scabbard in the spirit of that day—May its strokes be directed with such energy as speedily to force the enemy to a just and reasonable peace."[29] Hoping that Canada would be won by war, a Raleigh citizen cried, "Canada—May her Star be speedily added to our Constellation." But another declared, "Our maritime Rights . . . are the objects of the War, and they will not be abandoned."[30] When the tide of battle turned against American forces, the Wilmington citizens could still say: "Eternal war with all its privations and concomitant horrors, in preference to a peace that does not recognize and acknowledge our every right as a sovereign and independent Nation."[31] Enraged by England's use of Indian troops and the burning of the public buildings in Washington, a Raleigh crowd cheered the toast,

May the war in which we are engaged be carried on with ability and vigor, tempered with humanity; and may our enemy become sensible that a resort to wanton conflagrations, and the employment of the Scalping Knife, disgrace a civilized nation.[32]

North Carolinians were anxious for peace and praised President James Madison's "Mission to Russia: It proves to the world, that whilst we are fighting for our Rights, we are willing to avail ourselves of the first occasion of negociating an honorable peace."[33]

28. Raleigh *Star,* 5 July 1811.
29. Raleigh *Register,* 17 July 1812.
30. *Ibid.,* 10 July 1812; 9 July 1813.
31. *Ibid.,* 17 July 1812.
32. *Ibid.,* 9 July 1813.
33. *Ibid.*

Patriotic though they were, North Carolinians could find little about which to boast in the Peace of Ghent. The best they could do in 1815 was to recognize "Our late Ministers at Ghent." In 1816, they toasted "Our Navy—bold, enterprising and successful," "The Army of the United States—they fought bravely," and "Peace to the World"; but it was 1817 before they declared, in "The Last War—We plucked the laurels from the Crown of the conquerers of Napoleon." Finally, in 1820, they recognized "General Andrew Jackson—the immortal Hero of New Orleans," and condemned "The Hartford Convention—Commenced in iniquity, carried on in malignity, and ended in disgrace."[34]

The form of July Fourth celebrations gradually evolved and by 1820 had assumed a fixed pattern that changed very little until the coming of the Civil War. In the early days, the upper classes —gentlemen, government officials, the military, the Society of the Cincinnati, the Association of '76, and professional men, including lawyers, doctors, and preachers—in a word, what the press regularly called "men of Respectability"—were the chief participants, with the populace merely lookers-on. Most celebrations were held in the larger cities and county seats with only an occasional one at a country church, a crossroads store, or a tavern in the rural areas.

The day would begin with the ringing of bells at dawn, followed by cannon or musketry salutes at sunrise. During the early morning, various military organizations would parade the streets and go through their evolutions for the benefit of the populace. The people would then march in regular procession to a church, courthouse, or some other chosen place for the exercises. A newspaper account of a Raleigh celebration reports:

The following was the order of the procession:
The Marshall of the Day on horseback and in uniform, Herald, Band, Infantry, Cavalry, Male students and teachers of Academy, Female students, Ladies, Police, Government Officials, The Reverend Clergy, Orators of the Day, The Governor, and Files of Infantry and Cavalry.[35]

34. Raleigh *Minerva*, 7 July 1815; 12 July 1816; 11 July 1817; Salisbury *Western Carolinian*, 18 July 1820; Raleigh *Star*, 7 July 1820.
35. Raleigh *Minerva*, 7 July 1808. See also Raleigh *Star*, 5 July 1810.

In most cases there was also a designated position in the procession for visitors.

The public exercises consisted of prayers, an oration, the reading of the Declaration of Independence, the singing of patriotic airs, and occasionally the rendition of instrumental music. When these were concluded, the select group of ladies and gentlemen would adjourn to a tavern, hotel, or sometimes a private home, where they were served an "elegant and sumptuous dinner." After dinner, the ladies would retire, and the gentlemen would drink thirteen regular toasts, one for each state, and numerous voluntary ones in fine wines and imported liquors. One group in Georgia drank eighty-seven toasts. In the afternoon, the ladies would entertain at an "elegant tea party" at which there might also be vocal and instrumental music and dancing. The day would be concluded by a "splendid ball . . . given to the Ladies" by the gentlemen.[36]

With the coming of the Jacksonian epoch, there was a diminution of formalism and ceremony, but an increase in hilarity and boisterousness in the celebrations. With the decline of class distinctions, the people participated to a much greater extent. In fact, all business and labor came to a stop, and everybody celebrated. Ladies and gentlemen were still present and popular leaders were in charge, but all groups were officially recognized. The working men and "Mechanics Societies" were given positions of importance.[37] In a single procession in Norfolk, Virginia, in 1831,

tailers, hatters, blacksmiths, carpenters, stone-cutters, tanners and leather dressers, cordwainers, coppersmiths and other workers of metal, printers, ropemakers, gunsmiths, and finally the Norfolk Marine Society, and The School Teachers,

in that order, had their designated position.[38] And the streets of

36. Edenton *State Gazette,* 16 July 1790; Raleigh *Minerva,* 7 July 1808; Raleigh *Star,* 5 July 1810.
37. Raleigh *Register,* 28 July 1836.
38. Washington *United States Telegraph,* 8 July 1831.

the county seats "were filled to overflowing with the generous yeomanry of . . . the country" districts.[39]

The crowds, composed of men, women, and children, yea "all the little niggers in town," yelled and shrieked and screamed like mad.[40] These crowds, however, were assembled with a purpose that was serious, almost holy. They "listened attentively to lengthy prayers" distinguished for "fervent piety and patriotism," and greeted the Declaration and the oration with enthusiastic applause.[41] Instead of a dinner for a select few, barbecues were prepared for everybody. At one barbecue, "long tables groaned beneath the fat of the land, [and] notwithstanding a well-directed and prolonged attack by all there . . . the reenforcements constantly furnished . . . drove the armed hosts, with reluctant step, from their entrenchments."[42] Of food there was enough and to spare. After everyone had eaten, the "call for Voluntary toasts was answered with promptitude and alacrity." But instead of drinking the toasts in Madeira and imported liquors, as the early assemblies had done, these "motley crews" drank domestic wines and liquors, or even lemonade.[43] And instead of indulging in "elegant teas" and "splendid balls," they closed their festivities by engaging in square dances or watching a "successful and beautiful assention of a Balloon in the evening."[44] Beginning with July 4, 1836, the newspapers reported a new type of excitement, the "occasional popping of squibs," better known today as firecrackers.[45]

The Moravians, first to celebrate officially the Fourth in North Carolina, became less enthusiastic in their observance of the day as the celebrations became more boisterous. Their exercises had at first consisted largely of sermons, prayers, and a "singstunde with instrumental accompaniment." But on July 16, 1811, the

39. Salisbury *Carolina Watchman,* 10 July 1846.
40. *Ibid.,* 15 July 1837; Raleigh *Register,* 13 July 1853.
41. Salisbury *Carolina Watchman,* 15 July 1837.
42. *Ibid.,* 10 July 1846.
43. Hillsboro *Recorder,* 8 July 1841.
44. Salisbury *Carolina Watchman,* 15 July 1837; Raleigh *Star,* 7 July 1836.
45. Tarboro *Free Press,* 9 July 1836.

Salem Board "noted with regret that shooting as a sign of rejoicing, which we had tried to prevent, was carried on by several of the younger Brethren" on July 4. The next year, the Board noted with regret that a letter of one of the conferences warning against worldly manifestations of joy on July 4 was disregarded by the young men, who stuck cockades in their hats. In 1814, the secretary recorded in the minutes:

Disapproval is expressed concerning the behavior of the younger people on the fourth of this month, who made a noise by shooting in the Square and out of the Brothers House. In addition they have repeatedly occupied themselves with marching, soldier fashion, with drum and fife, near the town in the evening.

This action, said the Board, "must be considered disorder and must be suppressed." The Board ordered parents to warn their children, masters their apprentices, and choir officers the "Single Brethren." Evidently, the warning bore fruit, for in 1815 the Fourth was "observed in a solemn manner"; in 1817, "the anniversary . . . was more still and quiet in our town than it has been in many years"; in 1818, there was "little celebration"; and in 1819 and 1820, the celebration consisted of only "a singstunde with instrumental music" and a sermon by the distinguished Lewis David von Schweinitz.[46] One concession, however, had been made to the youth. Beginning in 1815, and continued thereafter, the sermon for the Fourth was delivered in English, rather than German.

Two new movements, the Sunday school and the temperance crusade, attempted to capitalize on the popularity of the Fourth during the Middle Period. The Guilford County Sunday School Union, an auxilliary of the American Sunday School Union, had charge of the exercises in Greensboro in 1834.[47] And in Raleigh, in 1851, over four hundred Sunday school children from the Baptist, Methodist, Presbyterian, and other Missionary churches gathered in the Presbyterian Church. They listened to the read-

46. Fries, *Records of the Moravians*, VII, 3150, 3180, 3237, 3259, 3368, 3402, 3439.
47. Raleigh *Register*, 15 July 1834.

ing of the Declaration, heard an oration, sang songs, and in the evening attended a session devoted to speechmaking.[48]

The temperance movement was better organized and had a more definite program than the Sunday schools; hence, it exerted greater influence on the Fourth. The Washington Temperance Society of Mecklenburg County was joined by a large body of the citizens of Charlotte in its celebration in 1842. They listened to the reading of the Declaration of Independence, heard two prayers, and drank more than fifty toasts, twenty-five to temperance, all "in *pure cold water.*" The male members carried a banner, made of white silk by the women members, inscribed: "To guard against a practice which is injurious to our health, standing and families, we as gentlemen pledge ourselves not to drink any spirituous or malt liquors, wine or cider."[49] They sang "Cold Water," one stanza of which reads:

> Here's to the Cup of Cold Water—
> The pure, sweet cup of cold water;
> For nature gives to all that lives
> But a drink of the clear cold water.[50]

Every toast offered at the Wilmington celebration of 1847, conducted by the Wilmington Temperance Society, made reference to temperance. A typical one reads: "The day we celebrate —may its next advent find every member now present faithful to his 'pledge,' and our number doubled."[51] That same year, the "Concord Division No. 1 of Sons of Temperance" joined in a local celebration. A newspaper correspondent reported that, despite the fact that only cold water and iced lemonade were used in drinking toasts, "The racy pun, the sparkling jest, and witty repartee circulated most merrily."[52] And at each celebration in Raleigh from 1845 through 1851, Sons of Temperance, Raleigh Teetotalers, and other temperance groups joined Sunday school

48. Raleigh *Star,* 9 July 1851.
49. Charlotte *Journal,* 14 July 1842.
50. *Ibid.*
51. Wilmington *Journal,* 16 July 1847.
52. Raleigh *Standard,* 14 July 1847.

children, numbering from three hundred to four hundred, and the citizens of the town in the Fourth of July exercises.

Even the official July Fourth celebrations in Washington experienced the leveling influence of the rise of the common man during the Middle Period. In addition to "the vapid orations, stupid toasts and execrable speeches; hot meats and cold wines; the customary laudation of the nation, and the quantum of headaches that follow the usual indulgence," a visitor in Washington reported the new "squibs and popguns"; the "commingling of all the central functionaries with citizens of every class" in the White House; and a band of "Sunday school children marched through the walks of the capitol grounds."[53]

What might be considered a typical Fourth of the antebellum period took place at Charleston, South Carolina, in 1843. The citizens of the town were awakened at dawn by the bells of St. Michael's, in whose pews on Sundays sat the aristocracy of the Cotton Kingdom. But on this holiday, the bells of St. Michael's called to worship all classes of citizens. As the clangor of the bells died away, cannon on the battery boomed a salute across the sleepy harbor. Gradually, the sidewalks filled with people—men, women, and children, black and white. The Charleston Light Dragoons paraded down the avenue to the waterfront; the Sixteenth and Seventeenth regiments of infantry and a battalion of artillery followed. Near the reviewing stand, occupied by the officials, were assembled men in tall hats and women in hoop skirts. When the troops were drawn up at attention, the United States cutter *Van Buren,* riding at anchor in the harbor, fired a salute; the artillery battery replied; and the infantry raised its muskets and fired a round to complete this part of the ritual.

The crowd then dispersed, but after a short interim new processions were formed. The Society of the Cincinnati and the Association of '76, their members few in number and now feeble old men, moved slowly to the First Baptist Church, where they heard prayers and an oration by a member of the '76. Meanwhile, the

53. Elizabeth Fries Ellet, *Court Circles of the Republic, or The Beauties and Celebrities of the Nation* (Philadelphia: Philadelphia Publishing Company, 1872); p. 308.

Washington Society had marched to St. Mary's, where it heard prayers, an oration, and the Declaration of Independence.

A third procession made up of temperance societies marched through the streets to the New Theatre where, after prayers and an anthem, Albert Rhett addressed "a numerous, brilliant and gratified audience of both sexes." After "a brief allusion to the grateful and hallowed occasion," Rhett took "the boldest and highest ground in favor of total abstinence." In the afternoon, thirteen hundred Sunday school children, preceded by ministers, teachers, and a "band of music," marched to the Presbyterian Church. There the exercises consisted of a prayer, a religious parody on the Declaration of Independence, an original poem, and an oration on the blessings of liberty and the higher blessings of Sunday schools, all delivered by boys. Appropriate anthems were sung by a girls' choir. The exercises were followed by a picnic of box lunches, and games. The day was concluded by fireworks at Tivoli Garden during the evening.[54] A North Carolina celebration similar to this one would have included also a dinner or barbecue, regular and voluntary toasts, and probably a dance in the evening.

The orator and his oration played a significant role in the celebrations. The orator was selected by a committee in charge of arrangements; and throughout the country, some of the most distinguished statesmen, preachers, lawyers, and editors were pressed into service. But in North Carolina, the orators, while selected from the above-named professions, were relatively unknown. Joseph Gales, Jesse R. Bynum, Jesse Speight, and James Branch addressed July Fourth crowds; but the better-known Nathaniel Macon, Archibald D. Murphey, William Gaston, Willie P. Mangum, William A. Graham, and Judge Thomas Ruffin seem not to have done so.

The early orators had a chance at originality of thought and expression, and some of them delivered thought-provoking as well as stirring addresses. David Ramsey, the South Carolina historian

54. Charleston *Courier,* 5 July 1843. See also Ralph Henry Gabriel, *The Course of American Democratic Thought: An Intellectual History Since 1815* (New York: The Ronald Press, 1940) , 96–97.

who in 1778 "delivered the first oration that was spoken in the United States, to celebrate this great event," was again the orator in Charleston, in 1794. He not only traced the colonial and revolutionary history of the United States, as most speakers did, but he reminded his hearers that they, as American citizens, enjoyed "advantages, rights, and privileges, superior to most, if not all, of the human race. . . . We [said he] have hit upon the happy medium between despotism and anarchy." According to Ramsey, we have freedom and equality of opportunity; we are all equal under the law; we have free press, free speech, and no state church. Tolerance and equality leads to peace between factions. And we can look forward to continuing peace, progress, and prosperity. "To what height of national greatness may we not aspire?" he asked. There was no limit, replied he, if the United States would educate all its people and maintain peace with all nations.[55] Ramsey painted an idyllic picture of peace, liberty, and equality, yet he passionately believed in the future growth and progress of the United States. His vision was that of the American dream.

By mid-nineteenth century, however, the phraseology of July Fourth orations had become so hackneyed and timeworn that one orator, the Reverend Mr. Moore of Virginia, spent considerable time in explaining his difficulty in preparing anything either fresh or acceptable to his audience. Said he:

> The situation of a Fourth of July orator now is like that of a man at the third table of a public dinner, who has left to him little more than scraps and empty dishes. All the rhetoric and logic of the occasion have been used up, and there is really not a respectable metaphor left. The American Eagle—a very respectable bird in its way—has been so plucked and handled that it has become as tame as a barnyard fowl. The British Lion has been so belabored and becudgeled by an indignant eloquence that he roars as gently as a suckling dove. The Stars and Stripes have been so vehemently flourished above admiring crowds of patriotic citizens that there is hardly a rhetorical shred left of them, and even that is somewhat the worse for handling. Even classic antiquity—Hercules and the serpent, Julius Caesar, Demosthenes, Greece

55. David Ramsey, *An Oration Delivered on the Anniversary of American Independence,* July 4, 1794, pp. 1–20.

and Rome—have so long been compelled to perform annual muster that they have really become exempt from military service. Even patriotism is not in season, because it is not near enough the election. The very Union would almost be dissolved by eulogizing it at such a melting temperature as this. Even "the Ladies" have been deemed too exciting a topic for the orator on this heated occasion and hence has been monopolized by the committee on toasts, where its exciting character may be tempered by ice water and other cooling compounds. So it is obvious that the path of a Fourth of July orator . . . is like that spoken of in a popular song not unknown in this community, "A hard road to Travel."[56]

Nevertheless, a few North Carolina orators found some new ideas to emphasize. The Reverend Joshua Lawrence, speaking in Tarboro in 1830, warned against a state-supported church. Said he:

I tell you that in my candid opinion, that the independence and liberty of our country is in more danger at this time from priestcraft, than it has ever been since the revolution, from all the nations of the earth, or any past or present source whatever; and I wish to remind you, that united we stand, divided we fall, a prey to the tyranny of kings or priests. Yea, if you suffer the priest by law to ride on your back, you will soon, I assure you, have to carry a king behind him.[57]

T. Loring, speaking at Wilmington in 1833, chose to emphasize the preservation of the Union against the threat of nullification and secession. He declared that "the most effectual safeguard of our liberties will be found in public education."[58] An orator at Tarboro in 1844 chose to speak on "The Importance of Female Education." Pleading for equal rights for women, he argued that liberty and freedom could be maintained only by an educated citizenry.[59] In the crisis of 1850, a Tarboro orator exhibited intellectual courage, as well as love of the Union.

Surrounded by an audience, whose sentiments on the topics it was his duty to discuss he knew to be as opposite as possible, he yet by found-

56. Washington *National Intelligencer,* 15 July 1854.
57. The Rev. Joshua Lawrence, *A Patriotic Discourse, Delivered by the Rev. Joshua Lawrence, at the Old Church in Tarborough, N.C., on Sunday the Fourth of July, 1830* (n.p., n.d.) , p. 29.
58. Wilmington *People's Press and Advertiser,* 17 July 1833.
59. Tarboro *Free Press,* 9 July 1844.

ing his sentiments on those facts which all Unionists knew to be true and all secessionists felt to be true, impressed upon each and all the strict equality in importance of Southern Rights and Union, and made all feel that though the one was nearly essential to our glory and prosperity, it could not stand unless the other was respected.[60]

In like manner, an orator at Raleigh on the same day chose the Union as his theme, and "portrayed in a most impressive and masterly manner its value and importance to the maintenance of our liberties, and the safety, peace and prosperity of the whole country."[61]

Dr. J. N. Danforth, in an address on "Thoughts on the Fourth of July, 1847," reached a new high in originality of thought and courage of expression. He decried illiteracy and ignorance, the misery and cruelty of the state prison system, and the destitution of the poverty-stricken, and demanded that the state and the nation give every possible aid to the eradication of these evils. He likewise called upon the people to encourage progress in science, to improve the means of communication of ideas, as well as of things, and to extend equal political rights to all people. But his special plea was for pacifism.

Let us not deceive ourselves [said he], with the phantom of military glory, after which so many are grasping only to be disappointed. Military glory depends for its acquisition on war, and war is one of the most bitter and blasting conditions of humanity. It is the daughter of pride and the mother of all kinds of abominations and disasters. It is one of the greatest curses to which humanity was ever abandoned. It breeds idleness, intemperance, infidelity, and all manner of licentiousness. It robs wives of their husbands, and children of their fathers. As it authorizes murder on a large scale, so it affords the opportunity and shield for all sorts of petty murders and assassinations. It involves an enormous expenditure of money, and encourages all kinds of wastefulness, creating bloated fortunes for some, and ruining others. It converts peaceful fields into the arenas of horrid strife, making of them shambles for the shedding of human blood, and instead of the quiet, cheerful, golden harvest of nature, substitutes the gloomy harvest of death, where, instead of the grateful song of the reaper, may be heard the bitter oath and execration; instead of the tranquil toil of the husband-man, yielding fruit, may be seen the fierce tumult of armed men,

60. *Ibid.*, 12 July 1851.
61. Raleigh *Star*, 9 July 1851.

resulting in nothing but weeping widows, childless parents, and mourning brothers and sisters. . . . War introduces a train of evils which a whole generation is scarcely sufficient to repair, polluting the morals, [and] prostrating the barriers of society.[62]

Danforth further ridiculed the ideas of honor, glory, chivalry, and the *beau ideal* in warfare. It must have taken a good deal of moral and intellectual courage for a man to deliver such a philippic against war at the very time the United States was engaged in the popular war with Mexico. In recent times, a Danforth would have been thrown into prison for saying much less.

By and large, the Fourth of July orations reveal a common pattern of thought and feeling. The orator generally recited American colonial history and found the hand of God directing in every crisis and leading the colonists along the road to independence; he emphasized the love of liberty of the early Americans; he lauded the colonists for their long-suffering endurance of tyranny; he damned George III and the British government for their flagrant disregard of the rights of man; he glorified the heroism of American men and women in the bitter struggle for independence; he expressed reverence for the leaders of the Revolution, especially George Washington; and he praised the system of government established in the United States as the most perfect under heaven. He then urged his hearers to attack current problems in a spirit similar to that of the founding fathers. He pointed with pride to the wonderful progress of the country and expressed hope and faith in the future progress and greatness of the United States. Throughout the discourse, he indulged in Biblical quotations, classical allusions, and high-sounding phrases that made his speech a masterpiece "of oratory according to the canons of the day." But despite its bombast and platitudes, the Fourth of July oration "epitomized the whole pattern of American political thought and feeling. . . . [It] was . . . an invitation to patriotism . . . and [an] inspiration for loyalty to the nation."[63]

62. The Rev. J. N. Danforth, "Thoughts on the Fourth of July, 1847," *The Southern and Western Literary Messenger and Review*, XIII (July 1847) , 502–505.
63. Merle Curti, *The Roots of American Loyalty* (New York: Columbia University Press, 1946) , pp. 140–141.

While not as important as the orator, newspaper editors played a significant role in the Fourth celebrations. They were often called upon to deliver an address; but more important, they published plans for the day, tried to whip up enthusiasm on the part of the people, wrote an annual editorial on the Fourth, always printed an account of the day's festivities—often including the address in full, and occasionally reprinting the entire Declaration of Independence.

In the 1830s, northern newspapers reported a decline in interest in the festivities in that section. They declared that in many towns and cities the day passed without any observance, and they noted general apathy on the part of the people. North Carolina editors, almost without exception, expressed satisfaction that such was not the case in the Old North State and in the South generally. "Notwithstanding the apathy complained of in some parts of the Union," said the editor of the Raleigh *Register,* on July 6, 1839, "our national Jubilee was celebrated in this city with becoming honors." Ten years later, he declared, "there are but few places in the Union, where, in proportion to means and population, the day is celebrated with more lively enthusiasm" than in North Carolina.[64] "Unusual demonstrations," "much enthusiasm," "unusually animated gathering," and "unusually spirited" were descriptive phrases he used during the 1850s.

The editor of the Raleigh *Southern Weekly Post* corroborated the *Register's* views. He said, "While in other sections of our country the day is permitted to pass without any special demonstration, we are rejoiced to see that in North Carolina the spirit of patriotism burns as brightly as it did in the days of the Revolution."[65] In Tarboro, also, the people continued to celebrate the day with old-time vigor. In 1852, they did so with "more than usual enthusiasm."[66]

South Carolina editors found that the people of that state, too, were unflagging in their "devotion to the principles of the revolution." Year after year rolls on, but they are "determined to keep

64. Raleigh *Register,* 7 July 1849.
65. Raleigh *Southern Weekly Post,* 7 July 1842.
66. Tarboro *Southerner,* 10 July 1852.

burning for ever the vestal fire of liberty, kindled by our fathers in the temple of union," and they rejoice in the success of the "glorious experiment of popular self-government." South Carolinians had had their "reverses and trials," but nothing had transpired to shake their "confidence in the stability and permanence" of the principles of the Declaration of Independence and the value of the Union. On the "contrary, the experience of the past only brightens the hope of the future, that our career will continue to realize its full promise of individual happiness and national glory."[67]

However, a Wilmington, North Carolina, editor in 1851 recognized "a gradual abatement of the fervor which signalized the earlier celebrations. The heart of the nation is less powerfully moved. The chord of public feeling responds less strongly to the note of festivity."[68] Among the reasons which he offered for the decline was the repetitious nature of the celebrations which, attended year after year, tended to develop an attitude of boredom. Furthermore, a new generation, born and nurtured in peace and prosperity, did not and could not respond to the Fourth as did their forefathers, who had fought and bled for their independence.

Another Wilmington editor in the late 1850s admitted a declining interest in the Fourth throughout the entire South. He attributed the change to growing sectional divergence and charged northern abolitionists with responsibility. The harmony which the Fourth should engender, said he, in 1856, was being submerged by the "wild torrent of fanaticism" which was "sweeping over the North."

Thousands of preachers and orators at the North [said he] will avail themselves of the opportunity [on the Fourth] to instil hatred to the South and her institutions. . . . We cannot, therefore, look forward to the influence of the day with the same hopeful feelings that used to animate us on such occasions. . . . We cannot but think that the state of affairs is such as to induce a deeper and more thoughtful tone than usually characterizes the occasion. [69]

67. Charleston *Courier,* 4 July 1843.
68. Wilmington *Tri Weekly Commercial,* 5 July 1851.
69. Wilmington *Daily Journal,* 3 July 1856.

The next year, he declared that the liberty of the South was threatened by the North. Will we, he asked, be able to celebrate the centennial of the Fourth, which is only nineteen years off? He concluded that Southern orators could not content themselves "simply with glorifying over the great event in honor of which the day is celebrated." We may congratulate ourselves that we can still meet around a common altar, but "the more ominous question will obtrude itself on the mind—How long will this be so?"[70] Unfortunately, his speculations were true; in less than five years, his own city was to abandon the celebration of the birthday of the republic.

Let us revert to the profound influence that the expansion of political democracy, the development of party machinery, the direct election of public officials, and the widespread participation in politics by the people—which ushered in Jacksonian Democracy—had on the celebration of the Fourth of July. More people participated in the activities of the day, and the ceremonies took on greater political significance. The people began to express their preference for candidates and their views on public issues in their voluntary toasts, and even the regular toasts began to have a direct partisan flavor.

Strangely enough, North Carolinians did not display much interest in the institution of slavery. At least, only three toasts were discovered that bore on the subject *per se*. One expressed the hope that the Colonization Society's "endeavors to establish a colony of Free Blacks in Africa would be crowned with success."[71] An extreme proslavery man of Salisbury toasted "William Lowndes of South Carolina: the able asserter of the rights of the Southern States" in his opposition to the restriction of slavery in Missouri.[72] And in 1825, a bold antislavery man proposed "Freedom to the slave."[73]

But politics was a different matter. Everyone seemed to want to

70. *Ibid.*, 3 July 1857.
71. Raleigh *Star*, 7 July 1820.
72. Salisbury *Western Carolinian*, 18 July 1825.
73. Charlotte *Catawba Journal*, 12 July 1825.

express his views here. Hoping to secure greater influence of the people in the nomination of candidates, one western North Carolinian proposed that "The tomb of King Caucus . . . forever remain hidden, like that of Moses, lest the followers thereof might there worship instead of going to the holy temple of American Liberty."[74]

In presidential election years, great interest was displayed in the candidates. Andrew Jackson was most popular, but John Quincy Adams, Henry Clay, John C. Calhoun, and even Martin Van Buren were also toasted. One person, who evidently looked upon the followers of Jackson as poor, filthy Democrats, expressed the hope that Jackson's friends might "always possess health of body, peace of mind, a clean shirt, and a sixpence." Another offered a toast to Jackson that some people in 1952 would have thought appropriate for one of the candidates. It was as follows: "Americans, in the choice of your Presidents, beware of military chieftains, and let the usurpations of Caesar, Cromwell, and Napoleon be ever fresh in your memory."[75] One, who recognized Jackson's services on the field of battle but feared his statesmanship, declared that the people of "the United States owe [General Jackson] a debt of gratitude, but God forbid that the debt should be paid by placing him at the head of the Nation."[76] At a Fourth celebration in Tarboro in 1832, there were six toasts for Jackson, two for Van Buren, and two for Clay and one against him.[77] A double-barrelled toast proposed at Carthage reads as follows: "May the friends of General Jackson be as millions and the enemies of Henry Clay as ten millions."[78] At the same meeting, Clay was toasted as "the Champion of the West and Polar Star of the Senate." Samuel Barringer summed up the attitude of the anti-Jackson North Carolinians in 1837, when he drank to "The honest and deluded people of the American Republic," and

74. Salisbury *Western Carolinian,* 13 July 1824.
75. *Ibid.*
76. Tarboro *Free Press,* 25 July 1828.
77. *Ibid.,* 10 July 1832.
78. Fayetteville *Journal,* 18 July 1832.

called upon "the great and good Ruler of the Universe [to] send a safe and speedy deliverance from the late and present humbugging and expunging administration."[79]

The Whigs of the Tippecanoe Club of Salisbury really took over the Fourth in 1840. In obedience to its call, the most immense crowd of people that had ever been congregated in North Carolina assembled in Salisbury: *"Twelve Thousand* is the number officially reported by . . . the Grand Marshall of the Day." These people came from Guilford, Iredell, Cabarrus, Mecklenburg, Lincoln, Stokes, Davidson, Davie, and Rowan counties. A procession formed at the race ground and marched in platoons of eight to Factory Grove, one and one-half miles distant. "Banners waved: Trumpets sounded: The cannon spoke forth—musketry responded—Ladies waved their white handkerchiefs from the windows." In the parade was a log cabin drawn by six white horses. A barrel, marked "Hard Cider," was lashed behind. The toasts, the oration, the speeches were distinctly partisan, all for "Tippecanoe and Tyler Too" and none for "Van! Van! the used-up man." Only the reading of the Declaration of Independence reminded the participants that it was really Independence Day. The celebration continued until midnight, when "all was hushed. It was now the Sabbath."[80]

North Carolinians also played state politics at their Fourth of July celebrations. James S. White of Concord toasted his "Representative in Congress—H. W. Connor—A Tree without fruit. But where little is given, little is required! All we ask of him is never to be a candidate again."[81] Another voter at a Fourth celebration expressed the hope "That our Representative in Congress stay at home next session and feed his father's cattle for the Charleston market."[82]

But North Carolinians displayed greater interest in national problems during the Jacksonian period than in congressional and presidential candidates, if the number of voluntary toasts they

79. Salisbury *Carolina Watchman,* 15 July 1837.
80. *Ibid.,* 10 July 1840.
81. *Ibid.,* 15 July 1837.
82. Charlotte *Catawba Journal,* 17 July 1827.

offered is a true indication. It should be remembered, however, that issues were closely related to President Jackson's administration. Burton Craige of Salisbury castigated

The self-styled American System: By Corruption it was begotten, by *Corruption* it has been nursed, it is itself *Corruption*. The Father, the Nurse, and the Offspring must and will be buried in the same grave, dug by an incorruptible people.[83]

Another paid his compliments to the Woolens bill by saying, "We, the people, are not gulled by the sophistry of Philadelphia meetings nor [will we be] fleeced by Boston monopolists."[84] A native of Orange County hoped that "Agriculture and Commerce —moral supporters of a free republic . . . [would] never be sacrificed at the shrine of manufacturers."[85] Many preached the good old doctrine of hard work as the way out of economic depressions. As one put it, "Better Times! To bring about which let every man exert himself to promote industry, economy, and good morals."[86] There was little or no support for protective tariffs among North Carolinians during the Middle Period.

There was general support for federal aid to internal improvements as expressed in the Raleigh toast, "May success attend every practical scheme which has been formed for opening water communications and roads in the interior of the Country."[87] But when President Jackson vetoed the Maysville Road bill, majority opinion seemed to support a Tarboro toast that the veto was "a sure guarantee that under his administration the Federal Union will be preserved."[88]

North Carolina public opinion was divided, as respects the controversy between state rights and unionism, over nullification; but unionism was by far the stronger. Of the thirty toasts at one Fourth celebration, twenty-one favored unionism, and only two favored state rights. Representative of state rights is the follow-

83. Salisbury *Western Carolinian*, 11 July 1831.
84. Charlotte *Catawba Journal*, 17 July 1827.
85. Hillsboro *Recorder*, 10 July 1822.
86. Raleigh *Minerva*, 7 July 1820.
87. Raleigh *Star*, 7 July 1820.
88. Tarboro *Free Press*, 9 July 1830.

ing: "The Sovereignty of the States. . . . The powers of Congress being only delegated, are of necessity subordinated and not sovereign powers."[89] Union sentiment was much more strongly expressed. "Nullification," cried one, is "the child of South Carolina, may it wither and blast on the soil of its birth."[90] An extreme Unionist indeed must have penned the following: "Our Country and the Union of States;—Palsy to the brain, and leprosy to the hand of those that would attempt a separation."[91]

There were only a few toasts on the Bank issue, and those were divided. At Stantonsburg, a bank supporter proposed, "The United States Bank—may it be rechartered, after every species of opposition from the President and his adherents." An opponent responded, "The United States Bank—may it sink into oblivion."[92] Another, associating the bank fight with the preservation of the Union, declared,

Gen. Jackson, the hero of New Orleans, the profound jurist and able statesman—may his collision with the Bank and Senate, like all his martial efforts, prove successful; and his bold declaration ever remembered: "The Union must and shall be preserved."[93]

In the 1840s and 1850s, the chief political concern of North Carolinians, as of the people of the nation at large, revolved around the related issues of the Mexican War, slavery in the territories, and the threat to the Union. Judging by the tenor of the voluntary toasts given at the Fourth, North Carolinians were overwhelmingly pro-union in sentiment; certainly they spoke out openly against secession and in favor of the Union. Year after year, at their Fourth of July celebrations, they toasted the Union and its perpetuity. In 1844, a Raleigh meeting cheered the sentiment, *"The Union,* May it endure forever." And an orator fervently exclaimed, "May God avert so horrible a calamity as the destruction of the Union of these states. Nothing can justify it."[94]

89. *Ibid.,* 9 July 1830.
90. Fayetteville *Journal,* 18 July 1832.
91. Charlotte *Catawba Journal,* 15 July 1828.
92. Tarboro *Free Press,* 11 July 1834.
93. *Ibid.*
94. Raleigh *Standard,* 10 July 1844.

The next year, Wilkesboro citizens drank to "The Union of the States—As one, they are great and growing, free and happy, abhorred be the plotter of disunion."[95] At Gold Hill, a toast officially approved declared, "The Union of the States—May the arm be palsied that would strike a blow to disunite them."[96] When the threat of secession had been averted by the Compromise of 1850, a Fourth-of-July crowd cheered vigorously and enthusiastically the regular toast, "The Compromise of the Slavery question—Conceived in the spirit which led to our Unnion [*sic*], it will secure peace and concord to the family of States."[97] The same crowd cheered ten voluntary toasts to the Union, of which the following is typical: "The Declaration of Independence, and the Constitution of the United States—Liberty and Union, now and forever, one and inseparable."[98]

But North Carolinians were, by the mid-1850s, beginning to fear that disunion would come. The editor of the Raleigh *Standard,* commenting on the spirited celebration of July 4, 1854, said: "We sincerely trust that next Independence Day may bring along with it less of fanaticism and disunion, and more of the spirit of justice and patriotism among portions of our fellow-citizens of the non-slaveholding States." In 1856, however, the same editor declared:

We think we may safely say that the celebration of Friday last was the most animated and extensive one that ever took place in Raleigh, to commemorate our National Independence; and one that was more generously participated in and enjoyed than any of late years. . . . Nor do we think that a fear for the Union—a dread of the abandonment of the principles of the Constitution—or a suspicion of the abnegation of the truths of the Declaration of Independence, contributed in any degree to arouse the patriotic emotions of our people. It seemed to be a congregation of freemen for freedom's sake . . . an outpouring of joy and thanksgiving for the blessings and privileges inaugurated on the 4th of July 1776.[99]

95. Salisbury *Carolina Watchman,* 26 July 1845.
96. *Ibid.,* 17 July 1846.
97. Staunton, Va., *Spectator,* 10 July 1850.
98. *Ibid.*
99. Raleigh *Standard,* 8 July 1854; 9 July 1856.

As events moved into secession and war, the attitude of southerners toward the Fourth underwent a slow but subtle change.
Several towns in North Carolina—Hillsboro, Tarboro, and Wilmington—failed to make plans for, or to hold, formal exercises in
1859 and 1860. An editorial in the Raleigh *Standard,* July 5, 1861,
on "The 4th of July," said, "This revered day passed off with but
little notice in the South. Here [in Raleigh], no public demonstration was had whatever." Such celebrations as were held consisted
of military parades, prayers, and the reading of the Mecklenburg
Declaration of Independence and the National Declaration of
Independence. The crowds were more serious than theretofore,
and totally lacking in hilarity and the festive spirit. The people of
Watauga held "a serious meeting on July 4, 1861." Some 650
people gathered to watch the home guard drill for two hours, to
listen to an oration on "The Impending Crisis," and to cheer long
and loudly the following poem:

> For forty years now past and gone,
> We bore the tyrants rod;
> We wanted nothing but our own,
> Nor thirsted for their blood.
> We strove for peace in every way,
> Because we thought it right;
> But since that peaceful day is gone,
> We're now resolved to fight.[100]

When the Civil War actually began, southerners debated
whether July Fourth should be "recognized and observed by the
people of the Confederate States." The editor of the Wilmington
Journal summarized the argument about as follows: Some con-
tend that southerners took as large a part as northerners, if not a
larger one, in proclaiming and winning independence; hence, the
South is as "much entitled as the North can be, to retain the day
as an anniversary in her political calendar." Since the South has

as much right to the honors and glories of the first revolution as the
North she is obligated to assert the right . . . to . . . share in *that* as
much as any other portion of the common heritage, and should therefore . . . adhere to the 4th as a demonstration of our intention to as-

100. Raleigh *State Journal,* 24 July 1861.

sert all the historical prestige that attaches to the Southern portion of the first revolution.[101]

Those who opposed the continued celebration of the Fourth took the position that that day "belongs to the history of a union which no longer exists." Since the states comprising the Congress which declared independence in 1776 were at war and now constitute two nations, they could not meet together to celebrate the day. Hence, an "observance would be only a form without vitality." Indeed, the Declaration had now become a part of past history and, "like the English *magna charta* . . . laid down principles in which the whole world has a deep interest." The South, therefore, was not called upon to celebrate its observance in any peculiar way.[102]

The editor of the *Journal* thought the best plan would be to stop all public celebrations for the duration of the war. "When Peace comes once again these things will regulate themselves." The editor of the Raleigh *Register* saw the matter in a different light. He could see

no reason why the birth of Liberty should be permitted to pass unheeded wherever Liberty has votaries. . . . The conduct of the North in trampling the principles of 1776 under foot and throwing ashes on the memory of its forefathers is no sufficient reason [said he] for a failure by the South to recognize and celebrate the Fourth of July as the anniversary of the most glorious human event in the history of mankind. . . .

The accursed Yankees are welcome to the exclusive use of their "Doodle" but let the South hold on tenaciously to Washington's March and Washington's Principles and on every recurring anniversary of the promulgation of the Declaration, reassert the great principles of Liberty.[103]

The view of the Wilmington editor, rather than that of the Raleigh journalist, was followed. Southern towns ceased to celebrate the Fourth, other than to fire a salute of eleven instead of thirteen guns and to close their stores. There were no parades, no dinners, toasts, orations, or fireworks. One soldier in camp showed

101. Wilmington *Journal*, 27 June 1861.
102. *Ibid.*
103. Raleigh *Register*, 3 July 1861.

his disdain for the day by entering in his war diary: "July 4th. This day being the anniversary of the Independence of the celebrated United States, I made my first attempt at washing my own clothes."[104]

Conditions after the War were not conducive to the renewal of the celebration of Independence Day by southern whites. Newspaper editors, however, discussed the day and aired southern reactions. In 1866, the editor of the Wilmington *Daily Journal,* in a long editorial titled "The Fourth of July," analyzed the southern position. He declared that no people ever took an oath of allegiance "in better faith and with nobler intentions" than southerners took the oath required of them in 1865, and "Today the South would have been glad to have united with the North in honest and grateful rejoicings of this national holiday." But they were not permitted to do so. Instead, said he, "Their cheerful concessions were responded to by renewed exactions, evincing by degrees a determined purpose to degrade them." Southern leaders whose deeds "illustrated the mighty power of true patriotism . . . must be denounced by their own people as traitors, or, dead, their memories must be dishonored and their blood despised."[105]

The war, said the editor, had been over for more than a year; but, on the Fourth, "thousands of *loyal* tongues" in the North

will utter execrations against England's tyrant, as their chosen readers, with faultless articulation, read from the Declaration of Independence, that immortal document of our old *rebel* forefathers, how swarms of officers have been sent to harass the people and eat out their substance; how standing armies in times of peace, have been kept among them without their consent; how they have been subjected to a jurisdiction foreign to the constitution and unacknowledged by their laws; how taxes have been imposed without their consent; how they have been, in many cases, deprived of the benefits of trial by jury; how their charters have been taken away and their most valuable laws abolished; how the civil government has been made subservient to the military; how their seacoasts have been ravaged, their towns burnt, and the lives of their people destroyed; how domestic insurrection has been excited

104. A. F. Drake, "Civil War Diary." Manuscript in the possession of W. Magruder Drake, University of Southwestern Louisiana, Lafayette, La.
105. Wilmington *Daily Journal,* 6 July 1866.

among them; and how their petitions for redress, in the most humble terms, have been answered by repeated injury.[106]

And, continued the editor,

Throughout the length and breadth of the prosperous North, will countless multitudes, . . . blinded by the completeness of their success, respond with fanatical zeal to each separate count in the terrible bill of indictment, and denounce as disloyal and traitorous, those who might suggest that the substitution of "the present Congress" for "the present King of Great Britain" in that remarkable paper, would be but "submitting facts to a candid world."[107]

Knowing all these things, the editor concluded, the southern people, "whose self-respect has not perished with defeat," cannot welcome "the Fourth of July with senseless uproar and pretended rejoicing. They know and appreciate all that is implied in the due observance of this day. . . ." They will do all that duty requires, in order to be permitted to join with those of the North "as worshippers of Constitutional liberty," but they cannot and will not sacrifice their honor. "To-day, then, should be passed by our people in dignified silence. Rejoicings will be but the shallow pretences of cowardly natures; complaints are the welcomed echos of radical hate."[108]

North Carolinians agreed with the editor. The observance of the Fourth "was indeed a quiet one." Except for

the usual excitement shown by the freedmen on all holidays, no exhibition of feelings was given vent to by the people of Wilmington. Even the merchants kept their places of business open. There was no jubilee, no expression of joy, no national activities, which could not be expected of a people who have no cause for rejoicing apart from the present nationality, and who are yet excluded from a place in the Councils of the nation. . . .[109]

Similar neglect of the day was reported in most towns of the state. A Salisbury paper laconically reported, "The Fourth of July— Proclamation of General Amnesty" by President Johnson.[110] In

106. *Ibid.*
107. *Ibid.*
108. *Ibid.*
109. *Ibid.*
110. Salisbury *Watchman and Old North State*, 4 July 1866.

Raleigh, B. E. Moore delivered an oration to the freedmen, in which he said it "would be inappropriate" for him "to deal harshly with Great Britain" before the assembled freedmen because "that great country emancipated all her slaves thirty years ago."[111]

Some southern cities, however, did observe the day in 1866. In Nashville, Tennessee, there were parties, picnics, and excursions of all kinds. The Radicals invited everybody to their celebration "without distinction to race or color." But the "Yankees and Freedmen . . . didn't harmonize very well [and] some four or five of each . . . were killed." Parson William G. Brownlow and Judge Leonidas C. Houk both delivered orations. The latter declared, "There are but two parties in the United States—the patriots (or radicals if you will call us so) and the traitors or rebels, and Andy Johnson is the leader, abettor, and supporter of the latter." An ex-Confederate officer who was present on the occasion said: "all the late Confederates" attended the celebration, but "We didn't observe the day because we have any peculiar love or respect for it but because the undying, the never to be forgotten, Yankees said we wouldn't."[112]

The Negroes, northern Radicals, and native white Unionists—all those affiliated with the Republican party—of North Carolina celebrated the Fourth in 1867. But few Conservatives or Democrats joined in. In fact, it would not be far from the truth to say the celebrations were Republican rallies. The Democratic press commented adversely on them. The Charlotte *Times,* after dwelling ironically on the rebel spirit of the authors of the Declaration of Independence, said, "This parchment roll still stands, a monument to the memory of its author and signers, and in direct contravention to the acts and doings of the mighty men who now bear sway." The Raleigh *Sentinel* said: "The advent of the anniversary is hailed rather with feelings of sadness than with peans of joy. The Declaration still lives, but its vital ideas are vanquished." And the Wilmington *Journal* expressed the view that

111. Raleigh *Standard,* 11 July 1866.

112. James Horace Wilkes to Elizabeth Wilson, 5 July 1866. Letter in possession of Edward M. Steel, Jr., West Virginia University, Morgantown, W. Va.

it would have been pleased if General Sickles should have ordered a reading, by his officers, soldiery and subjects, of the Declaration of Independence. There are some wholesome lessons taught in that document, by which the commander himself might profit.[113]

In the early 1870s, the celebrations were again following the general pattern of pre-Civil War days: cannon were fired, the Declaration of Independence was read, and there were processions, prayers, martial music, and orations. But dinners, toasts, and evening balls were lacking.[114] More and more, however, the participation in the exercises was limited to Negroes.[115] The editor of the Hillsboro *Recorder* pretty well summed up the attitude of southern and North Carolina whites toward the Fourth in the centennial year in two editorials. In the one, he said:

The whites of the South have no interest in this day. The suggestions of the freedoms fought for and won by a whole people's united efforts have no charms for those who feel themselves conquered, and, in many parts of the South, still subject to a conqueror's capricious rule.

The day may come, but is not now, when it can again be a nation's holiday.[116]

In the second editorial, titled "The Hundredth Year of Nationality," the editor declared that the nation's prosperity had been "secured at the expense of constitutional principles." The nation

is now undoubtedly weakened in those fraternal bonds which once made the hearts of its whole people beat as one. . . . Theoretically one and indivisible, a portion of it is still sought to be governed as conquered territory, and the fires of hate are still fanned to consume it. Therefore the Southern people now look upon the fourth of July with halting interest and doubting patriotism, because it recalls the gaining of an independence they cannot exert and a perfect Union they cannot enjoy.

. . . As the Centennial of the birth of a free people, it is accompanied with so much contrast and contradiction of the family of States that we wait developments before we can accept it as the real time and the field for thorough conciliation and fraternization.[117]

113. Raleigh *Standard*, 10 July 1867; Salisbury *Carolina Watchman*, 8 July 1867.
114. Raleigh *Standard*, 7 July 1869.
115. Wilmington *Daily Journal*, 5 July 1867; Hillsboro *Recorder*, 8 July 1874; 7 July 1875.
116. Hillsboro *Recorder*, 8 July 1874; 5 July 1876.
117. *Ibid.*

Feeling as they did, southerners abandoned any pretense of celebrating the birthday of the nation. Furthermore, the Civil War changed the attitude of the North toward the day. The preservation of the Union, the triumph of nationalism, and the death of state sovereignty brought a new sentimental reverence for the Constitution. The abolition of slavery by constitutional amendment also placed righteousness on the side of the Constitution. Hence, more and more, the nation shifted emphasis from the Declaration of Independence to the Constitution of the United States, and the old-time Fourth passed into the limbo of history.

What, one might ask, was the general significance of the Fourth of July celebrations? In addition to mirroring the political issues of the day, as seen in the above descriptive account, an analysis shows that Independence Day had important and specific bearings on the life of both the state and the nation.

North Carolinians used the Fourth to foster a greater love for the state and to stimulate the development of the state in the interest of the well-being and happiness of the people. Their orations and toasts emphasized the part played by the people of North Carolina in the movement for independence and lamented the fact that historians had not paid more attention to the state's contributions to national development. One toast to the Declaration declared that the flag of independence was

First unfurled in the fields of North Carolina, it floated for a while as the pennon of a small but gallant band, shedding inspiration wherever the gleamings of its folds were seen; [and] when amplified and enlarged by other hands it spread itself to the world. . . .[118]

In the 1830s, it became a regular part of the exercises in North Carolina to toast the Mecklenburg Declaration and its author, Dr. Ephraim Brevard, and to read that Declaration often in advance of the national Declaration.[119] A Raleigh citizen toasted "The History of North Carolina. Unwritten because the historian grew diffident of his ability to chronicle her glory";[120] and a

118. Hillsboro *Recorder,* 11 July 1839.
119. Charlotte *Miners' and Farmers' Journal,* 12 July 1834; Hillsboro *Recorder,* 10 July 1844.
120. Raleigh *Standard,* 10 July 1844.

Tarboro orator chose as his theme, "North Carolina . . . and the many wrongs done by her historians." He condemned especially the refusal of some historians to accept the authenticity of the Mecklenburg Declaration.[121]

Some of the Fourth speakers decried the fact that North Carolina was known as the "Ireland of the Union" and the "Rip Van Winkle State." They declared that the state's "independence and consistency of principle" should give her pre-eminence among the states. Concrete proposals for raising the standing of the state are found in the toast, "A system of general instruction: the development of our internal resources: the pure and able administration of justice: Let these be the cardinal objects of the policy of North Carolina."[122] "The Old North State," a twelve-stanza poem "written expressly for the Fourth of July" in 1846, expresses love, patriotism, and loyalty to the state. The first stanza reads:

> North Carolina! I will toast to thee,
> Thy honor and name may not fall:
> Peace and happiness may'st thou always see.
> Death to him whom thy name miscalls.[123]

The July celebrants emphasized three lines of development designed to advance the prosperity and happiness of the people. These were internal improvements, constitutional revision, and education. They were zealous advocates of developing the economic resources of the state and saw a close relationship between skilled labor and internal improvements to this problem. Hence, they demanded "American workshops" that would "make us commercially independent, as we are politically free." And they toasted "Mechanism—a science, the sublimity and grandeur of which is only comprehended by the enlightenment of its votaries"; and "The mechanic Arts: may they be so fostered . . . as to enable us to be independent . . . for any article we require."[124] But it was internal improvement projects to which the people

121. Tarboro *Southerner,* 10 July 1858.
122. Raleigh *Register,* 8 July 1825.
123. Tarboro *Free Press,* 15 July 1846.
124. Raleigh *Minerva,* 7 July 1808; Raleigh *Standard,* 7 July 1841; Fayetteville *Observer,* 11 July 1848.

looked most for economic progress. A Charlotte crowd, on July 4, 1825, gave six cheers and a three-gun salute to the toast, "The Opposers of Internal Improvements. May they receive the anathemas of an enlightened [citizenry]."[125] A few years later, a Fourth crowd, in the same city, toasting "Internal Improvements," enquired: "While other states are marching onward, shall North Carolina suffer her energies to slumber, and her resources to lie dormant?"[126] North Carolina still lagged behind; and in 1841, the people were still pleading with the state authorities: "Give us a judicious system of Improvements, and North Carolina will rank, as she should rank, among the first of the States."[127]

In the early days, the state constitution was highly praised by the Fourth of July celebrants. In 1810, Raleigh citizens drank to "The Constitution of the State of North Carolina—Beneath its powerful and protecting wings, the poorest citizen sits in safety 'under his vine and under his fig-tree,' and none can make him afraid."[128] But by 1820, western North Carolinians were bitter because of the system of representation and restricted suffrage. A Salisbury July Fourth celebration demanded "A Convention of the free people of North Carolina—Justice imperiously demands it."[129] The next year, they expressed their sentiments in "The Day —can our fellow citizens in the East have forgotten that their brethren in the West are the descendants of the men of '76."[130] This was followed by "A Convention of the People of North Carolina—Peaceable if we can . . . forcible if we must."[131] Western North Carolinians received some concessions on representation in 1835, but they continued to demand free suffrage. On July 4, 1852, an Asheville crowd bitterly condemned John Keer, the speaker who had opposed any further extension of the suffrage. They charged that he had said "in plain English, a negro, stud

125. Charlotte *Catawba Journal,* 12 July 1825.
126. *Ibid.,* 8 July 1828.
127. Hillsboro *Recorder,* 8 July 1841.
128. Raleigh *Star,* 5 July 1810.
129. Salisbury *Western Carolinian,* 18 July 1820.
130. *Ibid.,* 31 July 1821.
131. *Ibid.*

horse, or jackass are as much entitled to representation in the Legislature as a POOR WESTERN MAN."[132]

There is no question, however, that North Carolinians put most emphasis on education as a means to advance the progress, prosperity, and happiness of the people. In the early days, before the state gave any support to education, the Fourth celebrations toasted "The Arts and Sciences," and expressed the hope that they might be improved and cultivated. One such toast reads as follows: "The progress of useful knowledge. May the arts and sciences be cultivated with success, and their great end be directed to the improvement of social happiness."[133] After the state university was chartered, but before its doors were opened, Raleigh citizens drank a toast to "The University of North Carolina—May it prove the nurse of science, and the guardian of freedom."[134] After its opening, the university was toasted every Fourth of July by groups all over the state. It was proclaimed "the parent of science and patriotism," the "nursery of science, the shield of our political freedom," and "The Pride and Ornament of the State."[135]

A native of Orange County, in 1822, expressed the hope that the people of the state would "learn to appreciate its value"; and a citizen of Charlotte declared that it ought "to be the glory and hopes of the church." By the 1840s, "The University with the Dialectic and Philanthropic Societies" were declared to be "Pre eminently the Pride of the State," and "The University Magazine" was "An additional light on the hill of science."[136]

But the most fulsome praise was given the university in a toast at Halifax:

The University at Chapel Hill: Rome from her seven hills, boasted of the diffusion of knowledge and power; from the hill just named,

132. Raleigh *Star,* 7 July 1852, quoting Asheville *Times.*

133. Wilmington *Chronicle and North Carolina Weekly Advertiser,* 17 July 1795; Raleigh *Standard,* 9 July 1794.

134. Halifax *North Carolina Journal,* 6 July 1795.

135. *Ibid.,* 9 July 1798; Raleigh *Star,* 26 July 1811; Charlotte *Catawba Journal,* 12 July 1826.

136. Hillsboro *Recorder,* 10 July 1822; Charlotte *Catawba Journal,* 8 July 1828; Raleigh *Standard,* 7 July 1841 and 10 July 1844.

North Carolina and many of her sister States, have seen and felt the rays of science and useful knowledge.[137]

The people showed an interest also in other educational institutions. In 1797, they toasted the university and "all other literary institutions."[138] Raleigh citizens in 1811 drank to "Learning the support of virtue, virtue the pillar of freedom."[139] By the 1820s, North Carolinians were not satisfied merely with "The University of North Carolina and all other literary institutions of the State," as they had been in 1797; they now toasted specific institutions, including the "Roanoke Literary and Scientific Institution," and they called for aid to "Literature, Arts and Sciences," "Our University and *Schools*," and "Free Schools."[140] In the 1830s, North Carolinians began to put their trust in public school education; and in 1841, a Fourth of July toast proclaimed that "the general diffusion of Education among the people is the birthright of Liberty."[141] "Common Schools," cried one Fourth of July celebrant, "When the school master is abroad the foes of Freedom tremble."[142] Some Fourth of July exercises actually centered around public school work. The July 4, 1847, celebration in Nutbush District, Granville County, witnessed by about four hundred ladies and gentlemen, consisted of an examination of the pupils of the public school taught by Danbridge B. Hillard, the reading of the Declaration of Independence, and a barbecue enjoyed by the school children, their parents, and assembled guests. The toasts and the oration extolled the virtues of public education.[143]

For the nation as a whole, the celebration of the Fourth nurtured loyalty, patriotism, love of the Union, and a veneration of the principles of the Declaration of Independence. It gave the

137. Tarboro *Free Press*, 25 July 1828.
138. Halifax *North Carolina Journal*, 10 July 1797.
139. Raleigh *Star*, 5 July 1811.
140. Raleigh *Register*, 10 July 1812; Tarboro *Free Press*, 17 July 1829; Raleigh *Minerva*, 9 July 1813; Raleigh *Star*, 7 July 1820; Charlotte *Catawba Journal*, 12 July 1825.
141. Hillsboro *Recorder*, 24 July 1841.
142. Raleigh *Standard*, 10 July 1844.
143. Raleigh *Register*, 21 July 1847.

people an opportunity to express their missionary zeal to spread democracy and representative self-government throughout the world, and to express their sympathy and support for revolutionary groups trying to establish independence. It also gave them a chance to hear the American eagle scream defiance to the enemies of the United States and to proclaim their manifest destiny to dominate the western hemisphere.

The desire to share their ideas and happiness with others caused Americans to hold out welcoming arms to exiles from other lands. "Our Country," cried one North Carolinian, "Dear Columbia, hail! A sanctuary for the good and a sacred asylum for the persecuted. May thy land be sacred to science and devoted to religion; and may Liberty always crown the spot of independence."[144] Even more generous were Americans with their sympathy and support for people in foreign countries who were trying to gain independence and establish republican governments. They toasted "Parliamentary reform to Great Britain and Ireland," "Permanent freedom and peace to the Republic of France," "The Republics of France and Holland: may their renovated governments be as happy to them as ours has been to us," and "the unfortunate Poles."[145] Americans sympathized especially with South America. "May she," said one North Carolina toast, "shortly emerge from a state of wretchedness and slavery, and taste the blessings of liberty and independence with her sisters of the North."[146]

Another toast to "Our Republican Brethren of Spanish America" prayed that "wisdom and valor would combine to insure their Independence."[147] When Colombia had secured her independence, North Carolinians toasted "The New Republic of Colombia—We hail the birth of a Sister of the South—May her future be as prosperous, as her struggle has been glorious." Pride was expressed in "The Patriot General Bolivar: may his future

144. Raleigh *Minerva*, 11 July 1817.
145. Halifax *North Carolina Journal*, 10 July 1793; 6 July 1795.
146. Raleigh *Star*, 26 July 1811.
147. Salisbury *Western Carolinian*, 11 July 1820.

conduct be such as to merit the envious appelation of the Washington of South America."[148]

North Carolinians also displayed great interest in the Greek struggle for independence. They drank toasts to "The Cause of the Patriot Greeks—May they be as successful in their struggles, as the heroes of the American Revolution, in subduing their enemies and erecting a free government."[149] Naturally, the Turks and the Holy Alliance, as enemies of the Christian religion and republicanism, were anathema to Americans. The Holy Alliance was characterized as "the nightmare of Europe," and its members as "the Cyclops of Despotism."[150] North Carolinians expressed the hope that "Liberty and Christianity [would] defeat the Turks and the Holy Alliance."[151] When Grecian independence was virtually assured, a Lincolnton, North Carolina, Fourth assembly drank to "Modern Greece; a little dim, beclouded star rising in the east; may it borrow its light from the Western Sun."[152] Nor were North Carolinians unmindful of "Irish Emancipation," and "the Poles fighting for freedom."[153]

But Fourth of July celebrants were not altogether unselfish in their devotion to the cause of freedom. There were among them "Big Americans" who often expressed the doctrine of manifest destiny. Some toasts proclaimed a desire to acquire specific territory—Canada; "The Floridas . . . [which] will ere long form a part of the American Republic";[154] Cuba; Texas; even the Central American states. Others seem to have been delivered merely that the people might hear the eagle scream—the following, for instance: "The Eagle of the United States—may she extend her wings from the Atlantic to the Pacific; and fixing her talons on the Isthmus of Darien, stretch with her beak to the Northern

---

148. *Ibid.,* 9 July 1822.
149. *Ibid.,* 9 July 1822.
150. Washington *National Gazette,* 11 July 1823.
151. Salisbury *Western Carolinian,* 8 July 1820.
152. Salisbury *Western Carolinian,* 21 July 1829.
153. Charlotte *Catawba Journal,* 21 July 1836; Tarboro *Free Press,* 9 July 1845. 1845.
154. Raleigh *Star,* 7 July 1820.

Pole."[155] A variant was: "The American Eagle—May she stick her beak in the North Pole, fan the Atlantic and Pacific with her wings, and switch her tail feathers over the Southernmost tip of South America." The expression of such ideas caused South Americans to begin to regard the United States as the Colossus of the North. And occasionally, a North Carolinian would warn the people of the United States that they must curb their lust for power and new territory if they were to remain the leader of moral forces among the nations of the world.[156]

The most significant feature of the Fourth celebrations was that they nurtured loyalty and patriotism. Everywhere, Independence Day served as a symbol of unity and nationalism. North, South, East, and West—even in distant lands, Americans gathered to read the Declaration of Independence and to pledge anew their allegiance to the flag. Daniel Webster expressed this sentiment in an oration in Washington when he said:

This anniversary animates and gladdens and unites all American hearts. On other days of the year we may be party men, indulging in controversies, more or less important to the public good; we may have our likes and dislikes, and we may maintain our political differences, often with warm, and sometimes with angry feelings. But today we are Americans all; and are nothing but Americans.[157]

A North Carolina orator put it more emotionally. He said:

With what wild tumultuous throbbings of pleasure does the blood bound through the hearts of American freemen, as this glorious day dawns upon this land of freedom. . . . O, what rays of light does the annual return of this great Western Jubilee of liberty send, far, far into the dark spots of oppressed distant lands.[158]

A North Carolina editor declared that the Fourth "is calculated to perpetuate those principles which rocked the cradles of our Independence, and nursed it into manhood."[159]

155. Merle Curti, *The Growth of American Thought* (New York: Harper and Brothers, 1943) , p. 412. The variant appeared in the Nashville, Tennessee, *Banner.*
156. Salisbury *Carolina Watchman,* 15 July 1856.
157. Daniel Webster, *The Writings and Speeches of Daniel Webster, National Edition,* 18 vols. (Boston: Little, Brown & Company, 1903) , IV, 297.
158. Wilmington *Journal,* 11 July 1845.
159. Salisbury *Western Carolinian,* 4 July 1820.

Finally, Americans were possessed of a missionary zeal to spread democracy and self-government throughout the world. They firmly believed they had a good thing; and, like the Communists of today, they were anxious to share it with others, even to the extent of forcing it upon them. Toasts, orations, and editorials on the Fourth said as much. Of hundreds of such toasts the following are representative: "The Principles of the American Revolution —Destined to revolutionize the civilized world." "May the pure principles of humanity extend their influence throughout the globe." "All Mankind! May every branch of the great family participate in the blessings of freedom and peace." "The political voyage of mankind—May their destination be true republicanism. May the World be freed from every enemy of the rights of man." And "The Nations of the Earth—May they soon have the peace liberty and blessings we have."[160]

An orator, urging his hearers to spread the American gospel of democracy and republicanism, said:

And let us remember that we are acting not merely for ourselves, but for the oppressed of all nations, who are looking to us for an example of wisdom and virtue, which may be to them a pillar of cloud by day, a pillar of fire by night to guide and cheer them onward. Are we not at this moment the mark and model for all the world? Do not greyheaded statesmen, learned writers and eloquent orators, constantly point for proof and illustration to these United States?[161]

These toasts and orations were not empty, meaningless phrases, but the sincere expressions of loyalty by a generation that was not ashamed of its patriotism.

160. Salisbury *Carolina Watchman,* 26 July 1845; Halifax *North Carolina Journal,* 17 July 1793 and 9 July 1794; Fayetteville *North Carolina Minerva and Advertiser,* 9 July 1796; Raleigh *Minerva,* 11 July 1817.

161. David L. Child, *An Oration Pronounced Before the Republicans of Boston, July 4, 1826* (Boston: Josiah B. Cloush, 1826), p. 39.

6

On Tour with President Andrew Jackson

Here, again, Green is touching the lighter side of history. This essay was read at a session of the Mississippi Valley Historical Association in Denver, Colorado, April 24, 1959, and published in the *New England Quarterly Review*, XXXVI (June 1963), 209–228.

THE NUMEROUS JOURNEYS OF PRESI-dents Franklin D. Roosevelt, Harry S. Truman, and Dwight D. Eisenhower have made presidential tours common-place events and have enabled millions of American citizens in every section of the United States—in fact, citizens of every state in the Union except perhaps the two recently admitted ones—to see a President face to face. Consequently the presidential tour has ceased to be an important state occasion, and a President on tour has lost the aura of yesteryear. The cartoonists have taken great delight in picturing Truman at the Florida beach resorts dressed in bizarre, multicolored sports clothes, and the pundits have bitterly condemned Eisenhower for golfing with his friends in Augusta, Georgia, when, according to them, important domestic issues were hanging in the balance and a bad international situation worsened[1]—a modern Nero fiddling while Rome burns. Such was not the case in regard to presidential tours a hundred years ago.

Of the fifteen men who occupied the President's office between 1789 and 1861, only four—George Washington, James Monroe, Andrew Jackson, and John Tyler—made formal and official tours

---

1. For examples of reaction to Eisenhower's tours, see *Time*, LXX, (21 October 1957), 24; New York *Times*, 13 January, 14 January, 11 October 1957.

of the country. Such an event in those days was not only a rare, but also a *great* occasion. Few people had an opportunity to see a President; but when they did, they gave him a royal welcome. A presidential visit to one state in 1859 caused an editor to write: "It is not often we catch a live President in North Carolina. Our printers never saw one before and we have not seen much of our printers since."[2]

George Washington, the first President, initiated official tours of the United States with a northern one in 1789; this was followed by an eastern one in 1790, and a southern one in 1791. On these travels, he visited all the thirteen original states. The Constitution had been adopted and a union formed, but neither in spirit nor in reality did a national government exist. Washington understood this and hoped by his tours to win the good will and the support of the people for the central government and thereby, as he said, "make the States a nation, . . . stir the people out of their pettiness as colonists and provincials, and give them a national character and spirit."[3] Washington thought his visits were successful, and at the end of his third journey wrote:

Tranquility reigns among the people. . . . They begin to feel the good effects of equal laws and equal protection. . . . Each day's experience of the Government of the United States seems to confirm its establishment and to render it more popular.[4]

Despite the popularity and success of Washington's tours, his immediate successors—John Adams, Thomas Jefferson, and James Madison—displayed no interest in making similar journeys. Bitter sectional feelings plagued their administrations, highlighted by the Virginia-Kentucky Resolutions of 1798, the opposition of the New England Essex Junto to Jefferson's policies, and the Hartford Convention of 1814. These dangerous shoals were temporarily submerged by the New Nationalism that followed the War of 1812; and James Monroe, hoping to destroy all partisan feeling, to bind all sections closer together, and to win support

2. Raleigh *North Carolina Standard,* 8 June 1859.

3. Archibald Henderson, *Washington's Southern Tour* (Boston: Houghton Mifflin Co., 1923) , p. 1.

4. *Ibid.,* pp. 338–339.

for the national policies of his administration, made tours covering the New England, the Middle Atlantic, the southern, and the western states. His expeditions appeared to be eminently successful. The New England press united in proclaiming the day of Mr. Monroe's arrival in Massachusetts "as the commencement of 'the era of good feelings.'" And the New Haven *Herald* declared that "the demon of party . . . [has] departed and [has] given place to a general burst of NATIONAL FEELING."[5] Southerners generally expressed the view that Monroe's tours had strengthened the Union and promoted the prosperity and happiness of the people. Westerners were even more profuse in their praise. A Kentucky orator, in welcoming the President, assured Monroe

that the western people do approve of your administration, and repose an entire confidence in your intentions and exertions to do away [with] *sectional* prejudices—to destroy the *bitterness* of party spirit; and to unite the nation in a social, commercial and military connection. We hope and believe, that, under your administration, our country will enjoy prosperity and happiness and be united in indissoluble bonds of affection and interest—and [we] believe . . . that your journeys through the United States are intended to accomplish, and have, in a great degree, effected these desirable objects.[6]

The Monroe era of good feelings was followed by one of bitter interparty disputes and threatening sectional controversies. Withdrawing into his self-righteousness, John Quincy Adams made little effort to mollify his political opponents or to assuage the mounting sectional tension. His administration was repudiated, and the Jeffersonian Republican party was rent in twain. Emerging as the leader of the new Democratic party, Andrew Jackson was elected President in 1828, and soon became the symbol of American Democracy. More than any of his predecessors, Jackson gave a sense of participation in the federal government to the common man, and he somehow succeeded in identifying himself and his administration with the people's interests.

But Jackson's first administration was a stormy one. Through

5. Washington *Daily National Intelligencer,* 19 July 1819.

6. *Niles' Weekly Register,* XII (12 July 1817) , 314; Washington *National Intelligencer,* 19 and 29 July 1817.

the ruthless use of the spoils system, Jackson eliminated his political opponents from office; and by rotation in office, he built up the leadership of his own party. He dismissed his cabinet members when they differed with him, and he openly flouted decisions of the Supreme Court. He supported Georgia in the Cherokee Indian controversy and removed the Indians west of the Mississippi, and, by the repeated use of the veto, he checked internal improvements and destroyed the Second Bank of the United States. He dealt a major blow to state rights in the nullification controversy and did more to establish and maintain national sovereignty than any President prior to Abraham Lincoln. He broke with John C. Calhoun, generally recognized as his successor in party leadership, and forced Martin Van Buren on the party as vice-presidential candidate in 1832. Although each of these issues made political enemies for Jackson, he and Van Buren were triumphantly elected in 1832.

Jackson's war on the United States Bank had aroused resentment in New England, but his championship of national sovereignty in the nullification controversy was very popular and, for the first time, he won support in that section in the election of 1832. He received more than forty-six percent of the popular vote and carried Maine and New Hampshire.[7] Convinced by the vote in the presidential election that a close affiliation with the President would be beneficial to them in state and local elections, New England Democratic politicians began to invite President Jackson to visit their section. On February 5, 1833, a committee representing a public meeting in Hartford, Connecticut, invited Jackson to visit New England and view her "institutions of Republican Freedom"; her commercial cities and manufacturing towns; her temples of worship, colleges, and seminaries; and to visit and mingle with her active and virtuous population and independent yeomanry. They pointed out that Jackson's vote had increased in Connecticut from 4,000 in 1828 to more than 11,000 in 1832, and

7. Thomas Hudson McKee, *National Conventions and Platforms of All Political Parties, 1789 to 1900. Convention, Popular, and Electoral Vote*, 3d ed. (Baltimore: the Friedenwald Co., 1900) , pp. 32–33.

they expressed the hope that his re-election would extend "the beneficial results" of his first term to the New England states during his second administration.[8] After consultation with his political advisers, the President replied on March 7, saying that he hoped to visit New England later in the year to examine "the republican institutions which her sons have raised with so much public spirit and success," and "to engage in personal intercourse with the citizens themselves."[9] President Jackson received similar invitations from numerous Democratic leaders and partisan groups throughout New England. Among these was one from a committee "in behalf of the Republican citizens of Boston," to which Jackson replied that it would be "particularly gratifying to me to embrace an opportunity of extending to yourselves and those you represent on this occasion, as well as to my fellow citizens generally, my personal respects."[10]

These exchanges set the tone and pattern of the tour: it was to be distinctly political and partisan, rather than formal, official, and nationalistic in nature. Only after the arrangements, private and political, had been completed did the cities and towns make plans for official public receptions. Leaders of the opposition party were unenthusiastic. Edward Everett reluctantly approved a public welcome in Charlestown, Massachusetts, only because of the office Jackson held and of his stand on nullification.[11] The Massachusetts Senate, learning from private sources that Jackson would be in the state, finally requested the governor "to extend the customary hospitality" of the state to the President.[12] Generally, he was accorded the "respect due to the chief magistrate of the nation by all parties" but "his special friends or partisans received him with great eclat and enthusiasm."[13] One report said that "the

8. Washington *Globe*, 15 March 1833.

9. *Niles' Weekly Register*, XLIV (6 April 1833), 82.

10. Washington *National Intelligencer*, 30 May 1833.

11. Washington *Globe*, 8 June 1833.

12. *Niles' Weekly Register*, XLIV (13 April 1833), 100.

13. Nathan Sargent, *Public Men and Events from the Commencement of Mr. Monroe's Administration, in 1817, to the Close of Mr. Fillmore's Administration, in 1853*, 2 vols. (Philadelphia: J. B. Lippincott & Co., 1875), I, 245–246.

[Democratic] mobs went wild in their jubilation, the popular enthusiasm was undoubted, but the aristocrats averted their faces."[14]

Jackson left Washington for New England on June 6, 1833, accompanied by Louis McLane, Secretary of State, Lewis Cass, Secretary of War, Andrew Jackson Donelson, his nephew and private secretary, and Colonel Earle, his aide-de-camp. He intended to go as far as Portland, Maine, with stops at major points on the way.[15] A citizens' committee from Baltimore, riding on a Baltimore and Ohio train, met the Jackson party twelve miles from the city. Jackson and his companions abandoned their horses and boarded the train which carried them into the city in a few minutes. Seba Smith, better known as Major Jack Downing, says in one of his letters, "We flew over the ground like a harry-cane. There isn't a horse in this country that could keep up with us, if he should go upon the clean clip."[16] Jackson himself enjoyed this, the first ride by a President in the "steam cars."[17]

Upon reaching the station, Jackson entered a barouche and rode through streets "filled with folks as thick as the spruce trees"[18] in a forest. The Jackson party met Black Hawk, the Indian chief, who had arrived in the city the same day. Major Downing was so chagrined to find that the crowds showed more interest in the Indian than in the President that he suggested to Jackson that he not permit Black Hawk to appear in Philadelphia.[19] In the evening, Jackson and Black Hawk attended

14. Andrew Cunningham McLaughlin, *Lewis Cass* (Boston: Houghton, Mifflin and Company, 1891) , pp. 149–150.

15. Washington *Globe*, 15 March 1833; Andrew Jackson to Martin Van Buren, 6 June 1833, Andrew Jackson, *Correspondence of Andrew Jackson*, edited by John Spencer Bassett (Washington: Carnegie Institution of Washington, 1926–1933) , V, 106–107.

16. Andrew Jackson to Andrew Jackson, Jr., 6 June 1833, *Correspondence of Andrew Jackson*, V, 107; Washington *National Intelligencer*, 8 June 1833; Seba Smith, *Life and Writings of Major Jack Downing of Downingville, Away Down East in the State of Maine*, 3d ed. (Boston: Lilly, Wait, Colman & Holden, 1834) , p. 213.

17. Marquis James, *The Life of Andrew Jackson* (Indianapolis: The Bobbs-Merrill Company, 1938) , p. 637.

18. Washington *National Intelligencer*, 11 June 1833.

19. Smith, *Major Jack Downing*, p. 213.

the Front Street Theatre, where, once again, according to Hezekiah Niles, "immense crowds of persons assembled to get a sight of Black Hawk,"[20] but ignored the President.

A delegation of citizens from Philadelphia went to Baltimore to conduct Jackson to the Friendly City. Their boat, *The Ohio,* was met at the Philadelphia Navy Yard by a crowd of thirty thousand spectators. A barouche drawn by four white horses carried Jackson to his lodgings through streets so densely crowded that a troop of cavalry was necessary to open passage. On Sunday, Jackson attended divine services at the First Presbyterian Church, which was so filled that "ladies jumped upon the seats of the pews to get a good look at the 'Hero.' "[21] After the service, the President shook hands with a young boy,

and then—what a scene! one upon another's head, they all extended their hands, but in vain! The General, using his powers of foresight, soon perceived what would be the consequence, immediately sounded a retreat; . . . he wisely slipped out by a private door, and eluded the mob.[22]

Monday was given over to celebrations and, since Philadelphia and Pennsylvania were Democratic strongholds, the party did itself proud. Jackson supporters poured into the city. The *American Sentinel* boldly proclaimed that Jackson's arrival "naturally inspired . . . a people ardently devoted to the Democratic principles which characterize the administration of the distinguished visitor."[23] And the Washington *Globe,* Jackson's official organ, responded that Jackson "was gratified to see the warm welcome extended to him by the good and true of . . . the party."[24]

Plans called for a parade through the streets, a review of troops, and a reception at Independence Hall. The President rode bareheaded through the streets for five hours and, consequently, suffered severe sunburn about the face and neck. A military band furnished music for the review, but the "loud shouts and huzzas of

20. *Niles' Weekly Register,* XLIV (13 June 1833) , 256.
21. Washington *National Intelligencer,* 13 June 1833.
22. *Ibid.,* 20 June 1833.
23. Quoted in the Washington *Globe,* 17 June 1833.
24. Washington *Globe,* 18 June 1833.

the people who completely filled the streets . . . drowned the noise of the military music.''[25] The mayor introduced the invited guests to Jackson at a reception in Independence Hall, but before this was completed, the mob rushed in, and the Hall was crowded to suffocation. Someone raised the windows, "and a ludicrous scene ensued; man, woman, and child, came tumbling out, from a height of six feet, some jumping, some diving, and some rolling.''[26] For two hours, the President stood and shook hands with uninvited guests. These included members of the faculty and student body of the University of Pennsylvania, the young Democrats from the city and surrounding districts, and thousands of plain, simple Jacksonian Democrats. Jack Downing declared that the President

shook hands with all his might an hour or two, till he got so tired he couldn't hardly stand it. I took hold and shook for him once in awhile to help him along, but at last he got so tired he had to lay down on a soft bench covered with cloth and shake as well as he could, and when he couldn't shake he'd nod to 'em as they came along. And at last he got so beat out, he could only wrinkle his forward and wink. Then I kind of stood behind him and reached my arm round under his, and shook for him about half an hour. . . . Then we concluded it was best to adjourn for to-day.[27]

Jackson was highly pleased with the favorable reception he received in Philadelphia. Writing to his son, he said that he would "not attempt to describe the feelings of the people," but he declared that his reception "surpassed anything I have ever witnessed." Even so he wished the "trip was over," and said that, except to the Hermitage and to the watering places, this was to be "the last journey I shall ever undertake.''[28]

The opposition press was highly critical of the partisan activities in Philadelphia. Duff Green, editor of the *United States Telegraph,* wrote that the Democrats marched the President "up

25. Washington *National Intelligencer,* 20 June 1833.

26. *Ibid.* See also issues for 13, 14, and 15 June 1833.

27. Smith, *Major Jack Downing,* p. 214. See also Philadelphia *National Gazette,* 11 June 1833, and Washington *National Intelligencer,* 15 June 1833.

28. Andrew Jackson to Andrew Jackson, Jr., *Correspondence of Andrew Jackson,* V, 109.

and down the streets, here there and everywhere, as if he were a wild beast to be exhibited gratis. It was disgraceful to all concerned." Green criticized the President for stooping to such low political trickery as kissing babies, flattering the women on their personal appearance, and patting the cheeks and stroking the hair of young boys. The "slavish and sycophantic adulation poured into his greedy ears," said Green, show the degeneracy of the age in taste, feelings, and principles.[29]

The Washington *National Intelligencer* found fault with Jackson for his response to

a hale buxom young widow's statement—that she had walked six miles to enjoy the rare felicity of shaking his hand—"Madam, I regret that I had not known your wishes earlier; I would certainly have walked half way to meet you."[30]

But the *Intelligencer* pulled out all the stops in its condemnation of the partisan conduct of the tour. It declared that "the whole matter and manner of receiving and showing the President . . . were of party origin and management." "The party leaders," said the editor, "were evidently disposed to make the most of their opportunity," but he placed the responsibility upon the President, who sanctioned and approved the plans.[31]

Commenting on what he called the adulation heaped upon the President in Philadelphia, the editor of the *Commercial Herald* said:

We protest, in the name of *Liberty,* and of that Democratic simplicity which is now converted into Royalty and its trappings, against all this war upon simplicity and the dignity of Freemen . . .[32]

which was designed only to serve partisan ends.

Jackson left Philadelphia on June 11, spent the night at Trenton, New Jersey, and arrived at New York City on June 12. Preparations for Jackson's reception had been under way for more than a week, and Democratic leaders in city and state had joined hands to give the President a rousing welcome. The city

29. Washington *United States Telegraph,* 14 June 1833.
30. Washington *National Intelligencer,* 22 June 1833.
31. *Ibid.,* 18 June 1833.
32. Quoted in Washington *National Intelligencer,* 18 June 1833.

had appointed nearly four hundred people, "generally persons of high standing and respectability,"[33] to its official committee. Among these were Philip Hone, noted business leader and Whig diarist, who was highly critical of the whole affair. The committee's ship, the *North America,* was boarded by Jackson and his party at Perth Amboy. The entire party was seated at the most splendid dinner Hone had ever seen served on a vessel. When the *North America* arrived at Castle Garden, Jackson received salutes from the guns on Forts Hamilton and Diamond and the forts on Bedloe's, Governor's, and Staten islands, as well as from numerous steamships and revenue cutters in the harbor. The Bay was "covered with vessels of every style and description," and "the wharves and housetops, and vessels were covered with people."[34]

More than one hundred thousand persons had assembled in the area around the harbor. Troops were drawn up on the Battery. The President mounted a horse and reviewed them, "but from the moment of landing all was confusion." The President made his way to the city hall, where he was received by Governor William L. Marcy and was then accompanied by the mayor and Vice-President Van Buren to his hotel. The streets along the way were lined by "a solid mass of men, women, and children, who greeted their favorite with cheers shouts and waving of scarfs and handkerchiefs."[35] Downing described them as "an ocean of folks" who were "cutting up capers as high as a cat's back."[36]

Two accidents occurred at Castle Garden. A seaman on board the revenue cutter *Alert* was wounded when firing a salute to Jackson. He lost both hands and both eyes. Washington Irving and James Buchanan collected $426.25 for his benefit, and he was immediately taken to a hospital for treatment.[37] Less serious was the collapse of the bridge from Castle Garden to the Battery. A large number of people fell into the water. No one was drowned,

33. Philip Hone, *Diary of Philip Hone, 1828–1851,* with an Introduction by Allan Nevins, 2 vols. (New York: Dodd, Mead and Company, 1927), I, 94–96.

34. New York *Journal of Commerce,* 13 June 1833.

35. Washington *National Intelligencer,* 18 June 1833.

36. Smith, *Major Jack Downing,* p. 216.

37. New York *Albion,* 15 June 1833; *Niles' Weekly Register,* XLIV (27 July 1833), 360.

but one man had his arm broken, and "some got a mortal duck-ing." Among the latter were Lewis Cass and A. J. Donelson.[38]

Seba Smith's Jack Downing, a Democrat favorable to Jackson, says that more than "a hundred folks splashed into the water, all mixed up together one on top of t'other," and that among them were two of Jackson's party, Lewis Cass and Levi Woodbury. The President directed Jack to save both of them but, said he, save Woodbury at all hazards, for "I can't spare him at any rate."[39]

Charles A. Davis's Jack Downing, a Whig and bitter opponent of Jackson, tells a different story. He describes the people going into the water "like frogs, and such an eternal mixing—colonels and captains, and niggers, and governors, and sailors, and all." He says Lewis Cass lost his wig, Governor William Marcy had "his pantaloons rip'd from the waist band clean down to the knee," and Martin Van Buren saved himself by

hanging on the tail of the Gineral's horse, and streaming out behind as straight as old Deacon Willoby's cue when he is a little late to meeting. Some folks said it looked like the "Flying Dutchman." . . . But never mind we snaked him out of that scrape as slick as a whistle.[40]

Jackson's four days in New York were filled to overflowing with parades; parties, both public and private; receptions by men's, women's, and mixed groups; inspections of navy yards and battle-fields; and visits to nearby towns. On his last day, he visited Newark, Paulus Hook, and Elizabethtown, New Jersey, passed in procession over three-fourths of New York City, attended three parties—the mayor's, General Morgan's and one at the Garden —and bowed to upwards of two hundred thousand people. He wrote that he had never before witnessed such a scene of personal regard as he did that day, and "never," wrote he, "has there been such affection before I am sure evinced." And "Party has not been seen here."[41]

38. Washington *Globe,* 17 June 1833.
39. Smith, *Major Jack Downing,* p. 216.
40. Charles A. Davis, *Letters of J. Downing, Major, Downingville Militia, Second Brigade, to His Old Friend, Mr. Dwight, of the New York Daily Advertiser* (New York: Harper & Brothers, 1834) , pp. 13–14.
41. Andrew Jackson to Andrew Jackson, Jr., 14 June 1833, *Correspondence of Andrew Jackson,* V, 109.

Philip Hone was inclined to agree on the sentiment and affection but not on party spirit. He admitted that Jackson was the most popular man the United States had ever produced, but he was not the ablest; John Quincy Adams was twenty times superior to Jackson. But Jackson was the idol of his party and had given the happy toast, "The Union—it must be preserved." This alone had gained him five hundred thousand votes.[42]

Some changes in the personnel of Jackson's party took place in New York. McLane departed for Washington, and Levi Woodbury joined up to accompany the President to New Hampshire. Martin Van Buren likewise accompanied the President the remainder of the trip. Politics were involved in all three cases. Cass wished to strengthen his political fences at home. Woodbury hoped to gain strength by his close association with the President in New England. Van Buren, Jackson's chosen successor, expected to reap the benefits of Jackson's public approval throughout New England.

The President, however, wished to confer with Van Buren in regard to the removal of the Bank deposits. He had written Van Buren from Washington that he wished his opinion on the perplexing subject before he finally acted. Amos Kendall had also written Van Buren, outlining the proposed plan so that Van Buren might be fully forewarned and forearmed.[43] The President discussed with Van Buren "some rough notes" in favor of removal and these, as modified, were incorporated into the paper which Jackson read to his Cabinet on September 18, 1833.[44] Jackson was informed that Van Buren's support of the plan would probably bring William J. Duane, the new Secretary of the Treasury, into the fold.[45] Jackson sent Duane a copy of the revised plan from

42. *Diary of Philip Hone,* I, 96–97.

43. Andrew Jackson to Martin Van Buren, 6 June 1833, *Correspondence of Andrew Jackson,* V, 106–107; Amos Kendall to Martin Van Buren, 9 June 1833, *Correspondence of Andrew Jackson,* V, 107.

44. *The Autobiography of Martin Van Buren,* edited by John C. Fitzpatrick (Washington: Government Printing Office, 1920). *Annual Report* of the American Historical Association for the year 1918 . . . II, 601.

45. Reuben M. Whitney to A. J. Donelson, 10 June 1833, *Correspondence of Andrew Jackson,* V, 129, n. 1.

Boston,[46] but when Duane refused to accept the plan, Jackson summarily dismissed him.

Jackson's trip from New York to Boston was hurried and uneventful. His stops were short and the happenings rarely interesting or significant. The hostile political climate of opinion probably accounts for these conditions. He stopped at Bridgeport for only one hour where, the press reported, "The 'Yankee gals' turned out in great numbers, and were particularly delighted with the 'Hero' of New Orleans."[47] He spent two days in New Haven, where he attended a public meeting at which the mayor and the governor delivered the usual platitudinous welcome addresses. He visited Yale University and on Sunday attended three church services, Episcopal, Methodist, and Presbyterian.[48] At New Haven, he also attended to some personal business. He ordered that his family carriage, now repaired, be sent home, and he purchased a new light vehicle for his own personal use. He expected both to be awaiting him when he returned to Washington.[49]

One new and significant note was injected in Jackson's tour of New England—an enthusiastic support of Jackson's strong stand on nullification. As he entered Norwich, Connecticut, the President was met by a "procession of several hundred ladies, each of whom bore a banner inscribed with the words of the memorable toast—'The Union—it must be preserved.' "[50] This theme was to follow him throughout the remainder of the tour. At Roxbury, Massachusetts, Jonathan Dorr offered a voluntary toast: "And may his powerful arm long remain renewed, who said—'The Union—It Must be Preserved.' "[51] And an Attleborough merchant, displaying cards with buttons stamped with palmetto leaves, badges that had been ordered by South Carolina nullifica-

46. Andrew Jackson to William J. Duane, 26 June 1833, *Correspondence of Andrew Jackson*, V, 111–112.

47. Washington *National Intelligencer*, 20 June 1833.

48. Washington *Globe*, 21 June 1833.

49. *Ibid.;* Andrew Jackson to Andrew Jackson, Jr., 17 June 1833, *Correspondence of Andrew Jackson*, V, 110.

50. Washington *Globe*, 25 June 1833.

51. *Ibid.*, 28 June 1833.

tionists, jokingly told Jackson that, since he had interfered with his business, he should feel in honor bound to take the buttons off his hands. Josiah Quincy, who reported this incident, said that it was Jackson's nullification "proclamation . . . which gave the author the hearty reception he received" in New England.[52] Such sentiments pleased Jackson. As Jack Downing said, the "Gineral was tickled with the Yankees. There is no nullification here . . . says he."[53]

Jackson's stay in Massachusetts consumed more than a third of the time of the entire tour. Because of the lack of strong partisan support of Jackson among the top political figures, the entertainment was much more formal and official and much less enthusiastic and boisterous than in New York and Pennsylvania. There were, however, a number of interesting and significant happenings in Massachusetts. Among them were the issue of Jackson's health, the conferring of an honorary degree on Jackson by Harvard University, the undercover political activities of local Jacksonian leaders, the conflict in political interests of Van Buren and the possible alliance of Webster and Jackson, the inspection of the manufacturing plants in Lowell, and the abrupt ending of the tour.

Josiah Quincy, who had been appointed a special aide-de-camp to Jackson by Governor Levi Lincoln, met the presidential party on the bridge spanning the Pawtucket River, the boundary line between Rhode Island and Massachusetts. The Pawtucket artillery fired such a heavy departing salute that many windows were broken, for which the state paid a goodly bill.[54] Quincy arranged for Jackson to enter Boston on horseback, but "civic etiquette was paramount," and Jackson was forced to dismount and ride into the city in a carriage with the mayor and other dignitaries.[55] The initial reception of the President was consistent with the character of the Boston people. "It was neither uproarious nor sycophantic

52. Josiah Quincy, *Figures of the Past From the Leaves of Old Journals* (Boston: Roberts Brothers, 1883) , p. 354.

53. Smith, *Major Jack Downing*, p. 217.

54. Quincy, *Figures of the Past*, p. 354.

55. *Ibid.,* p. 356.

—nor did it partake of that rude party exclusiveness which has disgraced some other places."[56] The first day was given over to a parade including fire engines, an official welcome by the governor, and a review of the Boston Brigade. The attitude of the people was "liberal and cordial,"[57] that of the authorities "honorable and respectable."[58] There was no mad scramble of handshaking by the President, merely dignified bowing and waving of the hand. Downing complained that the people did not hurrah as they did in New York and that they did "plaguey little talking."[59]

Jackson was escorted by a company of cadets, first, to Faneuil Hall, where he received the people; thence, to the State House, where Governor Lincoln officially welcomed him to Massachusetts and Boston. The Governor discoursed on the state's social, cultural, and economic progress, "not in a spirit of vanity but to show that they—symbols of prosperity and happiness—are the natural fruits of a republican form of government."[60] He assured Jackson that Massachusetts supported him when he had "triumphantly asserted" and maintained "national sovereignty and independence . . . against internal disaffection and disloyalty" in the nullification controversy.[61]

An amusing incident occurred when Jackson reviewed the Boston Brigade. The horse secured for Van Buren by Quincy was unruly and bolted when the artillery began to fire. He finally backed up against a fence which divided the Mall and the Common and refused to move. Jackson returned after taking the salute and inquired, "Where's the Vice-President?" Pointing to Van Buren and the horse, Quincy replied, "About as nearly on the fence as a gentleman of his positive political convictions is likely to get." Jackson laughed heartily and replied, "That's very true and you've matched him with a horse who is even more non-committal than his rider." Van Buren's sensitive partisans

56. *Niles' Weekly Register*, XLIV (29 June 1833), 281.
57. Boston *Atlas*, 22 June 1833.
58. Washington *National Intelligencer*, 27 June 1833.
59. Charles A. Davis, *Letters of Jack Downing*, p. 16.
60. *Niles' Weekly Register*, XLIV (27 July 1833), 360.
61. John Spencer Bassett, "Notes on Jackson's Visit to New England, June 1833," *Proceedings*, LVI (Boston: Massachusetts Historical Society, n.d.), 251–253.

accused Quincy of deliberately planning to put Van Buren in this ridiculous position.[62]

Jackson had been in ill health when he began his tour, and his condition gradually worsened. He consulted the famous Dr. Philip Syng Physic in Philadelphia and found temporary relief, but his condition became serious in Boston. He suffered infection of the throat, bleeding of the lungs, and severe pain in the back. Dr. J. C. Warren, who attended him, bled him profusely and ordered him confined to bed, where he remained for two days. Consequently, Jackson was absent from many functions (Van Buren pinch-hit for him), including the launching of the *Constitution,* and forced the postponement of the award of the Harvard honorary degree and the Bunker Hill celebration. John Quincy Adams, Jackson's implacable enemy, unjustly charged that Jackson was merely malingering. He said that Jackson "was so ravenous of notoriety that he craves sympathy for sickness . . . that is four-fifths trickery, and the other fifth mere fatigue."[63] In truth, Jackson's health became so bad that it forced curtailment of the tour into Maine.[64]

On June 26, Harvard conferred on Andrew Jackson the honorary degree of Doctor of Laws, much to the chagrin of John Quincy Adams and other alumni. This tempest in a teapot has been fully and satisfactorily covered by Andrew McFarland Davis, in the *Proceedings of the Massachusetts Historical Society.*[65] A brief description of the controversy will suffice.

Harvard's President Josiah Quincy felt that the university should follow precedent and award the President of the United States a degree. He consulted John Quincy Adams and asked him to support and to be present when the degree was awarded. Adams declined, saying that as

62. Quincy, *Figures of the Past,* pp. 357–359.

63. John Quincy Adams, *Memoirs of John Quincy Adams, Comprising Portions of His Diary from 1795 to 1848,* edited by Charles Francis Adams (Philadelphia: J. B. Lippincott & Co., 1874–1877), IX, 4–5.

64. *Niles' Weekly Register,* XLIV (5 July 1833), 305; Van Buren, *Autobiography,* p. 602.

65. Andrew McFarland Davis, "Jackson's LL.D.—A Tempest in a Teapot," *Proceedings,* 2d ser., XX (Boston: Massachusetts Historical Society, n.d.), 490–512.

an affectionate child of our Alma Mater, I would not be present to witness her disgrace in conferring her highest literary honors upon a barbarian who could not write a sentence of grammar and hardly could spell his own name.[66]

Quincy admitted that Jackson as a person was unworthy of literary honors but maintained that the university should honor him as the President of the United States, and he persuaded the Board of Overseers to vote the degree.[67]

A part of the exercises were conducted in Latin, which furnished the background for Jack Downing's apocryphal story that Jackson himself spoke some Latin to the audience. Charles A. Davis's Jack Downing has Jackson repeating a long string of Latin phrases.[68] Seba Smith's Jack Downing says that the General was about to close his speech when some wag said, "You must give 'em a little Latin, Doctor. Here he off hat again—'E pluribus unum,' says he, 'My friends, sine qua non.' That'll do, Gineral, says I." Smith declared that "the Gineral can't stomack anything now unless its got Latin in it, ever since they put a Doctor on him down there at Cambridge."[69]

The press entered the controversy, generally choosing sides on the basis of party affiliation, Democrats supporting and Whigs opposing the degree. The editor of the Boston *Atlas* declared that the granting of the degree "was a gratuitous piece of flattery . . . undignified, and uncalled for."[70] He even questioned the legality of the act because of the nature of the ballot. The editor of the *National Intelligencer* could understand "the motives of kindness and hospitality" that prompted the act, but declared it "a gratuitous dispensation of literary honors"[71] that no one could justify. The Boston *Globe* and *Niles' Register* defended the degree on the

---

66. Adams, *Memoirs*, VIII, 546–547.

67. Quincy, *Figures of the Past*, pp. 360–363; Washington *National Intelligencer*, 2 July 1833; Andrew M. Davis, "Jackson's LL. D.—A Tempest in a Teapot," pp. 490–512.

68. Washington *National Intelligencer*, 2 July 1832; Charles A. Davis, *Letters of Jack Downing*, pp. 19, 26; Quincy, *Figures of the Past*, pp. 363, 365.

69. Smith, *Major Jack Downing*, p. 217.

70. Boston *Atlas*, 27 June 1833.

71. Washington *National Intelligencer*, 1, 2 July 1833.

grounds of precedent. They pointed out that English universities granted honorary degrees to political figures and military leaders.[72] These arguments led the *National Intelligencer* to revise its judgment and to defend the degree as merited.[73]

After receiving the LL.D. from Harvard, Jackson moved on to Charlestown for the Bunker Hill celebration. Edward Everett, the orator of the day, frankly told Jackson that the place and occasion were not for adulation and that for Jackson the man there would be not "one word of compliment or flattery." Everett did express approbation for the "firm, resolute and patriotic stand" President Jackson had taken in "the late alarming crisis" in South Carolina, and the rôle he had played "in preserving the happy union under one constitutional head."[74]

Everett's lengthy speech was followed by a two-hour procession around the city and a party afterwards. The speech-making and long tour so fatigued Jackson that he was late for his scheduled appearance at Lynn, where he was too ill to attend the dinner given in his honor. Such also was the case at Marblehead and Salem. The Democrats blamed young Josiah Quincy for the absence of Jackson at the Marblehead dinner, and the local paper warned Quincy "never to show his face again in Marblehead as there is no telling what treatment he might receive at the hands of the enraged people."[75]

A great procession had been planned for Salem, but Jackson was so ill that, upon arrival in the town, he was rushed to his hotel and to bed. Fearing a repetition of the Marblehead incident, Quincy decided to carry on without Jackson. He and Van Buren rode in the presidential carriage. Quincy "rode bolt upright," but Van Buren bowed and acknowledged the applause. Since it was getting dark the crowd never knew that they were not cheering the "Old Hero."[76]

72. Boston *Globe*, 27 June 1833; *Niles' Weekly Register*, XLIV (13 July 1833), 323.

73. Washington *National Intelligencer*, 10 July 1833.

74. *Niles' Weekly Register*, XLIV (6 July 1833), 315.

75. Quincy, *Figures of the Past*, pp. 369, 371.

76. *Ibid.*, pp. 370–371; *Niles' Weekly Register*, XLIV (6 July 1833), 316.

Lowell was a different story. Jackson felt fine and was intensely interested in everything he saw in the city. All the mills were closed and the working girls participated in the parade. Some five thousand, dressed in white with different colored sashes identifying them with the mills for which they worked, marched four abreast. They bore green parasols, which they waved in salute. Jackson expressed a desire to see a mill in operation and one was opened and set going for his benefit. He was so much impressed that, according to Quincy, he talked of little else until they reached the state line the next day. Jackson later wrote that the mills filled him with admiration. They "were perfect, nothing in the world could exceed them." But, said he, "such establishments, conducted with such skill . . . would need no protection."[77]

From Lowell, the presidential party moved on to Portsmouth, New Hampshire. Here it became deeply embroiled in local politics. The Jackson partisans determined to have the exclusive reception of the President to themselves; this "caused a quarrel between them and the other citizens of the place, in consequence of which, the President was disgusted with their feuds, and turned his back upon them all."[78] The local Jackson leaders used their influence to speed the presidential party on to Concord for partisan purposes. The legislature, which had already finished its business, was to be held in session for fifteen days so the Jackson Democrats might receive the President and bask in the limelight of his prestige.[79]

Jackson became disgusted with such flagrant partisan action.[80] He wanted to be President of all the people, not a faction. His reaction to local political feuds, reinforced by his continued illness, caused him to cut short his tour and hurry back to Washington. The original plans for the tour had called for a final reception at Portland, Maine, on July 15, but at Concord, New Hampshire, on July 1, Jackson suddenly turned on his heel and,

77. Washington *National Intelligencer*, 6 July 1833.
78. *Ibid.*
79. *Ibid.*, 2 July 1833.
80. Washington *United States Telegraph*, 15 July 1833; *Niles' Weekly Register*, XLIV (13 July 1833) , 322; Washington *National Intelligencer*, 1 July 1833.

as fast as horse, carriage, and steamboat could carry him, he returned by way of New York and Philadelphia, without letting anyone in those cities know anything about it, and reached Washington on July 4, where his arrival was altogether unexpected and unprepared for. Whether it was a real illness or, as John Quincy Adams said, a combination of crafty sickness and collisions of rival servility between two factions in the Democratic party in Maine and New Hampshire, Jackson's Grand Triumphal Tour of New England ended on a sour note.[81] The extreme Whigs and aristocrats had averted their faces from the President, the people generally had accorded him only the respect due the Chief Magistrate of the nation, his close political friends had received him with great eclat and enthusiasm, and the Democratic mobs had gone wild in their jubilation. In the next elections, the Democratic forces captured Connecticut and Rhode Island and greatly increased their popular vote in Vermont and Massachusetts. The formal, nationalistic presidential tours of Washington and Monroe had been transformed by Jackson into a highly partisan political campaign. Hereafter, Presidents would use the personal tour to build up partisan strength and win political support for administration measures in Congress.

81. Adams, *Memoirs,* IX, 6.

7

Johnny Reb Could Read

"Johnny Reb" is one of two previously unpublished essays to be included in this collection. It was prepared as a paper for the Phi Alpha Theta luncheon held in Washington, D.C., on December 28, 1961, during a meeting of the American Historical Association. After Green returned to Chapel Hill, the manuscript was put aside and temporarily misplaced. Not until the summer of 1968, as Green moved from his campus office after more than thirty years, was this essay found among other papers.

The footnotes documenting it, however, were not found, and every subsequent search for them has proved futile. Despite this lack of accustomed documentation, both editor and publisher felt that the intrinsic merits of this essay have earned it a place in this collection—that withholding it because it lacks footnotes would be serving the uses of pedantry rather than the reader.

In his research, Green used a number of published memoirs and reminiscences of Civil War veterans, but his most important single source for this essay was the diary of Henry Kyd Douglas, a manuscript that he had edited for the University of North Carolina Press and that was published under the title *I Rode With Stonewall* (Chapel Hill: University of North Carolina Press, 1940). Douglas was Assistant Adjutant General on the staff of General "Stonewall" Jackson and, after Jackson's death, served as a staff officer to Generals Edward Johnson, John B. Gordon, Jubal A. Early, John Pegram, and John A. Walker.

J OHNNY REB WAS "'RARIN' FOR A FIGHT'" in the spring of 1861 but he soon found that soldiering was not a continuous fight: it could be, and often was, dull, boring, and monotonous. One Texas Reb wrote, in 1862: "None

can imagine, who has never experienced a soldier's life, the languor
of mind—tediousness of time, as we resume—day after day the
monotonous duties devolved upon." Professor Bell Irvin Wiley
has told us in his delightful and informative book, *The Life of
Johnny Reb,* that

Johnny Reb was, for the most part, a volatile, sociable person; his dis-
position, plus his innate love of fun, caused him to invent all sorts of
escapes from the boredom of camp life. So frequent and varied were
diversions . . . that a considerable number of men seemed to find
more pleasure than hardship in soldiering.

He concludes that music was perhaps the favorite recreation in
the Confederate Army. Other diversions which he mentioned
were sports, including football, baseball, wrestling, and boxing;
moot courts and debating societies; dramatics, minstrels, and the-
atricals; dancing; card-playing and gambling; attendance upon
religious services and revivals; and reading.

In the first glow of patriotism at the outbreak of the Civil War,
wealthy, educated planters and professional men enlisted in local
military organizations and marched in the ranks side by side with
small farmers and laboring men, many of whom were unlearned
and illiterate. Robert Stiles, who held a bachelor of arts degree
from Yale and had studied law at Columbia University, enlisted
in the Confederate Army. He later wrote that

the intellectual atmosphere of the Confederate camps was far above
what is generally supposed by the people of this generation. . . . Few
things have ever impressed me as did the intellectual and moral character of the men in the Richmond Howitzers. . . . To my delight . . .
I found throbbing and intellectual life as high and brilliant and in-
tense as any I had ever known.

Many college-trained men enlisted as private soldiers. In one
company alone there were twenty-eight college graduates, seven of
whom held the M.A. degree from the University of Virginia, and
an additional twenty-five theological students. Among the pri-
vates in the company was Robert E. Lee, Jr. This of course was a
unique company.

Many of these men were later commissioned officers, but a
considerable number chose to serve in the ranks throughout the

war. Among them was Crawford H. Toy, formerly a professor at Harvard University, who was found by one of his comrades, shortly after the battle of Cold Harbor, lying on the ground in his tent studying Arabic. Edwin H. Fay of Alabama, a graduate of Harvard University and a teacher in civilian life, in spite of the entreaties of his wife, who was also a college graduate, chose to serve as an enlisted man to the end of the war. And Frank M. Coker, a college graduate and a banker of Savannah, Ga., wrote his wife from Culpepper Court House in Virginia in 1862 that he had no military aspirations. "I have never tried to go higher than I am [he was a private], and I sometimes regret it on your a/c. Women naturally love title and display, and I doubt not that you would prefer to see me a 'Col.' or a 'Genl.'" Coker, however, preferred to spend his leisure time in reading rather than in working for a promotion. He was at that time reading an article in an unnamed magazine on the Bonaparte family. He made a copy of the article and sent it to his wife.

Intelligent and educated men were not content to spend their free time in frivolous activities. They preferred to engage in meditation or serious discussion, and to read and study. As one twenty-year-old native of Maryland, a graduate of Franklin and Marshall College, wrote his sister:

I've plenty of time for the study of mankind and character and for meditation on the various systems of philosophy I've read of. . . . But I find my principle pleasure in books of which I have as yet always succeeded in getting a supply. God bless the man who first invented books, he was a great benefactor to the race.

Such men read widely and also influenced others to read. Another wrote, "Our ideas of the life and business of the soldier were drawn from the adventures of Ivanhoe and Charles O'Malley, two worthies with whose personal history *almost every man in the army was familiar.*" The last clause in the quotation is highly exaggerated, but it has some significance in regard to widespread reading by Confederate troops. Still another soldier declared: "Books whiled away many weary hours. As Edmond Dantes, in the Count of Monte Cristo, came out from his twelve years of imprisonment 'a very well read man,' we ought to have acquired limitless lore; but reading at last palled upon our tastes, and we would none of it."

What sort of reading did Johnny Reb do, one might ask. The answer is that he read any and every sort of material that came to hand. Some who were wholly illiterate were inspired to learn to read. One colporter who spent one month in the hospitals in Richmond "conversed with hundreds of invalid soldiers and found forty-five who could not read." He gave them McGuffey's *First Readers.* Other illiterate Confederates were started on the road to learning with Webster's *Elementary Spelling Book,* more popularly known as the Blue Back Speller.

Religious literature—the Bible, tracts, and denominational periodicals—was especially popular with Johnny Reb. Many—probably most—soldiers left home with a pocket Testament given them by their loved ones or by the church with which they were affiliated; and, upon arriving in camp, they often joined reading clubs which chiefly utilized religious literature. One minister reported that there was a "very great demand for good reading of all sorts" in these clubs, and that the friends of the soldier could do nothing more acceptable to him than to send him "good books, papers, magazines, etc." Every major sect and several interdenominational bodies responded to this appeal.

The Baptist General Association Board published and distributed, in 1861, 6,095 New Testaments, 13,845 *Camp Hymn Books,* 40 different tracts, the issues of which totaled 6,187,000 pages, and "a large number of religious books." At its peak, this Board published and distributed nearly one million pages weekly. The Virginia Baptist Board, in 1862–1863, distributed 14,000 *Camp Hymn Books,* 31,000 Bibles, several thousand religious books, and some 30,187,000 pages of religious tracts. One Baptist minister, the Reverend W. J. W. Crowder of Norfolk, Va., distributed, between June 1 and September 1, 1861, a total of 1,163,520 pages of nine different tracts. The two most popular tracts were *Come to Jesus* and *A Mother's Parting Words to Her Soldier Boy* by J. B. Jeter. Two hundred and fifty thousand copies of the latter were distributed within one year.

The Methodist Episcopal Church, South, published and distrib-

uted, in 1863, some 15,000,000 pages of tracts, 15,000 *Soldiers'*
Almanacs, 45,000 Bibles, 50,000 *Hymn Books,* and two papers,
The Soldiers' Paper in Richmond, Va., with 50,000 copies and
The Army and Navy Herald in Macon, Ga., with 20,000 copies.

The Raleigh, N.C., Episcopal Committee published and distributed 20,000,000 pages of thirty different tracts. The Virginia
Sunday School Board distributed more than 30,000,000 pages of
tracts and the Petersburg, Va., Evangelical Tract Society published and distributed *The Army and Navy Messenger* and some
50,000,000 pages of 100 different tracts.

The American Bible Society contributed $100,000 to religious
publications in the South and distributed 150,000 tracts in the
Southwest. The British and Foreign Bible Society contributed
£3,000 and gave the Reverend Moses D. Hoge of Virginia 10,000
Bibles, 50,000 New Testaments, 250,000 tracts, and "many valuable religious books" to be distributed in the Confederacy. These
figures are stupendous. It must have been of this religious literature the soldier was thinking, when he said that "reading at last
palled upon our taste and we would have no more of it."

In addition to the above publications, J. W. Jones lists in his
Christ in Camp twenty-two religious and seven secular newspapers which the various church organizations circulated throughout the Confederate Army.

Newspapers were very popular with Johnny Reb, but frequent
movements of the armies and poor mail service made their delivery uncertain. Even so, many soldiers subscribed for their home-
town or state paper, read it avidly whenever they received it, and
then passed it on to their friends and comrades. From the newspapers, they kept abreast of what was going on at home and of the
general trend of military events. One young lieutenant made
frequent reference to war news he gathered from three Virginia
and two New York newspapers. Confederates welcomed Yankee
newspapers. They came by these infrequently by picking them up
on the battlefield or by exchange with Billy Yank. While encamped on opposite sides of the Rappahannock River in 1863,
Johnny and Billy worked out an exchange of southern tobacco for
northern newspapers. The Yanks sent the papers across the river

in miniature sail boats and Johnny Reb swam the river pushing a plank with a box of tobacco upon it. The Yanks then loaded the improvised raft with sugar, coffee, lemons, and candy as a bonus. Marcus C. Toney, a Tennessee private, reports that, while the rival armies were encamped on the Rapidan River, a Yankee soldier called to him, " 'How would you like a New York *Herald* . . . ?' I told him I would like very much to see it, as we did not get many papers now, and the ones received were printed on the reverse side of wall paper." The exchange was made.

On one occasion, a Yankee soldier received a number of southern newspapers containing extracts from northern Democratic papers denouncing President Abraham Lincoln and voicing Copperhead sentiments. He wrote that "our friends at home should not give such aid and comfort to the enemy." He feared it would mean that the northern soldiers would have to fight all the harder to win the war.

Among the southern newspapers often mentioned by Johnny Reb were the Richmond, Va., *Examiner,* described by one as "a partisan paper" and by another as "very brilliantly edited"; the Richmond, Va., *Whig, Dispatch, Sentinel,* and *Enquirer;* the Mobile, Ala., *Evening News;* and the Memphis, Tenn., *Appeal.* The northern papers most often mentioned were the New York *Herald* and the *World.* The individual soldier generally preferred a local home-town paper, or at least a home-state paper. For instance, Private Ike Hermann of Sandersville, Ga., subscribed to the Sandersville *Georgian.* And he placed advertisements in it for flour, chickens, butter, eggs, and potatoes—sweet potatoes, that is —which he had been authorized to purchase for an Atlanta hospital.

Since most soldiers were unable to get their home-town paper, they began to publish camp newspapers. Among these were *The Pioneer Banner, The Rapid Ann,* and *The Western Pioneer.* Probably best known was *The Vidette,* published irregularly by soldiers in John Hunt Morgan's command in 1862 and 1863. Its publication was uncertain and its circulation was limited, but "it afforded great entertainment to its publishers and their comrades" and to citizens in the vicinity. It had, at times, a number of brilliant young writers on its staff. Its articles never admitted the possibility of defeat and often "announced Confederate victories before they had occurred." It discussed political issues both Union and Confederate "and gave advice to both governments."

Such periodicals as *DeBow's Review, Southern Field and Fireside, The Southern Illustrated News, The Southern Literary Messenger,* and *Harper's Weekly* were eagerly read by the Confederate troops whenever they could be obtained.

Some ambitious soldiers sought reading matter which they hoped would be beneficial to their military advancement. One wrote:

I have commenced a course of military study today—for the present my textbooks are Hardee's *Infantry Tactics,* Mahan's *Field Fortifications* and *The Army Regulations.* I shall try to familiarize myself with them and then take others, such as Artillery, Ordnance, and I must also get Mahan's *Permanent Fortifications* which has just been published in Richmond—it was never before published.

Incidentally, this soldier later became a colonel. Other such studies were William Gilman, *Manual of Instruction;* Henry L. Scott, *Military Dictionary;* and Sallie R. Ford, *Morgan and His Men.* One reader characterized the last-named book as "wishy washy."

Those who had been lawyers or who looked forward to becoming lawyers read and discussed Vattel's *Law of Nations* and Philmore's *International Law.* Teachers and college professors studied French and German and read the Latin and Greek classics.

Most soldiers, however, read for pleasure, entertainment, and relaxation. Their tastes led them to history and biography, fiction, particularly romantic and historical novels, detective stories, and poetry. One soldier in camp near Sharpsburg in 1863 observed:

Now, if there be anything which the soldier needs in camp or bivouac, it is something to read. . . . At such a time the men need, as never so much before, books of a cheerful and moderately-exciting character, strong, bracing stories like . . . the wonderful character pieces of Charles Dickens, and those choice productions of our American authors.

Popular histories were Rollin's *Ancient History,* which one soldier said he "enjoyed very much," Thiers's *French Revolution,* in which the Confederates saw something of their own conflict, and Arthur L. J. Freemantle's *Three Months in the Southern States* (1863). The latter, favorably disposed toward the Confederacy, was immensely popular, and was reprinted in Mobile, Ala. David Hunter Strother, a Virginian who cast his lot with the Union and aided his northern cousin, General David Hunter, in his raids in the Valley of Virginia, observed that Freemantle "was evidently permeated with Southern views," but he grudgingly conceded that the account of the battle of Gettysburg was "graphic and penetrating."

A large number of American authors was read by Johnny Reb. A very incomplete list would include Joseph Glover Baldwin, *Flush Times in Alabama and Mississippi;* Augustus Baldwin Longstreet, *Georgia Scenes;* Edwin A. Pollard, *A History of the Civil War;* Carolyn Lee Hentz, *The Southern Planter's Northern Bride;* Harriett Beecher Stowe, *Uncle Tom's Cabin;* Nathaniel Beverley Tucker, *The Partisan Leader;* John P. Kennedy, *Swallow Barn;* David Hunter Strother [pseud., "Porte Crayon"], *Virginia Illustrated;* Augusta Jane Evans Wilson, *Mecaria;* and W. P. Craighill, *The Army Officers' Pocket Companion.* The evaluation of some of those books by the readers is both interesting and instructive.

The language in Hentz's book was pronounced "beautiful and the characters were well drawn except one or two," and the reader "dreamed away 40 hours over the book." A Mississippi boy spent "all day coughing and reading that damned Yankee lie *Uncle Tom's Cabin.*" When Nathaniel P. Craighill, a Virginia farmer, was handed his son's book without being told the author's name, he turned to the title page, and reading the name "changed color and shook with emotion. . . . his wife . . . looked at it a moment, then burst into tears." Craighill told the soldier who presented him the book that his son, a Union officer, "has three brothers in the other army. You must excuse the mother's weakness."

Governor Shepley of Louisiana discussed Nathaniel Beverley Tucker's *The Partisan Leader* with a Virginia soldier, and pronounced it "a prophetic book." He remarked how much more farseeing southern statesmen were than the northern. The soldier replied, "The truth is that the Northern people were too busy getting rich to study statesmanship."

David Hunter Strother, a Virginia Union soldier, was introduced to two Virginia ladies, owners of a plantation home. Said he:

> They had my book *Virginia Illustrated* and professed themselves admirers of my literature. But while they were doing the amenities, the Union soldiers got into the house and commenced to plunder . . . [the ladies'] trunks and bureaus. In the confusion, I mounted my horse and escaped.

One soldier said of Mrs. Wilson's *Mecaria,* "I like it very well—Russell Aubrey is well painted—Irene Huntingdon is magnificent—Electra Gay I don't like very much—Dr. Arnold is the good man of the story—he and Harvey the preacher." Another soldier, reading the same book, pronounced the characters insipid, the book not worth reading.

Many other American writers were read and mentioned by name but the titles of their books were not given. Among them were James Fenimore Cooper, Edgar Allan Poe, William Gilmore Simms, and Charles H. Smith, better known as a writer by his pen name, Bill Arp. It is interesting to note that David Hunter Strother, the soldier—author of several well-known books—reported a conference with Thomas Bangs Thorpe in New Orleans but made no reference to Thorpe's authorship of *The Big Bear of Arkansas* or to any of his other books.

Johnny Reb read much more of English, French, and German than of American authors. Scott, Bulwer-Lytton, Dickens, Thackeray, and Lady Emma Stuart-Wortley of the English; Victor Hugo and Alexandre Dumas of the French; and Mulbach, the German, were the most popular of the romantic novelists. Macaulay and Thiers were popular historians; and Byron, Shakespeare, Shelley, and Tennyson were the most popular dramatists and poets. All of these names appear over and over again in the Civil War diaries. Wilkie Collins was a very popular writer of detective stories.

Many less well-known names appear frequently in soldiers'

reading lists. One private read Osborn S. Fowler, *Phrenology Proved, Illustrated and Applied.* Sergeant Fay read Jules Michelet's *L'Amour,* which he assured his wife was "not an immoral book. I did not think so when I read it, nor do I think you will consider it so." Young Randolph McKim thought that the author of *Evelina* (Madame d'Aublay) portrayed "the simple truth in her deliniation of character. And the exalted morality of the book struck me with great force, even while ignorant of the literary period in which she wrote, when novels were generally vicious and always indelicate." He felt that Macaulay was unfair in his criticism of the author in denying her first rank among English authors.

The sources from which Johnny Reb drew his reading materials were manifold. Much of his religious literature was distributed by chaplains and colporters on the battlefields, in camps and in hospitals. The Soldiers' Library connected with the Lynchburg, Va., Hospital, supported by friends in all the Confederate states, contained eight hundred volumes of religious and miscellaneous books, a large number of tracts and pamphlets, files of religious newspapers published in the South, and files of several secular newspapers. The library was open on a regular daily schedule, and "hundreds of applicants were daily served from it." The Charlottesville Hospital Library contained files of five religious periodicals. The librarian reported that "Every Georgian wanted *The Index* [published in Macon, Ga.] and so of other soldiers: each wants to see a paper from *his own dear state.*"

Much reading matter came to soldiers by way of prison camps. One correspondent reported that "a mania for study" had begun at Libby in July 1863: "Classes were formed in Greek, Latin, German, French, Spanish, algebra, geometry, and rhetoric." Text books were obtained from the Richmond stores. The chaplain at Castle Thunder, a Presbyterian, "scattered documents every Sunday." The guards and Confederate soldiers in the vicinity of the prisons were permitted to share in these programs. Luke Blackmer of Salisbury, N.C., "placed his library of several thousand volumes" at the service of both Confederate soldiers and Yankee prisoners.

John Allan Wyth, a Confederate soldier incarcerated in Camp Morton at Indianapolis, Ind., reported that relatives and friends in both the Confederacy and the Union generously supplied him with books and newspapers; and, said he, "Many an hour in those days of desolation was utilized in reading, and especially in studying French." Someone sent Wyth a French grammar and he "almost learned it by heart." He also "read the Bible through three times while there." Wyth enjoyed especially the opportunity to read the Louisville, Ky., *Journal* while in prison. After being parolled, Wyth passed through Salisbury, N.C., where he had the pleasure of meeting William Tappan Thompson, author of *Major Jones' Courtship,* and discussing the book with him. He had read the book so carefully that he was able to quote long passages from it for Thompson.

Henry Kyd Douglas was another Confederate who was supplied ample reading material while a prisoner of war. He reported reading a large number of books, including five in French, two in German, and one in Latin, while at Johnson's Island and Fort Delaware. Some of the books, he purchased; some were sent by friends and relatives in both the North and the South; and some were supplied by prison authorities. From Point Lookout, he wrote that the Provost Marshal's wife and sister, "being Southern women . . . saw no harm in furnishing me books." Finally, after trial, conviction, and incarceration in Fort Delaware, he wrote his sister: "As I have the privilege of an excellent library, I spend my time with books as pleasantly as can be expected. I was given free access to the Fort Library, in which I read many books."

One Confederate, however, reported that he was denied all reading matter, both books and newspapers, "except now and then a Bible or a Testament," while in a northern prison.

On the contrary, Basil Duke wrote that "Many Confederate prisoners devoted themselves to really serious and profitable study. It was quite common for men previously entirely ignorant" of French and German "to acquire a tolerably good acquaintance with those languages." And "those who could afford to buy books might pursue almost any branch of knowledge they chose." He concluded, however, that some "preferred the dime novel."

Soldiers stationed in the vicinity of plantation homes found the owners happy to share their books. One soldier, camped near Fredericksburg for six months in 1863, borrowed more than fifty volumes from the library of Moss Neck plantation, the home of Richard Corbin, a private in General Lee's army. In the library "were shelves of books of all kinds, except military, and of all ages and languages, legal, medical, scientific, and agricultural, books for sportsmen and horsemen, and ladies' magazines." Among the books the soldier borrowed and read were "Tennyson, Browning, Ossian, Shakespeare, Thackeray, Dickens, and a cart load of novels." The same soldier borrowed thirty-odd volumes from Mt. Airy, and the neighboring plantation of Dr. Andrew S. Meem.

As the northern armies overran the South, Billy Yank had no hesitancy in taking books from private homes. One Yank reported finding John P. Kennedy's *Swallow Barn*, Porte Crayon's *Virginia Illustrated,* and copies of *Harper's Magazine* in one Virginia farmer's home. Another found in a farmer's home a biography of Rufus Choate which he took and sat up until after midnight reading.

Soldiers purchased books, read them, and then passed them on to their comrades. The diary of one Virginia soldier records two purchases in Richmond and an order on Livermore and Company in New York City. George Cary Eggleston bought in Charleston, S.C., Owen Meredith's *Tannhauser,* bound in coarse wallpaper, for which he paid $7.00, and a set of Dickens's *Works,* well printed and bound in black cloth for $4.00 per volume.

Some soldiers brought books from their homes. Randolph H. McKim, a nineteen-year-old soldier of Virginia, was one who did so. Among the books he reported reading in the fall and winter of 1861–1862 were a life of Spencer, Spencer's *Works,* Madame d'Aublay's *Evelina,* Macaulay's *Essay on d'Aublay,* Carlyle's *Heroes and Hero-Worship,* and Humbolt's *Travels.* McKim sent to the University of Virginia for his "books among them some nice editions of the classics that belonged long ago to my father,—only to lose them all when we suddenly broke camp in the spring."

Johnny Reb was able to pick up books discarded by his comrades or his enemy on the battlefield or along the line of retreat.

For example, after the battle of Malvern Hill in 1862, General "Stonewall" Jackson asked for a novel to read. He was handed "a yellow backed novel of the sensational type that had been picked up on the battlefield." After reading it, he said that it had been a long time since he had read a novel and it would be a longer time before he read another. Finally, it might be noted that soldiers in transit from one station to another or on furlough might be given reading material at the Wayside Inns set up by women to care for soldiers who were sick or in need. Women also served in hospitals as nurses' aides and read to the sick and wounded soldiers. In spite of all this support, there were many complaints from Confederate soldiers of the lack of adequate reading material. There were some squeamish, self-righteous Johnny Rebs who urged others not to read books which, to their limited vision, were immoral. One of this group, a Mississippian, took firm ground on this matter. Said he:

> If you can't get good books to read do not read any. any composition of fiction falsehoods calculated to excite the mind, to a great extent should not be read by anyone. I have seen too many brilliant minds of young men almost ruined, just in this way, during the war. One of my mess who had an excelant mind, read novals a long time. he conclded a short time ago to study grammar if i would instruct him & of cors i could not refuse, but it is the hardest work i ever saw for him to keep his mind on it. he is a gorgian.

Fortunately, his ilk was a small minority in the ranks, and there was a great deal of reading done by Confederate soldiers. Two case studies will suffice to illustrate individual reading.

An Alabama sergeant read and evaluated four novels, a minister's memoirs, four poetry items, one Latin book, three magazines, and read ten different newspapers published in Alabama, Tennessee, Mississippi, and Louisiana. A Tennessee soldier, whose unpublished diary of the war is in the Southern Historical Collection at the University of North Carolina, lists the titles of twenty books he read. He gives critical evaluations of most of these books —including ten novels, four of which were by Bulwer-Lytton; five books on military science; two French books; and three histories. Of Thiers's *French Revolution,* he says:

Today I read the death of Danton—in Thiers Revolution. What a wonderful man himself—well did he say "I go into the Pantheon of History." When one has such rivals as he—was it well to say "I would rather be guillotined than to guillotine?" I am inclined to believe that we in our revolution have been entirely too mild—too many traitors in words and deeds, both now walk the earth free and untrammeled—it looks as if we doubted our own cause when we are so loath to spill blood. Let the guilty die.

Henry Kyd Douglas, born in Shepherdstown, Va., September 29, 1840, attended Franklin and Marshall College in Pennsylvania, and had begun a legal career in St. Louis, Mo. When news that his native state had seceded reached him in St. Louis, he hurried home, enlisted as a private in the Second Virginia Infantry, and served throughout the war. He was severely wounded at Gettysburg, was captured and remained in prison until exchanged, March 18, 1864. Douglas read more widely during the war than any soldier I know. His diary lists more than two hundred books which he read between December 11, 1862, and February 25, 1865. He recorded his views of and reactions to many of these books. In addition, there are scores of references to books which he did not identify by author or title.

Douglas had a catholic interest, as shown by the wide range of his reading. He read the Bible and other religious literature; military science and tactics; periodicals and the daily press; history and biography; government and politics; Latin, French, and German books; humorous essays and literary criticism; and poetry and fiction.

On December 11, 1862, he wrote: "I always finish the day by reading several chapters of the New Testament." Three days later, after a hard day's battle and a reprimand from his officer, he wrote: "I am almost too weak to write—at least coherently—tonight—so I will stop, and read some in the Testament in Job on patience. . . ."

It was, of course, natural that Douglas would read in military science. His "Diary" discloses that he used at least six books in this field and that he read and studied them over and over again. Five of those Douglas used were pirated editions of works written for and used by the United States Army.

Douglas kept up with current news in three Richmond, Va., papers: the *Dispatch,* the *Sentinel,* and the *Whig.* He subscribed regularly for the *Dispatch,* paying for it twenty cents per copy. He secured northern papers quite often, picking some of them up on the battlefield, and reading others brought to headquarters by visitors. He often mentioned the New York *World,* "Northern papers," "Yankee papers," and "New York papers" in his letters and diary. Douglas also read *Harper's Weekly.*

Douglas had a deep and abiding interest in history and biography. During the war, he read Markinfield Addey, *Stonewall Jackson, The Life and Military Career of Thomas Jonathan Jackson, Lieutenant General in the Confederate Army* (1863). He "found it readable although very full of gross errors. It praises him very highly, but the author does not understand the character of his hero." Other northerners knew little more of Jackson than Addey, according to Douglas. At Johnson's Island, Douglas spent his "time principally in reading, and contradicting, explaining or confirming many rumors with regard to my lost chief—General Stonewall Jackson. It is very amusing to hear the various ideas they have of him. Observations of this kind have been a source of much entertainment to me." Douglas read John S. C. Abbott, *History of Napoleon Bonaparte,* 2 vols.; *Napoleon and his Maxims;* Count Philippe Paul de Segur, *Histoire de Napoléon et de Grande Armée pendant l'Annee 1812,* 2 vols.; Samuel M. Schmucker, *The Public and Private History of Louis Napoleon the Third, Emperor of the French; with Biographical Notices of his Most Distinguished Ministers, Generals, Relatives and Favorites, and a Narrative of the Events of the War in Italy* (1859); Sir Jonah Barrington, *Personal Sketches of His Own Times* (1853); and Joseph G. Baldwin, *Flush Times in Alabama and Mississippi, a Series of Sketches* (1853).

In the field of government and politics, Douglas read President Jefferson Davis's *Messages* and *Proclamations* and Robert M. T. Hunter's *Speeches* in the Confederate Congress. He found the President's *Message,* published January 15, 1863, "a firm, dignified and able document." Davis's *"Proclamation* declaring that General Benjamin Beast Butler and his commissioned officers, if

taken shall not be treated as prisoners of war but shall be exe-
cuted—in retaliation for the unheard of atrocities that scoundrel
has been committing in New Orleans" was a most satisfying one
to Douglas.

Among foreign languages, Douglas read French, German, and
Latin. He read at least five volumes in French. The foreign
language reading, except Latin, was done while in prison at
Johnson's Island and Fort Delaware. This would indicate that he
was driven to this type of reading while in prison or else was
unable to secure it when in the Confederacy. Douglas read Horace while in camp, as well as in prison. On one occasion, he
mentions having his own copy of *Satires,* and, on another, he tells
of proving the *pons asinorum* from books borrowed from his
friends.

Douglas read the more solid works in literary criticism when
nothing else was available. On February 5, 1863, he began Hugh
Blair's *Lectures on Rhetoric,* but soon grew tired of it and turned
to a sentimental novel, *Cyrilla,* by the Baroness I. Taulphoeus,
which he reread and declared a "very good book" to be written
"by a woman." Several volumes of Leigh Hunt's writings, including *Antiquity; Autobiography,* 2 vols.; *Selections from English
Poets; Recollections of English Authors;* and *Imagination and
Fancy,* were read. It is interesting to note that every entry about
Hunt mentions "a nice toddy of which I cheerfully partook," or a
"bottle of fine whiskey" that added to the enjoyment of the
criticism. Much of Shakespeare was read at different times but
elicited no comment. Charles Lamb's *Essays,* however, were
highly commended.

Douglas was inordinately fond of poetry. He himself wrote
poems while in prison at Johnson's Island, and he often exchanged original verse with Mrs. Richard Corbin of Moss Neck
Plantation. He read, and reread three times, Elizabeth Barrett
Browning's *Poems.* Other English poets who claimed his attention
were Oman, Ossian, Thomas Moore, Robert Browning, and
Owen Meredith (Edward Robert Bulwer-Lytton) whose *Tannhauser* was first published in America by S. H. Goetzel of Mobile,
Ala., in 1863. But Alfred Lord Tennyson was Douglas's favorite

poet. He read him over and over again, whether in the Valley, at Moss Neck, at Johnson's Island, at Fort Delaware, or in the hospital at Baltimore.

On January 1, 1863, Douglas wrote in his "Diary":

Tonight I have been reading . . . Death of the Old Year (Tennyson) which I think the most beautiful poem on the subject I've ever seen. I wanted it last night. But I hope the complaint that the old year

> Give me a friend and a true, true love
> And the New Year will take 'em away

will not prove true in my case.

Three days later, he wrote:

Tennyson is my favorite poet, but I was struck tonight with the great truth and force of some passages which never attracted me particularly before the war. The beauty of poetry is appreciated only by those who happen to read it in the right time, place, and under the right circumstances. For this reason many passages which have cost the author most thought are least approved, because not read at the right time.

It was light sentimental fiction and the romantic English novel which claimed most of Douglas's time and attention, however. He read well over one hundred books of fiction. Of these, ninety-three were by English, twenty-five by American, and six by French authors. Among the better known English authors read by Douglas were Sir Walter Scott, Bulwer-Lytton (Edward George Earle Lytton) , Charles Dickens, Charlotte Bronte, Daniel Defoe, George Eliot, and William Makepeace Thackeray. Bulwer-Lytton led the list in number of volumes, with twenty-six; Scott follows, with twenty-one; Dickens, eight; Baroness I. Taulphoeus, five; Mrs. Ann Radcliffe, four; Thackeray and Miss Julia Pardoe, three each. Among the better known American authors Douglas read were James Fenimore Cooper, Edgar Allan Poe, Nathaniel Hawthorne, Nathaniel Beverly Tucker, William Gilmore Simms, and Mrs. Augusta Jane Wilson. Cooper led the list, with three, and Hawthorne and Wilson followed with two volumes each. Victor Hugo, Alain Rene LeSage, and Count Philippe Paul de Segur represent the French authors.

The quantitative distribution of Douglas's reading and his comments and critical evaluation of the authors and their works lend support to the view that educated southerners read chiefly from the English romantic school of writers. Douglas reread several of the Bulwer-Lytton novels. Among these were the four volumes, *What Will He Do With It?*, *Pelham*, *The Caxtons*, and *My Novel*. On March 24, 1863, Douglas wrote in his "Diary" that he had just begun to read *My Novel:* "Just one year ago I commenced it at Rudes Hill, in the Valley, but after reading half of it, we moved and the book was left behind. I hope I shall have an opportunity to finish it" this time. Five days later, on Sunday, he wrote: "I did not attend church as is my wont and duty. But I read some of *My Novel* much against my usual practice on such days." And then, as if to salve his conscience, he added: "I read in the Bible." His hope that he might be able to finish the book was fulfilled. April 1, 1863, he wrote: "Tonight 1:30 o'clock just finished *My Novel*." He then added: *"My Novel* is a Superior book of its kind. . . .—One of the best books I ever read." Eight days later, he finished Bulwer's *Pelham*, which he found "interesting, and a book of some genius." *The Caxtons* brought forth the laconic comment, "good book." Most of Bulwer's works were read in the winter and spring of 1863, when Douglas was largely free from military activity, and when he was out almost every night with some of the belles of the Fredericksburg neighborhood. This may account for the cryptic entry in his "Diary" of April 9, 1863:

Tonight I read *Falkland* (Bulwer) and I like it because I could appreciate it peculiarly at this time. Dear Posterity you will never know, I hope, why the story of *Falkland* should be long remembered by your ancestor; for I hope it has kept him from sinning a great sin.

Douglas enjoyed Scott's *Castle Dangerous* because it gave "a history of the house of Douglas, with a vein of romance (running) through it." The *Tales of a Grandfather, Being the History of Scotland from the Earliest Period to the Close of the Revolution 1745–46* in three volumes, Douglas found "very interesting," both because of his love of history and of his fondness of Scott. *Heart of Midlothian*, however, he thought was Scott's best. Douglas's "Recollections" are filled with quotations from and literary allusions to Scott's numerous books. He seems to have mastered the language and thought of Scott.

Douglas made few comments upon Dickens's works. He read *"Dombey and Son, David Copperfield,* and *Russell (James)"* on three successive days. *A Tale of Two Cities* and *Little Dorritt* he found were "light literature enough for some time." *Fair Maid of Perth* and *Little Dorritt* were both pronounced "first rate" books. Douglas's "Recollections" are packed with allusions to Dickens's characters.

Of the less known English writers, William Wilkie Collins and John Cardy Jeaffreson pleased Douglas most. He read Collins's *Woman in White* twice; the first time he found it "thrilling," the second, an "intensely absorbing book." Two days after the second reading of *Woman in White,* he read *The Dead Secret,* by the same author, but found it a "poor book." Jeaffreson's *Not Dead Yet,* read twice, had not only a "suggestive title" but also, for one engaged in a sanguinary conflict, was "a book that interested me (Douglas) very much."

Somehow, in spite of Douglas's love of women, he did not like their books. Charlotte Bronte "was a forceful writer for a woman, but I do not like the way *Villette* ends. It is otherwise an objectionable book." Mrs. Ann Radcliffe's *Mysteries of Udolpho, a Romance; Intersperced With Some Pieces of Poetry,* in four volumes, was "read hastily through" and found to be a very "mean book." Miss M. E. Braddon's *The Outcasts; or The Brand of Society* was found "uninteresting" and her *Eleanor's Victory: A Novel* was read through hurriedly. Augusta Jane Wilson's *Mecaria, or Altars of Sacrifice,* Douglas "read hurriedly but did not admire it." Julia Pardoe's *Wife's Trials, a Novel,* in three volumes, and Dinah Maria Muloch's *John Halifax, Gentleman,* were read, the second twice, but brought forth no comment. One woman, however, did win Douglas's warm praise. She was Baroness I. Taulphoeus. Douglas read three of her books, *Cyrilla, Initials,* and *Quits* twice each. They were pronounced a "good book," a "first rate book," and a "very good book," respectively. Each comment, however, was qualified by the statement, "to have been written by a woman."

Two anonymous English books attracted Douglas's attention. *Light and Darkness; or, The Shadow of Fate* he condemned as "a book that should be burned as it can have no effect, but a bad one." *Sword and Gown,* however, was "well written and at this time and under the circumstances interesting to me."

American authors won scant praise from Douglas. Poe and Simms were not even commented upon. Though he read three of Cooper's novels, only *The Last of the Mohicans* aroused much interest, and that only "towards the end."

Three books involving the sectional controversy were read by Douglas. Judge Nathaniel Beverly Tucker's *The Partisan Leader,* first published in 1836 by Duff Green under the pseudonym Edward William Sidney and reputedly suppressed, was republished in 1861 in the North as *A Key to the Disunion Conspiracy.* Douglas read it in 1863 and wrote: "Looked at as a book written so long ago it seems like prophecy on the prediction of the present Revolution and many of the incipient acts and present circumstances. (It is) . . . an apotheosis of the war. It is only interesting in that light—not as a novel."

Two books written in 1863, one by a Union soldier and the other by a Confederate, were read within a very few months after their publication. *Clarimonde: A Tale of New Orleans Life and of the Present War,* written by a member of the New Orleans Washington Artillery, Douglas found "unsatisfying." And *Shoulder Straps, A Novel of New York and the Army,* written by Henry Morford, a soldier of the Army of the Potomac, Douglas wrote his sister was "not worth reading."

One American book, Frank E. Smedley's *Frank Fairleigh: or, Scenes in the Life of a Private Pupil,* Douglas enjoyed immensely. Writing to his sister from Johnson's Island on October 13, 1863, and lamenting the fact that he had no female companionship in the prison, he said:

Indeed if some arrangements for Exchange are not soon made I shall be as ignorant of the sex as George Lawless was. Do you remember George the gay youth we read of in the book *Frank Fairleigh* over which you took such a hearty laugh several years ago? Well I have just read it over again and gave myself pains in the side by laughing so incessantly.

Douglas thoroughly enjoyed the French authors. Of Santaine's and Dubuc's *Picciola,* he wrote: it is "a good book, a very good book, but not the kind one, or at least I like to read in Camp." But he goes into rhapsodies over Victor Hugo. Hear him:

I was furnished with books, too, light and interesting, and one day a young gentleman, Mr. Samuel M. Smucker . . . brought me *Les Miserables* (popularly called "Lee's Miserables" by the Confederate troops) . It was just what I wanted in that place—plenty of reading for plenty of time, full of war and of love, full of wit, wisdom, everything; never before nor since have I ever enjoyed a book so much. It was translated, I remember, by a lady from Savannah, Georgia, during the war and being admirably done, was reprinted in the North. Anyone who has read it can well understand what a treat it would be at such a time and in such a place.

It might be noted that the time was July 15, 1863, and the place the Mercersburg Theological Seminary Hospital. Douglas had been severely wounded on July 3 at the battle of Gettysburg and was a prisoner in the hospital.

Considering the difficulties in securing reading materials, Johnny Reb did a remarkable amount of reading during the Civil War. He read more and better books than did his counterpart during World War I, if my memory serves me correctly. Of course, the Yanks in France had more interesting diversions than did Johnny. And a cursory sampling of published diaries and reminiscences of Union soldiers of the 1860s leads me to conclude that there was a great similarity in the reading habits of Billy Yank and Johnny Reb. They secured their reading materials from similar sources, although more publishing houses, bigger libraries, and better transportation and postal facilities made it easier for Billy than Johnny to acquire books. Even so, if one compares them, man for man—the well-educated with the well-educated, the poorly-educated with the poorly-educated, and the ignorant with the ignorant—Reb and Yank read about an equal number of books, read the same sorts of materials, in fact the same books, except that Johnny read more southern authors and newspapers than did Billy, and Billy read more northern books and papers; and their reactions and responses to what they read, except, again, in regard to books that dealt with North and South or the sectional conflict, were similar. [Examples: *Uncle Tom's Cabin* and Fremantle, *Three Months in the Southern States.*] Most of their reading was done in the general field of literature, English and French novelists and poets, where there could be little sectional application. Finally, it should be noted that there was a higher percentage of illiteracy in the South than in the North. Hence, there were more Johnny Rebs who could not read than Billy Yanks.

8

Higher Education of Women in the South Prior to 1860

This paper was read on July 25, 1962, in Farmville, Virginia, at the Institute for Southern Culture of Longwood College. This is its first appearance in print.

Education of women in the United States has been so exhaustively studied and written about that one might conclude that little or nothing remains to be said on the subject. One distinguished author, writing in 1959, noted that library catalogues contained some three hundred entries under "Women's Education," and that the subject claimed a special number under the Dewey classification system.[1] Much of this literature, however, bears the earmark of sectional interest, special pleading, and controversial claims. Southern writers have been prone to make exorbitant claims about the number, size, and quality of their colleges, and to emphasize firsts for the South; northern writers have discounted southern claims and pointed out that many of the "female colleges" in the Old South were not colleges, in fact —that the instruction given therein was inferior to that given in northern "female" institutions, and that none of the "female" colleges gave courses of study equal to that given in the men's colleges. And they counter with the statement that Oberlin College was the first degree-granting college to admit women, and that Vassar was the first women's college to give instruction of the same quality as that offered in the men's colleges.[2]

1. Mabel Newcomer, *A Century of Higher Education for American Women* (New York: Harper and Brothers, 1959) , p. 1.
2. See, for example, Thomas Woody, *A History of Women's Education in the United States*, 2 vols. (New York: The Science Press, 1929) , II, 161–167, 171–173 (hereafter, *Women's Education in the U. S.*) .

199

One writer has charged that some sections of the United States refused to allow girls "to attend any but the common or district school" until "the first half of the nineteenth century was well-nigh passed." In those sections, women "fought for every step of the way toward the recognition of the right to educational advantages equal to those provided for men." But such, says she, "was never the case in the South; for in every part of the South, from its earliest settlement, men recognized their obligations to their daughters as well as to their sons, and schools for girls were established all over the South as soon as conditions would warrant their maintenance."[3] She wrote a book to prove her assertions, and many southerners have accepted her position without questioning its validity.

As a matter of fact, the development of higher education for women ran a parallel course in the two sections. There was general opposition to formal education for women in both North and South until about 1800. Prior to that time, colleges were designed to train men for the professions—clergymen, lawyers, doctors—and for politics and government service. Since women were barred from all these positions, there was no need to give them college training. Women of the upper social and economic classes in the South received their education from governesses and were trained to manage their homes. Occasionally, they might attend classes in Latin, Greek, mathematics, and government taught by tutors hired to teach their brothers; and they might attend a private school where French, painting, needlework, music, and dancing were taught as a preparation for social life. The great majority of girls in the middle and lower classes grew up ignorant and illiterate, barely able to read and write. And many in fact could do neither.

Provisions for secondary education for girls and boys, South and North, began with the academy. The academies had their origin in the North but became more popular and widespread in the South, as public high schools were established in the North.

3. Isabella Margaret Elizabeth Blandin, *History of Higher Education of Women in the South Prior to 1860* (New York: The Neale Publishing Co., 1909), p. 9 (hereafter, *Higher Education of Women in the South*).

In 1850, there were 2,700 academies in the southern states, 2,100 in the middle states, and 1,000 in New England.[4] Some of the southern academies were state-supported. Such was the case in Georgia, where a system of land-grant academies was established. But most of the southern academies were sponsored by towns, churches, fraternal organizations, or individuals. In some states— Alabama, for instance—women organized "Female Educational Associations," or "Ladies Education Societies," to advocate and sponsor these institutions.[5] In Georgia, most of the academies were coeducational. In Alabama, they were about equally divided. In that state, over a period of twenty years, sixty-nine "male and female," fifty-three "female," and nineteen "male" academies were chartered.[6] In most states, however, the male academies far outnumbered the female schools.

Just when and where the first "female" academy was established is not known. The New Orleans Ursuline Female Academy was established in 1727.[7] Charleston, S.C., had its Female Academy in 1741,[8] and Augusta, Ga., in 1796.[9] These schools were of a special and limited nature, however. The first significant female academies in the South were established some ten to fifteen years later than in New England. Among the early ones were the Moravian Salem Academy in North Carolina (1802), and the Ann Smith Academy in Virginia (1807).[10] Many of the female academies gained a wide reputation and drew students from several states. Among these were the Elizabeth Academy in Mississippi (1818), the Lexington Academy in Kentucky (1805), the Nashville Academy in Tennessee (1817), the Marks Barhamville Academy in South Carolina (1828), and the Judson Female Insti-

4. Edgar W. Knight, *Education in the United States* (New York: Ginn & Co., 1929), p. 376.

5. Albert Burton Moore, *History of Alabama* (University, Ala.: University Supply Store, 1934), p. 338.

6. *Ibid.*

7. Catharine Frances, sister, *The Convent School of French Origin in the United States, 1727–1843* (Philadelphia: Sisters of Saint Joseph, 1936), p. 13.

8. Woody, *Women's Education in the U.S.*, I, 363.

9. Ellis Merton Coulter, "The Ante-Bellum Academy Movement in Georgia," *The Georgia Historical Quarterly*, V (December 1921), 21.

10. Woody, *Women's Education in the U.S.*, I, 341, 391.

tute in Alabama (1839).[11] Thomas Woody, whose *History of Women's Education in the United States* is generally recognized as the definitive one, compares very favorably the Elizabeth and Marks Academies with those of Catherine Beecher, Mary Lyon, and Emma Willard in the North.[12]

The Nashville Academy, chartered in 1817, had the largest and best-equipped plant and the largest enrollment of any female academy in the United States. In 1860, it had 513 students and 38 teachers. It offered two curricula: one in science, including mathematics and ancient languages as well as chemistry, botany, astronomy, zoology, and natural science; the other in the humanities, including modern languages, history, and belles-lettres. This academy, as did others, also offered the ornamental subjects: voice, instrumental music, painting, and drawing. It had a gymnasium and required calisthenics.[13]

Dancing at the Nashville Academy led to an open controversy between the principal, Dr. C. D. Elliott, who was an ordained Methodist minister, and the Reverend John B. McFerrin, editor of the Nashville *Christian Advocate,* the organ of the Tennessee Methodist Conference. The Academy gave dances, tableaux, and concerts regularly on Saturday evenings. On one occasion in 1858, the entertainment was arranged by the Negro servants of the Academy and included a "Virginia breakdown." Elliott, his faculty, and many Nashville citizens enjoyed the performance. Although the school was non-sectarian, McFerrin condemned the performance as sinful and contrary to Christian principles. Elliott replied that "if it is a sin to see a darkey dance the Virginia Breakdown and all whoever laughed at it are to be expelled from the church I shall find myself in good company."[14] But McFerrin

11. *Ibid.,* I, 382, 385, and 390; J. Winston Coleman, Jr., "Lexington as seen by Travellers, 1810–1835," *The Filson Club History Quarterly,* XXIX (July 1955) , 281; and Hennig Cohen, editor, *A Barhamville Miscellany* (Columbia: University of South Carolina Press, 1956) , p. iv.

12. Woody, *Women's Education in the U.S.,* II, 193.

13. F. Garvin Davenport, *Cultural Life in Nashville on the Eve of the Civil War* (Chapel Hill: University of North Carolina Press, 1941) , pp. 41–45.

14. *Ibid.,* pp. 44–45.

persisted and Elliott was divested of his orders. Elliott was supported by the Academy, however, and retained the presidency until 1866.[15]

The faculties of the female academies were generally well prepared. Many held the bachelor's degree and some, the Master of Arts. Many who taught in the church schools were trained as ministers. Some few of the teachers held the M.D. degree. Many of the teachers came from northern schools and colleges and a few, from European schools. Among the better-known teachers was Emily Pillsbury Burke, who had taught in New England academies before she removed to Georgia. She later went to Oberlin College, where she served as principal of the Ladies Department. She was dismissed from that post for kissing one of the male students in the hall of the administration building. And, believe it or not, she was reported to the president by the boy whom she had kissed.[16] Caroline Lee Hentz, the well-known author of several widely-read sentimental love stories, and her husband, Nicholas Hentz, who had taught first at George Bancroft's Round Hill School in Massachusetts and then served as Professor of French at the University of North Carolina, both taught in female academies in Kentucky, Alabama and Georgia.[17] Mrs. Almira Hart Phelps, a native of New England, was for many years a teacher at the Patapsco Female Academy in Maryland. Author of several books in botany, she was one of the two women to be elected to membership in the American Association for the Advancement of Science prior to the Civil War.[18] And Milo P. Jewett was president and professor at Judson Female Institute in Alabama for several years. He later persuaded Matthew Vassar to give money to establish Vassar College. Jewett was chosen president of the college,

---

15. *Ibid.*

16. Robert Samuel Fletcher, *A History of Oberlin College. From Its Formation Through the Civil War,* 2 vols. (Oberlin: Oberlin College, 1943) , I, 480–484.

17. "Caroline Lee Whiting Hentz," *Dictionary of American Biography,* 20 vols. (New York: Charles Scribner's Sons, 1928–1936) , VIII, 565–566.

18. "Almira Hart Lincoln Phelps," *Dictionary of American Biography,* XIV, 524–525.

but he became embroiled in a controversy over the curriculum and soon resigned.[19]

As Professor Thomas Cary Johnson, Jr., has shown, the "sweet girl graduates" of southern female academies and seminaries, might not have learned much Latin and Greek, but they had developed an interest in and gained an elementary understanding of mechanics, astronomy, botany, mineralogy, chemistry, natural philosophy, and zoology.[20] They had used chemical apparatus and telescopes, and made use of herbarium and cabinets of minerals and zoological collections in their experiments.[21] Professor Johnson might have added that they had also learned something of history, modern foreign languages, and literature.

The Academies stimulated an interest in teacher training and were forerunners of the normal schools. They gave women their first taste of higher education and aroused in them an interest in and a demand for college education of the same quality as that offered to their brothers in the men's colleges and universities. Women were not to attain the desired goal, however, without a long and bitter fight. First, they and their supporters had to convince the opposition that women were physically able and mentally capable of acquiring such an education; then, they had to show the need for and benefits to be derived from such an education; and, finally, they had to secure financial aid and support for the establishment of women's colleges.

The proponents of higher education for women found enemies among the women themselves. Emma Willard, in her "Plan for Female Education," said she hoped to establish a seminary for girls "as different from those appropriated to the other sex as the female character and duties are from the male."[22] Many opponents claimed that women were mentally inferior and could not grasp the sort of learning offered in the men's colleges. One

19. James Monroe Taylor and Elizabeth Hazelton Haight, *Vassar* (New York: Oxford University Press, 1915), pp. 42–45.

20. Thomas Cary Johnson, Jr., *Scientific Interests in the Old South* (New York: D. Appleton-Century Co., 1936), p. 106.

21. *Ibid.*

22. Anna Callender Brackett, editor, *Woman and the Higher Education* (New York: Harper and Brothers, 1893), pp. 1–2.

magazine writer said: "The great argument against the existence of this equality of intellect in women is, that it does not exist. If that proof does not satisfy a female philosopher, we have no better to give."[23] Such an argument may be an obtuse one, but women found it a most difficult one to cope with. Others argued that women could not stand the physical strain of college training, and, if they could, a college education would reduce marriages. Could those people have seen into the twentieth century, they would have known that co-education is the most effective matrimonial bureau ever set up.

Another objection to giving women a college education was that they could not make use of it. Practically no professional and business positions were open to women, and there were absolutely no openings in politics and government service. Edward W. Johnson of the Bedford, Va., Female Academy, said: "Women are not to be Navigators, Opticians, Almanac Makers, or Doctors. Why give them a half or quarter proficiency in that of which a whole knowledge would be useless to them? . . . Metaphysics, Logic, Political Economy, belong to the masculine offices and pursuits only, and cannot be brought into female education without wasting the time and injuring the perception, which should be employed in feminine things."[24]

Others tried to silence the proponents of college education for women by ridicule. The following stanza from a long poem, published in the *Southern Literary Messenger,* is typical of many such efforts.

> Shall they [our daughters], with flashing eye
>   and clanging tongue,
> Mount in the rostrum, lecture in the streets,
> And, in the arena of election strife,
> Claim with shrill voice, and rude disshevelled
>   locks,
> "Your Votes! Your votes!" Ye loud-mouthed
>   populace!

23. "The Intellect of Women," *Littell's Living Age,* LXIV (January 1860) , 184.
24. Richmond *Enquirer,* 3 November 1837.

> Nay;—Should that peach-like cheek but feel
>   the breath
> Of yonder foul-mouthed crowd, methinks its
>   bloom
> Should wither in the contact.[25]

And the editor of the Greensborough, N.C., *Patriot* (March 25, 1835) declared that the legislature of Kentucky had "made itself ridiculous by incorporating . . . Van Doren's College of Young Ladies" and granting the trustees and faculty the power to confer diplomas and degrees. He proposed that the degree M.P.L. (Mistress of Polite Literature, alias Mistress of Petticoat Law) be conferred on all ladies who completed the course of study at the college, and that the degree of M.F. (Master of Folly) be conferred upon Van Doren himself.

William Gilmore Simms, giving an address at the opening of the Spartanburg, S.C., Female College, spoke out "against women assuming the false position into which they would place their sex who are clamoring for equality and close companionship with men in all the sterner duties of life."[26] He thought woman's proper place was as wife, mother, and housekeeper, and he urged them to seek education suited to such duties. Another serious-minded opponent of college education for women argued that "the essential requisite for female education of a superior order, is to be found at home, under carefully selected and thoroughly prepared instructors." And the course of home study "should be prolonged to a maturer age . . . , and as a consequence of this, let the age of marriage be postponed at least to the age of twenty-five." Such a plan of education, the author declared, "would uplift society, the family, and also the standards of male education."[27]

Time and public opinion, however, were working in the interest of the movement for higher education for women. Jacksonian Democracy, with its philosophy of democracy and equality, was

25. L.S.M., "Woman's Progress," *The Southern Literary Messenger,* XIX (November 1853) , 700.

26. Charles F. Deems, editor, *Annals of Southern Methodism for 1856* (Nashville: Stevenson and Owen, 1857) , p. 126.

27. E.T., "Female Education," *The Southern Literary Messenger,* n.s., VI (September 1858) , 218–220.

helpful to the cause of women's education. The general movement for women's rights added some strength, although the two movements were not directly connected. Some leaders for women's education were outspoken opponents of woman suffrage. Mrs. Almira Hart Phelps of Patapsco Female Institute in Maryland was one of these.[28] Some feminists put major emphasis on political, economic, and legal rights, rather than on education. And the fact that feminist leaders were generally abolitionists drove a wedge between them and southern proponents of women's education. The establishment of a number of women's magazines was also beneficial to the cause of women's education. The *Southern Lady's Companion,* the *Magnolia,* and the *Southern Rose* all championed women's education, and the fact that they were edited by women strengthened their cause. Several of the southern literary magazines publicized the cause, although the editors might not favor it.

The campaign got under way in the 1820s and continued to gain strength to 1860. The list of men and women who wrote for the cause is a large one and contains ministers, political leaders, journalists, lawyers, doctors, planters, and educators. They delivered speeches to public gatherings, at college commencements, in churches and legislative assemblies. They wrote and published books, pamphlets, articles in periodicals, and letters in newspapers. Time permits reference to only a few of these leaders. We might begin with James Mercer Garnett, whose *Lectures on Female Education* which he delivered at his wife's school at Elm Wood, Virginia, deal largely with trivial matters. He did decry the low estate of the teaching profession and spoke in favor of the teaching of science in the female academies. The *Lectures* were published in book form and went through four editions.[29] The book was warmly praised by John Marshall, DeWitt Clinton, Bishop Richard C. Moore, and Dr. Frederic Beasley, Provost of the College of Philadelphia.

28. Emma Lydia Bolzau, *Almira Hart Lincoln Phelps* (Philadelphia: Privately printed, 1936) , pp. 377–400.

29. James Mercer Garnett, *Lectures on Female Education,* 4th ed. (Richmond· Thomas W. White, 1825) .

Much more significant was *An Address on Female Education*[30] delivered at the University of Georgia in 1835 by Daniel Chandler, a graduate of the University of Georgia and a member of the legislature of Alabama. This *Address* was directly responsible for the introduction of a bill in the Georgia legislature to establish a state female college. The bill failed; whereupon, a group of citizens in Macon, Georgia, organized a society and invited the Georgia Methodist Conference to join them in establishing a female college. The Conference did so, and, in 1836, the Georgia Wesleyan Female College was chartered by the Georgia legislature. This was the first woman's college in the United States authorized to grant the degree of Bachelor of Arts.[31]

Chandler's *Address* was an impassioned plea for women's education. Woman, said he, could master sciences and all the higher branches of learning. "She can comprehend them, in all their varied extent, and diversified ramifications. Give her an opportunity, and science will be her handmaiden—philosophy her companion—and literature her play-thing." Give her a chance and "she would enter the race for literary distinction, and struggle for the prize of scientific award . . . this would lead to improvement —improvement to distinction . . . intellectual acquisitions, employment, and pursuits." Women, said he, needed knowledge of ancient literature, philosophy, science in its progressive movements, general and natural history, chemistry, geometry, and mathematics. "Give the female the same advantages of instruction with the male; afford her the same opportunities for improvement, and she will struggle with the boldest mind, and outstrip in the proud race of distinction many of the favored objects of parental solicitude and legislative bounty." Chandler pointed out that there were in the United States sixty-one colleges with laboratories and libraries containing three hundred thousand books—

---

30. Daniel Chandler, *An Address on Female Education, Delivered Before the Demosthenian and Phi Beta Kappa Societies, on the Day after Commencement, in the University of Georgia* (Washington: William A. Mercer, 1835), p. 24 (hereafter, *Address*).

31. *American Universities and Colleges,* 7th ed. (Washington, D.C.: American Council on Education, 1956), p. 15.

"And to the disgrace of the nation be it spoken—not one dedicated to the cause of female education."[32]

A number of writers specifically challenged the long-held view that women were intellectually inferior to men, and they demanded the same rigid training for women that was given in the men's colleges. Charles L. Cocke of Hollins College wrote, in 1857: "The plan and policy of the school recognizes the principle that in the present state of society in our country, young women require the same thorough and rigid mental training as afforded young men."[33] He added, "It is my purpose to devote my life to the higher education of women in the South."[34] Doctor Lamar, in a commencement address at Wesleyan College in 1855, emphasized woman's need for "a solid education. His argument was unique. . . . He appealed to psychology."[35] He said: "No sexual difference in mind had ever been discovered or intimated [between man and woman]. . . . The sexes had always been classed together as coming under the same law. . . . If education, then, has the same *design* in each case . . . , the process for each should be the same."[36] Dr. Rufus W. Bailey of Mary Baldwin College wrote that, if the exact sciences and philosophy were to be confined to one of the sexes, he "did not hesitate to say these studies should be excluded from the men's colleges and given to the education of our daughters."[37] And Mary Bates, a teacher in a Pendleton, South Carolina, female academy, advocated a stiff regimen of studies for girls. She thought the academies devoted too much time to ornamental subjects. She warned that the fashionable airs of that day, "the bow, the twist, the skip, and other contortions—may be tomorrow as the extravagant customs of the Orientals."[38]

32. Chandler, *Address,* p. 10, *passim.*

33. Dorothy Scovil Vickery, *Hollins College, 1842–1942. An Historical Sketch* (Hollins College, Va.: Hollins College, 1942), p. 13.

34. *Ibid.,* p. 4.

35. *Annals of Southern Methodism* (1855), p. 171.

36. *Ibid.*

37. Mary Watters, *The History of Mary Baldwin College, 1842–1942* (Staunton: Mary Baldwin College, 1942), p. 17.

38. Mary Bates, "Female Education," *The Magnolia; or, Southern Appalachian,* n.s., II (January 1843), 66.

The general doctrine of the social value was found in many of the contemporary writings on education but the basic argument for women's education was one of human rights. Elias Marks, M.D., a teacher in the Columbia, S.C., Female Academy and founder of the better-known Barhamville Female Academy, developed this latter argument at great length in his pamphlet, *Hints on Female Education* (Columbia: A. S. Johnston, 1851). A few quotations will indicate the tenor of his argument: "Education applies to the human being, considered as a moral and accountable agent with an immortal nature, and having an imperishable destiny." "We consider the right education of woman essential to the general weal; it is the legitimate source of the moral character and political happiness of the people." "Inequality of rights . . . can only be based upon inequality of talents. . . . But that there exists any difference between the sexes, as it regards the sum of intellect, is one of those dogmas, which prescription has sanctioned."[39]

The campaign for higher education for women became closely associated with the development of public schools. The schools needed teachers, and it was generally admitted that women were well suited to teaching. The private schools and academies had drawn heavily on men and women from the northern states, especially the New England area. Furthermore, many girls of the planter class had attended schools in the North, and boys had attended both academies and colleges. With the growing hostility between the North and the South over the slavery issue, the proponents of higher education for women began to make use of this issue. "Let us stop sending our boys and girls to northern schools and colleges! Let us build female colleges in which we can train teachers for our children in the Schools!" was their plea. George Foster Pierce, first president of Wesleyan College, was guilty of using this argument, as did many other minister-presidents and teachers. Businessmen also appealed to this fear and advertised property as building sites for academies and colleges.[40]

39. *Hints on Female Education*, pp. 5, 6.
40. See Charleston *Mercury*, 31 December 1844, where F. H. Elmore advertised a site at Limestone Springs suitable for a school of standard instruction for the rising

C. K. Marshall, in an article, "Home Education," said: "Our sons and daughters return to us from their schools and colleges in the North with their minds poisoned by fanatical teachings . . . against the institution of slavery."[41] He proposed "that we educate our own teachers."[42] Albert Gallatin Brown devoted an entire speech, delivered as the commencement address at Madison Female College, Sharon, Miss., in 1859, to this theme. It is a diatribe against northern abolitionists and a clarion call to the South to protect its intellectual interests. The following quotation is typical:

> What is the tonic for the insidious northern influence? Let us have our own schools, academies, colleges, and universities. Let us rear and educate our own teachers.
>
> We want common schools in every neighborhood; we want academies, colleges and universities in three-fold the numbers that we have them now; and above all we want normal schools for the education of teachers, male and female.[43]

The sectional feeling unquestionably had an influence on the establishment of colleges in the South, but it is doubtful that a college growing solely out of such feelings could have made much contribution to education in its truest sense. Such institutions would not have sought the truth, but rather would have tried to indoctrinate their students.

The long crusade for higher education for women gradually awakened the southern people to the importance of and need for women's colleges, and they determined to do something about the problem. They first looked to the state governments for aid. There was precedent for such action, for the principle of governmental obligation to support higher education was recognized by the southern states with the dawn of independence, and it had been incorporated into the first constitutions of North Carolina

---

generation, which might do "much good, by a *safe and sound domestic education* for guarding their religious or civil condition from the insidious enemy. . . ."

41. C. K. Marshall, "Home Education at the South," *De Bow's Review*, XVIII (March 1855), 430–432.

42. *Ibid.*

43. Albert Gallatin Brown, *An Address on Southern Education* (Washington, Miss.: n.p., 1859), pp. 9, 11.

and Georgia. Both these states chartered state universities before the Constitution of the United States was framed, and North Carolina opened her university in 1795, Georgia, in 1801. Attendance in the universities was limited to boys, but Georgia provided for county academies, endowed with land; and, in 1785, Richmond, the first of these academies, was established. In 1786, a "female department" was added. These county academies prepared boys for the sophomore year in college, but the female department offered only English, French, mathematics, and the ornamental subjects.[44]

Tennessee took a second step toward providing higher education for women when Blount College, chartered in 1795 (now the University of Tennessee) opened its doors to women in 1804. This was the first college in the United States to admit women. For some unknown reason the practice ended in 1808. But it is fitting that the University of Tennessee today has dormitories named for the first five college co-eds in the United States.[45]

The Legislative Council of the Territory of Orleans (1803–1812), now the state of Louisiana, resolved "that the prosperity of every State depends greatly on the education of the female sex, in so much that the dignity of their condition is the strongest characteristic which distinguishes civilized from savage society."[46] The

44. Dorothy Orr, *A History of Education in Georgia* (Chapel Hill: University of North Carolina Press, 1950) , pp. 22–27 (hereafter, *Education in Georgia*) .

45. Stanley J. Folmsbee, *Blount College and East Tennessee College, 1794–1840* (Knoxville: The University of Tennessee, 1946) , pp. 22–27. [The distinction of being the first college in the United States to admit women is claimed for both Oberlin College (see p. 199) and Blount College. The reasons for this seem to be partly questions of semantics, chronological continuity, and differences in each school's approach to a policy for co-education. Oberlin College began admitting women students in 1833. It did not grant them equal status with men students, however, until some years later, probably about 1837, when its first women graduates received degrees. Blount College, unique in being this country's first nondenominational college, was chartered in 1794 and began operation in 1795. Old records list a number of women students enrolled at Blount College from 1804 to 1808, and histories of the school stress that it was the first college in the United States to admit women students on an equal basis with men students. In 1808, Blount College was closed and did not resume operation again until 1820. It then became, successively, East Tennessee College, East Tennessee University, and, finally, in 1879, the University of Tennessee.—J.I.C.]

46. Blandin, *Higher Education of Women in the South,* p. 9.

state, however, failed to implement this noble statement of the Council.

In 1820, the legislature of Alabama passed an act providing for a state university. One section of the act authorized "a branch of said university for female education."[47] This act, as amended in 1822, reads as follows: "There shall be also established three branches of said university for female education, to be located at such places as may be deemed by the Legislature for the public good, and the Legislature shall proceed to locate and fix the sites of said branches at the same time and by the same manner of election that the site of the principal university is to be located."[48] Unfortunately, financial difficulties prevented the legislature from carrying into effect this plan of a co-ordinate college for women in the university. But students of the Alabama Female Institute were later permitted to attend the lectures in science courses offered by Professors John W. Mallett and Michael Tuomey.[49]

In 1830, the Alabama legislature petitioned Congress, asking for a grant of two sections of land in each county to be used for "female academies."[50] Governor Israel Pickens was a strong supporter of this measure. He believed the request was consistent with national munificence and especially with the generous and refined sentiments of the age. Congress took no action on the petition.

There was a concerted effort in Georgia to secure the establishment of a state-supported college for women. Duncan Greene Campbell, a graduate of the University of North Carolina and a teacher in a female academy, introduced a bill in the state legislature in 1822, "to establish a public seat of learning in this State for the education of females."[51] In support of his measure, he said

47. *Acts Passed at the Second Session of the General Assembly of Alabama* (1820), pp. 4–6.

48. *Acts Passed at the Third Session of the General Assembly of the State of Alabama* (1821), pp. 3–8.

49. Johnson, *Scientific Interests in the Old South*, p. 110.

50. The memorial is quoted in Blandin, *Higher Education of Women in the South*, pp. 66–67.

51. Orr, *Education in Georgia*, p. 75.

that the present generation lived "in an age of improvement and enjoy[ed] the means of ameliorating the condition of all classes of society."[52] To the women was entrusted the early instruction of both sexes, and they should be educated in science and all learning so that they might develop "individual excellence," assure "the political security" of the country, and "contribute to the valuable store of literature, philosophy, and religion."[53] The bill was defeated, but Campbell secured the appointment of a committee of thirty, fifteen men and fifteen women, which should work for the cause. Campbell reintroduced his bill in 1825, but it was again defeated, much to the indignation of many people in the state. Letters were published in the state newspapers bitterly condemning the legislature. Arguments in support of the bill were that a women's college would stabilize and supply teachers for the lower schools and prevent people's leaving the state to obtain better educational advantages. A eulogy published shortly after Campbell's death said that "amidst the prejudices of his age, he [Campbell] called on his country to elevate the standard of female education," to enable women to improve the state in many ways, and to inculcate in the youth of the land the democratic doctrines so necessary for the preservation of the United States.[54] After Campbell's death, Benjamin H. Rutherford carried the banner for a women's college. His last effort came in 1834, when his bill to establish "The Female Institute of the State of Georgia" and to appropriate $25,000 for its support was defeated by a vote of 105 to 41.[55]

While none of these efforts to provide state-supported higher education for women succeeded, they are of some significance. They develop fully the concept of state support and control, and they foreshadow the major types of women's education that were to come at a later date: co-education on the same campus but with separate training programs; the co-ordinate woman's col-

52. John C. Butler, *Historical Record of Macon and Central Georgia* (Macon: J. W. Burke & Co., 1879), p. 118.

53. *Ibid.*

54. *Ibid.*, p. 120; and Orr, *Education in Georgia*, pp. 75–76.

55. On Benjamin H. Rutherford's work, see *Journal of the House of Representatives of the State of Georgia* (1834), pp. 63, 70, 148, 250.

lege; branches of the university; and the separate and distinct woman's college.

The failure of the state governments to carry through on any efforts to establish colleges for women led the proponents of women's education to seek other sources of financial aid. Local communities and fraternal organizations gave some assistance, but the various church organizations became their strong right arm. Citizens in some towns were inspired by local pride to build a college so that their daughters might not have to travel to distant cities or to other states to secure their education. A newspaper report of the establishment of a college in a small Georgia town in 1849 closed with the statement that "the citizens of the town . . . having felt for some years the inconvenience and impolicy of sending their daughters far from home to obtain a suitable college education . . . [decided] to set up a college."[56] Citizens of the town gave the grounds and erected a building or buildings, employed some person to take charge, and they had a college. These colleges almost invariably took the name of the town in which they were established. There was great rivalry in the towns for a college. When Spartanburg, S.C., established a female college, Greenville, Gaffney, and Anderson set out to do the same. Such appeals to local pride may not have been the best way to build colleges, but college administrations use the same competitive principle in the 1960s in their effort to secure money with which to raise faculty salaries.

Fraternal organizations, the Masons and Independent Order of Odd Fellows, were instrumental in establishing a number of women's colleges in the Old South. The exact number is not known, but it was at least twenty-five. Such institutions were often colleges in name only, existed for a short time, or were taken over by the town or one of the churches. The Odd Fellows of Abingdon, Virginia, decided to establish a college in that town. The members of McCabe Lodge, "feeling deeply sensible of the want of an institution for the education of the female portion of the Country," and "recognizing the importance of such an institution as

56. George White, *Historical Collections of Georgia . . . From Its First Settlement to the Present Time* (New York: Podney and Russell, 1854) , p. 561.

being one which tends more perhaps than any other to subserve the wants and wishes of this part of the State," resolved to establish a college "in which the female mind could be taught to its utmost capacity in all the various branches of learning as well as all the accomplishments of the fine arts."[57] Out of this grew Martha Washington College.

The religious denominations were responsible for establishing a vast number of colleges in the Old South, many of which were, at best, junior colleges. Others were of poor quality and did not long survive; but some of them were four-year colleges of high quality, have withstood the vicissitudes of time, and are still serving the region. The churches were motivated not only by their interest in the cause of education but also to propagate their respective church doctrines by training the youth in the proper faith. For instance, the Methodist General Conference, in 1820, called attention to the fact that "nearly all the seminaries of learning in our country, of much celebrity are under the control of the Calvinistic . . . principles, or otherwise managed by men denying the fundamental doctrines of the church."[58] It called upon Methodists everywhere to take steps to provide colleges suitable for the training of their children. This admonition had reference to boys but was applicable also to girls when the movement for female colleges began in the 1830s.

The churches joined forces with local interests and, more often than not, their female colleges bore the name of the town in which they were located. There was considerable rivalry between Methodists, Baptists, and Presbyterians in establishing these colleges. Governor George R. Gilmer, commenting on this rivalry in Georgia, said that Wesleyan College in Macon "has been conducted with the zeal and energy which characterize the people of that denomination [the Methodist]."[59] And Madison had "two of the

57. Edgar W. Knight, editor, *A Documentary History of Education in the South Before 1860*, 5 vols. (Chapel Hill: University of North Carolina Press, 1949–1953), IV, 412–415 (hereafter, *Documentary History*).

58. Nathan Bangs, *A History of the Methodist Episcopal Church*, 4 vols. (New York: Mason, Lane, and Sandford, 1839–1841), III, 105.

59. George Rockingham Gilmer, *The Literary Progress of Georgia. An Address Delivered in the College Chapel at Athens, Before the Society of Alumni, and at*

most flourishing female colleges in the state," one run by the Baptists, the other by the Methodists. "The Episcopalians [said he] have been struggling hard to imitate the admirable example of the Presbyterians, Baptists, and Methodists," and "Bishop Stephen Elliott now heads the Episcopal Female Institute in Montpelier."[60]

The first of the women's colleges authorized to grant the bachelor's degree was the Georgia Female College, chartered in 1836.[61] The original impulse for the college came from the people of Macon, Ga., who had organized a society for the purpose of establishing a college. Learning that the Georgia Methodist Conference was also contemplating such an institution, the citizens, believing that the Methodist Church possessed "facilities for carrying through so favorite a scheme beyond that of any other in the State," asked the Methodist Conference to assume the responsibility for the project. The church accepted the responsibility, and the college was opened in 1839[62] and granted its first A. B. degree in 1840. In 1843, a private citizen offered the college $8,000 as a scholarship fund if it would change its name to Wesleyan Female College, and it was so done.[63] George Foster Pierce, first president of the college, writing in 1840, said: "Two years ago the notion of a female college was laughed at as a Platonic idea—a mere dream—an impracticable fancy born in the reverie of some speculative mind, well meaning perhaps, but utterly ahead of sober sense and prudent wisdom. A Female College!—Anomalous, absurd."[64] But the institution was a success, and was but the first of several female colleges established in the southern states before 1860. In Georgia alone, at least a dozen institutions calling themselves colleges were established within twenty years. And an equal number were established in other

Their Request, on Thursday, August 7th, 1851 (Athens: William N. White, 1851), p. 44.

60. *Ibid.*

61. Butler, *Historic Record of Macon and Central Georgia,* p. 117.

62. Orr, *Education in Georgia,* p. 152.

63. *Ibid.*

64. George Foster Pierce, "The Georgia Female College—Its Origin, Plan, and Prospects," *Southern Ladies Book,* I (February 1840), 9.

southern states. Entrance requirements at Wesleyan and most southern female colleges, however, were not as high as those at men's colleges, nor was the course of study as severe.

In neighboring Tennessee, twelve years after the establishment of the Wesleyan Female College, the Tennessee Female Institute was chartered.[65] The name, upon bequest of $10,000, was changed to Mary Sharp College. Under its president, Z. C. Graves, the college required a course of study as thorough as its students' brothers had at their colleges and universities. Women would now have "the same knowledge, literary, scientific, and classical, that has been for so many generations the peculiar and cherished heritage of the other sex."[66]

Prior to 1860, the legislature of every southern state with the exception of Arkansas and Florida had chartered one or more women's colleges. Most of the colleges were founded and controlled by religious denominations. The Methodist Church established more colleges than any other church but was closely followed by the Baptist Church. The Presbyterian, Protestant Episcopal, and Roman Catholic churches, with fewer communicants, established fewer colleges for women. The fraternal orders, Masons and Odd Fellows, established a goodly number of colleges, and still others were established by local groups in towns and cities.

Alabama had established twenty or more colleges whose "courses of study . . . conformed to the general college curriculum of the times" and "offered excellent work in . . . college subjects."[67] Among the better known of these colleges were Athens Female College and the Alabama Conference College, both Methodist-controlled, and Judson Female College, a Baptist Institution.

65. *Acts of the State of Tennessee, passed at the First Session of the Twenty-Seventh General Assembly for the Years 1847–1848* (Jackson: Gates and Parker, 1848), p. 290–292.

66. Woody, *Women's Education in the U.S.*, II, 142, quoting *Mary Sharp Catalog, 1853–1854*.

67. Minnie Clare Boyd, *Alabama in the Fifties: A Social Study* (New York: Columbia University Press, 1931), pp. 124, 138; Moore, *History of Alabama,* pp. 336–337, 344.

The latter institution, chartered in 1841, was transferred to the Alabama Baptist State Convention in 1843. The Reverend Milo P. Jewett was president. In 1852, the college had a faculty of 11 professors and 190 students. The course of study was "comprehensive and thorough embracing all the solid and ornamental branches taught in the highest Female Seminaries in the United States." In addition to courses in mathematics, sciences, languages, and natural philosophy, the students attended lectures in the neighboring Howard College for men. It was a "college, in the highest acceptance of the term" and attracted "students from every part of the South West, and commands the patronage of intelligent parents and guardians, without reference to religious denomination."[68]

Women's colleges in the South had now come of age by 1860. They were ready to develop to their fullest. But war came, and the southern colleges suffered severe setbacks, as did all other institutions. Even so, the southern states had made significant contributions to women's higher education. They had laid foundations upon which both North and South were to build in later years.

68. *American Baptist Register for 1852* (Philadelphia: American Baptist Publication Society, 1853), pp. 421–424; see also Knight, *Documentary History,* IV, 396–397.

9

Thomas Prentice Kettell: Economist, Editor, and Historian

> Thomas Prentice Kettell was a shadowy figure in American history during the decade of the 1850s. He is important in the study of southern history because of his interest in the antebellum South and, more particularly, because of his *Southern Wealth and Northern Profits* (New York: George W. and John A. Wood, 1860). The book has long been out of print, and the University of Alabama Press decided recently to reissue it with Fletcher Green as editor. The new edition appeared in 1965 (University, Ala.: University of Alabama Press, 1965). Reprinted here in full is Green's essay on Kettell, which appeared in the new edition on pp. ix–xxv.

THOMAS PRENTICE KETTELL WAS AN outstanding spokesman of that group of pre-Civil War northerners who earnestly believed that it was possible to save their country from the horrors of a sectional conflict, who worked many years to prevent the threatened dissolution of the Union, but zealously supported the national government during the Civil War in the hope that military victory would achieve what thirty years of wrangling, negotiation, and compromise had failed to accomplish—namely, the preservation of a united North and South. Most of this northern group were linked by economic ties to the planters of the South. As merchants, shippers, and financiers, they largely depended upon the cotton trade for much of their prosperity; hence, they opposed governmental policies which they believed would disturb their connections with the South and the foundations on which their economic prosperity and well-being rested.[1] But the fact that their ideas and position were founded on selfish economic interests did not make their action dishonest or unpatriotic.

Antislavery writers often referred to New York City as the prolongation of the South, where "ten thousand cords of interest are linked with the Southern Slaveholder." In fact, New York was a stronghold of southern sympathizers. Her newspapers regularly carried advertisements addressed specifically to southerners, urging them to visit their stores which specialized in merchandise designed exclusively for the southern trade. Many of the New York business firms had branches in southern cities, and some few New York stores were branches of southern business enterprises.[2] Many New York shipping merchants would have found it almost impossible to carry on a profitable ocean-going commerce without cotton, tobacco, and other raw materials produced in the South. They also depended upon southern products to purchase return cargoes from Europe, for despite the large quantities of western corn and wheat which poured into New York by canal and railroad, the chief cargo of European-bound ocean packets was cotton. Furthermore, since a large number of southern products were exported from New York City, the coastal vessels were laden with goods destined for the southern cities.[3] One contemporary account estimated that New York merchants annually sold merchandise to the five cotton states valued at \$131,000,000 and that the total business with the five states was above \$200,000,000.[4]

The movement for southern economic independence which got

1. For an excellent treatment of this subject, see Philip Sheldon Foner, *Business & Slavery; The New York Merchants & the Irrepressible Conflict* (Chapel Hill: University of North Carolina Press, 1941). See especially pp. vii, 1–5 (hereafter, *Business & Slavery*).

2. *The Southern Trade: An Epitome of Commerce North and South, Etc., with a Directory of Prominent New York Houses Interested in Southern Trade.* [This was published in New York by E. K. Cooley, and a publication note in the May 1860 issue states that it was a semi-annual publication.—J.I.C.] See advertisement pages.

3. Robert Greenhalgh Albion, *The Rise of the New York Port, 1815–1860* (New York: Charles Scribner's Sons, 1939), pp. 95–96.

4. Stephen Colwell, *The Five Cotton States and New York* (Philadelphia: [n.p.], 1861).

under way in the 1830s filled the merchants of New York with fear, not because they were worried by the Southern Commercial Conventions, but because of the influence of the abolition movement. The merchants feared that, because of the sectional controversy over slavery, "New York" printed on a box of merchandise would symbolize to the southerners hostility to slavery and southern rights. Above all, they feared the struggle over slavery would lead to the dissolution of the Union, thereby achieving what direct trade conventions, commercial conventions, and propaganda campaigns could not accomplish. Hence,

a vast majority of New York merchants regarded the agitation of the slavery question and the interference with the rights of Southern slave holders as inexpedient, unjust, and pregnant with evils.[5]

It was not a question of morals with the merchants, but of millions of dollars in southern trade which would be jeopardized. One of them wrote to Samuel J. May, a New York abolition leader:

We cannot afford, Sir, to let you and your associates endeavor to overthrow slavery. It is not a matter of principle with us. It is a matter of business necessity. . . . we mean, Sir, to put you abolitionists down, by fair means if we can, by foul means if we must.[6]

Thomas Prentice Kettell, son of Thomas Prentice, Sr., and his wife, Hannah Dawes Pierce Kettell, was born in Boston, Massachusetts, in 1811. His forebears had left England and first settled in Charlestown, Massachusetts, in 1634. Among Thomas's colonial ancestors were architects, merchants, ministers, and soldiers. His father, a merchant, served for twenty-four years in the state senate. Thomas was educated in the Boston schools, but as a youth displayed an avid interest in commercial pursuits, and on occasion accompanied his father on trading voyages to the North Atlantic port cities. He was employed for some years in a Boston hardware store, and then went to Europe as a representative of various exporting firms. He visited many of the leading cities of Europe, became acquainted with leading merchants—several of whom he later used as subjects for biographical sketches in Ameri-

5. Foner, *Business & Slavery*, pp. 13–14.
6. *Ibid.*

can journals—but most important for his future career, he studied "the course of general operations of international commerce, with a view to reconcile the practical workings of trade with the general practice of the economists."[7]

Upon his return to the United States in 1837, Kettell settled in New York City, where he began his career as a writer, publicist, and editor in the fields of commerce, finance, and industry, in which he was to attain not only national but international recognition. In fact, Freeman Hunt, in 1849, wrote that Kettell ranked along with McCulloch, Macgregor, Taylor, Tucker, and Carey as the leading authorities in the field of economics.[8]

James Gordon Bennett, founder and editor of the New York *Herald,* had, in 1835, begun a series of articles dealing with economic conditions. He employed Kettell, in 1837, to do a series titled "Money Articles," which

became famous throughout the commercial and financial circles of Europe and the United States, and the public, those with money to invest as well as the Bulls and Bears . . . derived great benefit in having the financial affairs of the world daily spread before them.[9]

Prior to 1837, the public press had not systematically followed commercial events nor exerted itself in the advocacy of economic measures distinct from party politics. Kettell changed this. He determined to expose pernicious conditions and practices in commercial and financial matters and to suggest judicious issues. His articles were penetrating and informative and soon attracted general attention throughout the United States and in the major financial and commercial cities of Europe. From 1837 to 1843,

7. *"Commercial Sketches with Pen and Pencil. Thomas Prentice Kettell," Hunt's Merchants' Magazine,* XX (June 1849), 618–627. Portrait facing p. 576.

8. Freeman Hunt, "The Editor to His Friends and Patrons," *Hunt's Merchants' Magazine,* XXI (July 1849), 143–144.

9. Frederick Hudson, *Journalism in the United States, from 1690 to 1872* (New York: Harper and Brothers, 1873), p. 434. There is a controversy over the authorship of the articles. Hudson claims that Bennett was the author, but modern authorities recognize Kettell as the author of the "Money Articles." See Alfred D. Chandler, Jr., *Henry Varnum Poor: Business Editor, Analyst, and Reformer* (Cambridge: Harvard University Press, 1956), p. 335, n. 37, who says Kettell even originated the Bennett series.

during which period the series regularly appeared, they acquired an almost "oracular authority with statesmen and merchants."[10]

The press generally was high in its praise of the "Money Articles." The Boston *Courier* [in 1840] printed with approval the statement of a leading merchant of that city that Kettell was a "man of extensive knowledge of the mercantile affairs of the country, and a mind of uncommon shrewdness in observation."[11] Francis P. Blair of the Washington *Globe,* in 1841, characterized Kettell as a

man of principle, of judgment, of information. His views of the Exchequer scheme are characterized by honesty and patriotism, and by the judicious and practical considerations which have given so much deserved weight to his notices of the monetary concerns of the country.[12]

The Hartford (Connecticut) *Times* declared,

These articles are among the best, if not the very best that are written for the American Press, on the monetary affairs, public or private, of the country. The author is not . . . a blind partisan, but a clear headed, honest, and most able collector and disseminator of facts.[13]

Complimentary reports came in also from abroad. The *Times* (London) wrote:

The New York *Herald* has been one of the most powerful instruments in the United States in exposing the frauds, bubbles, and stock-gambling machinery which our fund managers had organized in America for robbing the land and labor of that country, as they have robbed this since the days of Walpole. For correctness of detail, research, industry, sound political economy and decided talent . . . [the] Money Articles have not yet been equalled on this side of the Water.[14]

Members of both houses of Congress—one contemporary writer said "nearly every member of the Senate"—publicly acknowledged Kettell's ability to expose the evils of the financial system. They spoke of "the clearness of his style, the perfect mastery of his

10. Chandler, *Henry Varnum Poor,* p. 101.
11. Quoted in "Commercial Sketches," pp. 624–625.
12. *Ibid.*
13. *Ibid.*
14. *Ibid.*

subject . . . the fullness and accuracy of his information, and the soundness of his judgment." William Allen, senator from Ohio, remarked, in 1842, that

for a year or two past they ["Money Articles"] have, in general, displayed a very uncommon industry and ability, and greatly aided in displacing error and exposing frauds and corruption with which the country has been so long afflicted through its corporations, its currency, its stock jobbers and paper [stock] mongers.

And Thomas W. Bagley, a representative from Virginia, declared that the "Money Articles were written with an ability which the whole country acknowledged."[15]

Possessed of vigorous intellect, clear perception, and rare sagacity, Kettell grasped the essence of a problem and presented it with a force and clearness that carried conviction. His "Money Articles" constitute a valuable commentary upon the stirring economic and financial problems of the late thirties and forties and gave him a reputation as one of the ablest and soundest economists of that day. Freeman Hunt declared that Kettell was one of the most forceful writers on political economy in the country, that he had "done more to impart a respectable character to the tone of the press on that subject than any other," and that he was entitled to a high rank among the economic reformers of the day, "a class of men whose labors effect a world of good, while the laborers are scarcely known even by name to those who profit most by their exertions."[16]

The reputation and fame he gained by the "Money Articles" opened for Kettell a wider field of activity. In January 1846, he was appointed editor of the *United States Magazine and Democratic Review,* the semi-official organ of the Democratic party and the spokesman of the expansionists, or "Young America" element of that party in the 1840s and 1850s. He held the post until December 1851. He contributed four signed articles to the *Review* during that period, three of which were concerned primarily with the South. These were "Stability of the Union," "The South." and "The Methodist Church Property Case."

15. *Ibid.,* p. 624.
16. *Ibid.,* p. 627.

The theme of "Stability of the Union," based on official United States data, was that the industrial and material well-being of the North depended largely upon the production of raw materials in the South, which in turn depended upon slave labor. Kettell maintained that the South produced the greater part of the national wealth of the Union and that the North gained, through the influence of her capital and the operation of federal laws, bounties, tariffs, etc., a large proportion of that wealth. He also criticized the abolition attacks upon slavery.[17]

In "The South," Kettell claimed that his first article had made a strong impression on the North and had resulted in "a manifest subsidence in the suicidal cry against Southern institutions." His study of commerce, capital, and industry had convinced Kettell "of the criminal folly of attempting to disturb the only conditions upon which a society may almost be said to exist." He declared that the chief articles of American trade and commerce were the raw materials produced by slave labor in the South. In return for their servitude, "the Africans receive civilization and Christianity in addition to physical support." Without their servitude, the "Negro slaves would still be Pagan cannibals." And if "civilization and Christianity are things of value" they should not "be left out of the account of black remuneration for service by those [the northern abolitionists] who profess to hold the precepts of Scripture, as they understand it, to be the highest law of our government."[18] This defense of slavery and criticism of the abolitionists was highly pleasing to southern slaveholders.

Kettell's view of the attempt of the Methodist Episcopal Church [North] to deny the Methodist Episcopal Church South its share of the property held by the parent church before the division in 1845 may be summed up in his statement that "the thieving spirit of philanthropy which bred this schism for the sake of robbing the South . . . was stimulated and nurtured by English

17. Kettell, "Stability of the Union," *United States Magazine and Democratic Review,* XXVI (January 1850), 1–16.

18. Kettell, "The South," *United States Magazine and Democratic Review,* XXVIII (February 1851), 139–147.

Methodists."[19] He is bitter in his condemnation but ignores the fact that the Reverend Orange Scott, who first seceded from the church, was a native New Englander, not an English Methodist.

Relinquishing his post as editor of the *United States Magazine and Democratic Review,* Kettell became owner and editor of the *United States Economist* in 1852. He patterned his magazine after the London *Economist* and adopted as a subtitle "A weekly journal devoted to political economy, finance, commerce, manufactures, and agriculture." He gave to the *United States Economist* a reputation unequaled by that of any of its competitors and established an editorial policy that remained with the *Economist* for nearly thirty years. His financial and business analyses often surpassed those of his chief competitor, *Hunt's Merchants' Magazine.* He also gave his readers general political and foreign news, and his broad knowledge, good sense, and sound judgment assured his readers of his reliability.[20]

In the field of transportation, and especially railroads, Kettell's *Economist* was the major competitor of Henry Varnum Poor's *Railway Journal.* Kettell's articles were more general and not always accurate, but they were always suggestive and cleverly written. Kettell furnished the American people much information on railroads during the 1850s and sponsored the Illinois Central, which was of much interest to southerners because of its tie-up with the Mobile and Ohio road in the first federal land grant to railroads. The *Economist* also provided its readers with valuable information on political as well as economic problems. In fact, its editorials carried almost as much weight on business conditions both here and abroad as did the London *Times.*[21]

Kettell began to write for *Hunt's Merchants' Magazine* in 1845, when he published an article on "British Commercial Policy." It was soon followed by "A Hamburg Merchant in His Counting

19. Kettell, "The Methodist Church Property Case, U.S. Circuit Court, Southern District of New York, 1851," *United States Magazine and Democratic Review,* XXIX (October 1851) , 382–383.

20. David P. Forsyth, *The Business Press in America, 1750–1865* (Philadelphia: Chilton Books, 1964) , p. 86.

21. Chandler, *Henry Varnum Poor,* pp. 33, 101, 221.

House" and "Commercial Treaties of the United States: With Reference to the Progress of Commercial Freedom." All three of these articles grew out of travel and studies in Europe, supplemented, of course, by research in America. In November 1847, Kettell began his great series on "State Debts of Europe and America." Twelve chapters were published (1847–1858), covering all of the eastern and midwestern states. Maryland was the only southern state studied. In some 155 pages, Kettell gave a thorough and exhaustive treatment of this question, delving into the financial burdens and the significance of state debts for the people. The articles are noted for the research and ability that went into them, and they constitute the most comprehensive and reliable account of the debts, finance, and resources of the several states studied. As such, they are a most valuable storehouse of data for the historian.

When Hunt died, on March 2, 1858, he was succeeded as editor by Kettell, who also continued to edit the *United States Economist* until he sold it in 1859. Kettell edited *Hunt's Merchants' Magazine* until 1861. While editor of the *United States Magazine and Democratic Review,* Kettell had begun to write for James Dunwoody Brownson DeBow's *Commercial Review of the South and West,* published in New Orleans.

Between September 1847 and September 1856, Kettell contributed eight articles to *DeBow's Review.* In the two articles on "Progress of American Commerce, Agriculture, and Manufactures," Kettell analyzed the credit system and warehouse exchanges, discussed banks, imports, and exports, especially southern commodites, and concluded that these gave to the South and nation "promise of greater and more lasting prosperity than perhaps any which the commercial world has heretofore witnessed."[22] In "The Money of Commerce" and "Currency and Banks," Kettell emphasized the importance of private capital and the banks of New Orleans. He related the southern export trade to the Bank of England and the French banking practices. He dealt also with state banking policies and warned of the injurious effects of state

22. The two articles appear in *DeBow's Review,* IV (September 1847), 85–95, and (November 1847), 326–337. The quotation is found on p. 85.

financial legislation.[23] In "The Commercial Growth and Greatness of New York," Kettell described the growth and significance
of the port and its role in the shipping, commercial, and financial
life of the South.[24] In "The Industry of the South," Kettell discussed recent developments in manufacturing and, basing his
interpretations on the abundance of raw materials, labor, capital,
and markets, predicted a bright future for textiles, lumber, and
tobacco.[25] "Stability of the Union," a reprint from the *United
States Magazine and Democratic Review* and analyzed above, was
probably Kettell's most significant contribution to *DeBow's Review*.[26]

But "The Future of the South" was the most pleasing to his
southern readers. It is primarily a discussion and defense of the
institution of slavery as it existed in the South. Kettell declared
that the cotton which had "enveloped the commercial world, and
bound the fortunes of American slaves so firmly to human progress, that civilization may also be said to depend upon the continual servitude of the blacks in America." The cotton textile industry formed an indissoluble cord, "binding the black who was
threatened to be cut off [from] human progress," for "the black
race . . . has made no progress whatsoever [in Africa]. They were
without invention, almost without language, and destitute of the
faculties or the wish to advance." Kettell further argued that
American wealth and power were largely based upon the culture
of cotton, which in turn depended upon slave labor. Northern
shipping was basically in southern commodities, which in turn
paid the duties on imports. In fact, the economic prosperity of both
North and South depended upon southern staples. Truly, cotton
was king! The only trouble was that the textile industry was
located too far from the source of cotton. But that would change.
England had had the advantage, prior to 1830, because of her
control of the ocean. New England now dominated the industry,

23. *Ibid.,* VI (October-November 1848), 243–264, and IX (October 1850),
412–416.
24. *Ibid.,* V (January 1848), 30–44.
25. *Ibid.,* XII (February 1852), 169–181.
26. *Ibid.,* VIII (April 1850), 348–363.

but she was losing, and control would soon shift to the South. Kettell concluded:

There are conditions which shadow forth the greatness and power of the South, and as she rises in power and wealth she will elevate the black race with her. She will have, however, to encounter the zealous hatred of rivals whose philanthropy will be developed as her prosperity increases. It is, however, through the long lesson of industry taught by white surveillance, that the great work of regeneration of the black race can be accomplished.[27]

However far from truth or reality these views may have been, Kettell's words were as sweet music to his southern readers.

Three of the articles discussed above, with slight changes in titles, were reprinted in DeBow's *Industrial Resources of the Southern and Western States,* 3 vols. (New Orleans: DeBow's Review, 1852, 1853). They were "New York," "Union—Its Stability," and "The Future of the South."[28]

A sequel to Kettell's article, "The Stability of the Union," which as already noted was published in three periodicals, was his "Strength of Union—Magic of Cooperation," which appeared in 1860. The editor of *The Southern Trade,* in which "Strength of Union" was published, introduced it with the statement that Kettell had presented

facts and figures . . . in a clear and concise manner, showing the all-pervading influence of Southern productions on the commerce and wealth of the country and exposing the fallacies sought to be imposed on the credulous, by the fabrications of "Helper's Impending Crisis."[29]

The editor hoped—in vain, as time was to tell—that the article "would commend itself to the calm reflection of every thinking man."[30]

27. *Ibid.,* XXI (September 1856), 308–323.

28. See Vol. II (1853), 154–164; Vol. III (1853), 357–367 and 37–45.

29. Kettell, "Strength of Union—Magic of Cooperation," *The Southern Trade: An Epitome of Commerce North and South, Etc., with a Directory of Prominent New York Houses Interested in Southern Trade,* No. 2 (May 1860). Kettell's article begins on p. 5, moves to even-numbered pages 6–26, and is continuous on pages 28–32. I have been unable to locate but one copy, that in Widener Library, Harvard University.

30. *Ibid.*

Kettell developed his argument historically. England was the first of the great nations to reap the benefits of the commercial and industrial revolution of the last half of the eighteenth century. She did this through her exploitation of India and the development of the continental and West Indian colonies through forced labor of more than two and one-half million Negro slaves. In the nineteenth century, the United States forged ahead through prosperity based upon profits drawn from the compulsory labor of other races of men. The North supplied manufactured goods to the South and in return received raw materials produced by slave labor. The North exchanged manufactured goods—hardware, drygoods, shoes, groceries, and so on—for the raw materials of the South.

In other words, the South had the wealth, while the North acquired the profits. And every person in the North shared in these profits. Nevertheless, some northerners—abolitionists—had begun to quarrel with the manners and customs of the South and attempted "to force upon them a new system of morality." In doing so, they were driving a wedge between the two sections which neither really desired. If the North "should supinely permit a few unscrupulous politicians, clerical agitators, and reprobate parsons to hasten . . . [their] most wanton attacks upon the institutions of their best customers," piety would be their only "reward and their crown of martyrdom" might be, in fact, "an idiot's cup." In conclusion, Kettell maintained that the North had already suffered economically because of the abolition attacks upon slavery.

This state of things cannot but be of pecuniary injury to the North, even when the present distrust shall have passed away, and the loyalty of the whole people for the Union, its compromises, its duties and obligations shall have manifested itself so strongly as to bury forever in oblivion those politicians who seek advancement by agitating purely sectional issues.

And he earnestly pleaded with northerners to cease their attacks upon the South "before any further serious difficulties grew out of . . . [the disturbed] state of the public mind."[31]

31. *Ibid.,* pp. 24, 26, 32.

Kettell's supreme and final effort to convince the northern people that it was to their best interests to cease their attacks upon the South and her institutions, especially slavery, in order to preserve the Union, was the publication of *Southern Wealth and Northern Profits, as Exhibited in Statistical Facts and Official Figures: Showing the Necessity of Union to the Future Prosperity and Welfare of the Republic* (New York: G. W. & J. A. Wood, 1860). As the title indicates, his approach was entirely economic. There was no attempt to meet the moral argument of the abolitionists. This was his strength and his weakness. Exaggerated, and even false his arguments might be; yet, they were widely accepted in some circles; but they were of no weight to those who found slavery a great moral issue. Hence, there was no hope of bringing the two groups together. Furthermore, by 1860, Kettell had himself reached the stage where he would not listen to those who disagreed with him. Too long had he repeated his own arguments. He was immovable. He castigated his opponents in extremely abusive language. If they did not agree with him, they were corrupt, unscrupulous, slanderers, prevaricators, and reprobate parsons.

The publisher's blurb—probably written by Kettell himself, for it has the tone and phraseology as well as the substance and ideas of his earlier writings—is a forthright statement of the author's views and purpose. It reads:

This able work addresses itself peculiarly to the *patriotism* and *interests* of the *American people,* at this juncture, when it has become the duty of every good citizen, whatever may be his political creed, to aid in spreading the light of that truth which alone is depended upon to "combat error where the press is free." The press and the pulpit have stirred up domestic strife by broadcast misrepresentations of the South and her institutions, and the greatest exertions have been made to create a belief in Southern decrepitude and distress as a result of slavery. In the present volume the official figures are concisely produced and analyzed, exploding those INCONCEIVABLY ERRONEOUS ASSUMPTIONS and FABRICATIONS of "Helper's Crisis," which tend to irritate the South, mislead the North, and create sectional dissensions, for the sole benefit of unscrupulous politicians.

The immense WEALTH PRODUCED AT THE SOUTH is clearly demonstrated, and the expenditure and ACCUMULATION of that

WEALTH AT THE NORTH, where it stimulates industry, employs shipping, constructs palaces, builds railroads, occupies land, raises rents, impels trade, conferring affluence upon many and competence upon all, are clearly traced and made vividly manifest.

The welfare of this Union, the existence of the American nation, and the industry of Western Europe, are DEPENDENT upon the APPRENTICESHIP of the BLACK race to useful industry. They are working out, by an indispensable servitude, their passage from the brute condition to a semblance of manhood. The Diety has manifestly appointed the white race to drag forth, through the operation of servitude, those black savages from their cannibal lair in the African wilds into the light of the Gospel and the knowledge of the true God.

By the same operation, MODERN CIVILIZATION, which takes date from the ORIGIN of the SLAVE TRADE, has reached its present development. This glorious progress is sought to be arrested by clerical agitators, unprincipled office seekers, and CORRUPT FABRICATORS of SLANDERS upon SISTER STATES. These despise the best gifts of the Almighty, and reject his organization of creation; and, seeking fellowship with an inferior race, strive to plunge back into that slough of barbarism whence it has required three centuries to escape.

The simple truth alone is requisite to stem the torrent of disunion, strife, desolation, and bloodshed thus let loose, and the pages now offered contain that truth in a concise and clear form.[32]

Southern Wealth and Northern Profits was favorably received in the South, where Kettell's free trade principles, sympathetic attitude toward slavery, and his interest in southern economic development had long been known. Moderate southerners hoped the book might be helpful toward a compromise that would prevent secession, whereas radicals hoped it would further the cause of secession.

James D. B. DeBow devoted seventeen pages to an analysis and review of the book.[33] He spoke of Kettell as

one of the ablest political and statistical writers, who has for nearly thirty years, in various publications, illustrated the industrial conditions of the Union, and sustained, by incontrovertible facts, their mu-

---

32. This copy is taken from the outside back cover of the 1860 paperback printing.

33. *DeBow's Review,* XXIX (August 1860), 197–213.

tual dependence, demonstrating the wealth, resources, and self sustaining power of the Southern States.

He declared the book deserved a place upon every table, for it was an important campaign document in

the struggle between the adherents of law and the Constitution and the powerful body of disorganizers which, under the banner of Lincoln, Seward, and Sumner, threaten the existence of the government and even of republican institutions.

He closed his review with the statement that the book would, in the hands of the conservative men of the North, "prove an engine of tremendous power against the black and treasonable designs of Seward and Lincoln." The wish was father to the thought but alas, for DeBow, Hinton Rowan Helper's *The Impending Crisis of the South: How to Meet It,* which Kettell had attacked, was much the more influential in the election.

The Southern Literary Messenger, reviewing Kettell's book after the election and the organization of the Confederate States of America, used Kettell's arguments to bolster secession, rather than to try to prevent it as DeBow had done. It declared that if every newspaper south of the Mason and Dixon line would get a copy of Kettell's book,

it would have at hand a vast treasury of facts and figures with which to abolish at once, and forever, those pernicious sheets which are playing traitor to their own section by copying the infamously false statements of the northern press, and thus alarm our people with the preposterous idea that, when the worst comes to the worst, the Abolitionists can easily subjugate the South.[34]

As was to be expected, northerners vigorously attacked *Southern Wealth and Northern Profits.* Newspapers and periodicals generally condemned it, and at least one individual, Samuel Powell of Pennsylvania, published a thirty-one-page reply, under the title *Notes on Southern Wealth and Northern Profits.*[35] Emphasizing Kettell's southern bias, Powell refers to his work as "the very

34. *Southern Literary Messenger,* XXXII (February 1861), 159–160.
35. [Samuel Powell], *Notes on "Southern Wealth and Northern Profits"* (Philadelphia: C. Sherman and Son, 1861).

text-book of the mad movement [Secession] of the hour . . . [which] cannot fail to provoke the most stern indignation." He characterized Kettell's statement that slave labor was more advantageous than free as a "fatal error." He found Kettell in error also in regard to the quantity and value of southern products, that "slaves were well fed and well clothed," and that the North benefited unduly from protective tariffs and fishing bounties. He was especially bitter because of Kettell's strictures on abolitionists; he, in turn, castigated the southern secessionists who, with "subtile cunning . . . intentionally sow the seeds of sectional hatred, to ripen into the poison fruit of treason and national destruction." It is clearly evident that he had Kettell in mind when he wrote the above statement. In fact, he charged that Kettell deliberately held up to his readers the idea of "the annihilation of the North . . . its fields grown with weeds, its ships rotten, its factories and towns in ruins, their people departed . . . ." Powell admitted that Kettell's book was full of facts but charged that the author was "incapable of developing a single important truth from the whole of them."

The reader of the reviews of *Southern Wealth and Northern Profits* inevitably comes to the conclusion that the book had little or no influence on its readers in 1860–1861. It only confirmed them in the views they already held in regard to slavery and the sectional controversy.

Epilogue

Kettell had been sincere in his efforts to persuade the North that her interests, both economic and political, would be best served by recognizing the constitutional guarantees of slavery; but when secession and war came, he loyally supported the United States government. He found himself at loose ends, however, for his connection with *Hunt's Merchants' Magazine* was abruptly ended in January 1861. His economic views and political philosophy were no longer acceptable to his northern readers, and he turned, during the war years, to historical writing.

In 1862, Kettell published a *History of the Great Rebellion* (Worcester, Mass.: L. Stebbins, 1862–1863), in which he traced the sectional controversy over secession, discussed the formation of the Confederate States' government, the raising of armies and the immense financial resources of the United States, and praised the patriotism, enthusiasm, and loyalty of the northern people. A second volume appeared in 1863. In the preface, Kettell said that, in giving "the views of leading opponents," he had avoided "tracing their present position . . . to remote causes operating in past years." He further explains that the "Introduction and Chapter I" were written by someone other than himself; hence, "by this means were introduced sentiments that may appear to the reader far more partisan than historical." For these reasons, Kettell "disclaims all responsibility." He further explains that his own narrative was "written from a Union point of view." For that, he "neither desires to apologize nor expects an apology will be required." At least, he had recanted and hoped to get a favorable northern hearing.

A revised and complete *History of the Great Rebellion* was published in 1865. In this edition, Kettell wrote that

Passion must . . . become cool, prejudices be softened, and the light of truth illumine many passages, at present obscure, before effects can be traced to their proper causes, and such a history be written as will bear the unmistakable imprint of accuracy and impartiality. . . .[36]

Evidently, he was not yet ready to yield entirely on the views he had expressed about sectionalism and slavery in the years before the war.

Kettell's next works were more nearly in line with his pre-Civil War interests. In 1866, he published *The History of the War Debt of England; the History of the War Debt of the United States, and the Two Compared* [New York: n.p., 1866]. This was followed by *Eighty Years' Progress of the United States* (Hartford, Conn.: L. Stebbins, 1867), a co-operative work treating the economic and industrial growth of the nation.[37] Kettell contrib-

36. Thomas Prentice Kettell, *History of the Great Rebellion* (Hartford, Conn.: L. Stebbins, 1865), p. [iii].

37. [An earlier two-volume edition had been published by Stebbins from his New York office in 1861. The contributors to this work were well-known men, Horace Mann being one of them.—J.I.C.]

uted three chapters on colonial trade and manufacturing, three on transportation, three on cotton textiles, two each on paper and woolens, and one each on shoes and firearms. Kettell avoided sectional issues and comparisons of northern and southern development. Only once did he express his views on the sectional issue of slavery in such manner as to criticize the North. That had to do with the abolition of the foreign slave trade in 1808.

Kettell also attempted to re-establish himself in the publication field. He left New York City for San Francisco, where he for a short time edited the *Alta California.* He also attempted to re-establish himself in trade publications, and in August 1867 became editor of the San Francisco *Mercantile Gazette and Prices Current Shipping List and Register.* But despite his great reputation and long experience, this trade journal failed and ceased publication on October 16, 1867.[38]

When and where Thomas Prentice Kettell died I have been unable to learn. Strange as it may seem, I have found no obituary notice, nor does he appear in any of the biographical dictionaries. The only biographical sketch located was that printed in *Hunt's Merchants' Magazine* in 1849. One can only surmise that his championship of the South and slavery caused Kettell to become the forgotten man of his generation. Even so, it is difficult to explain how a man who contributed so much to American life and was toasted by the press during his lifetime as "one of America's most brilliant editors," "the major spokesman of American bankers and merchants on issues of political and economic interest," and as "the writer on political economy who did more to impart respectable character to the tone of the press on that subject than any other man," could have dropped totally out of sight.

38. Forsyth, *The Business Press,* p. 80.

10

William Watson Davis:
Introduction to the 1964 Edition
of William Watson Davis's
The Civil War and Reconstruction in Florida

> William Watson Davis was a product of the Dunning School. He
> was an able scholar, yet one who was never as well known as some
> members of the group. His book, *The Civil War and Reconstruc-
> tion in Florida,* was published in 1913 in New York by Columbia
> University, and then remained out of print for many years. In
> 1964, it was selected by the Florida Quadricentennial Commission
> for republication in a facsimile edition. The University of Florida
> Press assumed responsibility for publication, and Fletcher Green
> was asked to prepare the introductory essay. Green's essay on
> Davis and his writings, reprinted here in full, appeared on pp.
> xiii–xliii of the facsimile edition (Gainesville: University of
> Florida Press, 1964).

WILLIAM WATSON DAVIS, AUTHOR OF *The Civil War and Reconstruction in Florida,* (Columbia University Studies in History, Economics, and Public Law, vol. LIII [New York: Columbia University Press, 1913]) was born in Pensacola, Florida, February 12, 1884. His great-grandfather was the famous Matthew Livingston Davis of New York City. Journalist, businessman, politician, close friend and second to Aaron Burr in his fatal duel with Alexander Hamilton, Matthew Davis won an unsavory reputation when, as Grand Sachem of Tammany Society, he was accused of fraud in munici-pal contracts. He was found guilty but was finally exonerated in a second trial in the New York City Court. Davis engaged in a profitable trade with South America, was New York correspondent of the London *Times,* and wrote a life of Burr, who had left his papers in Davis's possession.[1]

Matthew Davis's son, John Eayres Davis, upon reaching majority, decided to seek his fortune in the South and moved to Georgia. He settled near Columbus and became a successful cotton planter and factor. He married Sarah Caroline Cropp, daughter of a South Carolina cotton planter who had removed to Alabama some few miles across the Chattahoochee River from Columbus. Loyal to his adopted state and region, John Davis joined the Confederate Army and was killed in battle. He left his widow with three daughters and two sons, one of whom was named Matthew Livingston for his grandfather. The war had dissipated the Davis wealth; and shortly after its close, Mrs. John Eayres Davis moved to Pensacola, where she ran a boarding house. Her son Matthew worked as an office boy for D. F. Sullivan, a lumberman. After Sullivan married one of Mrs. Davis's daughters, Matthew became a partner in the Sullivan lumber firm. Matthew Davis married Annie Laurie Lane of Virginia, and to this union were born five children, the eldest of whom was christened William Watson Davis. In 1887, Matthew Davis moved to Oak Grove, some fifteen miles from Mobile, Alabama, where he built a milldam, a sawmill, a store, quarters for white and Negro laborers, and developed a prosperous lumber industry of his own. Mrs. Davis died when William Watson was twelve years of age.

Watson, as the boy was called, grew to be six feet tall, roamed the woods and fields around Oak Grove, hunted and fished, became an expert horseman, knew everybody for miles around, and absorbed the lore and stories of the Civil War and Reconstruction years. He attended Wright Military Academy in Mobile, from which he was graduated at the age of sixteen. In 1899, he entered Alabama Polytechnic Institute at Auburn (now Auburn University), where he was a brilliant student. He studied under Professor George Petrie, a distinguished teacher and historian whose influence was decisive in crystallizing Davis's early interest in the

1. "Matthew Livingston Davis," *Dictionary of American Biography,* 20 vols. (New York: Charles Scribner's Sons, 1928–1936), V, 138–139.

Civil War and Reconstruction into a firm determination to make a professional career in history. In Professor Petrie's "Historical Seminary," Davis was trained in methods of historical research, introduced to the use and criticism of secondary and primary source documents, and wrote historical papers and essays which were later published. With his first-hand knowledge of the lumber industry, he wrote a paper for Professor Petrie on "The Yellow-Pine Lumber Industry in the South." Stirred by the terrible disaster of the Galveston flood of 1900, he wrote a paper on that subject. He also took an active interest in the college debating society, where the students discussed current issues, political problems, and historical questions. On one occasion, Davis chose to defend England's position in the conflict with the Boers of South Africa, which at that time was highly unpopular in Alabama. So well did he plead his case that he won the decision and made for himself a local reputation as an able speaker. He enjoyed the triumph and continued to develop his talent for speaking; and in his later professional career, he became a public speaker much sought after by university groups and civic clubs.

Davis was graduated with the Bachelor of Science degree in 1903. Professor Petrie was so favorably impressed with Davis's ability that he offered the young man an assistantship in the department of history. Davis accepted the appointment and won his Master of Science degree in history at Alabama Polytechnic Institute in 1904. Recommended by Professor Petrie, Davis applied for and was awarded a University Fellowship by Columbia University, where he went to study under the nationally known historian, William Archibald Dunning. He was thus to become one of the "Dunning School" of Civil War and Reconstruction historians. He greatly admired Professor Dunning but did not form the close tie with him that many students did.

Davis worked reasonably hard but took time from his studies to explore New York City, which fascinated him. The city had many points of interest for a rural southern boy with highly developed intellectual interests. Besides, Davis made the acquaintance of some of his New York relatives for the first time.

After finishing his residence program at the university, **Davis** went to France and spent a year at the Sorbonne. He also read and studied at the Bibliothèque Nationale. The study in France awakened in Davis an interest in European affairs, and he, with some fellow American students, decided to establish a journal devoted to news of and comments upon the European political scene, the journal to be circulated in the United States. Unfortunately for the venture, his father's lumber mill at Oak Grove was burned, and the young man was forced by financial conditions to abandon the project and return to the United States. With Professor Dunning's support, Davis secured an appointment as an assistant professor of history at the University of Kansas in 1912. The next year, he won his Doctor of Philosophy degree from Columbia University and at Kansas was promoted to the rank of associate professor.

Shortly after going to the University of Kansas, Davis met Miss Roxana Gage Henderson of Cambridge, Massachusetts, who was visiting friends in Lawrence, Kansas. They married in 1915 and retained their home in Lawrence until 1960. They had one son, Edward Lane Davis, presently professor of political science at the State University of Iowa.

When World War I came, Professor Watson Davis, having attended a military preparatory school and served as captain of his military company at Alabama Polytechnic Institute, participated in the early days of the SATC program at the University of Kansas. Desirous of more direct participation in the war effort, Davis volunteered for service with the Red Cross. He was accepted, commissioned, and ordered to France, where he saw duty in the front lines. After the war, he served with the Army of Occupation in Germany. He had escaped injury during the war but had a serious bout with influenza in Germany. He was nursed back to health by the German family with which he was billeted and long held them in fond remembrance.

Returning to the University of Kansas, Davis was made professor of history in the 1920s and named chairman of the department of history in 1936, a post he held until 1949. He ended his teaching career in 1954. Professor Davis offered courses in United States, Latin American, and Far Eastern history. He had a deep interest in diplomatic history, government, and political science, but his major interest was the Civil War and Reconstruction era. His courses in this era were very popular. In a poll conducted by the Alumni Association of the University of Kansas, Davis was chosen among the top ten professors of the university for the teens, twenties, and thirties. He was often called upon to discuss problems in history, politics, and government by university groups and civic clubs. Davis took a keen interest in athletics, especially football, and served as a faculty representative on the University of Kansas Athletic Council. He was a member of the Kansas State Historical Association, occasionally read papers to that organization, and served as a member of its board of directors from 1937 until his death in 1960.[2]

Davis's non-professional interests centered in travel and the great outdoors—fishing, hunting, and exploring out-of-the-way places in the South, the Rockies, Canada, and New England. While on leave of absence from the University of Kansas in 1934–1935, he visited the Far East and traveled in Japan, Korea, and China. On his return, he gave numerous public lectures on those countries, and he read a paper, "Japanese Viewpoints on Far Eastern Problems," before the Kansas History Teachers Association in 1938. After retirement in 1954, Davis continued to reside in Lawrence until 1960, when he moved to Iowa City, Iowa, to be with his son. Professor William Watson Davis died April 5, 1960, and was buried in the family plot in the church cemetery of Oak Grove.[3]

Davis's Published Writings

Watson Davis was an intelligent and ambitious young man and early began a publishing career. His association with Professor Petrie stimulated his desire to write; and while a student at

2. *Kansas Historical Quarterly*, VII (February 1938), 223; XXVII (Spring 1961), 124.

3. I am deeply indebted to Professor Lane Davis of the State University of Iowa and to Miss Margaret F. Davis (sister of William Watson Davis) of "Return," Oak Grove, Mobile, Ala., for much of the data in this biographical sketch. Miss Margaret F. Davis to Fletcher M. Green, 26 February 1964; Professor Lane Davis to Fletcher M. Green, 28 February 1964; letters in possession of the author.

Alabama Polytechnic Institute, Davis published three articles, in reputable magazines, and a historical monograph which was twice reprinted. A brief analysis of Davis's published works, chronologically arranged, will give an insight into his research interests and some understanding of his contributions to American historiography.

"The Yellow-Pine Lumber Industry in the South"[4] was his first. Doubtless the fact that his father was a lumberman and that Davis himself grew up in Oak Grove, the center of his father's milling industry, where he daily saw the backwoods whites driving the two- and four-mule, or ox-drawn, log carts and wagons, and the Negro workmen engaged at the mills sawing lumber, stimulated this study. After a brief survey of the major belts of yellow-pine timber of the United States as they existed in 1904, the author described the methods by which the timber was cut and the lumber sawed and marketed in the southern belt. He emphasized the failure of the labor unions to organize southern labor which, as he analyzed it, consisted of "backwoods whites in the logging" and "negroes[5] in the manufacturing department." He was favorably disposed toward organized labor, whereas public opinion in the South generally was hostile in 1904. But in discussing the white and Negro laborers, he clearly showed his acceptance of the concept of white supremacy and Negro inferiority. He declared that the Negroes were inclined to drift into the towns, to loaf, to shirk their work, and "were unreliable." And, said he, "negroes as a class lack the aggressive enterprise of the Caucasian."[6] It is surprising that this rural southern youth expressed strong support of the conservation of natural resources at a time when the conservation movement was in its infancy. He deplored "the ruthless destruction and waste going on in the Southern forests" and the "loss of new growth by carelessly set and uncontrolled fires." He called upon the southern lovers of trees and native game to work in conjunction with the United States

---

4. *The American Monthly Review of Reviews,* XXIX (April 1904) , 443–450.

5. Davis followed a practice, generally accepted in his day, of not capitalizing "Negro."

6. "The Yellow-Pine Lumber Industry in the South," p. 449.

Forestry Service to save these resources. He concludes: "If it succeeds, not only will a great economic problem be solved, but a thing of beauty [will] be created for the future sons of our land."[7] From whence this youth derived these ideas one can only surmise, for he cites no reading on the subject. But we do know that, in roaming the woods around Oak Grove, he had seen ample evidence of this destruction. And, since Alabama Polytechnic Institute was a land-grant college, his attention had probably been called to the need of conservation by his professors in history and agriculture.

"The Monroe Doctrine and Perry's Expedition to Japan,"[8] Davis's second publication, was inspired by the Russo-Japanese War, which many Americans considered a threat to United States interest in China. Davis took the position that Russia had been a menace to the United States from the day of its independence. He saw the Monroe Doctrine stemming directly from the Russian ukase of 1821, by which Russia proposed to extend her control southward to 51° on the Pacific coast of North America, and in which she warned vessels of all nations against trespassing within one hundred Italian miles of the coast. And he maintained that the Perry expedition of 1854 was intended by the United States to draw Japan into her commercial-economic orbit in her conflict with Russia, particularly in support of United States interests which had developed with China since the Cushing Treaty with China in 1844.

Davis's third publication, "Antebellum Southern Commercial Conventions,"[9] was one of the first attempts by a scholar to evaluate the significance of the commercial conventions held from 1837 to 1859 on the development of southern unity. Davis maintained that the conventions worked for the development, not only of

7. *Ibid.,* p. 450.
8. *The Cosmopolitan,* XXXVII (June 1904) , 219–225.
9. Alabama Historical Society, *Transactions, 1904,* V, No. 7, 153–202.
   Ibid., Reprint No. 34 from *Transactions* (Montgomery, 1906) , pp. 153–202.
   Ibid., in Alabama Polytechnic Institute, Historical Seminary, *Studies in Southern and Alabama History, Papers by Members of the Historical Seminary, George Petrie, Ph.D., Professor,* 2d ser. (Montgomery: Alabama Polytechnic Institute, 1906) , pp. 53–102.

domestic, but also of foreign trade. The leaders envisioned railroad and canal construction within the South and railroad connections between the South and the Pacific Coast, steamship lines from southern ports to the Amazon River valley and to English and continental European ports, and southern banking houses in England and Europe. Moreover, Davis emphasized that the southern leaders advocated the idea of federal aid to southern railroads and steamship lines. He saw sectional squabbles over slavery and the tariff as the basic cause of the failure of the conventions to accomplish their goals.

"How Galveston Secured Protection Against the Sea"[10] is the story of the rebuilding of the city of Galveston, Texas, after the great flood of 1900. Davis's attention probably was drawn to this disaster because some of his relatives had moved to Galveston after the Civil War. Davis recounts the story of the campaign for reform of the city government, the herculean engineering feat of building the great seawall and of raising the city's land surface above sea level, and of the successful drive for financing the great undertaking. He praised the new "Commission Form of City Government" as a significant advance in municipal government, and concluded that

From the conception of the idea in the gloom of failure and destruction to the present wonderful achievements the keynote has been—public spirit. The people of Galveston, rich and poor, are bearing the expense of these engineering triumphs.[11]

The editor of the London *Review of Reviews* remarked that "Among many wonderful chapters of civic romance, one of the most remarkable is that of Galveston as told in the *American Review of Reviews* by Mr. W. Watson Davis."[12]

Davis's fifth work, *The Civil War and Reconstruction in Florida*,[13] will be analyzed, discussed, and evaluated after an analysis

10. *The American Monthly Review of Reviews*, XXXIII (February 1906), 200–205.

11. *Ibid.*, p. 205.

12. *The Review of Reviews* (London), XXXIII (February 1906), 171.

13. Columbia University Studies in History, Economics, and Public Law, LIII (New York: Columbia University Press, 1913).

of the criticisms of the Dunning School made by the Revisionists.

In his sixth, "The Federal Enforcement Acts,"[14] Davis admits that the methods of the Ku Klux Klan were "notoriously violent and bloody"; that the southern whites kept the Negro from voting by methods with which the state officials and courts could not cope; that witnesses feared to give testimony, and grand and petit juries feared to make presentments or return verdicts adverse to southern whites; and that southern whites did not deny such violence. But, said he, "the purpose of the Enforcement Acts was not to secure the rights of the Negro but to insure Republican victory at the polls." Implicitly, therefore, he condoned white lawlessness. Furthermore, said he, by enacting such legislation, the national government had "deserted the principles in political procedure" which had made democracy as known in the United States a practical and working system. He concluded that the Acts "did not square with public consciousness either North or South." Whether correct or not in his judgment, Davis would, if living today, observe a great shift in "public consciousness" in regard to the Negroes' civil rights in the South as well as in the North. And the hindsight of today would deny categorically the judgment Davis made in 1913.

His last published work was "Flight Into Oblivion. By A. J. Hanna. A Review," published in the *Florida Historical Quarterly,* XVII (January 1939), 227–236.

As the record shows, Davis began his publishing career when only twenty years of age, and in a period of ten years, published three articles in nationally known magazines, one historical monograph that was twice reprinted, a chapter in a book whose contributors included several nationally recognized historians, and a book in the Columbia University *Studies* that was generally recognized as a significant contribution to the historiography of Reconstruction. But having gotten off to such a flying start, he

14. *Studies in Southern History and Politics.* Inscribed to William Archibald Dunning, Ph.D., LL.D., Lieber Professor of History and Political Philosophy in Columbia University, by His Former Pupils, the Authors (New York: Columbia University Press, 1914), pp. 205–228.

published nothing more except one book review. Since Davis's papers and correspondence are not available to the student, one can only speculate as to the explanation of the cessation of Davis's publication at such an early age. Was his devotion to his family so great that he never found time for research and writing? We note that he was married one year after his last publication. Did his experience in World War I have something to do with the decline in interest? Was it that Davis derived greater satisfaction from teaching than from research and writing? Since Davis's major research interest was in the South, might an explanation be found in the scarcity of southern sources in the University of Kansas library? Again, Davis enjoyed public speaking and was often called upon to address public audiences on problems of current interest. He was a popular speaker and he might have found speaking more rewarding than research. All these and other factors may have been influential, but I surmise that most important was Davis's love of the great outdoors and his pleasure in traveling. He himself explained his failure to attend the national association meetings by saying that he found a trip to Alabama at Christmas-time more important than going to the meeting. Whatever the explanation, it is no exaggeration to say that the historical profession lost something when William Watson Davis called it quits in 1914, so far as research and publication were concerned.

The Dunning School

William Archibald Dunning (1857–1922) was one of the first to make a scientific and scholarly investigation of the Reconstruction period in United States history. A product of John William Burgess's seminar at Columbia University, Dunning wrote sympathetically of the South. In his first book, *The Constitution of the United States in Civil War and Reconstruction, 1860–1865* (New York: J. F. Pearsen, 1885), he described the plans of the Radicals, under the leadership of Thaddeus Stevens, for punishing the southern Confederates as being "passionate fancies of fanatics more extreme than the Southern fire-eaters who had precipitated the Civil War." In his *Essays on the Civil War and Reconstruc-*

tion (New York: Macmillan Co., 1897), he described the administrative and political process of Reconstruction as "one of the most remarkable achievements in the history of government," but he decried the goal of the Reconstruction Acts as "purely political." His *Reconstruction: Political and Economic, 1865–1877* (New York: Harper & Brothers, 1907) was long accepted as the standard treatment of the period, and it has not yet been entirely replaced. In this book, Dunning turned to the national scene, whereas his students directed their attention largely to the individual southern states. As Dunning saw the Reconstruction, the social, economic, and political forces that "wrought positively for progress are to be found in the record, not of the vanquished but of the victorious section" (p. xv). Furthermore, "In this record there is less that is spectacular, less that is pathetic, and more that seems inexcusably sordid than in the record of the South" (pp. xv–xvi). Running through the book was the racist view that "The negro had no pride of race and no aspirations or ideals save to be like the whites" (p. 213). For this reason, said Dunning, the Negro desired social equality, mixed schools, and equal entrance into hotels and theaters.

Professor Dunning attracted a large number of able students to his seminar on Reconstruction. Many of his students, largely from the South, chose under his guidance to investigate the process of Reconstruction in one of the secession states. Listed in order of the publication of their works, they were: Charles Ernest Chadsey, *The Struggle Between President Johnson and Congress over Reconstruction* (New York: Columbia University Press, 1897); Edwin Campbell Woolley, *The Reconstruction of Georgia* (New York: Columbia University Press, 1901); James Wilford Garner, *Reconstruction in Mississippi* (New York: Macmillan Co., 1901); Walter Lynwood Fleming, *Civil War and Reconstruction in Alabama* (New York: Columbia University Press, 1905), Charles William Ramsdell, *Reconstruction in Texas* (New York: n.p., 1910); William Watson Davis, *The Civil War and Reconstruction in Florida* (New York: Columbia University Press, 1913); Joseph Grégoire deRoulhac Hamilton, *Reconstruction in North Carolina* (New York: Columbia University Press, 1914); Clara

Mildred Thompson, *Reconstruction in Georgia* (New York: Columbia University Press, 1915) ; and Thomas Starling Staples, *Reconstruction in Arkansas* (New York: Columbia University Press, 1923). Chadsey was a native of Nebraska and Woolley, of Illinois; all the others were southerners. Thompson and Staples were native Georgians; the others were natives of the states on which they wrote. As Woolley's title indicates, he looked upon Reconstruction as a policy of the federal government on a state; the others were interested primarily in conditions within the state. All of the authors save Miss Thompson are deceased. In addition to the books listed above, we should note that Fleming was the editor of *Documentary History of Reconstruction,* 2 vols. (Cleveland: Arthur H. Clark, 1906), and *The Sequel of Appomattox* (New Haven: Yale University Press, 1919). We should include also *Studies in Southern History and Politics, Inscribed to William Archibald Dunning . . . by His Pupils, the Authors* (New York: Columbia University Press, 1914). There were contributors to this volume who did not write a special study on state Reconstruction, while some who did write special studies did not contribute essays to the *Studies.* Dunning and his students— again, let me emphasize, largely southerners—who wrote on Reconstruction came to be known generally as the "Dunning School." Several of them established national reputations in the field of Reconstruction history.

The writings of the Dunning School were generally favorably received at the time of their publication, and continued in good repute until about 1940. E. Benjamin Adams found Dunning, *Reconstruction: Political and Economic,* of "extraordinary excellence" in which "the analysis of causes and situations is keen and correct. Both subjects and men are treated with eminent fairness and justice." Noting Dunning's sympathy with the South, Adams said: "The book cordially recognizes the patience, patriotism and, in the main, wisdom shown by Southern people in the terrible and, to great extent, needless sufferings through which they were made to pass."[15]

---

15. *American Historical Review,* XII (January 1908) , 371–373.

Edmund G. Ross, reviewing the first of Dunning's students' dissertations on Reconstruction—Chadsey, *The Struggle Between President Johnson and Congress over Reconstruction*—pointed out that the author painted the Radical congressional leaders as strong-willed men who were able to force unquestioning compliance with their plans and thus ruled with an absolute despotism that absorbed for a time not only executive but also judicial powers in the reorganization of the seceded states. "The winner [the North] was imperious and too often disdainful and revengeful." Ross described the author's concluding statement that the record of "the whole period is marked by blunders and prejudices on both sides; that the spirit of compromise could find no place in either's plans" as "blunt but truthful." The judgment was as "complete, fair and intelligent . . . as is possible in the space devoted to it."[16] One scholar jointly reviewing Woolley's and Garner's books said that a reader could infer that one was written by a northerner and the other by a southerner, but that the reader would have to "concede to both writers the purpose to be fair." Woolley, said the reviewer, did not "attempt a close study of Southern conditions and Southern character, but criticizes freely the motives of the Northern leaders in Reconstruction and the policy they adopted." On the other hand, Garner was "extremely shy of criticizing the acts of Congress and does not generalize about the policy," but he "recounted dispassionately" the "humiliations of his people" and "carefully weighed out praise and blame to Northerners in Mississippi." And "So far as impartiality is honesty neither [Woolley nor Garner] leaves anything to be desired."[17]

William Oscar Scroggs, an economist, said that Fleming treated Reconstruction

as something more than a political maneuver, as a process affecting churches, schools, trades, and professions, as well as politics and civil administration. The author's sympathies are decidedly with the South,

16. *Ibid.*, III (October 1897), 159–161.
17. William Garrott Brown, *American Historical Review*, VII (April 1902), 582–584.

but the work is free from bitterness or prejudice, and is on the whole as impartial an account as one can expect from any writer on this subject.[18]

Dunning's comparison of Fleming and Garner is a penetrating one. Fleming, Dunning wrote, presents "a great mass of social and economic as well as political facts with a marked Southern bias in their interpretation." Garner "deals chiefly with the legal and political movements, in a rigidly judicial spirit."[19] Ellis Paxon Oberholtzer said, of Fleming's *Sequel of Appomattox,*

we have no higher authority on this theme. . . . That he is a partisan he never tried to conceal, but none can come out of an investigation of Southern conditions after the war, no matter how cursory, without a disgust which will be reflected on the written page. To justify such abominations would completely condemn one's historical instincts as well as moral sense. . . .[20]

Walter Flavius McCaleb found Ramsdell, *Reconstruction in Texas,* "extremely temperate" and "judicious." But when Ramsdell dealt with "the relations between state officials and military commanders . . . [he] has shown Sheridan's shortcomings in unmincing words."[21]

An anonymous reviewer described Davis, *The Civil War and Reconstruction in Florida,* as a narrative of "absorbing interest" in which the author brought in national politics and events so that the reader may better comprehend developments on the state scene. "The author's attitude is usually that of a dispassionate looker-on, although now and then he expresses clearcut conclusions. . . ."[22] William E. Dodd found Davis's book in "good clear style which reads well," and "The contentions of the writer are so cogently presented that the reader is not likely to dissent."[23] To John H. Russell, Davis's book showed "that the war entailed in

18. *American Historical Review,* XI (July 1906) , 943–944.
19. *Reconstruction: Political and Economic,* p. 353.
20. *American Historical Review,* XXV (April 1920) , 520.
21. *Ibid.,* XVI (January 1911) , 368–369.
22. *Ibid.,* XIX (January 1914) , 404–405.
23. *Journal of Political Economy,* XXI (November 1913) , 871–872.

fact a temporary industrial revolution," but he complained that the author was "guilty of padding" the account in striving for "literary style."[24]

William K. Boyd described Hamilton's *Reconstruction in North Carolina* as a well-told story of extravagance and corruption, the rise and violent action of the Ku Klux Klan, Governor Holden's use of force, and his impeachment. Boyd declared that the author's "warm sympathy with the struggle for redemption from radical misrule" left the impression that he gave the Reconstructionists "no mercy" and "in some cases" did not give "due consideration to extenuating circumstances."[25]

John H. T. McPherson described Thompson's *Reconstruction in Georgia* as a "candid and impartial treatment" of the subject. In her own words, Miss Thompson found "the personnel engaged in the Reconstruction administration" of Georgia "was not entirely bad, was even quite good in some members." She also found "the Freedmen's Bureau . . . an important constructive force towards economic adjustment in the immediate transition from slavery to freedom," although it "was badly mismanaged" and some of its "agents taught the freedmen to mistrust the whites" so that the agents might "manipulate the helpless black voters for their own aggrandizement." The reviewer agreed with Miss Thompson that "Reconstruction in Georgia meant a wider democratization of society" for the poor white, as well as the Negro.[26] Arthur Charles Cole, in his review of *Reconstruction in Georgia*, noted that the author "emphasized the special contributions which Reconstruction made in political and social equality and to education in Georgia."[27] Cole was also high in his praise of *Studies in Southern History and Politics*, the co-operative work of Dunning's students. He said,

There can be no doubt that they [the authors] have kept their minds open to the teaching of a sane and scientific brand of history and with their master have rejected rampant sectional prejudice for a broad-

24. *American Political Science Review*, VIII (February 1914) , 137–138.
25. *American Historical Review*, XX (July 1915) , 869–871.
26. *Ibid.*, XXI (October 1915) , 162–164.
27. *Mississippi Valley Historical Review*, III (June 1916) , 113–115.

minded tolerance, a temperate sympathy, and a critical understanding.[28]

Historians generally used the term "Dunning School" to include Dunning and his Columbia University students whose major research interest was the Civil War and Reconstruction. Their interpretation of the Reconstruction era was generally accepted by the historical profession and soon permeated the school textbooks. It was later popularized by two journalists, Claude G. Bowers in *The Tragic Era: The Revolution after Lincoln* (Boston: Houghton Mifflin Company, 1929) and George Fort Milton in *The Age of Hate: Andrew Johnson and the Radicals* (New York: Coward-McCann, 1930) and came to be almost universally accepted by the American people as the correct interpretation of that period in United States history.

The Revisionists

Despite the general acceptance of the Dunning School interpretation, there were, almost from the beginning, a few scattered voices of dissent. And, since the Dunning School displayed a strong prejudice against the Negro's role in Reconstruction, it is not surprising that Negro historians were among the first to criticize their interpretation. William Edward Burghardt Du Bois, in his article "Reconstruction and Its Benefits," argued that Reconstruction brought advance and progress in several areas, including a great upsurge in Negro education.

This great multitude rose up simultaneously and asked for intelligence. . . . There is no doubt that the thirst of the black man for knowledge . . . gave birth to the public free-school system of the South.[29]

He also maintained that Reconstruction brought beneficial economic legislation and broadened the base of political democracy in the South. Du Bois's claims were exaggerated, but there is truth in his position.

28. *Ibid.*, pp. 108–112.
29. *American Historical Review*, XV (July 1910), 781–799.

John Lynch, a Negro Republican officeholder in Mississippi during Reconstruction, told his story of those years in *Facts of Reconstruction* (New York: Neale, 1913) . In it, he advanced the thesis that Negroes and whites collaborated in efforts for political reform in that state, but that these efforts were cut short because of the Radical program. A few years later, the Negro historian Alrutheus Ambush Taylor wrote three books dealing with the Negro's role in Reconstruction in South Carolina, Tennessee, and Virginia. In *The Negro in South Carolina During Reconstruction* (Washington: Associated Publishers, 1925) , Taylor took the Dunning School to task for their treatment of the Negro. "Self-interest," said he, ". . . impelled them to select such facts as would establish their view"; hence, "their books were practically worthless in studying and teaching the history of Reconstruction." Carl Russell Fish, in a review of the book, said no one could accept "any such sweeping indictment."[30]

Taylor renewed the attack in 1938, charging in "Historians of Reconstruction" that Dunning's students were "so biased and prejudiced that they wrote with little regard to dispassionate presentation of facts" in their effort "to prove the Negro not capable of participating in government and to justify the methods of intimidation and fraud used to overturn the Reconstruction governments." Taylor admitted that Dunning himself had "in the main, written dispassionately," but insisted that "his writings were greatly influenced by his students"; hence, Dunning "found occasion to extenuate, if not to justify, the black codes." Taylor maintained that Reconstruction was beneficial in that it established equality of all men before the law, made free public education available to both races, established a greatly improved judicial system, and provided the Negro with economic benefits through labor contracts and land tenure.[31]

Horace Mann Bond, Negro historian and educator, directed his attack at the Dunning School's failure to recognize social and economic reforms brought about by Reconstruction. The title of his article, "Social and Economic Forces in Alabama Reconstruc-

30. *Ibid.,* XXX (April 1925) , 653.
31. *Journal of Negro History,* XXIII (January 1938) , 16–34.

tion," indicates his approach to the problem.[32] And W. E. B. Du Bois, in *Black Reconstruction: An Essay Toward a History of the Part Which Black Folk Played in the Attempt to Reconstruct Democracy in America, 1860–1880* (New York: Harcourt, Brace and Co., 1935), emphasized the accomplishments of the Negro during Reconstruction, the social, economic, and political benefits derived therefrom, and what he interprets as Negro-poor-white political alignment. This work was so highly prejudiced and colored by Marxian philosophy that it failed to gain general acceptance. It was, nevertheless, an antidote to the Dunning School.

Whether Carl Lotus Becker was correct in "Everyman His Own Historian" (*American Historical Review*, XXXVII [January 1932], 221–236; and *Everyman His Own Historian* [New York: Appleton-Century-Crofts, 1935], pp. 233–255), where he developed the idea of subjective emphasis and relativism in judging the past by the climate of opinion of the present—or, as J. B. Black put it, "every age interprets the record of the past in light of its own ideas"—United States historians were prepared, by mid-twentieth century, to reinterpret the Reconstruction period in a much more favorable attitude toward the Negro than that of their predecessors and to recognize more beneficial results from Reconstruction. A number of historians took up their pens to attack the Dunning School interpretation. In fact, they conducted a veritable crusade for the cause. Among others, Francis Butler Simkins,[33] Howard Kennedy Beale,[34] T. Harry Williams,[35] and John Hope Franklin[36] fired broadsides at the past generation of Reconstruction historians.

32. *Ibid.*, XXIII (July 1938), 290–348.

33. Francis Butler Simkins, "New Viewpoints of Southern Reconstruction," *Journal of Southern History*, V (February 1939), 49–61.

34. Howard Kennedy Beale, "On Rewriting Reconstruction History," *American Historical Review*, XLV (July 1940), 807–828.

35. T. Harry Williams, "An Analysis of Some Reconstruction Attitudes," *Journal of Southern History*, XII (November 1946), 469–486.

36. John Hope Franklin, "Whither Reconstruction Historiography?" *Journal of Negro Education*, XVII (Fall 1948), 446–461; "Reconstruction," in *Problems of American History*, 2d ed., edited by Richard W. Leopold and Arthur Stanley Link (Englewood Cliffs, N.J.: Prentice-Hall, 1957), pp. 329–363.

These younger historians differ somewhat in their approach to Reconstruction historiography and emphasize different aspects of the Dunning School interpretation; but they agree on major points and, in fact, often repeat each other. Beale's article was more general in approach and more comprehensive in scope than that of any of the other writers. An analysis of his criticisms will, therefore, provide a general understanding of the views of the new Revisionist School. Beale surveyed the literature of Reconstruction from its beginning to 1940, criticized and evaluated its strength and weakness, and suggested new approaches to the problem. He maintained that the Dunning School had exaggerated the "sordid political and economic motives of the Radicals" and overemphasized the harm done to the South during Reconstruction. They were prejudiced against Negroes, carpetbaggers, scalawags, and Republicans and glorified ex-Confederates and Democrats. They greatly magnified the tax burdens, the size of the Reconstruction debts, the useless expenditures of the Reconstruction legislatures, and the fraud and corruption of the Reconstruction state governments. Beale admitted that some of the Dunning School saw the social and economic implications of Reconstruction, but he argued that they did not grasp their significance. Furthermore, they greatly exaggerated the control which the Negro exercised in state governments, and according to Beale they looked at Reconstruction as a local or regional process and ignored its national significance.[37]

Beale noted that modification of Reconstruction historiography had set in, and that a new interpretation was under way. He declared that younger southern scholars were leading the way to a fuller and more accurate understanding of Reconstruction. Vernon Lane Wharton had "presented facts that are revolutionary in their significance." Horace Mann Bond "illuminated the role of business interests" in the Reconstruction of Alabama. Comer Vann Woodward, in his treatment of the "New Departure Democrats," had "brought understanding to what has been a veritable

37. Beale, "On Rewriting Reconstruction History," p. 808.

'darkage' in American [political] history." Francis Butler Simkins and Robert H. Woody "have been unusually fair minded toward the Negro and the white Reconstructionists and have shown interest in social and economic forces."[38] But this was only a beginning. Beale said the time had come when historians generally should

> study the history of Reconstruction without first assuming, at least subconsciously, that carpetbaggers and Southern white Republicans were wicked, that Negroes were illiterate incompetents, and that the whole white South owed a debt of gratitude to the restoration of "White Supremacy."[39]

Beale sounded a clarion call for further study, new approaches, and a sounder and more nearly correct interpretation of Reconstruction. He thus became the spearhead of the new Revisionist School as opposed to the old Dunning School.

Following Beale's call, the Revisionists have chipped away at what one of them called

> the prejudiced version of Reconstruction laid down around the turn of the century by Rhodes, Burgess, and Dunning, developed by Fleming and some of the individual state historians of the period, and widely popularized, in 1929, by Claude Bowers' zestful work of imagination, *The Tragic Era*.[40]

The Revisionist interpretation has been implemented in hundreds of articles and scores of monographs, and has been accepted as an article of faith by many, probably a large majority, of the professional historians.

But in 1959, Bernard A. Weisberger, an ardent Revisionist, lamented that there was "no synthesis of this material in a good general history of Reconstruction." He noted that E. Merton Coulter, "the author of the only full-sized treatment by an academic historian since 1940," had declared that he felt that

> there can be no sensible departure from the well-known facts of the Reconstruction program as it was applied to the South. No amount of

38. *Ibid.,* p. 809.
39. *Ibid.,* p. 810.
40. Bernard A. Weisberger, "The Dark and Bloody Ground of Reconstruction Historiography," *Journal of Southern History,* XXV (November 1959) , 428.

revision can explain away the grievous mistakes made in that abnormal period of American history.[41]

Weisberger characterized this statement as an indignant rejection of the entire notion of revision, and concluded: Coulter's book "is no contribution to understanding. In point of fact it is something of a setback."[42]

Weisberger also was unhappy because many of the textbooks still followed the Dunning School. Among those he singled out for disapproval were those written by John D. Hicks, Samuel E. Morison and Henry Steele Commager, and Robert E. Riegel and David F. Long; but he was especially severe in his condemnation of "Thomas A. Bailey's *The American Pageant,* a highly popular one-volume text." Quoting and paraphrasing two sentences from the book, Weisberger concluded, "No doubt this is as stirring for students as a showing of *The Birth of a Nation* but it is not much more accurate."[43]

In 1961, a beginning was made to fill the two gaps in the Revisonist interpretation of Reconstruction with the publication of John Hope Franklin's general treatment of the problem, *Reconstruction: After the Civil War* (Chicago: University of Chicago Press, 1961), and David Donald's revision of James G. Randall's well-known textbook, *The Civil War and Reconstruction* (Boston: D. C. Heath, 1937). Franklin treats Reconstruction as a national rather than a sectional problem, emphasizes the shortcomings of Presidential Reconstruction, explains the corruption under the Radicals as a national malaise, extols the virtues of the Radical program, and emphasizes the beneficial social, economic, and political reforms of the period. He has given extended and favorable coverage to the role of the Negro. In *The Civil War and Reconstruction,* second edition (Boston: Heath, 1961), Donald has, as he himself expressed it, "taken full advantage of the important revisionist work that has been completed in recent years and . . . tried to show Negroes, carpetbaggers, and scala-

---

41. *Ibid.,* p. 434. See also E. Merton Coulter, *The South During Reconstruction, 1865–1877* (Baton Rouge, La.: Louisiana State University Press, 1947), p. xi.

42. Weisberger, "Dark and Bloody Ground," p. 434.

43. *Ibid.,* p. 436.

wags in a fuller and fairer light." He has given a much fuller treatment to agriculture, business, and labor, but "rejected the economic interpretation of the Reconstruction period in favor of a more complex pattern of intergroup rivalries." He explains the corruption of Reconstruction in the South as a "part of the whole tawdry age."[44] Donald emphasizes the role of the Negro, champions the carpetbagger and scalawag, and maintains that Reconstruction brought beneficial results to the South in the area of social, economic, and political reforms. Over-all, the tone of this edition is much less pro-southern than the original one of 1937.

La Wanda Cox and John H. Cox, in *Politics, Principle, and Prejudice, 1865–1866: Dilemma of Reconstruction America* (Glencoe, Ill.: Free Press of Glencoe, 1963), have reinterpreted the struggle between President Andrew Johnson and the Radical Republicans in the Revisionist spirit. They have taken a very favorable view of the Radicals; and, under their treatment, Johnson loses some of the stature which he had obtained with the Dunning School and all of the aura in which Claude G. Bowers and George Fort Milton clothed him. It is interesting to note, however, that there are differences between the Beale, the Cox, and the Eric L. McKitrick (all in the Revisionist School) assessments of Johnson's role in Reconstruction.

Since the Revisionists were attacking a well-established and firmly entrenched interpretation of Reconstruction, it was only natural that they carry the battle to the enemy and use any and all available weapons. Hence, they sometimes took positions that were vulnerable. They exaggerated the sins of the Dunning School and magnified the benefits of Reconstruction and the role of the Negro in bringing those benefits to fruition. They had a tendency to write in terms of absolutes, and their tone was often adamant and unyielding. In other words, prejudice and bias are not the exclusive possessions of the Dunning School. And if the Dunning School position was too far to the right, the Revisionists have moved too far to the left. The pendulum, with time, will doubtless swing back and come to a position somewhere between

44. James G. Randall and David Donald, *The Civil War and Reconstruction,* 2d ed. (Boston: Heath, 1961), pp. vi–vii.

the two schools of thought, but to the left of center. One thing is certain: there is, at present, no single account of Reconstruction that satisfies the two schools.

My own sympathy is with the Revisionists, rather than with the Dunning School. Even so, I would point out what seem to be fallacies and weaknesses in the Revisionist interpretation. They admit that the Dunning studies are "detailed, thorough, and generally accurate," but condemn them because they "show hostility to the Negro, the carpetbagger and the scalawag," and take a regional rather than national point of view. One would observe that the critic who admits that he "drew heavily upon the research of the Dunning School" should go slow in condemning their interpretation unless he himself had researched the sources on which the interpretation was made. And since most of the studies are limited to a single state, they could hardly be other than state and regional. The Revisionists have muddied the historical waters by including nearly all the writing done on Reconstruction from 1895 to 1940, and much of it thereafter, in the Dunning School—or the "Dunning Type," as some of them prefer to call it. Thus, we find Revisionists including in the Dunning School the writings of men trained at the Universities of Chicago, Johns Hopkins, North Carolina, Pennsylvania, and Wisconsin. And to correct the misinterpretation of these "detailed, thorough and generally accurate" studies, the Revisionists sometimes offer a single short article published in a local historical journal. These articles may be excellent (indeed, I hope they are, for some of them were written by my former students), but they are highly specialized and are not broad enough to offset a book-length study of Reconstruction in a state. And if "Fleming's distortions [in *The Civil War and Reconstruction*] are corrected" in an article of seventeen pages, as the author of one of the Revisionist books says, the distortions were evidently neither numerous nor significant. Another Revisionist was either careless with facts or guilty of grave distortion when, attempting to establish youthful background sympathy for a pro-southern attitude, he named six authors who, he says, were over twenty-one years of age in 1901. The source he cites shows that one of the six was born in 1900.

The Revisionists often disagree among themselves in evaluating the works on Reconstruction. A few examples will suffice. Weisberger condemns E. Merton Coulter, *The South During Reconstruction,* as offering "no contribution to understanding [Reconstruction]. In point of fact it is something of a setback"; whereas, Franklin says that a "just treatment of this crowded and chaotic period [Reconstruction] makes heavy demands upon any writer's scholarship, judgment and literary skill," and concludes: "Mr. Coulter's book ably meets most of these demands." Franklin links James W. Patton, *Unionism and Reconstruction in Tennessee* (Chapel Hill: University of North Carolina Press, 1934), with Simkins and Woody, *South Carolina During Reconstruction* (Chapel Hill: University of North Carolina, 1932) "Among the studies that deal with the larger social and economic picture" of Reconstruction; whereas Donald links Patton's work with James W. Fertig, *Secession and Reconstruction in Tennessee* (Chicago: University of Chicago Press, 1898) as "Dunning-type" works. Both Franklin and Donald praise Allan Nevins, *The Emergence of Modern America, 1865–1878* (New York: Macmillan Co., 1927), for its excellent and balanced coverage of Reconstruction; Donald places it among "Three general works [that] stand largely outside of this historiographical controversy." Nevins cites Fleming's and Garner's studies of Reconstruction as "Among those of special merit and thoroughness," and those of Ramsdell, Davis, Hamilton, Thompson, and Staples as "excellent." Those studies are the basic works of the Dunning School, which Franklin and Donald condemned as unsound in their treatment of Reconstruction. The wide discrepancy in the evaluations of the Dunning School writings by the Revisionists has some bearing on the validity of the latter School's interpretation of the period. If they cannot agree on the value of their sources, how can one be confident in their interpretations? Furthermore, one should note that the Revisionists make considerable use of the Dunning School studies and often cite them in support of interpretations in which they agree.

Two major criticisms of the Dunning School are that they overemphasized the corruption of the Radical state governments and overlooked beneficial social, economic, and political reforms. Actually, the two schools of thought are not too far apart on these issues, and the two may be reconciled. The Dunning School, writing on individual states, found, exposed, and condemned corruption whenever it existed. It loomed large in the devastated and poverty-ridden South, and they treated it as a local problem.

The Revisionists admit, generally frankly and candidly, that corruption existed in the southern states, but they try to relate it to the general national picture. Carl N. Degler says:

> There is no denying the disreputable character of all too many of the Radical state governments. Certainly the history of Louisiana, South Carolina, Florida, and Alabama during this period provides rather painful examples of what corruption can be and what government should not be.

On the other hand, he declared that Mississippi "under Radical Republican rule enjoyed a government as administratively honest as most Democratic ones," and he cites James W. Garner, *Reconstruction in Mississippi,* in his support. Georgia, too, "showed a marked moderation in her government, a lesser degree of reconstruction evils, less wanton corruption and extravagance in public office." And Degler cites C. Mildred Thompson, *Reconstruction in Georgia,* in support.[45]

David Donald admits, "There is a great deal of evidence to substantiate the familiar charges that these Radical governments in the South were corrupt."[46] Both these Revisionists, however, relate corruption in the southern state governments to corruption in the northern states and in the federal government. Degler says:

> Though not at all excusing the Radical frauds, the corrupt climate of the times does make it clear that the Radical pilferings were little more than particular instances of a general postwar phenomenon.[47]

In similar vein, Donald writes:

45. Carl N. Degler, *Out of Our Past: The Forces That Shaped Modern America* (New York: Harper, 1959) , pp. 226–227.
46. Randall and Donald, *The Civil War and Reconstruction,* 2d. ed., p. 624.
47. Degler, *Out of Our Past,* pp. 226–227.

With no attempt to minimize these frauds, the historian must attempt to put them in perspective. The entire postwar era, it must be remembered, was one of graft and exploitation; no political party and no section of the country escaped the malign influence.[48]

Both schools, then, recognize the corruption and trace it to the abnormal conditions of Reconstruction times; but the Dunning School studied the individual state problem, while the Revisionists were concerned with the national picture. It should be observed, however, that the stench was no less obnoxious in the South because its corruption was less than that in the North.

In regard to social and political reforms, the Revisionists have confused the issue by generalizing about the action in the southern states as a group; hence, they overlook the variation from state to state. Several of the Dunning studies recognize that various social, economic, and political reforms were incorporated into the state constitutions and political practices during Reconstruction. This is particularly true of James W. Garner, *Reconstruction in Mississippi*, C. Mildred Thompson, *Reconstruction in Georgia*, William W. Davis, *The Civil War and Reconstruction in Florida*, and William L. Fleming, *Civil War and Reconstruction in Alabama*. Garner devotes an entire chapter to the economic aspects of Reconstruction and another to educational development. He notes that, in 1876, "the public school system which they [Radical Republicans] had fathered had become firmly established, its efficiency increased, and its administration made somewhat less expensive."[49] Thompson emphasized the work of the Freedmen's Bureau in education and its constructive role in the economic adjustment of the Negro. And she reported that Reconstruction in Georgia meant a wider democratization of society for poor whites, as well as Negroes. Fleming's work contains a mass of data on social and economic life, and he emphasizes that Reconstruction in Alabama was not confined to politics

48. Randall and Donald, *Civil War and Reconstruction,* p. 624.

49. James W. Garner, *Reconstruction in Mississippi* (New York: Macmillan Co., 1901), p. 370.

and government but was concerned with religion, education, the professions, and trade and industry.

Davis and the Revisionists

The Revisionists aimed their criticisms at the Dunning School as a group, and did not check the individual author against their standards. In fact, they practically ignored William Watson Davis and *Civil War and Reconstruction in Florida*. Howard K. Beale does not mention Davis in "On Rewriting Reconstruction History," nor does Bernard A. Weisberger, in "The Dark and Bloody Ground of Reconstruction Historiography." John Hope Franklin lists Davis's book, without comment, in *Reconstruction: After the Civil War*. David Donald lists Davis's study of Reconstruction twice in the bibliographical section of *Civil War and Reconstruction*, 1961 edition; the first reads, "On Florida the standard work is William W. Davis, *The Civil War and Reconstruction in Florida*"; the second, "The Dunning-type work on Florida is William W. Davis. . . ."[50] Donald does not cite Davis in the text, although James G. Randall had cited it in the first edition (1937) of that work, and described it as "The best work on Florida."[51] E. Merton Coulter cites Davis's work a number of times in *The South During Reconstruction, 1865–1877,* as does Francis Butler Simkins in *History of the South,* 3d ed. (New York: Knopf, 1963). One may gather, therefore, that the Revisionists have generally discarded Davis as unsound, but that historians of the old school still consider him trustworthy.

Let us test Davis by checking his book against the major criticisms of the Revisionist School: first, the claim that the Dunning School let race prejudice blind them to the Negro's role in Reconstruction. Davis certainly made no attempt to hide his acceptance of the concept of white supremacy and Negro inferiority. The United States Supreme Court had long since declared the Civil Rights Acts unconstitutional and had upheld state laws requiring separation of the races, and the nation as a whole had accepted

---

50. Randall and Donald, *The Civil War and Reconstruction,* 2d ed., pp. 758, 780.
51. James G. Randall, *The Civil War and Reconstruction* (Boston: D. C. Heath, 1937), p. 867.

and applied the concept of racial inferiority in dealing with racial groups in newly acquired territory. Within this frame of reference, Davis was able to deal with the Negro sympathetically and understandingly. He approved the application of antebellum laws restricting free Negroes to the freedmen in the Black Code of 1866, but declared that "The negro was in need of protection when dealing with unscrupulous whites, Northern or Southern. He was also in need of some aid in earning a living under the new régime of freedom."[52]

Davis believed the Freedmen's Bureau was founded on a false assumption, namely "that the Southern black unaided would not obtain justice from the Southern white," and that its operation was "arbitrary [and] bureaucratic." Nevertheless, he praised its work in many fields, including distribution of food to the destitute, maintaining an orphanage, insane asylum, hospitals and distributing free medicine to Negroes, aiding Negroes to locate homesteads on federal lands, instituting written contracts for labor between white employer and Negro laborer, and in organizing and superintending schools for Negroes.[53]

In another connection, Davis noted with satisfaction that ex-Senator Stephen D. Mallory; J. D. Wolf, an ex-Federal Army officer; and Hayes Satterlee, an aged Negro, representing three social groups—southern white, northern white, and southern Negro—addressed a mass meeting and urged amicable cooperation of the races. He later expressed regret that the movement had failed.

Davis never attempted to hide his belief that Negroes generally were ill-prepared for participation in politics and government, and he often castigated them for shiftlessness and venality. But he found some individual Negroes able, honest, and well-prepared, and gave them a full meed of praise. For instance, in discussing the personnel of the Constitutional Convention of 1868, he

52. Davis, *Civil War and Reconstruction in Florida*, p. 378.

53. *Ibid.*, pp. 380–386. Davis gives about as much credit to the Bureau for its good work in these and other areas as does Joe M. Richardson, "An Evaluation of the Freedmen's Bureau in Florida," *Florida Historical Quarterly*, XLI (January 1963), 223–238. See also George R. Bentley, "The Political Activity of the Freedmen's Bureau in Florida," *Florida Historical Quarterly*, XXVIII (July 1949), 28–37.

pointed out that "two or three [of eighteen Negro members] . . . had evil reputations; and would have done better in jails than in legislative halls"; but "The most cultured member of the Convention [composed of eighteen Negroes, sixteen carpetbaggers, twelve scalawags, and two Conservative southerners], probably, was Jonathan Gibbs, a negro." He characterized Robert Meacham, a mulatto, as "an intelligent though troublesome man," and William U. Saunders, "a 'Baltimore negro,'" an ex-barber proved to be the most prominent negro politician in the convention as well as one of the shrewdest . . . men there."[54]

Davis devotes two chapters in his book to lawlessness in Florida. He admits that most of the offenders were native whites, and he is forthright in his condemnation of individual and group action. Southern whites "deliberately determined to get rid of local political [Republican] leaders and negroes"; their criminal action was "systematic and organized"; they were guilty of "cold blooded murder and assassination"; they deliberately killed an upstanding Jewish merchant because he "expressed opinions derogatory to 'white supremacy'"; their whippings were "disgustingly brutal"; and the "criminal demoralization [among the Southern whites] . . . was frightful." Recognizing the evils inherent in people taking the law into their own hands, Davis permits his racial prejudice to justify such action. He concludes:

Men formed the habit of defying the law and resorting to violence to attain their ends. The Southerner was certainly face to face with negro domination foisted on him by Federal law. He arose to protect his own unwritten laws in order that his property, his self-respect, and his family might not be injured or destroyed. He resorted to physical violence under cover, in one of the most sinister and interesting contests of modern times. And in this contest *for a very necessary supremacy* a foul crime was committed by white against black. Innocent people suffered. There is no mercy and scant justice in social adjustment.[55]

Turning now to the Revisionist charge that the Dunning School exaggerated and overemphasized the political corruption,

---

54. Davis, *Civil War and Reconstruction in Florida*, pp. 494, 496.

55. [The closing quotation is taken from Davis, *Civil War and Reconstruction in Florida*, p. 586; the italics are the editor's.—F.M.G.] For a new treatment of this lawlessness, see Ralph L. Peek, "Lawlessness in Florida, 1868–1871," *Florida Historical Quarterly*, XL (October 1961), 164–185.

high taxes, and excessive debts of the Radical Republican state governments, we note that Davis devoted relatively little space to the question of political frauds. In most cases which he discussed, he concluded that the Conservatives had overstated their case; at least, they were unable to prove their charges against the Radicals. For example, the Conservatives charged fraud in the election of delegates to the Constitutional Convention of 1868. They had sworn testimony that "crowds of negroes from Alabama" had been brought into Florida and voted, and General George G. Meade admitted that there was "prima facie evidence . . . that . . . the Reconstruction laws" were not "strictly adhered to." In spite of such evidence, Davis concluded, "no good documentary evidence is extant demonstrating that fraud was resorted to."[56] He reached a similar judgment in the charges of fraud in the state elections of 1868.[57] He dismissed the charge that Governor Reed had knowingly signed illegal bonds, with the statement that "the trial did not develop any substantial proof of the allegations."[58] And he balanced the Conservative claims that the Radicals resorted to chicanery and extreme execution of federal law to control the election of 1872, with the statement that the "Conservatives resorted to threats of lawless violence to keep the negroes from the polls."[59] In the election of 1876, he found both parties tarred with the same corrupt brush.

Only in the matter of state bonds did Davis find the Radicals guilty as charged. He declared that "the state officials had either been fools or knaves, or both." "Bribery was open and shameless," but it was not the certainty of "partisan politics, but rather the amount and shameless nature in handling public funds or performing a public trust" that impressed Davis. Even so, he noted that

antebellum quarrels between Democrats and Whigs, or even between factions of the Democratic party, had produced ugly charges of dishonesty, of a deliberate seeking after monopolistic control of the state's credit for individual and partisan ends.

56. Davis, *Civil War and Reconstruction in Florida,* pp. 497–498.
57. *Ibid.,* pp. 526–527.
58. *Ibid.,* p. 631.
59. *Ibid.,* pp. 526–527.

And "Some of these charges were based on truth."[60] Such positive pronouncements certainly clear Davis of the Revisionist charge that blind partisanship prevented the Dunning School from seeing corruption in the Democratic ranks.

Discussing the state debt, Davis noted that it had increased under the Radical Republican administration from $523,856.95 in 1868 to $5,620,809.55 in 1874, nearly 900 percent, but he remarked that "a public debt might be a 'public blessing' and is not in itself necessarily indicative of bad government." He found that schools had been liberally supported and that the state prison had been reorganized. On the other hand, he rang the changes on misuse of public funds. Consequently, the people had not received adequate returns for the money spent on public roads, buildings, jails, and railroads, and no colleges, normal schools, or seminaries had been built. Furthermore, there had been much graft and corruption. Even so, Davis found that the legislature had passed "many measures [which] were meant honestly and were wise." These included school laws, regulation of insurance companies, and fees of officials which were "certainly a step toward a sound reform." Davis's evaluation of the Radical fiscal policy was not overly critical, nor did he overemphasize the problems of finance.[61]

Davis's treatment of carpetbaggers and scalawags differs in some particulars from the views of the Revisionist School. Davis found that both terms, as used during Reconstruction, were loaded with opprobrium and contempt. He noted that the Conservative native white Floridian had little regard for either group. From the first, they received the carpetbaggers somewhat coldly, and they deliberately ostracized the carpetbaggers after they joined the Negro in politics. The Conservatives considered the "Yankee carpetbagger a meddlesome interloper who spread the pernicious doctrine of social equality and sought selfish gain in politics." Davis quotes a personal interview with a Conservative who said the carpetbaggers he had known were a "dirty set—unscrupulous and pandered to the negroes. They mixed with the

60. *Ibid.*, pp. 663–664.
61. *Ibid.*, pp. 679–683.

blacks on terms of social equality."[62] Davis observed that the Conservatives did not look upon the carpetbagger as a new neighbor who needed help to get established and hoped to find white friends in his new home.

The Florida Conservative detested the scalawag—the native white Radical Republican—almost as much as he did the carpetbagger. As one Radical put it: The Conservatives

make no distinction about men who have joined the Republican party. A Northern man is "a damn Yankee" who came here to rule and a Southern man who joined the Republican party is "a damn scalawag" and there was no honesty about him; he was a traitor to his country and to his race.[63]

Davis observed that the Conservative looked upon the scalawag, not as an old neighbor who honestly differed from the Conservative white on political issues, as Democrats and Whigs had differed before the Civil War, but as a turncoat, a recreant to his race who sought political advancement at any cost.[64]

Davis himself saw carpetbaggers—he estimated their maximum number at about three hundred—as divided into at least two classes. First, there were the "birds of passage," whom the press characterized as unprincipled, selfish northerners who ignored the welfare of the state and sought political office so they might prey upon the people, after which they would move on to greener pastures. The second class, an honest group, some of whom had come to Florida during the war as army or governmental officials, now sought to become planters, merchants, or professional men. They sought primarily neither temporary jobs nor political office, but rather to make homes where business and professional opportunities were promising. But, said he, "some of these became as bad as birds of passage."[65] Davis recognized among carpetbag

62. *Ibid.*, p. 481.
63. *Ibid.*, p. 609.
64. *Ibid.*, p. 479.
65. *Ibid.*, pp. 476–477. For a Revisionist view of the carpetbagger in Florida, see George Winston Smith, "Carpetbag Imperialism in Florida, 1862–1868," *Florida Historical Quarterly*, XXVII (October 1948), 99–130; XXVIII (January 1949), 260–299.

leaders some men of intelligence, education, honesty, and strength of character who made real contributions to the state.

Davis also saw at least two groups among the scalawags—he estimated their number at about two thousand. First was the majority, "men of no particular reputation—good or bad—and of mediocre enlightenment."[66] These men came from the poor whites, small farmers, and laboring men—the yeoman class—and were largely former Democrats. The second, a much smaller class, included representatives of the upper, well-to-do educated class— planters, professional men, and political leaders. This group contained both former Whigs and Democrats.

Davis and the Revisionists do not agree on the character and distribution of the scalawags. W. E. B. Du Bois says that some of them were unquestionably self-seeking adventurers, renegades, men who "sold themselves for office"; others were poor white trash.[67] David Donald maintains that "In most of the Southern states . . . these 'scalawags' come from the planter, mercantile, and industrial classes," and that they were almost entirely former Whigs.[68] Davis shows that most of the Florida scalawags came from the lower and middle class and that their leaders were divided between former Whigs and Democrats.

There has been no general Revisionist study of Reconstruction in Florida, as there has been of some of the southern states. John Edwin Johns, *Florida During the Civil War* (Gainesville: University of Florida Press, 1963), brings a fresh view to the wartime problems, but has not greatly modified Davis's interpretation. Several excellent articles published in the *Florida Historical Quarterly,* some of which have been characterized as "Revisionist in spirit," have tended to change Davis's interpretation about special points, but they do not materially alter his general interpretation. One is, therefore, safe in saying, as did James Garfield Randall in 1937, that William Watson Davis, *The Civil War and Reconstruction in Florida,* is still the best work on that subject.

66. Davis, *Civil War and Reconstruction in Florida,* p. 494.
67. Du Bois, *Black Reconstruction,* p. 347.
68. Randall and Donald, *Civil War and Reconstruction,* p. 627.

11

Some Aspects of the Convict Lease System in the Southern States

Joseph Grégoire de Roulhac Hamilton was for four decades a distinguished member of the University of North Carolina faculty. At the time of his retirement, in 1948, *Essays in Southern History* (Chapel Hill: The University of North Carolina Press, 1949) was prepared as a *Festschrift* by his former students and Fletcher Green was the editor. Green's own contribution, "Some Aspects of the Convict Lease System in the Southern States," appeared as Chapter VII, pp. 112–123.

THE PROBLEM OF THE CONTROL OF CON-victs in such manner as to render them least trouble-some and expensive to the government and at the same time to insure them humane and proper treatment has always been a perplexing one. It has involved not only protecting and safeguarding the rights of others, but also the attempted reformation of the criminal so that he may once again take a proper place in the life of his community. Prison practices of the United States, inherited from England, have gone through several stages of development, each adding some reformatory principles and practices to its predecessor; not yet has the ideal solution of the problem been found.

During the last quarter of the eighteenth century, the American states began to substitute imprisonment for the death penalty for all except the more heinous crimes. This was done because of the gradual acceptance of the philosophy that the chief end of punishment was to prevent the criminal from doing further injury to society and to "prevent others from committing the like offence," not "to torment a sensible being, nor to undo a crime already committed"; and in the belief that punishment could be

reformative only "when compassion and humanity shall penetrate
the iron gates of dungeons."[1] At that time, the local jail, the chief
prison at hand, was found entirely unsuited to reformatory functions, and the states began to establish new and more up-to-date
prisons, where the prisoners were doomed to solitary confinement
or else set to work at various productive tasks. Overcrowding,
disruption of industry, difficulty of discipline, and other evils led
reformers to condemn bitterly the common jails and prisons.
Consequently, during the second quarter of the nineteenth century, two new and rival penitentiary systems were developed.
These were the Pennsylvania, or solitary confinement, and the
Auburn, a practical compromise between separate confinement
and congregate labor under a silent system.

The latter system was largely shaped by Louis Dwight of the
Boston Prison Discipline Society. Dwight was more concerned
with the redemption of unfortunate sinners than the punishment
of criminals. In order to reclaim the sinner, Dwight and his
followers organized Sabbath schools and introduced Bibles and
religious services into the penitentiaries. But another and more
significant feature of Dwight's program was the development of
prison industries. Shortly after the Auburn prison was established, an enterprising citizen applied for and was given a contract to operate a factory within the prison walls using convict
labor. Soon, this and other penitentiaries were realizing a net
profit from the labor of convicts, over and above all expenses.[2]
Here, then, was one answer to the problem of maintaining a state
prison without taxing the people for its support. While the penitentiary system was concerned with the reformation of the convicts, as well as punishment—it was designed to give the prisoner
time to meditate upon his sins and to teach him a trade—profits
from the convict's labor soon became the central idea in the
operation of the penitentiary. The American distaste for taxation

1. Cesare Beccaria, *An Essay on Crimes and Punishments with a Commentary by
M. de Voltaire* (English translation, Edinburgh: n.p., 1788) , p. 51. See also Blake
McKelvey, *American Prisons: A Study in American Social History Prior to 1915*
(Chicago: University of Chicago Press, 1936) , p. 2.

2. McKelvey, *American Prisons,* pp. 6–12.

was proverbial, and the burden of supporting an ever increasing number of idle convicts had been a major cause for popular dissatisfaction with early prisons.

Three major systems of employing convict labor had developed prior to the American Civil War.[3] These were the Public Account, the Contract, and the Lease. Under the Public Account system, the state itself managed and supervised the work of convicts who were generally engaged in manufacturing enterprises within the prison walls but sometimes in internal improvement projects for the state outside the prison. The convicts labored for the state, not for the pecuniary benefit of any individual or corporation. The state had entire control over the convict, and guards, foremen, wardens, and supervisors were state officials. This was generally regarded as the ideal convict labor system.[4]

The Contract system, however, was the more prevalent one. Under it, the prison officers advertised for bids for the employment of the prisoners of their respective institutions, the highest bidder generally securing the contract. The contractor engaged to employ a certain number of convicts at a fixed sum, the prison or state furnishing power, sometimes machinery, and on rare occasions, even tools for the convicts. The prisoners were generally employed within the walls, and the state did not surrender its control over the convict; it hired only his labor to the contractor who, in turn, expected to make a profit on convict labor.[5]

In 1883, Zebulon Brockway introduced the Piece-Price modification of the Contract system, whereby the contractor had nothing whatever to do with the prisoners or their work. The contractor merely furnished the warden with material ready for manufacturing, and the prison officers returned the finished article, made by convict labor, to the contractor and received a fixed price per piece.[6] This method was quite similar to the old domestic manufacturing system.

3. U.S. Bureau of Labor, *Annual Report of the Commissioner, 1886, Convict Labor* (Washington: Government Printing Office, 1887) , p. 4.
   4. *Ibid.*, pp. 379–380.
   5. *Ibid.*, pp. 311, 372–373.
   6. *Ibid.*, p. 379. See also McKelvey, *American Prisons*, p. 95.

Under the Lease system, the state would lease to the highest bidder all or part of the convicts for a fixed sum; the lessee would meet all expenses of management, including housing, protection, food, clothing, and guarding, connected with the employment of the prisoners. He was also given complete authority over the control and punishment of the prisoners, subject, of course, to the terms of the lease, and might sublease them at will. The state was relieved of all obligation and responsibility, and the payments by the lessee were clear profits to the state.[7]

In degree of more or less excellence, the operations of penitentiaries under Public Account, Contract, and Piece-Price

whether under official directors or contractors were harmonized with those features of the prison management that looked to the secure detention, the health, the discipline, and the moral reformation of the prisoners, the execution of the law's sentence upon him in its closest and furthest intent, and, if possible his return to the outer world, when he must be returned, a more valuable and less dangerous man. . . .[8]

It was the absence of many of these features, and often of all, that made the difference between these systems and that known as the Lease.

Prior to the Civil War, the southern states had developed their penitentiary systems along the same general line as those of the northern states. Since Negro slaves, constituting a large element of the population, were largely disciplined and punished for their crimes either on their respective plantations or in special courts, the prison population of the South was relatively smaller than that of the North. Nevertheless, all the southern states—except the two Carolinas and Florida, in which convicts were imprisoned in county jails—had established state penitentiaries by 1860. Most of these were of the modified Auburn system and were managed under the Public Account or the Contract system. Some of the southern penitentiaries had inaugurated what, for that day, were progressive reforms. The Baltimore prison early established spe-

7. U.S. Bureau of Labor, *Annual Report of the Commissioner, 1886,* p. 381.
8. George Washington Cable, "The Convict Lease System in the Southern States," *Century Magazine,* XXVIII (February 1884) , 584.

cial women's quarters and employed a chaplain to conduct Sunday classes. The Richmond prison was the first in the United States to use honor badges and the grading system as rewards for good behavior.[9] The Baltimore and Frankfort prisons were among the first to provide dining room accommodations. The Louisiana penitentiary conducted model cotton and shoe factories and gave its inmates training in the skills. Tennessee, in 1836, was the first state to grant a reduction of sentence for good behavior over a period of years.[10] Edward Livingston of Louisiana formulated a prison plan for model reform schools for juveniles, houses of correction for minor offenders, and two grades of imprisonment. The prisoner was to be given a certificate of good behavior, promoted to better quarters, and given the privilege of associating with like good-conduct prisoners as a reward for good behavior.[11] Unfortunately, no state adopted Livingston's program in its entirety.

On the other hand, Kentucky, in 1825, gave Joel Scott a five-year contract for its penitentiary at $1,000 per year, and thus inaugurated the Lease system, although Massachusetts had, in 1798, permitted wardens to hire the labor of prisoners to anyone who worked them near enough to the prison to permit the warden to exercise general supervision. Scott built cell blocks modeled on the Auburn system, a dining room, a chapel, model and profitable factories, and maintained excellent discipline.[12] He was in good repute with Dwight and the Boston Prison Discipline Society, and his management of the penitentiary was considered exemplary. Alabama followed Kentucky in 1845 by leasing her penitentiary. While imprisonment in these two state institutions was degrading, it was not more so than that in most state prisons, North as well as South. Enoch Cobb Wines and Theodore William Dwight, two distinguished penologists, concluded in 1867 that there was "not a state prison in America, in which the reforma-

9. McKelvey, *American Prisons*, pp. 19, 26.
10. *Ibid.*, p. 43.
11. Edward Livingston, *Code of Reform and Prison Discipline* (Washington: Gales and Seaton, 1828).
12. William C. Sneed, *A Report on the History and Mode of Management of the Kentucky Penitentiary* (Frankfort, Ky.: J. B. Major, State Printer, 1860).

tion of the convict is the supreme object of the discipline."[13] In fact, the development of prosperous prison industries was the most earnest concern of the wardens in all state prisons, and the penitentiary that was least expensive was considered most successful.

The Civil War greatly affected the prison policies of the southern states. It halted the development of the penitentiary system; and the social, economic, and political unrest of the Reconstruction period fixed the Lease system upon the South almost to the exclusion of other forms of labor. The cruelty and brutality which followed has rarely been equaled in modern times. One student of American prison history has concluded that "since the Civil War, the southern states from a penalogical point of view never really belonged to the Union."[14]

Specific factors influencing the shift to the Lease system are obvious. The penitentiaries of several of the states had been burned or otherwise destroyed during the war, and others had been so damaged as to be unusable.[15] The state governments were bankrupt, and there was little property upon which to levy taxes to secure the funds necessary for rebuilding. The poverty and unrest of the post-war years caused a great increase in the number of white criminals, and the abolition of slavery brought the problem of Negro criminals to the fore. Prior to 1865, the Negro had been controlled and punished by his owner and only rarely came before the courts. As a freedman, he became subject to the civil and criminal law in like manner with the white man. Since the federal government did little to give the new freedmen economic security, and since the freedmen were possessed of no property, the Negroes were dependent upon the fruit of their labor for the

13. Enoch Cobb Wines and Theodore William Dwight, *Report on the Prisons and Reformatories of the United States and Canada, Made to the Legislature of New York, January 1867* (Albany, N.Y.: Van Benthuysen & Sons, 1867), quoted by McKelvey, *American Prisons*, p. 39.

14. McKelvey, *American Prisons*, p. 172.

15. The Georgia and South Carolina penitentiaries were burned by federal troops; those of Alabama, Arkansas, Louisiana, Mississippi, Tennessee, and Texas were badly damaged and misused during the war; and that of Virginia was burned when Richmond was evacuated.

necessities of life. Few white landlords had money with which to pay wages; moreover, they distrusted the free Negro as a worker, and many were guilty of acts of aggression against him. Hence, facing starvation, the Negro turned to thievery and robbery and was caught up in the toils of the law.

The large criminal population, white and black, entailed greatly increased expenditures for food, clothing, and guards and for penitentiaries in which to house the convicts. The impoverished states did not have and found it impossible to secure additional funds. On the other hand, railroad companies, lumbering, mining, and other business interests were anxious to secure cheap labor that they could easily control. What more natural, then, than that the states should lease their convicts to private industry, escape the heavy costs of building penitentiaries and caring for large numbers of criminals, and, at the same time, secure much-needed revenue for their depleted treasuries? Under these circumstances, the southern states ignored the trend in the North, where model prisons were being built and where programs of reformation were being instituted. They chose, instead, to follow the path of least resistance and to lease their convicts for ready money.

The first of the new leases were instituted by the provisional and military governments on a temporary, short-term basis. The Republican Reconstruction governments accepted the Lease as the solution of the convict labor problem and the "home rule," or Bourbon, Democratic governments greatly expanded the system and instituted long-term leases. The Georgia legislature, one of the first to turn to the Lease, considered the possibility of rebuilding its penitentiary, burned by federal troops in 1865 but, anticipating a great increase in Negro convicts, decided to look for a new solution.[16] In December 1866, it authorized the governor to farm out the penitentiary to the highest bidder, provided the state should be relieved of all expenses connected with the upkeep of convicts.[17] Governor Charles Jones Jenkins did not see fit to act,

16. Judson Clements Ward, Jr., "Georgia Under the Bourbon Democrats, 1870–1890," (Unpublished doctoral dissertation, University of North Carolina, 1947), p. 379.
17. Georgia, *Acts* (1866), pp. 155–156.

but General Thomas Howard Ruger, the military governor, in May of 1868, leased one hundred convicts to the Georgia and Alabama Railroad for one year. The railroad was to bear all expenses of housing, guarding, feeding, and clothing the convicts and pay the state $2,500 for their labor. The lessee was given full power to discipline and control the convicts.[18] Rufus Brown Bullock, Republican governor of the state, followed Ruger's lead and leased all the state convicts. Under the Bullock leases, the state was not paid for its convicts but was relieved of all expenses.[19] The short-term leases required the lessees to "treat convicts humanely" and "to feed them well," but forbade them "to inflict . . . corporal punishment upon the convicts unless absolutely necessary to secure discipline."[20] The law of 1874 required the lessee to provide "humane and kind treatment" for the convicts and to segregate "those convicted of crimes involving great moral turpitude" from others.[21]

When the Democrats regained control of the state, they accepted the Lease system and in 1876 the legislature passed an act authorizing the governor to lease all the state's convicts to the highest bidder for a period of twenty years. Under this act, three companies were formed and agreed to pay the state $500,000 for the convicts for the period. The state was relieved of all expenses except the salary of a penitentiary physician and that of a chaplain whose duty was "to aid in reforming the moral character of the convicts."[22]

Shortly after its erection in 1841, the Alabama penitentiary was leased to private individuals, but the state warden retained full responsibility over the convicts, who were to be worked within the prison walls. This system, really a Contract, was continued until 1862, when the state resumed full management. Federal troops released the convicts in 1865 but returned the badly-damaged

18. Antoinette Elizabeth Taylor, "The Convict Lease System in Georgia, 1866–1908" (Unpublished master's thesis, University of North Carolina, 1940), pp. 7–8.

19. Georgia, *Report of the Principal Keeper of the Penitentiary* (1872–1873), p. 22.

20. Taylor, "Convict Lease System in Georgia," p. 23.

21. Georgia, *Acts* (1874), p. 28.

22. Georgia, *Acts* (1876), pp. 42–43.

penitentiary to the state; the next year, the prison and its inmates were leased to private contractors; and in 1867, the lessees were permitted to work the prisoners outside the walls. The lessees fed, clothed, and housed the convicts but paid the state nothing and even failed to repay a state loan of $15,000 negotiated for the repair of the penitentiary.[23] One student of the problem declared that "During the entire Reconstruction period, Alabama convicts were poorly, if not actually corruptly managed," and entailed a financial burden on the state.[24]

When the Democrats gained control of the Alabama legislature in 1874, they determined to revise the leases so as to realize revenue for the state. Short-term leases, from one to five years, were negotiated with railroads, iron and coal mining companies, and planters at from $2.50 to $5.00 per month per convict, and the state began to reap considerable profits.[25] Nevertheless, criticism of the system led by Doctor Jerome Cochran, state health officer, caused Warden John Hollis Bankhead to recommend changes. He proposed to concentrate all convicts at one place near the mines where the larger portion of them were working, so that they might be supervised directly by himself and the prison physician. Following Bankhead's suggestion, the legislature made some modifications in the system. Heretofore, the counties had been permitted to lease their convicts directly, rather than to sentence them to the state penitentiary, and the lessees had secretly agreed to divide their bids among the counties and thus prevent competitive bidding. The state, in 1883, assumed control over county convicts and put a stop to county leasing;[26] and in 1887, all convicts were concentrated at the Pratt Mines and on two Black Belt plantations. The next year, the Tennessee Coal, Iron and Railroad Company acquired the Pratt Mines convicts and secured a ten-year lease from the state.[27]

The Mississippi Penitentiary was partly destroyed during the

23. Allen Johnston Going, "Bourbon Democracy in Alabama, 1870–1890" (Unpublished doctoral dissertation, University of North Carolina, 1947), p. 387.

24. *Ibid.*, p. 390.

25. Alabama, *First Biennial Report of the Inspectors of Convicts to the Governor,* (1886), pp. 3–6.

26. Going, "Bourbon Democracy," p. 391.

27. Alabama, *Inspectors Report* (1888), pp. 1–2.

war, and General Alvin C. Gillem, the military governor, farmed
out all the state convicts to Edmund Richardson, a planter, paying him $18,000 per year for maintenance and $12,000 for transportation.[28] Gillem's Republican successor, Governor James Lusk
Alcorn, opposed this system. He was unable to abolish it but did
obtain some revenue for the state from the leases.[29] When the
Democrats came to power in 1876, they leased all convicts to
Jones S. Hamilton, a counterpart of the "Robber Barons" of the
North and West, who, in turn, subleased to various planters,
railroad companies, and levee contractors. Later, the state leased
all convicts to the Gulf and Ship Island Railroad and, in 1887,
forbade subleasing.[30] So corrupt was the railroad that its lease was
later cancelled, and the state returned to individual leases.

The story of convict leasing in Arkansas, Louisiana, Tennessee,
and Florida parallels that of Georgia, Alabama, and Mississippi.
Arkansas, after experimenting with short leases under which the
state paid a small fee for the support of each convict, under
Democratic control turned to a single fifteen-year lease, whereby
the state received $25,000 annually. Louisiana entered into a
twenty-year lease at $20,000 for the first year but with increasing
returns with the increase in the number of convicts. Tennessee
leased all her convicts to the Tennessee Coal, Iron and Railway
Company for $101,000 annually. Florida had no state prison prior
to the Civil War but, in 1866, secured the federal arsenal at
Chattahoochee, where "during the eight years of reconstruction,
the boodlers in charge housed an average of eighty-two convicts at
a total cost of $234,473."[31] The Democrats changed the system and
leased the convicts from year to year, trying to improve the state's
bargain. So cruel and barbarous were conditions in the Florida
lease camps that one of the guards characterized the penitentiary
as "the American Siberia."[32]

28. Mississippi *House Journal* (1870), Appendix, p. 58.
29. Vernon Lane Wharton, *The Negro in Mississippi, 1865–1890* (Chapel Hill:
University of North Carolina Press, 1947), p. 238.
30. *Ibid.*, p. 242.
31. McKelvey, *American Prisons*, pp. 175–176.
32. J. C. Powell, *The American Siberia; or, Fourteen Years' Experience in a
Southern Convict Camp* (Chicago: H. J. Smith & Co., 1891).

The remainder of the former slaveholding states fall into a somewhat different category; they followed wholly neither the practices of the states of the Lower South nor those of the North. Texas at first employed her convicts on state-owned railroads and, after the roads were sold to private interests, confined the convicts in the penitentiary where they were worked under the Public Account system. The convict population of the state grew so rapidly that a second prison was built. The two soon became inadequate, and the convicts were scattered over the state at railroad and bridge construction, mining, iron-blasting, and farming. Under these private contracts or leases, the penitentiary superintendent maintained efficient inspection, regulation, and control of the convicts.[33] Kentucky, North Carolina, and South Carolina, like Texas, followed a combination of Public Account-Contract-Lease system and escaped some of the worst evils of leasing as practiced in the Lower South. The North Carolina Constitution of 1876 prohibited the state from surrendering the control of state convicts to the lessee. Missouri combined Contract, Public Account, and Piece-Price. Maryland, Virginia, and West Virginia followed the Contract system, where the penitentiary was the center of convict labor.[34] Outside of the South, only Nebraska, New Mexico, and Washington leased convicts to private industry after the Civil War.

The evils of the Lease system were self-evident. In the first place, the system was based primarily on the economic motive: revenue for the state and profit for the lessee. If there was no collusion of government and businessmen at first, it soon developed; and high-ranking public officials lined their pockets with the sweat, blood, and tears of convict laborers. Governors Joseph Emerson Brown and John Brown Gordon were members of the Three Penitentiary Companies which leased Georgia's convicts for a twenty-year period. Edmund Richardson utilized convict labor in Mississippi to become the biggest cotton planter in the world. Jones S. Hamilton, who dabbled in both Republican and

33. McKelvey, *American Prisons*, p. 177.
34. See tables in U.S. Bureau of Labor, *Annual Report of the Commissioner, 1886, Convict Labor*, pp. 82–87.

Democratic party politics in Mississippi, was another who made a fortune from convict-lease labor. And John Hollis Bankhead, warden of the Alabama penitentiary, founded a long and powerful line of politicians in that state. Efficient lobbies were maintained and newspaper support was bought up by the lessees, and there is evidence that the prison, or convict, gang was closely tied up with the Bourbon Democratic machines;[35] the tie-up was also close between the local courthouse rings and the lessees. Pressure was brought to bear on officials to arrest, and the courts to convict, all offenders, so that the lessees might secure more convict laborers for their fixed payments.[36]

The Lease system had a distinct color tinge. In most states, Negroes made up an overwhelming majority of the convicts; in all, their number was considerably higher than their population percentage. The infamous "Pig Law" of Mississippi seems to have been especially designed to ensnare Negroes. Certainly, under it, the number of Negro convicts increased by leaps and bounds, and convict-leasing became a big business in that state.[37] Of the 1,239 convicts in Georgia in 1878, 1,124 were Negroes. Of this number, 36 were women, while only 2 of the 115 whites were women.

The incarceration of young boys and girls, first offenders, with old and hardened criminals under the Lease system was a flagrant disregard of the reclamation ideal. Among the convicts leased in Georgia in 1883 were 137 boys between eleven and seventeen years of age. In 1886, there were 30 boys under fifteen; in 1897, 34 boys and 2 girls under fifteen; and in 1904, there was 1 boy only eight years old.[38] In 1874, Tennessee leased 123 convicts under eighteen years of age; 54 of these were under sixteen, 3 were twelve, and 1 only ten years of age.[39] Of 981 Arkansas convicts in

35. Rebecca (Latimer) Felton, *My Memoirs of Georgia Politics* (Atlanta: The Index Printing Company, 1911), pp. 438–439; "Report on Prison Rings," Tennessee *House Journal* (1879).

36. Governor James M. Smith of Georgia said the lease system increased the number of convicts by securing "a more rigid and proper enforcement of the laws." Georgia *Senate Journal* (1872), p. 139.

37. Wharton, *The Negro in Mississippi*, p. 237.

38. Taylor, "Convict Lease System in Georgia," p. 78.

39. John Berrien Lindsley, *On Prison Discipline and Penal Legislation, with Special Reference to the State of Tennessee* (Nashville: Printed for the Robertson Association, 1874), p. 38.

1895, 105 were between twelve and fifteen years of age. And in 1882, Texas had 509 convicts under twenty years of age, 1 of whom was only seven years old.[40] Manifestly, what these states should have done was to build reformatories for their juvenile offenders.

The chief evil of the Lease system was its cruelty and barbarity, its disregard for human life. Despite the fact that most leases contained such phrases as "care should be taken to preserve the punitive and reformative character of the Penitentiary," reform was ignored, and southern "penal institutions instead of tending to reform, . . . [became] veritable nurseries of crime, anarchism and degradation." One Tennessee critic maintained that, of the nearly 5,000 convicts released from the penitentiary of that state over a thirty-year period, "none practically are reformed, but most all are cultivated in crime, contaminated, debased, degraded and embittered."[41]

Jesse De Vaney, a Georgia guard who whipped Aaron Bryan, a Negro convict, to death, declared: "I whipped him for impudence and for refusing to work; . . . I whipped [him] on the bare skin—shirt turned up and pants [turned] down."[42] Despite such practices, one legislative report praised the state lessees because they had "reduced the present system of farming out convicts to a complete success as well to the state as to themselves,"[43] and this evaluation was generally accepted by the state officials and a majority of the citizens.

But from the very beginning, there was severe criticism of the conditions of convicts under the Lease. Some newspapers pointed out the evil conditions in all the states. The Mobile *Register* of February 15, 1875, declared that Alabama convicts, "Laboring with manacled limbs in swamps and sleeping in the unwholesome atmosphere . . . died like cattle in slaughter pens."[44] The Huntsville, Alabama, *Gazette,* a Negro Republican newspaper, dedi-

40. George Washington Cable, *The Silent South—Together with the Freedman's Case in Equity and the Convict Lease System* (New York: C. Scribner's Sons, 1885), p. 176.

41. Knoxville *Journal,* 10 March 1893.

42. Georgia, *Senate Journal* (1870), Pt. 1, p. 320.

43. Georgia, *Report of the Principal Keeper of the Penitentiary* (1872–1873), p. 4.

44. Quoted by Going, "Bourbon Democracy," p. 394.

cated itself "to the abrogation of the inhuman, barbarous and vicious convict labor system."[45]

Liberal and progressive leaders, businessmen, ministers, and teachers condemned a system that advertised to the outside world that they were a barbarous people. Organized labor attacked the system, especially in Tennessee. Women like Mrs. Rebecca Latimer Felton of Georgia and Miss Julia Tutwiler of Alabama organized crusades against the Lease, which they described as not only a disgrace to the state, but a disgrace to civilization. Physicians attacked the practices of the lease camps that impaired the health and contributed to the moral degeneracy of the inmates. The mortality rate was so high in Tennessee that a physician's report declared: "Before these figures humanity stands aghast and our boasted civilization must hide her face in shame."[46] In both Georgia and Florida, there were lease camps containing, at one time, twenty-five or more illegitimate children born of convict mothers. Finally, political leaders were aroused, and legislative reports exposed the evil conditions: men and women, stripped naked and beaten in the presence of others with leather straps studded with wooden shoe pegs; Negroes, beaten with heavy whips until the blood oozed from the open wounds, and these beatings repeated day after day, opening old wounds and making new ones, until death finally released the unfortunate victim. These and many other whippings, "the most brutal ever inflicted by one human being upon another,"[47] forced the state governments to abandon the Lease.

Mississippi led off in 1890, when a provision was incorporated in the constitution that forbade the lease of any convict "to any person or persons or corporation, private or public . . . after December 31, A.D., 1894." Tennessee acted in 1895, after several years of strikes and disorders involving convicts and free labor in the mines. Troops had been called out to suppress the disorders, and even these joined the strikers. Governor Hoke Smith called a

45. Going, "Bourbon Democracy," p. 425.
46. P. D. Sims, "Report of the Committee on Prisons in Tennessee," Tennessee State Board of Health, *Second Report, October 1880 to December 1884,* pp. 312–313.
47. Georgia *House Journal* (1895) , p. 829.

special session of the Georgia legislature that abolished the Lease in that state in 1908. Florida acted in 1924, only after the brutal whipping to death of a young North Dakota convict by a penitentiary guard (because the convict refused to shine the guard's shoes) had inflamed public opinion throughout the nation. North Carolina retained her modified Lease system longer than any other state. That state finally abolished it in 1933, when control of the state convicts was transferred to the Public Works Commission.[48] Unfortunately, the county chain-gang system for working public roads that was substituted for the Lease in several states was almost, if not altogether, as bad. This was notably true of Georgia. And southern penal practices still contain vestigial evidence of a system that left a trail of dishonor and death that could find a parallel only in the persecutions of the Middle Ages or in the prison camps of Nazi Germany.

One finds it difficult to explain why a civilized people would have for so long tolerated the barbaric Lease system. Why did not the people smash the evil thing? How could anyone, even a guard in a convict camp, treat his fellow man with such fiendish cruelty as thousands and thousands of men, women, and children were treated in prison camps scattered throughout the South? Economic conditions which prevailed during the last quarter of the nineteenth century are a partial answer. The southern states, devastated by war, needed rebuilding; and the political leaders, both northern and southern, seized avidly upon industrialization as the one sure road to economic recovery. The industrialists were not averse to exploiting human labor, as the long hours and low wages of the country testify. Neither did the governments hesitate to aid the employer as he exploited the laborer. Congress enacted a Contract Labor Law, and the state legislatures gladly leased convicts to private industry. As a consequence, contractors in the North and West used immigrant contract laborers, and those of the South used convicts to build railroads, to mine coal, iron, and

48. Hilda Jane Zimmerman, "Penal Systems and Penal Reforms in the South Since the Civil War" (Unpublished doctoral dissertation, University of North Carolina, 1947), pp. 387–390. This work is by far the best account of the abolition of the Lease.

phosphates, to cut timber, and to manufacture brick. They were even used to construct government buildings. Were not all of these beneficial to the economic well-being of society? Why, then, should anyone condemn the labor system by which they were brought about? So reasoned southerners; and the southern Bourbon Democrats saw no incongruity in taking convict blood money and earmarking it for public education.

The prevailing race feeling also helps to explain why the southern states retained the Lease system until well into the twentieth century. There was practically no sympathy for the criminal and little more for the Negro. Since a large part of the convicts were Negroes, the state governments, controlled by the whites, could easily ignore reforms that would so largely redound to the benefit of the blacks. Of less importance but of some significance was the fact that the number of women prisoners was proportionately far less in the South than was the case in the North. Had the number of white women convicts been large, an appeal to the sense of chivalry and protection of women might have been effective in overthrowing the Lease system.

Another factor in the apathy of the people was the fact that the Lease camps were generally located in isolated areas, where the evils of leasing were hidden from public view. The convicts were scattered in the swamps and forests at lumber camps, in the hill and mountain sections at coal and iron mines, in the rural areas on large cotton plantations; others were located at railroad and construction camps, where one who had no economic interest at stake seldom saw them. Hence, the masses of people were actually unaware of the evil conditions that obtained.

Significant, too, was the fact that there were few trained prison workers in the South. Prison wardens and supervisors in the North in increasing numbers began to look upon their work as an honorable profession, and took pride in developing standards and techniques of prison discipline and reformation. Not so in the South, where wardens, guards, and other penitentiary employees were either political appointees or men selected by the lessee for the purpose of driving the convict laborer to secure a maximum output. Consequently, the majority of prison employees in the

South had no interest in their profession and little interest in the well-being and reclamation of the convicts under their control.

Those people who did see the degradation and feel shame for the evils of the Lease were able to force piecemeal reforms that ameliorated the worst features of the system. Miss Julia Tutwiler of Alabama organized an Anti-Convict League, composed of teachers, preachers, miners, workingmen, and merchants, and memorialized the legislature for reform. Similar groups in other states followed suit. The attacks upon the citadel of intrenched interests gradually brought results. First offenders were segregated from hardened criminals; reformatories were established; separate women's prisons were provided for and women prisoners removed from the Lease camps; laws were passed to shorten the hours of labor and to lighten the tasks of convicts; religious services were made available in the camps; books and schools were provided; the state boards of health began to take an interest in the health of convicts; and some attention was paid to recreation and the general social and spiritual welfare of the convicts. Baseball teams were organized; and the convicts were furnished musical instruments with which they gave band concerts. Paroles were granted and long-term sentences were shortened for good behavior.

In the twentieth century, the better penological trends of the North and West have had their counterparts in the South; but the decentralization which came with county chain gangs retarded the advance of reform. Hence, much remains to be done in the field of prison reform before the southern states can claim a modern, reformative penal system.

12

Resurgent Southern Sectionalism, 1933–1955

> This essay was Green's presidential address to the December 1955 meeting of the North Carolina Literary and Historical Association. In it, Green notes the difference between twentieth-century southern sectionalism and southern nationalism of the mid-nineteenth century; also, while looking at the South's past, he expresses his hope for the future of the region. The choice of topic was most timely, in view of the South's reaction to the 1954 *Brown* vs. *Board of Education of Topeka* decision. Publication of this address was in the *North Carolina Historical Review*, XXXIII (April 1956), 222–240.

A STUDENT OF THE HISTORY OF THE United States during the twentieth century, and especially since 1933, observing the sweep and power of the nationalizing movement, would unquestionably agree with the statement of Elihu Root made in 1905 that "our whole life has swung away from old state centers, and is crystallizing about national centers."[1] The overwhelming importance of the national government under Franklin Delano Roosevelt and the New Deal and Harry S. Truman and the Fair Deal has brought support for and fear of national control of nearly every facet of human life—agriculture, industry, communication, health, education, and social security—from maternity aid to death benefits, or, as the English phrase it, from the womb to the tomb.

---

1. Quoted by Frederick Jackson Turner, *The Significance of Sections in American History; with an Introduction by Max Farrand* (New York: Henry Holt and Co., 1932), p. 287 (hereafter, *American History*).

The Great Depression, the Second World War, the cold war against Russia, and the hot war against Communism have caused a real revolution in the American philosophy and concept of government far removed from the Jeffersonian view that that government is best that governs least. Today, the general attitude is "Let the federal government do it." And this attitude has not been seriously checked by Republican control under President Dwight David Eisenhower. The Communist scare has led the federal government to employ undercover Federal Bureau of Investigation agents in school and college classrooms. And recent Supreme Court decisions have opened public schools, parks, golf courses, buses, trains, and public waiting rooms that had long been closed by southern states to Negro citizens. Certainly, the trend is away from state centers and toward control by the federal government.

But if we take a longer and backward view of our history, we will find that the United States is, in reality, a federation of sections, rather than a union of individual states. In political matters, the states act as groups, rather than as individual members of the Union and are responsive to sectional interests and ideals. They have leaders who, in Congress and political conventions, speak for the sections, confer and compromise, and form combinations to formulate national policies. In other words, party policy and congressional legislation emerge from sectional contests and bargainings. Congressional legislation is hardly ever the result of purely national considerations. And when we study the underlying forces of social and economic life and the distribution of political power in the Union, we find that sectionalism antedated nationalism, and that it has endured, although sometimes obscured by political forms, throughout our entire history.[2]

There are, of course, varying degrees of sectionalism. The most extreme form was that exhibited in the struggle between the North and the South over the slavery issue, which saw the emergence of a southern nationalism that culminated in the organization of the Confederate States of America and the American Civil

2. *Ibid.*, pp. 321–322.

War. Gradually, the wounds of that conflict healed and, by 1900, the North and the South were once again united. The new national spirit was made manifest when Fighting Joe Wheeler and Fitzhugh Lee, Generals C. S. A., led troops in Cuba during the Spanish-American War as Generals, U.S.A. Legend says that General Wheeler forgot himself and, while charging up San Juan hill, yelled, "Come on, Men! Give those Yankees hell."[3] Even so, Wheeler and his men were American, not southern soldiers.

There is, however, another kind of sectionalism which, as Frederick Jackson Turner so interestingly pointed out in his *The Significance of Sections in American History,* has lain dormant but may, under sufficient provocation, gain vitality at any time. This sort of sectionalism does not threaten the unity of the nation, but it makes itself manifest through a feeling of distinctness and separateness from others—in a word, Consciousness of Kind. It may be of economic interest, of mores and customs, of public attitudes, of cultural patterns, or even a manner of speech. The tests of such sectionalism may be found in the methods by which an area resists conformity to a national pattern—by mental and emotional reactions, or by a combination of votes in Congress and in presidential elections. This type of sectionalism gives a distinctive quality to a region. In this sense, New England, the Middle States, the Old Northwest, the Great Plains, the Mountain States, the Pacific Coast constitute sections no less distinct than the South. Each has its peculiar geographic qualities, its economic resources and interests, its particular political bent, and its own social and cultural patterns. One may not be able to define exactly their specific differences, but they undeniably exist. Frederick Jackson Turner said that, in this sense, "one of the most avowedly sectional portions of the Union" was and still is New England. And he devoted five pages in his book to depicting her sectional characteristics.[4] He noted that the Boston press has long urged the section to act as a political unit, and that the six states had formed a New England States Commission of seventy-two

3. Paul Herman Buck, *The Road to Reunion, 1865–1900* (Boston: Little, Brown and Co., 1937) , p. 306.

4. Turner, *American History,* pp. 329–333.

members, twelve from each state, that met in annual conference to formulate political and economic policies for the section.

But it is of the South I propose to speak. I believe that the Great Depression of the 1920s and 1930s, followed by the New Deal, constituted the provocation that aroused the dormant sectionalism of the South. Southerners suffered severely during the depression and reacted violently to the New Deal. They either accepted FDR wholeheartedly and swallowed the New Deal hook, line, and sinker, or they hated Roosevelt and fought the New Deal stubbornly and viciously. The two points of view may be illustrated by the story of the public school teacher and the reaction of the governor of a southern state. The teacher, so the story goes, was drilling her pupils in the benefits derived from the New Deal and indoctrinating them in the Santa Claus-like quality of Roosevelt. She asked, "Who gave us this beautiful new school building?" The children, properly coached, answered in chorus, "Mr. Roosevelt." "Yes," said she, "and who gave us these fine desks, charts, maps, and blackboards?" The reply was, "Mr. Roosevelt." Having exhausted the objects inside the schoolroom, she looked outside and asked, "Who gave us the playground and its equipment of slides and swings?" "Mr. Roosevelt," they replied. And, finally, "Who gave us the beautiful lawn with its shrubs and flowers?" One youngster, his sense of justice aroused, cried out in a shrill, small voice, "God." Whereupon the other children shouted, "Throw that Republican out." Speaking for the second point of view, Governor Sam Houston ("Sad Sam") Jones of Louisiana wrote:

New Deal policies . . . have continued to kick an already prostrate South in the face. . . . [President Roosevelt] has allowed his New Deal to close down the horizons of the masses of Southern people, increase their handicaps, darken their future; he has permitted a senseless policy to continue whose end result can only be to impoverish the rich and pauperize the poor.[5]

Let us examine the evidence of this insurgent southern sectionalism. In what areas does it manifest itself? I believe it can be seen

5. Sam Houston Jones, "Will Dixie Bolt the New Deal?" in *The Saturday Evening Post*, CCXV (6 March 1943), 20 (hereafter, "Will Dixie Bolt?").

in every major field of human interest, and that it has been growing stronger ever since the early 1930s. But time permits a brief discussion of only a few fields, and I have chosen to present emotional and social attitudes, cultural life, general welfare activities, economic life, and politics.

Emotional and Social Attitudes

The overwhelming and crushing defeat of the Confederacy in 1865 left the people of the southern states with a defeatist attitude, an inferiority complex, a tender skin to criticism, and a fear of ridicule. The victor naturally dictated the patterns of life and looked upon the South as backward and uncivilized. Southerners were on the defensive and often found criticism when northerners were merely stating facts.

This touchy attitude lingers on after ninety years and, in the 1930s, southerners, resenting Secretary of Labor Frances Perkins's statement that "A social revolution would take place if shoes were put on the people of the South," charged that she was "poking fun" at southerners for their poverty and that she accused them of going barefooted like peasants and country yokels. "Why, even the mules of the South wear shoes," indignantly rejoined one southern senator.[6]

In like manner, they resented President Roosevelt's *Report on Economic Conditions in the South* and the President's statement that the South constituted the nation's economic problem number one. In truth, this study was designed to explore economic conditions in the South and to point the way to economic recovery and prosperity. Nevertheless, civic clubs, chambers of commerce, state legislatures, governors, and representatives and senators in Congress roundly condemned the publication and adopted and presented resolutions of censure and protest to the Congress.[7]

---

6. Stetson Kennedy, *Southern Exposure* (New York: Doubleday & Co., 1946), pp. 1–2. See also Thomas D. Clark, *The Southern Country Editor* (Indianapolis: Bobbs-Merrill Co., 1948), p. 334; Virginius Dabney, *Below the Potomac: A Book About the New South* (New York: D. Appleton-Century, 1942), p. 25 (hereafter, *Below the Potomac*).

7. Kennedy, *Southern Exposure*, pp. 2–3.

More significant was the fear of the breakdown of social mores because of Roosevelt's interest in the advancement of the Negro. Governor "Sad Sam" Jones of Louisiana charged that it was the purpose of the New Deal to force social relations between the two races, and that Roosevelt planned to use World War II as an instrument to force social equality.[8] Southerners heard, believed, and retold over and over again rumors that Mrs. Eleanor Roosevelt was organizing Eleanor Clubs among Negro cooks and maids to get them out of the kitchen in order to force white women to perform the menial duties of housework. H. A. Jessen, secretary of the South Carolina Sheriffs Association, in an address before that body, declared that the attitude of the Roosevelt administration on race relations was "an insult to every white man and woman in the South." He said also that no South Carolina sheriff would dare call on the Federal Bureau of Investigation, for fear that he "might commit an act that the Administration would consider unfair to its Eleanor constituents."[9] Southerners declared that there was no race problem. They claimed that they understood the Negro and could get along with him, if northerners would only keep their noses out of affairs that did not concern them.[10] This emotional reaction had both bad and good effects. On the one hand, it led to an increase of mob violence and a renewal of Ku Klux activities; on the other, it led to co-operation of whites and Negroes who organized the Southern Regional Council in 1943 that has done effective work in the improvement of race relations in the South.[11] Southerners still resent northerners who come into the South to champion the Negro, especially when they feel that they are interfering in affairs in which they have no concern. Witness for instance the feeling aroused by the activities of the NAACP in the Till murder case in Mississippi.

8. Jones, "Will Dixie Bolt?", p. 21.

9. Undated clipping, the Charlotte *Observer.*

10. Dallas *Morning News,* 20 November 1944. See Waldemar E. Debnam, *Then My Old Kentucky Home Goodnight* (Raleigh: [n.p.], 1955), pp. 117–118, for a recent expression of this feeling.

11. Charles S. Johnson and others, *Into the Main Stream, a Survey of Best Practices in Race Relations in the South* (Chapel Hill: University of North Carolina Press, 1947), pp. 5–11.

A curious episode in southern emotionalism was the revival of interest in the Confederate cap and flag. The cap was widely worn by children and teen-agers. The flag was waved by college boys and girls at football games, worn as an emblem on their jackets and raincoats, and flown from their automobiles. Furthermore, southern boys in the United States armed forces, at various points throughout the world, were reported to have flown the flag from United States warships or from their company and regimental standards. Both the flag and the cap became far more familiar than they had been at any time since 1900. Some northerners reacted violently. The mayor of Newark, New Jersey, was reported in the daily press to have issued an order that anyone displaying either the cap or the flag in that city would be guilty of subversive action and would be punished accordingly.

Cultural Life

The 1930s also witnessed the development of a new regionalism in cultural life. It was made manifest in many ways—in scholarly organizations, informal groups, publications, literature, and official action in the field of education. In all of these, there was particular emphasis on the South and southernisms. For instance, there was organized in 1934 a Southern Historical Association, with emphasis not on history per se, but on southern history. It was followed by the Southern Political Science Association, the Southern Economics Association, the Southern Sociological Association, the Southern Humanities Conference and the Southern Council on International Relations. And there were the Southern Book Parade, the Southern Newspaper Publishers Association, the Southern Training Program in Public Administration, the Southern Writers Conference, and the Southern Educational Film Production Service.

Emphasis was placed on the South, both in name and content, in a continuing stream of books and periodicals. The Louisiana State University Press began the new ten-volume *History of the South* and the multi-volume *Southern Biography Series*. North Carolina countered with the *Southern State History Series* and a *Documentary History of Education in the South*. Both these and

other university presses issued numerous excellent books dealing with the southern region. The pre-Civil War *Southern Literary Messenger* was revived, and new periodicals with "southern"
in the title flourished. Among them were the *Southern Review,*
the *Southern Patriot,* the *Southern Magazine, The South, The
South Today,* the *Southern Frontier,* and the *Southern Packet.*
The *Journal of Southern History* refuses to publish any article
that does not deal with the South. Even the federal government
succumbed to southern regional publication and issued reports on
Southern Economic Conditions, Southern Labor, and *Southern
Industry.* In fact, the South has become the best-documented
section in America.

Southern literary writers, as they did before the Civil War,
turned their attention to the southern region and the southern
theme. They wrote of the southern Negro, the southern poor
white, the southern frontier, southern society, southern glamor
and romance, southern drama, and even of southern religion.
Much of this writing was of excellent quality, and there were
Pulitzer Prize winners in nearly every field of endeavor. Among
them are Julia M. Peterkin on the Negro, Caroline Miller and
Marjorie Kinnan Rawlings on the frontier, Margaret Mitchell on
glamor and romance, and Paul Green on the drama. William
Faulkner has won world-wide fame in winning the Nobel Prize in
literature for his analysis of southern society. And the South has
become, in reality, the literary capital of the nation.[12]

In education, there was organized the Southern Regional Council, with a Board of Control and central offices in Atlanta. Fourteen states joined in and made appropriations of more than
$1,500,000 the first year. It provided for exchange of students in
medicine, dentistry, forestry, and veterinary science from one
state to another.[13] More recent is the Southern Fellowship Committee, with headquarters in Chapel Hill, administering a fund of

12. See Donald Davidson, "Why the Modern South Has a Great Literature,"
Vanderbilt Studies in the Humanities, I (Nashville: Vanderbilt University Press,
1951), pp. 1–17; and Louis D. Rubin, Jr., and Robert D. Jacobs, editors, *Southern
Renascence: The Literature of the Modern South* (Baltimore: Johns Hopkins Press,
1953).

13. New York *Times,* 5 September 1950.

several million dollars, and granting fellowships and research aid to graduate students and scholars on a regional basis. It might be noted, however, that this fund was made available by one of the national foundations.

General Public Welfare

Liberal and progressive southern leaders—ministers, journalists, educators, and statesmen—have been concerned also about the general well-being of the southern people. It should be noted that there have been several Pulitzer Prize winners in this field, as well as in literature. Among them are George E. Godwin of the Atlanta *Journal,* for exposing vote frauds in Georgia; Louis I. Jaffe of the Norfolk *Virginian-Pilot,* for advocating the rights of the Negro; Robert Latham of the Asheville *Citizen,* for championing political independence and liberalism; and W. Horace Carter of the Tabor City *Tribune* and Willard Cole of the Whiteville *News Reporter,* for exposing the Ku Klux Klan activities in North Carolina in 1952–1953. For lack of time, two or three examples of work in this area will have to suffice, although the activities of leaders extend over a wide sphere—including farm tenancy, health, labor, education, civil liberties, race relations, law enforcement, and many others.

The Southern Policy Committee was organized in 1935, to investigate and publicize the need for reform in southern life. From this committee came numerous short reports on the evils of farm tenancy, poor health conditions, and the lack of medical care and hospitalization in the South, the burden of the poll tax as a prerequisite for voting on the poorer whites as well as Negro citizens in the southern states, and the lower wages and longer hours of laborers in southern industry as compared to those of the workers in the North.[14]

The Southern Conference for Human Welfare, organized in 1938 in Birmingham and designed "to promote the general welfare and to improve economic, social, political, cultural, and

14. Dabney, *Below the Potomac,* pp. 306–308.

spiritual conditions of the people of the South,"[15] offered the Thomas Jefferson Award to the person judged to have done the most during the year for the betterment of the southern people. Two winners of this award were Frank P. Graham, then president of the University of North Carolina, and Hugo Black, at that time United States senator from Alabama and, at present, Associate Justice of the United States Supreme Court. Unfortunately, this organization fell under the control of the leftist group and was branded as communist and subversive in a report of the United States House of Representatives Un-American Activities Committee, but was ably defended by Dr. Walter Gellhorn of Columbia University in the *Harvard Law Review*.[16] While its aims were laudable, and while it did, at first, accomplish worthwhile things, its usefulness has dwindled away.

The Southern Tenant Farmers Union, organized when about sixty-eight percent of southern farmers were tenants and sharecroppers, was another such organization whose goal—improvement in the conditions of the rural farm work—was praiseworthy. But it, too, fell under the leftist control and consequently failed in its major purpose.[17]

Economic Development

The Civil War and Reconstruction left the southern people poverty-stricken. Certainly, if they were ever going to recover from the effects of that tragedy, they should have done so by 1930. And, indeed, they had made rapid strides economically. Nevertheless, they had not been able to close the economic gap between them and the northerners, for the North had advanced just as

15. Southern Conference for Human Welfare, *By-Laws* (Nashville: [n.p.], 1946) ; Katherine DuPre Lumpkin, *The South in Progress* (New York: International Publishers, 1940) , pp. 228–230.

16. For a sympathetic appraisal of the Conference's work, see Kennedy, *Southern Exposure*, pp. 360–363. The report of the Un-American Activities Committee and Dr. Walter Gellhorn's article are summarized in *The Southern Patriot*, V (December 1947) , 8.

17. Dabney, *Below the Potomac*, pp. 129–130; Kennedy, *Southern Exposure*, pp. 279–280; Lumpkin, *The South in Progress*, pp. 130–132.

rapidly as the South. Like the runner in a race who falls behind, the South must advance more rapidly than the North if it is to close that gap.

Smarting under poverty, southerners were stung by what they believed were the taunts in the President's *Economic Report on the South*. Thirty southerners, representing the fields of business, journalism, labor, law, education, and religion, meeting in Atlanta, Georgia, declared that many of the ills set forth in the President's Report resulted from things done or left undone by the national government. "The nation's treatment of the South," these representative southern leaders declared, "has been that generally accorded colonial possessions. The South does not ask a preferred status; what it asks is equality of opportunity within the Union."[18] *The Manufacturer's Record,* published in Baltimore, Maryland, published a series of editorials designed to refute what it called "the stigmatic statement that the South is 'the nation's No. 1 economic problem.' " It attributed the pamphlet and the statement to interests and sections jealous of the South's industrial progress, to northern fear of losing factories to the South, and to "unworthy political motives."[19]

Southern political leaders complained that Roosevelt and the New Deal did nothing to solve the economic problems of the South; rather, they charged that the Roosevelt administration adopted policies that aggravated them. Governor Jones of Louisiana charged that the federal government continued to dole out only seven percent of war industries to the southern states until the Southern Governors Conference threatened to bolt the party. Even then, said he, "rank discrimination continued," and only $2,000,000,000 out of $38,000,000,000 in war contracts went to the South. Richard B. Russell of Georgia charged in the United States Senate that disbursements of United States Relief Agencies

18. Quoted in an editorial, "Equality of Opportunity Asked for the South," in the Atlanta *Journal,* 17 January 1939. Two books that emphasize the colonial status of the South are Walter Prescott Webb, *Divided We Stand* (New York: Farrar & Rinehart, 1937) and Avraham G. Mezerik, *The Revolt of the South and West* (New York: Duell, Sloan and Pearce, 1946).

19. *The Manufacturer's Record,* CVII (August 1938), pp. 13–14.

through November 30, 1938, amounted to $78.80 per capita. The amount in the southern states ranged from a low of $28.40 in North Carolina to a high of $69.50 in Florida. In contrast, eighteen northern and western states ranged from $81.00 in Wyoming to a high of $127.00 in Montana, and New York received $106.80 per capita. Russell charged, and supported his charge with figures, that a similar disparity existed in the wages paid southern and northern WPA workers. For instance, the average paid North Carolina WPA workers was $32.00, while those in Rhode Island were paid $84.63. Similar disparities existed in the AAA payments to southern corn and cotton growers and western corn and wheat growers, and in PWA grants to the states. These conditions, charged Russell, magnified the inequalities that originally existed between North and South.[20]

In 1942, Representative Wright Patman of Texas blasted the Congressional War Plants Corporation, established to aid manufacturers engaged in war or essential civil production, for having "accomplished virtually nothing in the South."[21] Others complained that such war industries as were established in the South consisted largely of training camps and shipyards that would of necessity fold up with the coming of peace, whereas the industries established in the North were heavy goods and tooling industries that would continue to benefit the North long after the war was over.

And southern-born Thomas Parran, Surgeon General of the United States and a noted figure in public health service, charged that the federal government spent 40 cents per capita for public health but that the highest expenditure in the South, where the need was actually the greatest, was 23½ cents in Florida.[22] Still others charged that, of $400,000,000 spent during the war for research by the federal government, less than five percent went to southerners.

While irate southerners complained, others went to work and organized the Southern Economic Council, the Southern In-

20. Quoted in the Atlanta *Journal,* 4 February 1939.
21. Durham *Morning Herald,* 7 December 1942.
22. Atlanta *Journal,* 4 February 1939.

dustrial Council, and the Southern Association of Science and Industry, whose purpose was to influence industrial and economic progress in the South. This latter body, under the leadership of Thomas Boushall, president of the Bank of Virginia at Richmond and an alumnus of the University of North Carolina, declared that "Southerners were . . . given to platitudinous observations rather than specific and dynamic action," that "the South was experiencing a multiplicity of mediocrity," and that "loyalty to traditions of the South interfered with southern zeal to solve Southern [economic] problems." The Association began a campaign to revitalize the South through education, an appreciation of the opportunities and resources of the South, and by an inventory of southern resources. To achieve these goals, it marshalled the ablest staff the South could produce. Its work was partially responsible for the increase in the number of industrial plants in the South from 34,143 in 1935 to 44,779 in 1945, and an increase in the value of manufactured products from $7,500,000,000 to $20,600,000,000.[23] Other such research agencies working toward the same general goal are the Southern Research Institute at Birmingham, the Institute of Textile Technology at Charlottesville, and the Herty Research Foundation at Savannah.

Notable advances have been made all along the line. The Southern Newspaper Publishers Association played a major role in the coming of the paper pulp and newsprint industry to the South. The TVA, a New Deal agency, has done much to develop hydroelectric power and to diversify industry in the South. Able and aggressive industrialists have led in the development of new industries as well as in work to expand textiles, tobacco, furniture, and other older industries. Cities and states, through their industrial commissions, have secured new industries; and, by advertising, southern industries have enticed many northern plants into the South. Now, the shoe is on the other foot, and northern states, industrialists, and labor leaders are protesting to federal authorities that the southern states are stealing their industries.

In 1948, Lieutenant Governor Arthur Coolidge of Massachu-

23. *Ibid.,* 19 July 1946.

setts, speaking to the Greater Lawrence Chamber of Commerce, charged that "Dixie Claghorns" were "kidnapping the Massachusetts textile industry." They were, said he, "robbing Northern Peter to pay Southern Paul." He proposed "to fire an opening gun in a new industrial war between the North and South."[24] And Seymour Harris, professor of economics at Harvard University and chairman of the New England Governors Textile Committee, declared on November 9, 1955, that "The South is fighting the Civil War all over again in trying to take away our industry."[25] New England congressmen, led by John W. McCormack, Democrat, and Joseph W. Martin, Jr., Republican, both of Massachusetts, have organized to put an end to the dispersal of new defense plants. On March 20, 1955, they asked Defense Mobilizer Charles E. Wilson for preferential defense contracts.[26] In August 1955, the New York *World-Telegram* "charged Southern states with assuming the role of a 'reverse carpetbagger' by attempting to entice storm-hit industries to rebuild in the South."[27] Governor Abraham Ribicoff of Connecticut declared: "I can't imagine anything more ghoulish. . . . I am shocked that in this tragic time any Southern state would try to come and steal our industries. This is really a new low."[28] Governor George Bell Timmerman, Jr., of South Carolina, wired in reply, "I am shocked that you would issue such a statement."[29] Governors LeRoy Collins of Florida, Frank Clement of Tennessee, and Luther Hodges of North Carolina likewise expressed condemnation of Ribicoff's charges.[30]

Political Action

Much of the new southern sectionalism stems from political conditions. Long the region of Democratic party supremacy, southern Democrats largely dominated congressional committees when the Democratic party controlled Congress. The South, too,

24. Durham *Morning Herald,* 13 April 1948.
25. *Ibid.,* 10 November 1955.
26. New York *Times,* 27 June 1951 and 20 March 1955.
27. Durham *Morning Herald,* 28 August 1955.
28. *Ibid.,* 26 August and 23 October 1955.
29. *Ibid.*
30. *Ibid.*

could block the nomination of any unsatisfactory Democratic presidental candidate, through the two-thirds rule. But FDR persuaded the Democratic convention to abrogate this rule in 1936, and southern Democrats thereby lost power. Forgetting that the Roosevelt Democratic administration brought them the chairmanship of nearly all the committees in both houses of Congress; four members of the cabinet; three Associate Justices of the Supreme Court; several top posts in the foreign service; the head of the Reconstruction Finance Corporation; and the chief presidential assistant—and resenting both Roosevelt's attempted packing of the Supreme Court and his attempted purge of conservative southern Democrats in 1936, southerners organized for opposition to the Roosevelt administration. They set up the Southern Caucus in Congress to keep a sharp eye on federal policies. They had, in 1934, organized the Southern Governors Conference, in an effort to secure unity of action in support of southern economic and political interests. This latter body has been very influential in the partially successful fight on freight rate differentials between the official or northeastern states and the southern territory, the establishment of the Southern Regional Educational Board, and the effort to secure new industries for the South.[31]

Less successful, but more vocal, has been the Southern Governors Conference, in its opposition to federal action in regard to the extension of the suffrage and civil rights to the Negro. When the Supreme Court struck down the white primary in 1944, state legislatures repealed all laws governing the primary. Some states adopted new constitutional restrictions—the Boswell Amendment of 1946 in Alabama, for instance—but the courts invalidated these. Georgia, Mississippi, and South Carolina adopted new registration procedures. Judge J. Waties Waring declared the South Carolina action unconstitutional. Today, large numbers of Negroes register and vote in all the southern states.[32]

31. Robert Alexander Lively, *The South in Action: A Sectional Crusade Against Freight Rate Discrimination* (Chapel Hill: University of North Carolina Press, 1949), pp. 46–48. Dabney, *Below the Potomac,* p. 310.

32. V. O. Key, Jr., *Southern Politics in State and Nation* (New York: A. A. Knopf, 1949), pp. 625–637.

When Harry Truman advocated a broader program of Civil Rights for Negroes in 1948, many southern Democrats refused to go along with his nomination and organized the State Rights party, generally ridiculed as the Dixicrat movement. Nominating J. Strom Thurmond of South Carolina and Fielding L. Wright of Mississippi as their candidates, the State Rights party won the electoral vote of four southern states and a very sizable popular vote in all the others.[33] And in 1952, southern conservatives, bitterly opposing the loyalty oath imposed by the Democratic convention, refused to support Adlai Stevenson, the Democratic nominee and, led by such men as Governor James F. Byrnes of South Carolina, Senator Harry F. Byrd of Virginia, Governor Allan Shivers of Texas, and Governor Robert B. Kennon of Louisiana, southern Democrats bolted the party, and Eisenhower carried seven southern states and secured a large popular vote in the others.[34] Most of these disgruntled southerners, however, are unhappy over the turn of events. They found no relief from the pressure for civil and equal rights for the Negro. President Eisenhower appointed Earl Warren Chief Justice of the Supreme Court and, under his leadership, the Court unanimously struck down the "separate but equal" idea of Negro education in the South. Today, the Lower South is seething with unrest, and Georgia, Mississippi, and South Carolina have already taken steps to abolish the public schools. A special session of the Virginia legislature has been called, to consider a proposal to amend the state constitution so as to legalize state aid to private education.[35] North Carolina, long known for its progressivism and its moderate stand on race relations, is aroused and divided. Governor Luther H. Hodges's effort to secure voluntary acceptance of segregated schools has brought considerable criticism in many quart-

33. Alexander Heard, *A Two-Party South?* (Chapel Hill: University of North Carolina Press, 1952), pp. 25–26.

34. *The World Almanac and Book of Facts for 1953* (New York: New York World-Telegram, 1953), p. 50.

35. After this paper was written, the Virginia legislature passed by an overwhelming vote—93 to 5 in the House of Representatives and 38 to 1 in the Senate—a bill to submit to the people a change in the state constitution. New York *Times*, 6 December 1955.

ers. His reference to the NAACP as an outside body has been particularly displeasing to the Negro citizens. More recently, the North Carolina legislature's Committee on Education was reported to be considering a plan for the abolition of the state's public school system. What the solution of this difficult problem will be, no one can with confidence predict. The future is undeniably dark.

The South has at least learned that it cannot expect support from the Republican party on its segregation policy and has grown lukewarm to the Eisenhower administration.[36] Senator Lyndon Johnson of Texas has been working for some time to unify southern Democrats, and the Southern Governors Conference, at its meeting in Point Clear, Alabama, in October 1955, proposed that southern Democrats act as a unit, in order to gain greater influence in the Democratic convention and control both the platform and the candidates for the presidency and vice-presidency in 1956.[37]

Jonathan Daniels, editor of the Raleigh *News and Observer,* has been highly critical of this sectional political attitude. He says that

No Southerner will ever be nominated for the Presidency until he first becomes a national figure. . . . So long as Southerners . . . "insist" upon seeking sectional advantage they will invite retaliation from every other section . . .[38]

Thomas L. Stokes, Georgia's Pulitzer Prize-winning columnist, also criticized the action of the Governors Conference. He declared that southern Democrats were conducting a political civil war against the northern wing of the party.

Only the South, [said he] still exists as a distinct political entity. . . . Nothing exists elsewhere in this respect—or "The East," or "The Middlewest," or "The West." Nor do you find politicians in those geographical divisions constantly planning, as they do in the South and as the governors did again here, to form a cohesive bloc to regain for "the

36. See editorials, "Republican Party's Impact on the Solid South," and "Any Signs that Two-Party South is Imminent," in the Durham *Morning Herald,* 4 and 5 October 1955.

37. Durham *Morning Herald,* 18, 19, and 22 October 1955.

38. See editorial, "The Senatorial Complex," the Raleigh *News and Observer,* 22 October 1955.

South" what is called its "proper share" in the direction of the Democratic Party.[39]

But Stokes was wrong in regard to the unique character of southern political sectionalism. Two days after Stokes made his observation, mid-western party leaders, meeting in Chicago, "organized the Mid-western Democratic Conference," and adopted a resolution demanding that the national Democratic party accept and incorporate in its platform a series of planks recommended by the Midwestern Conference.[40]

I have recounted in some detail the story of the resurgence of a militant southern sectionalism. But what does it mean? It seems to be a mixture of bad and good, a warning and yet a glowing promise. There is a very close—in fact, an almost exact—parallel in this story and that of southern sectionalism in the 1830s and 1840s. For lack of proper leadership and because of the breakdown of the processes of democratic government, the people suffered the great tragedy of the Civil War. The South must see to it that that part of the story does not repeat itself; in fact, there is no danger of that, for the sectionalism of today has none of the aspects of southern nationalism that characterized that of the nineteenth century. Southerners must see to it that discrimination against minority groups, whether of race, class, or creed, is ended, that the processes of democratic government are strengthened and broadened so that the government can cope with demagogic leaders and subversives at home and with Communists abroad. In doing this, freedom of thought, freedom of speech, and freedom of individual action must be safeguarded and preserved. In other words, the individual must be assured of the opportunity to develop along his own bent and must not be forced to conform to any fixed mold or pattern.

There is also a promise in the new sectionalism. Out of it have come, during the last twenty years, many good things. No other section of the nation has made such rapid strides in education, in industrialization, and in general economic well-being. No other section has produced so many significant literary figures. Along

39. Thomas L. Stokes, "A Familiar Paradox," and "Feeling Their Oats Again," in the Durham *Morning Herald*, 21 and 24 October 1955.
40. New York *Times*, 23 October 1955.

the entire front, the South has been closing the gap and catching up with the rest of the nation. The South is today a new frontier, a land of hope and promise for the future, to her own people and to the people of all America.[41] But there is still much to be done. The South is still economically poor and poorly educated. It should make the best use of its economic resources to further the well-being of the people—all the people—rich and poor, black and white, tenant farmer and industrial laborer, the professional and the business man. It must educate its young people and give them an opportunity to make the most of their talents, whatever they may be. It must close entirely the gap between North and South, both cultural and economic, so that the best southern brains and leaders will not be drawn to the North by greater opportunities, but will remain in the South to contribute to her progress.

The South must once again take her rightful place in national life. Between 1776 and 1860, with only one-fourth of the political people, the South furnished nearly two-thirds of the national political leadership—Presidents, cabinet members, legislative policy makers, diplomatists, and jurists. Those leaders formulated national policies and translated them into action. They contributed largely to the building of America. Only when they put section above nation, denied to many equal rights and opportunities, and tried to curb freedom of thought and speech did they lose control. How can a political reformation be brought about? It can be done by the people. They must choose and elect to office militantly-aggressive liberal and progressive statesmen who will be concerned with the well-being, the prosperity, the happiness, and the progress of all the people of the South and the nation. Then will the promise of the new southern sectionalism be fulfilled.

41. For progressive changes in the South, see "The Deep South Looks Up," *Fortune*, XXVIII (July 1943), 95–100, 218, 220, 223–225; Wilbur Zelinsky, "The Changing South," *Focus*, II (15 October 1951), 1–5; "The Industrial South," *Fortune*, XVIII (November 1938), 44–54, 118, 120, 123, 126. The latter article states that, while the South may be "the nation's economic Problem No. 1" to the President, it is "to many industrialists, the nation's No. 1 economic opportunity."

Index